GOD IS A CONSERVATIVE

KENNETH J. HEINEMAN

God Is a Conservative

Religion, Politics, and Morality in
Contemporary America

NEW YORK UNIVERSITY PRESS

NEW YORK AND LONDON

NEW YORK UNIVERSITY PRESS
New York and London

© 1998 by New York University

Library of Congress Cataloging-in-Publication Data
Heineman, Kenneth J., 1962–
God is a conservative : religion, politics, and morality in
contemporary America / Kenneth J. Heineman.
p.   cm.
Includes bibliographical references and index.
ISBN 0-8147-3554-1 (alk. paper)
1. United States—Politics and government—1989–   2. United
States—Politics and government—1945–1989.   3. Presidents—United
States—Election—History—20th century.   4. Conservatism—United
States—History—20th century.   5. Religion and politics—United
States—History—20th century.   6. United States—Moral conditions.
I. Title.
E839.5.H45   1998   98-11093
976.92—dc21   CIP

New York University Press books are printed on acid-free paper,
and their binding materials are chosen for strength and durabiltiy.

Manufactured in the United States of America

10   9   8   7   6   5   4   3   2   1

For
Theresa Ann Heineman
and
Natalie MacKenzie Heineman

Contents

Preface

This is a work of broad social commentary, not an academic monograph intended for a handful of specialists. My intention is to reach a larger audience of readers who are interested in American politics, moral debates, and recent history. I make a number of observations on contemporary moral politics while, I hope, writing a story that will sustain reader interest. A traditional scholarly book would have subsections and repeated tag lines signaling every time an analytical statement was coming in sight. The scholar might even dispense with chronology and organize ideas around certain concepts such as American foreign policy and evangelicals, religious conservatives and race, and so on. Most folks, however, mark the passage of political time in four-year intervals—in other words, presidential elections. We do not tend to think of presidential politics in terms of carefully segregated themes that span several decades.

For better or for worse, a far larger proportion of Americans vote in presidential elections than in state legislative contests. People are more likely to know the names of the major presidential candidates than who represents them on city council, the school board, and in Congress. Presidential elections are national contests, providing Americans with the opportunity to pass judgment every four years on various economic and social developments. For that reason they are useful in bringing out the interplay of local, sectional, and national politics. Presidential elections also underline the success, failure, and future of particular voter coalitions.

An academic specialist would probably say that everybody knows that in 1988 Al Gore (not George Bush) first accused Michael Dukakis of letting black prisoners out on weekend furloughs to rape white women. Or, that in 1976 Jimmy Carter ran to the right of Gerald Ford on moral issues, seeking endorsements from Pat Robertson and the very religious leaders who would go on to found the Moral Majority and help Ronald Reagan defeat the southerner four years later. Or, that Ralph Reed of the Christian Coalition tried to turn social conservatives against Pat Buchanan and helped give the 1996 GOP presidential nomination to Bob Dole. (Moral conservatives felt betrayed when Dole subsequently announced that he wished to soften GOP opposition to abortion.) I am not so sure that these are generally well-known facts outside (or even necessarily inside) academia and the newsroom.

I am happy to admit up front that I do not accept the tenets of modern liberalism. Then again, I am uncomfortable with what often passes for contemporary conservative politics. Basically, I am a New Deal conservative in that I believe government has a responsibility to protect deserving, hardworking citizens. Ultimately, however, people have to accept the consequences for the moral and economic choices they make. Large, impersonal institutions—the federal government, the corporation, the national labor union, the university, and the media—cannot save people from their own self-destructive tendencies. The elites (Democratic or Republican) who run such institutions may often be part of the problem. Moreover, I do not like a political system that frequently compels citizens to choose between two equally unpleasant "leaders"—Teddy Kennedy or Jesse Helms. Then again, perhaps in a society that has become as culturally polarized as ours there can be no other choices but extreme ones.

Of course, moderation, or compromise, or "pragmatism" for the sake of getting along has its downside. Heated argument and the shattering of consensus can be good things for a democracy. (They may even be unavoidable.) Since the sixties, left-leaning figures in the media and the university have attempted to silence dissenting voices by arguing that criticism of racial quotas, criminal rights, and abortion was racist, sexist, and fascist. Conversely, all federal legislative initiatives and judicial rulings that promoted the causes of social liberalism were good, progressive, and properly understood to be compensating various oppressed groups for past persecution. Now that voters have applied the brakes, and even Bill Clinton had to, at least publicly, disavow his ties to gay, feminist, and civil rights groups, social liberals have modified their tactics. They now condemn their conservative critics as "divisive." Folks like Pat Robertson and Pat Buchanan should just keep quiet. I can discern no logical reason as to why the National Organization for Women and the National Abortion

Rights Action League are not equally as "divisive" as the Christian Coalition and the conservative Heritage Foundation.

A little less hypocrisy among our cultural elites would be nice. But don't misunderstand me. I have been just as frustrated with the Right. A few years ago, while attending a seminar at the Heritage Foundation, former Attorney General Ed Meese held forth on the accomplishments of the Reagan administration. Now, Ronald Reagan was not as bad a president as liberal historians like Arthur Schlesinger, Jr., and Garry Wills would have you believe. Then again, Reagan had his failings. I asked Meese about one such failing; the fact that the law-and-order president saw crack abuse and drug-related murders skyrocket during the eighties. Meese replied that the White House had reduced drug abuse among its target constituency—meaning white, middle-class suburbanites. After Meese's session, a southern conservative and former U. S. attorney, who had nothing good to say about affirmative action, shook his head and told me he was appalled. As he saw things, poor, law-abiding black people living in the ghetto had the same right not be shot down by dope pushers as suburban whites.

I learned two things from this encounter. First, I am not an Ed Meese conservative. Second, morally upright conservatives are probably more attuned to the aspirations of ordinary people than those who purport to lead the GOP. This may be true as well for individuals on the Left. That was part of the argument I advanced in *Campus Wars*, a history of student antiwar activism in the sixties. There were people in the ranks of the New Left who did not celebrate the violence of the Black Panthers and castigate the morally conservative white working class. Such activists, however, did not set the political agenda for the New Left and its offspring—social liberalism. Indeed, reasonable activists were often politically marginalized and generally forgotten by the media and the academy.

There are in the ranks of contemporary liberalism a few folks whose political vision is profoundly ethical. This book does not question the religiosity of people like Jimmy Carter or Congressman John Lewis of Georgia. The problem with the post–New Deal Democratic Party is that Teddy Kennedy helped destroy Carter and that Jesse Jackson, not John Lewis, speaks for the civil rights establishment. Just once has Jesse Jackson sounded like Lewis—when he lamented that while walking down the street he felt safer around whites than young black males. Jackson quickly "clarified" his remarks, once again blaming the problems of the black underclass on white racism. Lewis does not doubt that racism persists in America, but he thinks that poor people need to behave morally. With Lewis, honest argument over racial quotas is possible. With Jackson, you run the risk of being dismissed as divisive or branded a racist.

Now that I have laid out the structure and view of *God Is a Conservative*, I should tell you a little bit about the research undergirding this work. One of the difficulties in doing contemporary social commentary is gaining access to archival documents. I found that many donors placed restrictions on their papers. Most often, organizations and individuals insisted that their papers could not be examined, or at least quoted from, for a period of fifteen years from the date of their donation. In some cases, donors required that their papers be sealed until the time of their death or until everyone mentioned in their papers was dead. This meant that my archival research had to stop just short of the 1984 presidential election. Other archives imposed even more onerous restrictions on their materials. If nothing else, at least I was spared from additional travel. This helps to explain, in part, why the amount of archival research declines and the number of book, newspaper, magazine, and journal citations increases by the fifth chapter.

Nearly every person mentioned in *God Is a Conservative* has left behind memoirs, articles, interviews, and the like. That would not have necessarily been the case in a bygone era. In the thirties, Roosevelt administration players mostly kept their own counsel—at least until FDR died. Even then, their memoirs trickled forth over the span of five decades. In contrast, Reagan, Bush, and Clinton staffers regularly knifed one another in the media and wrote instant memoirs at the end of their (often short) tenure in office.

The research for, and writing of, *God Is a Conservative*, would not have been possible without the assistance of a number of people. I express my heartfelt thanks to Janyce Nasgowitz and the wonderful staff of the Billy Graham Archives, Wheaton College; William McNitt, Geir Gundersen, and the exceptional archivists at the Gerald R. Ford Library at the University of Michigan; and Kevin Cawley, Wendy Clausen, and the extremely helpful staffers at the University of Notre Dame Archives. At the Lancaster Campus of Ohio University, I gratefully acknowledge the indispensable assistance of our reference librarian, Julia Robinson, our interlibrary loan staffers, Amber Landis and Tammy Walker, and our library director, Susie Phillips. For a regional campus, we have a truly outstanding library and a staff willing to go the extra mile to locate somewhat obscure books and journal articles. The Gerald R. Ford Presidential Library and the Ohio University Research Committee provided small but vital grants that paid for photocopying, lodging, meals, and mileage.

At New York University Press, Colin Jones and Niko Pfund generously gave me their time, ideas, and encouragement. They *are* appreciated. Several friends provided great advice and stimulated my thinking: Curt Miner, Kevin Dunphy, John Zimmerman, Helen Killoran, Mel Small, Andy Dowdle, and Kyle Sinisi. I must also thank Charlie Alexander, Paula Baker, and Lon Hamby for supporting my grant applications.

Finally, I thank my wife for her woman-on-the-street commentary and keeping our delightful baby diverted on the weekends. We were extremely lucky to be blessed with a daughter who took naps, established a regular nighttime sleeping schedule early in her life, and messed up her diapers and demanded feeding all in good humor. Regional campus faculty have larger teaching loads than our main-campus counterparts and seldom receive course reductions. Consequently, every minute of writing time Theresa and Natalie gave me was essential. Not for nothing have I dedicated *God Is a Conservative* to them.

Introduction
Heaven Can't Wait

Twenty-two years after Leonard Bernstein hosted a cocktail soiree and fund-raiser for the Black Panther Party, liberal chic was back in style. A *smiling* Yoko Ono, as always wearing large sunglasses whether outdoors or in, stood next to a laughing Jann Wenner. In the sixties Wenner proved that one could be a hip capitalist, packaging the counterculture to millions of youths who smoked dope, protested against the Vietnam War, and had money to spend on records. Now the publisher of *Rolling Stone*, who would shortly leave his wife for a man, was aglow. What had made Ono and Wenner so happy as they sipped cocktails into the night? Just two weeks before, Bill Clinton had been elected president. Even if Clinton had won only because Ross Perot split the Republican vote, Boomer liberals were determined to take their victories where they could. Their joy was understandable. For twelve years they had been lost in a Republican wilderness. During his reign as governor of California, Ronald Reagan had cracked down on antiwar protesters at Berkeley. In the eighties, President Reagan gave rhetorical support to a constitutional ban on abortion. A father figure from their worst nightmares, Reagan had cast a pall over the protest generation's youth. Now the conservatives were banished, never to return.[1]

Unlike Ono and Wenner, a few blue-collar union men expressed dismay at the prospect of a Clinton presidency. As the governor of Arkansas, Clinton gave tax breaks to anti-union corporations. By the eighties, Arkansas had become a haven for low-wage employers like Wal-Mart and Tyson Foods. Wal-Mart was so pleased with the governor that the corporation appointed Hillary Rodham Clinton to its board of directors.

Certainly hanging out in the boardroom was more fulfilling than trying to teach law students at the University of Arkansas.

Just as telling was Clinton's relationship with gay activist James Hormel. A wealthy industrialist and generous Clinton campaign contributor, Hormel was a champion of equal rights for homosexuals. Unfortunately, Hormel did not extend the same consideration to his employees. In the eighties, the Hormel corporation broke the meat-packers union at its midwestern plants. Many workers lost their jobs; others returned to Hormel, where they received reduced wages and a loss of health benefits. The backbone of the Democratic Party since the thirties, when John L. Lewis established the Congress of Industrial Organizations, blue-collar unions possessed few friends among lifestyle liberals. Hormel, slated to become a U.S. ambassador, saw no contradiction between his political pronouncements and his business operations.

All of this would have come as no surprise to Alex Barkan, the former political director of the AFL-CIO. A feisty working-class Jew, Barkan argued that after the 1968 election the Democratic Party had been taken over "by those phony liberals and feminists." To the aging AFL-CIO leadership, nothing was more disturbing than watching white-collar unions like the National Education Association promote multiculturalism, women's liberation, and alternative lifestyles. In an era when good-paying industrial jobs were disappearing, the Rustbelt union chiefs believed that organized labor should focus on bread-and-butter issues, not the cultural agenda of middle-class professionals. (In 1996, 42 percent of the AFL-CIO's membership was made up of white-collar, public-sector employees —most of whom were affiliated with the American Federation of State, County, and Municipal Employees. Overall, just 15 percent of the nation's work force belonged to a union.) Boomer liberals were delighted that North Carolina senator Jesse Helms took aim at their friend. A former segregationist and ally of the tobacco lobby, Helms discredited any cause with which he was associated.[2]

The conservative writer Peggy Noonan did not receive an invitation to trade bon mots with Ono and Wenner. That however, did not deter her from expressing an opinion of Clinton. She did not appreciate that Clinton—who had evaded the Vietnam draft—compared himself to John Kennedy, a World War II combat hero. Although Kennedy and Clinton both came to the White House while in their forties, the similarities ended there. As Noonan argued, "Kennedy's generation was not shocked to be governing at the age of forty-three. They had already been men for twenty years."[3]

A child of the Catholic preserves of Long Island, Noonan had flirted with the counterculture. But in 1971, during a peace march on Washington, she grew disgusted with the protesters' anti-American sentiments. Noonan concluded that her McGovern campaign button would make a better marijuana clip than political statement. This began her ideological odyssey. By the eighties, Noonan was a Reagan speechwriter. In 1988, she wrote the acceptance speech George Bush delivered at the Republican National Convention. Her words became the core of President Bush's "vision thing." Noonan embraced voluntarism and hoped to spark "a thousand points of light" that would illuminate the nation. All everyone had to do was just help one another. Boomer liberals ridiculed the speech, failing to understand that most Americans think of themselves as charitable people. On the other hand, Bush expressed himself so poorly that Noonan's ideas were easily lost in the translation.[4]

There was at least one other Boomer conservative who shared Noonan's skepticism of contemporary liberalism: Newt Gingrich. A Pennsylvania carpetbagger, Gingrich had spent two decades on his march from Atlanta to the House Speaker's chair. In 1994, with the apparent implosion of Clinton's presidency, the Republicans captured the Senate and gained control over the House for the first time in forty years. Gingrich promised to bring about a conservative revolution, yet closed his first speech as House Speaker by exalting the godfather of twentieth-century liberalism:

If you truly believe in representative self-government, you can never study Franklin Delano Roosevelt too much. He did bring us out of the Depression. He did lead the Allied movement in World War II. In many ways he created the modern world. He was clearly, I think, as a political leader the greatest figure of the twentieth century. And I think his concept that we have nothing to fear but fear itself, that we'll take an experiment, and if it fails, we'll do another one—and if you go back and read the New Deal, they tried again and again. They didn't always get it right, and we would have voted against much of it, but the truth is we would have voted for much of it.[5]

Gingrich and Noonan spoke for Sunbelt Protestants and northern Catholics who had been firmly Democratic until the late sixties. As Gingrich had said on the fiftieth anniversary of Roosevelt's death, the remarkable fact about the New Deal was that it addressed the economic needs of

Mississippi racists and Chicago blacks. In the thirties, southern Protestants who refused to vote for a Catholic at the top of the Democratic
ticket went along with federal legislation that protected the rights of Polish-American steelworkers in Pennsylvania. Roosevelt, who earned the
lasting hatred of the Coors and DuPont families, forged an electoral majority out of minorities. Southern white Protestants, northern black Protestants, urban Catholics and Jews, and Ivy League professors voted Democratic. Culturally, these groups had nothing in common. Only the crisis
of the Great Depression and the military challenges posed by Nazi Germany and the Soviet Union kept them together. The New Deal Democrats
offered something to everybody: labor laws to urban Catholics, color-
blind hiring policies on federal projects to northern blacks, and agricultural subsidies to white southerners.[6]

A great weakness of the New Deal coalition was that the Democrats
could not afford the defection of any group. Although most American
voters were Protestant, Roosevelt never received the majority of their
votes. What there was of a Democratic Protestant vote came from southern whites and northern blacks. If civil rights ever became an issue, the
Democrats would be in trouble. Likewise, the Democratic Party had to
keep the loyalties of Catholics. Next to southern evangelicals, Catholics
were the most anti-Communist and socially conservative voters in the
nation. Michael Novak, a Slovak son of Johnstown, Pennsylvania, recognized just how conservative Catholics were while arranging campaign
stops in 1972 for Sargent Shriver, the Democratic vice-presidential nominee:

Shriver was greeted with scarcely veiled disdain, I thought, by workers at the gates
of the Homestead [Pennsylvania] Steel mills—my own kind of folks, who would
normally be with us by upwards of 89 percent. In Joliet, Illinois, on a factory
floor where I encountered dozens of Slovak faces that made me think of my
cousins in Johnstown, workers did not want to shake McGovern-Shriver hands.
Trying to find out why, I met with our "advance person"—a young woman
wearing a miniskirt, high white boots, and a see-through blouse, with a large pro-
abortion button on her collar. On that factory floor in 1972, the clash of social
classes and cultural politics could scarcely have been more discordant.[7]

By the seventies, Roosevelt's party lay in ruins. College students, professors, and community activists were championing everything from a
military withdrawal in Vietnam to affirmative action and gay liberation.
Liberal reformers captured the Democratic Party's presidential nomination machinery in 1972. The chief objective of Boomer liberalism was to

achieve freedom from repressive moral authority. Abortion rights and sexual experimentation were part of this Boomer liberationist ethos. Upon graduation, such liberals became journalists, professors, and film-makers. Although few in number, their cultural influence was enormous.

If Boomer liberals won control of Hollywood, the news media, and liberal arts faculties, they lost the war for the hearts and minds of the American electorate. (As sixties radical Todd Gitlin lightly put it, "The Right took over the government, the Left took over the English depart-ment.") In 1972, George McGovern saw workers, Catholics, and white southerners vote for Richard Nixon. (They did not yet support a straight Republican ticket, believing that their local Democratic representatives remained reliable New Dealers.) Even though McGovern was a World War II veteran and the son of a Methodist minister, he became identified with the countercultural excesses of the sixties. Worse, his followers tossed Richard Daley and George Meany out of the Democratic National Con-vention. Replacing the Chicago machine boss and the AFL-CIO president—both Catholic—with Jesse Jackson and Gloria Steinem was not savvy politics. Catholics accounted for one-quarter of America's elec-torate, blacks and Jewish feminists little more than 10 percent.[8]

Four years later, Jimmy Carter barely managed to defeat Gerald Ford, whose pardon of Nixon in the aftermath of the Watergate scandal made him one of the weakest Republican candidates ever nominated. Carter paraded his southern, evangelical origins for all to see in 1976, winning back enough Dixie votes from the Republicans to secure the White House. On the other hand, Carter's Southern Baptist rhetoric made a number of northern Catholics nervous. So desperate did the situation become during the election that Carter made repeated campaign trips to Pittsburgh. He had enough priests in his retinue to risk being mistaken for a cardinal. In 1980, as the nation reeled from inflation, humiliation overseas, and a suspicion that Boomer liberalism was promoting a break-down in public morality, evangelicals deserted Carter in droves. Although Reagan was a product of Hollywood and a divorced man who had strained relations with his children, he seemed more moral than Carter. Meanwhile, many Catholics became Reagan Democrats.

To Moral Majority founder Jerry Falwell, who did much to bring about Carter's defeat, God was the ultimate lawgiver. In contrast, Boomer lib-erals emphasized individual choice. God or government should not ban abortion or punish homosexual acts. Regardless of which side had the better sense of where moral authority originated, as Boomer liberalism lost at the ballot box, it also hurt the mainstream Protestant denominations. In reaction to the liberal stances of Episcopalian and Presbyterian church leaders, membership in fundamentalist and Pentecostal churches has grown sevenfold. Resentful of their declining fortunes, and frightened by the Religious Right, Boomer politicians and clergy condemned social conservatives like Falwell and Pat Robertson. According to the social liberals, Falwell and Robertson were attempting to breach the alleged constitutional wall separating church and state. Conservatives countered that the Religious Left had already politicized the church in the sixties by supporting civil rights and opposing the Vietnam War. Martin Luther King, Jr., and Father Daniel Berrigan, *not the Moral Majority,* first scaled the judicial barriers between church and state.

While the initial impetus for civil rights and peace in the sixties came from the churches, many Boomer liberals lost sight of the religious roots of social reform. Berrigan earned great acclaim from Boomer liberals for his protests at American missile sites. On the other hand, the Boomer Left could not fathom why Berrigan also engaged in nonviolent demonstrations at abortion clinics. To Berrigan, following Catholic teaching that all human life is sacred, opposing nuclear war and abortion were complementary, not contradictory, acts.

In 1983, at a Washington rally against American foreign policy, the sixties counterculture briefly rose again. Aging hippies and college students staged bizarre political theater. Some protesters held "die-ins," complete with chalk lines drawn around their corpses. Others dressed up as Reagan's UN ambassador and menaced the crowd. After Peter, Paul, and Mary played their repertoire—as 50,000 demonstrators pretended to remember the lyrics—Rev. Jesse Jackson spoke. To the surprise of the politically uninitiated, white feminists booed Jackson from the stage. Although a sharp critic of Falwell's anti-Communism, Jackson was also an opponent of abortion and gay rights. Jackson's liberal allies viewed him only as a civil rights champion, forgetting that he was a Baptist minister as well. In terms of theology and culture, Jackson had more in common with Falwell than he did with secular liberals. The inability of liberals to recognize that most Americans are religious and can be excited by moral exhortation has tickled conservatives for more than two decades.

As a media advisor to Nixon in 1972, Patrick Buchanan had urged the White House to put the Vietnam War behind it and to concentrate on cultural issues. According to this pugnacious Catholic conservative, campus and urban unrest, abortion, pornography, and gay liberation were the issues around which to build a new Republican majority. Meanwhile, Michael Novak advised McGovern's campaign, hoping to return the Democrats to their socially conservative, economically populist roots. Novak failed and gradually moved to the Right. During the civil rights revolution, Falwell had criticized King for politicizing the church. God and politics did not mix. By the seventies, in the wake of the Supreme Court's decision to legalize abortion, Falwell had a change of heart. With his moral universe turned upside down, Falwell followed King in becoming a crusader against government tyranny. In 1979, Falwell founded the four-million-member Moral Majority. Protestant evangelicals had at last found an organized political force to represent them, accounting for 25 percent of the Republican vote. Most of these religious conservatives hailed from the South, which, as early as the Civil War, had twice the number of Protestant churches and worshipers than could be found in the North.

The Moral Majority and Pat Robertson's Christian Coalition—founded a year after his failure to win the 1988 Republican presidential nomination—have their differences. Falwell has walked away from his dream of capturing Congress and the White House. Indeed, Cal Thomas, a former Moral Majority media advisor whose syndicated newspaper column is read by millions, has exhorted evangelicals to set individual examples of commendable Christian behavior rather than focusing exclusively on the ballot box. Falwell and Thomas have urged some degree of Christian separatism from the secular culture.

In contrast, Robertson has enthusiastically embraced the ballot box. After all, evangelicals and religious traditionalists represented one-third of the electorate and 40 percent of the Republicans' primary voters in the nineties. Despite grand visions of achieving national political power, however, Robertson has been frustrated. In 1996, Christian Coalition director Ralph Reed, who was in diapers when President Kennedy was assassinated, learned that he could not reliably deliver his group's votes to the preferred Republican primary candidates. The bonds between leaders and rank and file in the Christian Coalition of the nineties are not as tight as those in the forties-era CIO. In 1996, Reed and Robertson endorsed Bob Dole because they loathed Buchanan's anti-corporation rhetoric. Nearly half of the Christian Coalition voters in the Louisiana and Iowa caucuses supported Buchanan.

As fundamentalists, Falwell and most of the rank and file of the Moral Majority never thought that America could be made perfect through federal intervention. Punishing immoral behavior would make America a better place but not a paradise. As Pentecostals, Robertson and many Christian Coalition supporters believe that the Second Coming of Christ is imminent. Heaven's thousand-year reign will begin on the earth soon. Consequently, Christian conservatives must help prepare the way for the establishment of Christ's earthly Kingdom. This is a theology, as well as a program for political action, that Baptists and Catholics find troublesome.

Sunbelt Protestants and northern Catholics have their differences as well. Catholics were much more likely to join labor unions in the thirties and undertake collective social action than Protestants. The union movement of the thirties (and afterwards) failed miserably in the most Protestant region of the country—the South. Catholic communalism and Protestant individualism continue to be at odds. Catholic conservatives like the patrician William F. Buckley, Jr., and the neoconservative Michael Novak are not welcomed in the ranks of the Sunbelt Right. While the southern wing of the conservative movement is a champion of the free market, Buckley, Novak, and Patrick Buchanan have contended that where corporate practices undermine the family, business must give way to social regulation. To Catholic conservatives, eliminating American jobs and relocating overseas in search of cheaper labor, or producing obscene, violent movies and rap music are morally unjust corporate acts.

Catholic and Protestant conservatives also have contrasting ideas concerning federal power and economics. Sunbelt conservatives are more individualistic than their northern Catholic counterparts. As Falwell has observed on numerous occasions, "God is in favor of freedom, property, ownership, competition, diligence, work, and acquisition. All of this is taught in the word of God, in both the Old and New Testaments." In 1996, Christian Coalition leaders reassured the business community that they were "the most libertarian group in America," interested only in having the government outlaw abortion, not plant closings. Buchanan's economic populism and Novak's call for moral capitalism were not positions embraced by Reed.[9]

Even though many Catholics voted for conservatives in the seventies and eighties, they did not join the Moral Majority in great numbers. Most Catholics chose to work within their church organizations to lobby against abortion or place pressure on the television networks to clean up their acts. Just one-third of the Moral Majority's membership was Catholic, and the same was true of the Christian Coalition in the nineties. When Sunbelt Protestants in the nineties express support for Buchanan, they dwell upon his social conservatism and ignore his economic populism. Buchanan's Catholic supporters place equal emphasis upon social and economic concerns.

The Heritage Foundation, a leading conservative think tank in Washington, began attacking Buchanan in 1992 and has long ignored Catholic critiques of unbridled capitalism. Free-market champions such as Joseph Coors exercise great influence at the Heritage. When William Bennett spoke at Falwell's Liberty Baptist College in the eighties, a student expressed amazement that Reagan's education secretary believed in God. After all, he was Catholic. Bennett, a product of northern New Deal sensibilities, earned the scorn of Senator Helms for having written kindly of the civil rights movement. Moreover, Sunbelt conservatives did not appreciate how animated the scrappy philosophy professor became whenever he recounted the time he was assaulted by Mississippi thugs for defending Martin Luther King, Jr.[10]

Every so often the theological cracks within the Religious Right are exposed for all to see. Religious Right activist and Pentecostal minister Jimmy Swaggart reached a television audience of three million weekly and had an operating budget of $30 million in the early eighties. While condemning Boomer liberals for promoting pornography, Swaggart proclaimed that Catholics were not Christians and, consequently, were destined to burn in hell. Swaggart, who temporarily lost his pulpit after being caught performing kinky sex acts with a Louisiana prostitute, was not atypical.

The Bob Jones University Press was a major publisher of anti-Catholic books and tracts in the seventies and eighties. Indeed, university president Bob Jones even referred to Pope Paul VI—the church leader who urged abstinence rather than birth control in the sixties—as the "arch priest of Satan" and "the anti-Christ." It should be recalled that the Reagan Justice Department had sided with Bob Jones University in its struggle to avoid racial integration. Boomer liberals who reported on the case focused on the racial issues involved but failed to mention the Christian school's record of anti-Catholicism. This is not too surprising. Catholics, who are often socially conservative and white, are not on the liberals' list of approved minority groups. More surprising was the sight of the Reagan administration allying with anti-Catholic fundamentalists. It would be difficult to conjure a more effective way to wreck the conservative religious coalition that brought Reagan to power in 1981.[11]

When the *American Spectator*, the entertaining tabloid of the conservative movement, ran a favorable story on Pope John Paul II in 1995, one evangelical took great offense. Her letter to the magazine's editor echoed the sentiments of Swaggart and Bob Jones:

There are foundational reasons why Protestants reject Catholicism and its doctrines. This country was founded mainly by Protestants who used the Bible rather than the Catholic Church as their guide. . . .

Do you really want to promote Catholicism? You're opening a Pandora's box if you do. Are you ready to defend faith/works salvation, praying to Mary and Catholic saints, the rosary, the Mass and sacraments, the Pope as head of the Church, etc.? These are not quaint and harmless traditions; either they are true or they are heresies. Many Catholic traditions contradict the Bible and its teachings.

America's first culture war, the one pitting Protestants against Catholics, has not been entirely supplanted by the new struggle between religious conservatives—both Catholic and Protestant—and Boomer liberals.[12]

Choosing to ignore theological and cultural divisions among social conservatives and to depict the Religious Right as a monolithic movement, Boomer liberals have been making some questionable judgments regarding the issue of race as well. Many progressives have asserted that the conservative assault on federal programs that began in the seventies was racially motivated. Because 60 percent of the black middle class is employed by some local, state or federal agency, and because the Democratic Congress and liberal judges have promoted affirmative action, any criticism of hiring quotas and welfare is seen as inevitably racist. Boomer liberals have long ignored the fact that blacks provide pollsters with very conservative responses to questions dealing with abortion and pornography. To Bennett's dismay, southern Protestants have not exploited the values gulf between middle-class white liberals and working-class black Democrats.

Catholics and southern whites initially became Republicans for different reasons. While both groups came to resent coercive federal power, southern whites were reacting against the imposition of civil rights from Washington. Catholics—the great beneficiaries of federal intervention since the New Deal—did not fear civil rights. Many Catholics moved to the Right when the federal courts sanctioned abortion and liberal judges failed to curb a violent crime rate that has risen 560 percent since 1960. Today, southern religious conservatives reject racial segregation, although in Mississippi it is understood that the Democratic Party is for blacks and the Republican Party for whites.

Rather than accusing religious conservatives of being racist, an inquiry might be made of their attitude toward Jews. A number of liberals have charged that Robertson's ideas are lifted from the anti-Semitic tract *Protocols of the Elders of Zion*. Conservative Jews such as Adam Meyerson of the Heritage Foundation are quick to defend Robertson. On the other hand, one does not see many thirtysomething evangelicals joining Adam Bellow, John Podhoretz, and Lisa Schiffren on their Georgetown pub crawls. The class and intellectual gap between conservative Jews educated at Harvard and Christian activists who graduated from Liberty Baptist is too great to make for easy social mingling. Jews *are* the most liberal cultural group in the country. With its emphasis upon the here and now (with no plans for the Resurrection), Judaism is more inclined to use government to build a better world than is orthodox Christianity. There is a class as well as a theological dimension that should be noted. Jews are the most affluent religious group in America, Pentecostals the poorest.[13]

To some conservatives, Jews are suspiciously overrepresented in the ranks of politically correct academics, immoral Hollywood screenwriters, gay activists, and record producers for gangsta rap performers. Lisa Schiffren might even *want* to be on the cover of *Rolling Stone*: She wrote Dan Quayle's "Murphy Brown" speech, crusades against illegitimacy, and rocks to the "Pulp Fiction" soundtrack. Will she go medieval on Clinton's butt in '96? (The answer was no, but how much could a social conservative do on behalf of a divorced career politician like Bob Dole? Then again, how much *would* a social conservative do on behalf of a candidate who wanted the GOP to be more tolerant of prochoice Republicans?)

Jews are not the only group whose ways are alien to Christian conservatives. Beyond the persistent Catholic and evangelical strains, there are cultural tensions between old-money Protestants and evangelicals. Although alcohol is Satan's drink—often the cause of family breakup and crime—the Christian Coalition advances its moral crusade with support from the Coors beer empire. That political reality does not stop Robertson's staff from visibly wincing whenever the obligatory cases of Coors are hauled out at Heritage Foundation get-togethers. Pentecostals usually flee the scene; Catholics and libertarians drink deeply and debate the merits of censoring Hollywood. If bored by that, libertarians might then ogle the Coors television and billboard advertisements. The message Coors appears to be sending is that blondes with impressive cleavages will be attracted to frisky, beer-drinking men—none of whom are members of the Christian Coalition.[14]

Of great concern to Republican businessmen is the support Buchanan receives from religious conservatives. So desperate did the Heritage Foundation's financial backers become in 1996 that they encouraged millionaire Steve Forbes to enter the Republican primaries. He immediately attacked Buchanan for fomenting class warfare while championing a flat tax that would net the wealthy millions of dollars. The class gulf between those who play the polo fields and those who work the assembly lines is no less than the cultural gap dividing Jews and Southern Baptists. Paradoxically, such captains of industry, while touting conservative values, would not give a second thought to hiring a liberal Columbia graduate over a conservative product of Liberty Baptist. Whenever morals conflict with the bottom line, it becomes difficult to tell Republican businessmen and Boomer liberals apart.

In many ways the class and cultural divisions afflicting the Republicans mirror those that tore apart the New Deal coalition. If it is hard to picture Yoko Ono and Alex Barkan meeting in a bowling ally for beer, chips, and political fence-mending, the imagination reels at the thought of Robertson and Buchanan debating the moral regulation of capitalism over several glasses of stout. One possible question immediately presents itself: Will religious conservatism become just as politically irrelevant as Boomer liberalism? Probably not. After all, since the sixties it has been evident that there is a moral majority in America—although not quite the one Falwell envisioned. If this were not so, issues such as abortion, pornography, crime, drug addiction, and family dissolution would not resonate with so many voters. There has been a Republican presidential majority since 1972. The Republican capture of Congress in 1994, even if conservatives subsequently lose control of it, still underlines the reality that Americans have rejected many of the tenets of Boomer liberalism. Yoko Ono should also not think that her stepson Julian Lennon is a typical Clinton-loving member of the Baby Buster generation. In 1990, for the first time in nearly sixty years, a plurality of registered voters under the age of thirty were Republicans. The next-largest bloc of young voters identified themselves as independents. New Dealers and Boomer liberals are not replenishing their ranks.

A probable scenario for the future of American politics, and of social conservatism and economic populism in particular, would be this: the Democratic Party continues its decline, becoming no more than 25 percent of the electorate. Meanwhile, at least two new Republican parties appear. As Sunbelt Protestants and free-market champions berate the Big Government credo of Boomer liberals, the second Republican Party would position itself between the two extremes. It would advocate a conservative social agenda, as well as populist economic policies. Buchanan might well be the John the Baptist of this movement. His political baggage and polarizing rhetoric, however, would prevent him from becoming the leader of a reconstituted New Deal Republican Party.

God Is a Conservative proposes to examine the nature of morality-based politics and the rise of social conservatism since the sixties. This social history of moral politics hopes to answer the question implied above: Will Christian conservatism prove to be as ineffectual, divisive, and obnoxious as Boomer liberalism? How do race relations fit into this discussion of morality and politics? Could Boomer liberals lose blacks, one of their most reliable constituencies, if they become convinced that conservatives are not racists? And one more question. With traumatic economic dislocation already here, and with more on the horizon, are moral politics a diversion from our pressing problems, or a cure for what ails the nation?

CHAPTER ONE

Reaping the Whirlwind
1968

Rev. Nelson Bell of Montreat, North Carolina, had not been in good humor ever since the Supreme Court, in *Brown v. the Board of Education* (Topeka, Kansas), ruled that racially segregated schools were unconstitutional. He had been beside himself when his son-in-law, Rev. Billy Graham, formed a friendship with a black Baptist minister named Martin Luther King, Jr. Although Bell could endorse Graham and King's crusade against sexually suggestive rock 'n' roll lyrics, the North Carolinian had no use for civil rights activism. To Bell's relief, Graham had not been a forceful advocate of the Montgomery, Alabama, bus boycott that King led in 1955 and 1956. On the other hand, Bell's son-in-law insisted that his revival meetings, whether held in the North or the South, be racially integrated. Given this history, the letter that arrived at Bell's home in the spring of 1968 was most welcome. Writing shortly after King's assassination, a Charlotte television station director informed Bell:

I wrote to ABC ... hopeful that they might cease the glorification of Martin Luther King and turn to something that would serve a constructive purpose.

Somebody needs to do something to try to save the republic from suicide. It appears obvious that no politician in sight possesses both the will and the ability to do it.

Kindest personal regards.

Cordially,
Jesse Helms[1]

Other white southerners were no less exasperated with the civil rights movement. Following the race riots that swept the nation in 1968, a Chattanooga woman complained to Bell. "I am heartily tired," she wrote, "of having the matter of color used as a criticism and accusation against the churches because they have not thrown open their doors to the colored race, who would probably be most dissatisfied were they to become members of a white congregation, except in the case of a very few." Bell readily agreed with the sentiments expressed by his correspondents. Three years earlier, when the Watts neighborhood of Los Angeles had gone up in flames, King demanded the resignation of the city's white mayor and police chief. Although unemployed black youths had started the riot, King blamed the white power structure for the destruction of property worth $40 million. Bell countered that it was agitators like King who had provoked the riot. As far as Bell was concerned, King and his ilk, not the Los Angeles Police Department, had the blood of thirty-four people on their hands. "The unfortunate thing," Bell apprised the pastor of a Louisville Presbyterian Church, "is that we now have an element in our society who consider themselves above the law, and when they break it, consider themselves martyrs if they are punished."[2]

In the city where King first rose to national prominence, the Montgomery *Advertiser* delivered a strange eulogy to the slain activist. While King was "at least glib and adroit in the guile by which he managed to flummox an alarming number of Americans," his successor as leader of the Southern Christian Leadership Conference, Rev. Ralph Abernathy, could be described only as "an unprincipled and unspeakable bum without any redeeming qualities whatever." The Montgomery *Advertiser* gleefully reminded its white readers of the 1958 incident in which a jealous, hatchet-wielding husband had gone after King's protégé. Montgomery's blacks closed ranks behind Abernathy, even though he was guilty of seeking "unnatural sex acts" with another man's wife. While the enemies of the civil rights movement spread tales about Abernathy's adulterous behavior, Yankee journalists often refused to listen. Against a backdrop of Ku Klux Klan bombings of black churches and the murder of civil rights activists, liberals refused to report on the moral gap between the public and personal behavior of some civil rights leaders. In any event, the large billboards along Alabama roadsides that depicted King as a Communist only made northern reporters more hostile toward the white South.[3]

To the northerners who watched the civil rights struggle unfold on the evening news, there seemed to be two Souths: one black and one white. Quite clearly, shotgun-wielding yahoos in pickup trucks were intent upon brutalizing blacks. At the same time, however, opinion surveys of white southerners conducted four years before the passage of the 1965 Voting

Rights Act revealed that 95 percent thought that blacks should have the right to vote. A slim majority of southern whites even stated that they did not mind sharing a bus seat with a black. One Greensboro, North Carolina, textile mill supervisor in 1968 best summed up the complicated mind-set of white southerners. While he boasted that if rioting blacks tried to set fire to his house he would "tie them up in the street and burn them," the sixty-year-old supervisor supported the 1964 Civil Rights Act, which banned discrimination in public accommodations. "I ain't for holding the colored down," he told a pollster.[4]

The problem for white southerners was not just racial. Their experience with a failed revolution, a humiliating military occupation, and a century of grinding poverty led many southern whites to be suspicious of the federal government. They were stern believers in self-help, protective of their property rights, and, having lived with economic limits, had no sense that there was enough to share with less fortunate whites, let alone blacks. When Montgomery's civic leaders spent $100,000 to commemorate the centennial of Jefferson Davis's inauguration as president of the Confederate States of America, southern whites were doing more than symbolically slapping civil rights activists in the face. They were thumbing their noses at the arrogant Yankees in Washington.[5]

With the end of the Civil War, southern blacks embraced the federal government and the Republican Party as their personal champions. Conversely, southern whites became ardent Democrats and foes of Big Government. (Their opposition to Big Government did have its limits. Southern planters expressed warm appreciation for the cotton, peanut, and tobacco subsidies that Franklin Roosevelt provided.) Few northerners in the early sixties sympathized with the white South's view that not serving blacks at a restaurant was a basic right of private property ownership. Two northerners who did believe businesses had a constitutional right not to serve blacks were *National Review* editor William F. Buckley, Jr., and Robert Bork—then a little-known member of the Yale Law School faculty. According to the Yale professor, relying upon Congress and the federal courts to promote racial equality was more obnoxious to constitutional law and property rights than segregation itself. Bork was not going to be invited to a lot of Manhattan soirees.[6]

In spite of the southern racial divide, and in spite of the 1962 riot at the University of Mississippi that killed two men when racists tried to stop a black from enrolling as a student, there were hopeful developments. A year after the "Ole Miss" riot, the Mississippi State University basketball team quietly sneaked out of Starkville in order to compete in the NCAA tournament at East Lansing, Michigan. Stealth was necessary since Governor Ross Barnett had forbidden white Mississippi athletes from playing against colleges with black players. Even though they lost to an integrated Loyola of Chicago team, applause and cheers shook the rafters of the auditorium as the Mississippians shook hands with their black and Catholic counterparts. "Ole Miss" may have been the school of choice for Deep South gentlemen, but the cotton choppers in Starkville showed that they had far more class.[7]

If one believed the rhetoric of the 101 Dixie congressmen who pledged their unyielding opposition to public school integration in 1956, blacks and whites lived completely separate from one another. In reality, there had always been places in the segregated South where members of both races found harmony, craps games, sex, and bootleg whiskey. At night, far off the state routes and deep in the cotton fields, a humble sharecropper's cabin would be transformed into a raucous "blind pig." Black bootleggers, who invested pennies in the manufacture of moonshine, would happily charge thirsty white folks sixteen dollars a gallon for their wares. Only the handful of patrons who were still standing as the morning sun arose felt cheated. Black musicians on their way to Chicago were known to raise the roof at the reefer-drenched blind pigs.[8]

The culture spawned on the margins of southern life was shocking to religiously upright whites and blacks. One had only to listen to the lyrics of hillbilly music and rhythm and blues to hear the voice of moral depravity. Themes of adultery, drinking oneself blind, illegitimacy, and spousal murder predominated. It was no wonder that when the music of poor blacks and whites moved North and became repackaged as rock 'n' roll and country-western, Billy Graham and Martin Luther King, Jr., were aghast. To the consternation of God-fearing Baptists, the music they so despised reflected unwelcome truths. As early as the thirties, the South had the highest illegitimacy and syphilis rates in the nation, and six Dixie states ranked first in the incidence of black-on-black homicide.[9]

Yankee reformers mistakenly believed that the white power structure sought only to keep lower-class blacks in check. Little did they know that lower-class whites were also targets. When disfranchisement swept the South at the beginning of the twentieth century, almost all blacks, as well as a third of whites, lost the right to vote. Moreover, while northern liberals pointed to the 3,400 blacks who had fallen prey to lynch mobs since the end of Reconstruction, they failed to note that 1,300 whites had met the same fate. Paradoxically, the middle-class whites and blacks who fought each other over civil rights had long been united in a culture war against the dissolute members of their respective races. Near Plains, Georgia, during the Great Depression, a man sexually assaulted a ten-year-old black girl. After he attacked a white police officer, area residents shot the pedophile. Although liberals chalked this incident up as a "mob lynching" of an innocent black man, they could not have been more wrong. Blacks and whites wanted the molester executed. The issue here was morality, not racism.[10]

As champions of moral order, the ten million members of the segregated Southern Baptist Convention regarded the civil rights movement as less than Christian. In 1965, a handful of black college students in Tuskegee, Alabama, sought to attend worship services with whites. The deacons of the Baptist church gave new meaning to the song "Onward Christian Soldiers," pummeling their black counterparts. At Georgia's Mercer University, a Southern Baptist college, a white minister lost his pulpit when he criticized his deacons for barring blacks. Birmingham's white clergy closed ranks in 1963. They decried King for claiming to lead a nonviolent movement that thrived upon the provocation of "hatred and violence." King countered that God's commandments transcended secular segregation laws. Consequently, blacks had a moral imperative to march in the streets. It was not their fault that the Birmingham Police Department responded by beating and hosing down helpless black children. Southern black and white clergy were reading from different Bibles.[11]

Dismayed that black ministers were bringing their political agenda into the sanctuary of God's house, the pastor of the Thomas Road Baptist Church chastised King. From Lynchburg, Virginia, a community whose name had become part of America's cultural landscape, Rev. Jerry Falwell argued in 1965 that blacks should heed the words of Jesus. The Savior, after all, believed that individual sin, not discrimination and segregation, was the crux of humanity's problems. Moreover:

If church leaders feel that the church should take part in social reforms, then I am forced to ask why the church is not concerned about the alcoholism problem in America. There are almost as many alcoholics as there are Negroes. Three times as much money is spent annually in America for liquor as for education. More money is spent annually for tobacco than for support of religious institutions. There seems to be a good bit of hypocrisy evident here. Why is the church not concerned about the liberal trend in our theological schools? Why is there not a like display of concern about the lowering of moral standards among young people today?[12]

The dynamic young minister had good reason to believe that religious crusades against alcohol and immorality were more important than "the alleged discrimination against Negroes in the South." Falwell's father, a dance-hall operator from the wrong side of the tracks, had killed his brother during a heated argument. Although the elder Falwell had acted in self-defense, he never forgave himself and subsequently committed the slow suicide of an alcoholic.[13]

Falwell's unwillingness to confront racial discrimination was understandable. Like many white clergymen, he could not escape the peculiar history that had shaped southern Christianity. Slavery had existed in the South more than a century before a Virginian planter named Thomas Jefferson had written that all white men were created equal. Southern planters enslaved Africans, yet felt morally obliged to convert them to Christianity. English evangelical George Whitefield preached the Gospel to blacks in the eighteenth century while seeking to extend slavery to Georgia. When the abolitionist cause swept northern Baptist congregations in the nineteenth century, southerners decided to secede. Founded in 1845, the Southern Baptist Convention championed slavery, temperance, and biblical inerrancy. While northern Baptists had no problems outlawing alcohol and believing that everything in the Bible should be taken literally, human bondage was another matter.[14]

Separation from their co-religionists in upstate New York and New England had a number of consequences for the Southern Baptists. Where Yankees championed public schooling, with the understanding that the schools would teach Protestant values, Southern Baptists balked. Dixie's Protestants feared that an anti-religious secularism would inevitably infect public schools. Consequently, Mississippi did not establish a public school system until 1919, eighty years after New England. In the South's segregated schools, black teachers received half the salary of whites. As late as 1945, the majority of southern teachers, black or white, did not have college degrees. Local school boards did, however, make sure that the teachers were Christians.[15]

At the beginning of the twentieth century, a number of Protestant congregations in the North embraced the Social Gospel. Here was a theology of reform that emphasized the economic foundations of social injustice and argued that government had a role in combating poverty. Hailing from the more affluent Protestant sects, advocates of the Social Gospel also tended to reject the doctrine of biblical inerrancy. In short order, the sectional schism that arose from the dispute over slavery evolved into a theological conflict over religious practice and the responsibility of government to change economic and racial relations. Those who embraced the fundamental tenets of Protestantism became known as fundamentalists. Drawn from the ranks of the lower middle class, fundamentalists scorned the Social Gospel. To Southern Baptists, reformers like Martin Luther King, Jr., were the Pharisees of the modern world. Hiding behind their clerical garb, they sought to subvert the message of God's church.[16]

Through the fifties, liberals and fundamentalists found one area of agreement: Catholics and Communists posed serious threats to American religious freedom. Rev. Norman Vincent Peale, an author of religiously tinged self-help books, and Martin Luther King, Sr., warned against a Vatican takeover of America if John Kennedy were elected president in 1960. A nominal Catholic who thought that the commandment against adultery was merely a suggestion, Kennedy could not believe that the father of the civil rights leader was a bigot. It never occurred to Kennedy that there might have been a religious reason behind why the Kings were named after the leader of the Protestant Reformation.[17]

One other group in the South had remained voiceless in the region's political affairs, partly by choice and partly by economic circumstance. While fundamentalists were revolting against a federal government that championed civil rights, Pentecostals seemed to be at peace. Although most Americans in the sixties did not know the difference between Pentecostals and fundamentalists, Southern Baptists and members of such holiness congregations as the Assemblies of God did not need to be told. Pentecostals believed in faith healing and spirit possession. God could make them speak in ancient tongues and thereby reveal His word. Unfortunately, God was not the only spirit close at hand. Satan also dwelled among the wretched of the earth, constantly tempting them with moonshine and illicit sex. Many of the wizened Okies who left the Dust Bowl for California during the Great Depression were Pentecostals. Unlike John Steinbeck's fictional characters in *The Grapes of Wrath*, these stoic individualists declined federal assistance and scorned farm-labor organizers. (For that matter, real Okies would not have warmed to any lyrics from "The Battle Hymn of the Republic," a *Yankee* Civil War song.)[18]

Sin was not an abstract concept to Pentecostals. They expected that everyone, including their religious leaders, would succumb to temptation. In 1926, when Los Angeles evangelist Aimee Semple McPherson apparently went off to a "love nest" and then tried to cover up by claiming to have been kidnapped, her followers were understanding. The intellectuals were not so forgiving. Sinclair Lewis mocked McPherson in *Elmer Gantry*, his searing indictment of money-grubbing fundamentalists and lusty Pentecostals. If Lewis had closely studied the people he purported to write about, he might have discovered a few seeming anomalies. White and black Pentecostals often worshipped together. Indeed, in the dirt-poor reaches of Louisiana during the forties, Jimmy Swaggart preached to his black friends while his cousin, Jerry Lee Lewis, hung out in blind pigs learning rhythm and blues. When respectable white southerners enacted poll taxes and literacy tests as part of their effort to disfranchise blacks, they likewise had the Lewis and Swaggart families in mind. You just never knew when Jesus was going to tell the Pentecostals that the planters were servants of the Devil.[19]

Not every Pentecostal came from a deprived background. Occasionally, a privileged individual discovered that life without an ever-present God lacked meaning. In Lexington, Virginia, in a universe far from Lynchburg, where Jerry Falwell struggled to overcome family tragedy, a southern aristocrat was born. The much-indulged second son of Senator A. Willis Robertson, Pat Robertson could have been mistaken for one of the princely Tarleton twins in *Gone With the Wind*. Rural poverty and the Great Depression never touched Pat Robertson. In college, his friends came from the ranks of the dissipated gentry. Roommate John Warner, with the *Social Directory* at his side, scanned the yearbooks from nearby women's colleges looking for a suitable heiress to marry.[20]

Pat Robertson followed the conventional path set for a southern gentleman. From college he entered the military, then graduated from Yale Law School, and soon embarked upon a career as a businessman. The next logical step would have been to return to Virginia and prepare for election to Congress. For Robertson, however, life remained empty. By the fifties, the Virginian decided to become a clergyman and serve the poor. Forsaking his family's wealth, Robertson went to a Brooklyn garden spot known as Bedford-Stuyvesant. Desiring to live as Jesus did among society's outcasts, Robertson, his wife, and their children moved into a rat-infested church center. Robertson racially integrated churches in the New York City area, ministered to the poor, and led a Bible study group for Jews interested in converting to Christianity.[21]

His experiences in Bedford-Stuyvesant taught the senator's son a few things. Robertson watched one man father sixty children, each of them on welfare and condemned to lives of poverty. As far as Robertson was concerned, there was too much government around—showering checks upon the undeserving poor and sapping their desire to work—and not enough churches. At the same time, the Pentecostal broke sharply with his father on the question of race. Senator Robertson had taken his place among other southern congressmen who vowed to defeat the civil rights movement. His son accepted blacks as brothers in the Holy Spirit:

I was much more open toward assimilation to the blacks in society than were the Old-Guard Southerners. I was uncomfortable with the massive resistance that went on, the unwillingness to allow black people into school, and segregation in general, which put one class of people down. They had a feeling of white superiority. That was their culture and it was a blind spot, although those people were mostly Christians who just couldn't accommodate the emerging status of blacks.[22]

When Robertson came home, it was to preach, not to run for political office. Learning of a ramshackle UHF television station for sale in Norfolk, Robertson bought it for a few thousand dollars. The Pentecostal could not have known in 1961 that he was helping to give birth to a Christian counterculture. Robertson's Christian Broadcasting Network (CBN) gradually acquired television and radio stations across the country. Wherever Appalachian Pentecostals migrated north during World War II, from the hills of Alabama, Kentucky, and West Virginia, to the boom towns of Akron, Columbus, and Detroit, CBN had an audience. While the news media devoted much of its time to chronicling the youth rebellion of the sixties, the Christian counterculture went largely unnoticed. When Hollywood made the Pat Boone vehicle, *The Cross and the Switchblade,* New Yorkers hooted the Pentecostal hero who preached among impoverished blacks and Puerto Ricans. More often, these outlandish Pentecostals did not even intrude that much into the lives of the smart set. In any event, so long as such southerners kept to themselves and did not vote, who cared if they watched CBN, sent donations to Oklahoma's Oral Roberts, and joined the "Pentecostal Rotary"—the Full Gospel Business Men's Fellowship?[23]

The action in the religious world, so liberal reporters and politicians believed, was to be found in the respectable Protestant denominations and among progressive Catholics. Religious orthodoxy was out, while civil rights and protest against the escalating Vietnam War were in. Desiring to make the church more appealing to Catholic college students, some East Coast priests brought radical politics and rock 'n' roll music to the Mass. At countercultural Masses—held in activist centers rather than the parish church—clergy and laity substituted Beatles' songs for more traditional hymns. After reading passages from Henry Miller's erotic novel *Tropic of Capricorn,* the laity sang an offertory chorus of "A Little Help from My Friends." Instead of pictures of Christian saints hanging from the walls of the improvised church, parishioners were surrounded by photographs of activists like King and Malcolm X.[24]

Northern religious reformers marched with King and organized protests against America's anti-Communist foreign policy. Thomas Merton, a Trappist monk whose mystical writings were becoming the rage on college campuses, viewed the Vietnam War as a continuation of America's history of genocide and racism. Similarly, Father Philip Berrigan asserted that Western civilization was "the enemy of man." One Catholic theology professor compared Communist leader Ho Chi Minh to Jesus Christ and President Lyndon Johnson to Satan:

Depart from me, you cursed Americans, into the eternal fire for the devil and his angels; for I was a hungry North Vietnamese and you gave me no food, I was a thirsty Viet Cong and you gave me no drink, I was a napalmed child and you did not welcome me. . . . In fact, it is you who made me, the Vietnamese Christ, hungry and thirsty, an outlaw hiding out in my own forests, and it is you who maintain my suffering by bombing my people and villages and razing my land.[25]

In Milwaukee, liberal Catholics established a branch of the Christian Family Movement. This group advocated the busing of white students to black schools, arguing that racial integration would improve minority education. (Black Power advocates did not appreciate the implicit rationale behind busing; that their children could not learn without the intellectual stimulation of white students and teachers.) Suburbanites and parents who sent their children to private schools—like many supporters of the Christian Family Movement, for instance—would not feel the effects of busing. During a 1967 open-housing march, Milwaukee's working-class Poles waved baseball bats at the liberal Catholic priest who led the demonstration. Two years before that, Selma, Alabama, racists murdered Rev. James Reeb, a Unitarian minister and Boston civil rights activist. Viewing such incidents, and then linking America's racial troubles to the never-ending Vietnam conflict, Catholic, Jewish, and Protestant reformers came to a conclusion: The South, white workers, and a foreign policy–making Establishment in Washington had declared war on God.[26]

To the young whites and blacks who filled the ranks of the New Left, it did not matter if racist AmeriKKKa was waging war against God. Many activists worshipped at the altar of Ho Chi Minh, Mao Tse-Tung, Che Guevara, and Fidel Castro. Others were insatiable hedonists, reveling in immediate physical gratification through drugs and sex. Even if the number of gonorrhea cases among youths increased 200 percent during the sixties, few of them seemed concerned. There was no such thing as an incurable social disease. Nothing more was required to be rid of a sexually transmitted disease than a quick trip to the free clinic and a shot of penicillin. In San Francisco, where refrigerators could contain more LSD than food, straights and gays bragged about their sexual conquests. Many could mark a score in the triple digits. Antiwar activists at Berkeley enlisted in the cause, founding the militant Sexual Freedom League. Regular orgies, and the legalization of pornography and pedophilia, were but a few projects of the Bay Area freedom fighters. These folks were not seeing much of the inside of churches or synagogues on the weekends.[27]

Although the civil rights movement had been born in the black churches, with King deliberately calling his organization the Southern *Christian* Leadership Conference, the religiosity of its new recruits was minimal. As secular whites and blacks from the North did battle in Birmingham and Selma, fewer activists attended church or expressed a belief in God. By 1964, barely a third of white civil rights activists from the North thought religious belief relevant to the cause of social justice. God was dead. Describing his thoughts at his first antiwar demonstration, a member of the radical Students for a Democratic Society (SDS) best summed up the attitude of the New Left toward religion, "I felt the way I did when I gave up religion. I felt I had kicked something. I was free."[28]

A desire to "do my own thing," coupled with a hostility toward white workers, southerners, authority figures, and a government that waged war on Marxist guerrillas in Southeast Asia, formed the basis of New Left ideology. Cold War Democrats, the politicians who stood at the "vital center" of American society, represented the true adversaries of progressive reform. Some SDSers became revolutionaries, robbing banks, bombing military bases, and rumbling with white policemen—the occupation army of America's ghetto colonies. Other New Leftists sought control of the Democratic Party, intending to drive out its racist urban machine bosses and anti-Communist labor leaders. Still more dreamed of making "the long march through the professions," moving into positions of cultural power in the university, the media, and Hollywood. Radicals also entered the legal profession in order to shape the federal judiciary. Just as they nationalized the civil rights conflict, challenging repressive local ordinances in the federal courts, radicals planned other legal crusades. In their minds, northern communities that prohibited abortion and gay sex were little different from the southern states that sanctioned segregation.[29]

A few observers on the Right noticed that a growing number of young conservatives were no less hedonistic than their counterparts in the New Left. The *National Review,* reflecting the angst of its conservative Catholic editors, warned that the libertarians' rejection of Big Government could go too far. Scrapping a federal bureaucracy that interfered with the conduct of business was one thing, but the wholesale repudiation of all moral authority was another matter. Libertarians wanted to legalize marijuana and abolish the draft. (Only the poor would be compelled by the free market to enlist.) Even though the libertarian Right and the New Left stood at opposite ends of the political spectrum, they had much in common. Both wanted dominion over the federal government, with libertarians hoping to free business from health and safety regulations, and radicals wanting to outlaw racism and deny military support to anti-Communist regimes. Libertarians and leftists avoided the Vietnam War through college-student deferments, smoked pot (some even inhaled), and entered the ranks of the upper middle class. The libertarian Right usually could get along with the New Left; it was those Southern Baptists, orthodox Catholics, and angry white workers who were so troublesome.[30]

The black New Left was not without its own quirks. Although racism pervaded American society, black leftists frequently exaggerated their suffering for political ends. No objective white would have denied that blacks found it difficult to obtain decent jobs and housing in Lansing, Michigan, during the Great Depression. Yet Malcolm Little, upon becoming the Black Muslim leader Malcolm X, invented a story in which white supremacists murdered his father. Actually, a jealous husband had ambushed the senior Little. In the Ocean Hill-Brownsville district of Brooklyn in 1968, black militants accused white teachers and public school administrators of being racists. Many of the whites were liberal Jews who had marched in civil rights demonstrations. The black militants seized control of the school district's governing board, employing vicious anti-Semitic rhetoric to justify the expulsion of Jewish teachers.[31]

Black Panther leader Eldridge Cleaver argued that the rape of white women by black men represented "an insurrectionary act." Stokeley Carmichael, a leading proponent of Black Power, proclaimed that "every courthouse in Mississippi should be burnt down tomorrow so we can get rid of the [white] dirt." A militant black college student in Ohio informed a pollster that he welcomed rioting because it would drive all of the whites from the cities. However, this young man could not understand why "these Jew merchants keep coming back." Anyone who criticized the black militants' anti-Semitism and exhortations to violence against whites was scorned by the New Left. As victims of racism, blacks could not themselves be racist. In any event, the white radicals who went south had rejected the black clergy as "Uncle Toms." The *authentic* black people whom they came to rescue from oppression were—like Malcolm X and the Black Panthers—to be found in the prisons and blind pigs. Sure they were rough, but that made them real. Southern Baptists needed no more confirmation that the civil rights movement was an incubator of immorality.[32]

In the early sixties, liberal northerners expressed no little satisfaction that America's race problem was a *southern* problem. The Los Angeles riot of 1965 shook their complacency. By 1968, in the aftermath of one hundred race riots that killed 225 people and caused $112 billion in property damage, there was little cause for Manhattan to feel superior to Birmingham. Northern liberals were puzzled. After all, there had never been any racial disturbances in their white-collar neighborhoods and suburbs. The professors and lawyers of Brookline, Massachusetts, for instance, prided themselves on creating a community open to anyone in the upper middle class. Blacks, Greeks, Reform Jews, and Anglo-Saxon Protestants established excellent public schools, art galleries, and restaurants for the sophisticated diner. Everyone got along in Brookline. Why could *those* people in Boston, Buffalo, and Milwaukee not emulate their worthy example?[33]

It required little effort to discern who *those* people were that the liberal professionals found so distasteful: working- and lower-middle-class Catholics. Their friends generally referred to them as white ethnics. Less kind critics, namely suburban liberals and collegiate New Leftists, called them racist, hawkish hard hats. Along the eastern seaboard, most Catholics hailed from Italy and Ireland. The Irish and the Italians arrived in Boston and New York in the nineteenth and early twentieth century were met with discrimination in employment, housing, and higher education. Often as not, it was the Episcopalian grandparents of the liberal Brookliners who had discriminated against white ethnics like Panos Dukakis. (Faced with discrimination, Greeks and Jews were more prone to assimilate than

Slavs, putting their immigrant, blue-collar roots far behind them.) In the industrial centers of the heartland, representatives from corporations like U.S. Steel had gone to Croatian, Polish, and Slovakian villages to recruit workers. Slavs worked for pennies and appeared to be docile. Since many of the Eastern European Catholics hailed from the Austro-Hungarian Empire, the Presbyterian mill bosses mockingly labeled them "Huns" or "Hunkies." Southern black migrants pronounced "Hunkie" as "Honkie."[34]

White ethnic and black relations had never been cordial. During the 1919 steel strike, U.S. Steel, Bethlehem, and Republic recruited tens of thousands of black scabs from the South. Eighteen years later, recent black migrants sided with the mill bosses, defeating CIO organizing efforts in Johnstown, Pennsylvania, and the cities of Ohio's "Steel Valley"—Canton, Massillon, and Youngstown. Racial violence flared in the mill towns while National Guardsmen and company "goon squads" fired into the picket lines. Although black scabs became legendary in the Midwest, white Appalachian migrants also brushed aside the Catholic strikers. Catholics had no use for black or southern Protestant strike breakers. Indeed, ethnics would have given a much friendlier reception to a pro-CIO black than to Bull Connor, an enthusiastic member of U.S. Steel's Birmingham goon squad. For the Catholic New Dealers who had fought the labor wars of the thirties, there was no reservoir of goodwill toward Connor. When Birmingham's vicious police commissioner fought Martin Luther King, Jr., in 1963, the United Steel Workers Union and the United Automobile Workers sent money to the Southern Christian Leadership Conference.[35]

With the advent of the Second World War, nearly two million southern blacks headed to the Midwest and California. Once Dixie's cotton fields became fully serviced by mechanized pickers in the fifties, three million more black southerners went north. Chicago's black population grew from 492,000 in 1950 to more than one million by the end of the sixties. Whites who could afford suburban housing left the cities, leaving behind struggling Catholics and Appalachians. Convinced that Catholics possessed "white-skin privilege," upscale New Leftists came to regard working-class ethnics as part of the racist power structure that ruled America. They were deluded. In the sixties, two-thirds of Italian-Americans lived not much above the poverty level and only 7 percent had college diplomas. Similarly, four-fifths of Polish-Americans collected minimal wages and just half had completed high school. Postwar affluence for the typical Catholic, Southern Baptist, and Pentecostal meant having a car payment and a mortgage on a small bungalow. It did not mean living in a spacious Brookline abode and attending Harvard.[36]

In 1964, President Johnson announced his intention to build the Great Society, which would do away with racism and poverty. Civil rights legislation outlawed discrimination and protected black voting rights, while a host of social-welfare programs either expanded upon their earlier charter or were created whole cloth. In Chicago, Johnson's Community Action Program awarded grants to "authentic" black community leaders, in most cases bypassing the clergy. (Secular liberals wished to maintain the separation of church and state, and radicals disdained most black ministers. One Brooklyn minister conceded that the church was a "training ground for equipping folks with the middle-class values of upward mobility." Few black clergy called for the overthrow of capitalism.) Blacks were then expected to establish businesses that would ease unemployment in the inner city. Unfortunately, among the new minority business organizations created were the Vice Lords and the El Rukns. Ethnic Democrats were not amused that Washington bureaucrats were using their taxes to subsidize drug dealing, extortion, murder, and prostitution. Great Society liberals denied that there were any problems and accused critics of the Community Action Program of being racists. (President Johnson cut his losses, abandoning the Community Action Program.)[37]

During the sixties welfare programs for single mothers became more generous. With the poor receiving federal checks, subsidized housing, Medicaid, and food stamps, the cycle of poverty, crime, and illegitimacy would surely be broken. In 1965, one-quarter of black children did not have fathers. Nearly all illegitimate children lived in poverty. The next few years saw federal spending on the poor expand 400 percent, while the caseload for Aid to Families with Dependent Children (AFDC) rose 125 percent. In the same span of time, the number of single, black, teenage mothers grew 800 percent and the proportion of black children who did not have fathers went from one-quarter to one-third. The violent crime rate went up 126 percent as the number of murderers, rapists, and drug dealers thrown into prison fell substantially. Those most affected by violence were white ethnics and blacks. The affluent suburbs where Great Society liberals lived remained safe havens.[38]

The level of trust between ethnics and Protestant liberals had never been high. During the forties and fifties, in an era when ethnics were supposed to have become fully accepted members of American society, prominent liberal voices were heard criticizing Catholics. The National Education Association opposed providing public transportation to parochial schoolchildren. Taking the NEA's side, former first lady Eleanor Roosevelt claimed that efforts to give tax breaks to parents with children in parochial schools, or even transporting Catholic children, were part of a Vatican-directed scheme to seize control of American education. To the NEA and Eleanor Roosevelt, it did not matter that Catholics had to pay property taxes to support the public schools their children did not attend, as well as come up with parochial school tuition.[39]

Protestant educators had wanted to destroy the parochial school system since its inception in the nineteenth century. The passing of one hundred years had changed little in the public school establishment's attitude toward Catholic schools. It mattered hardly at all to the NEA, and to the editors of such liberal magazines as the *Christian Century* and the *Nation* that the bishops of New Orleans, St. Louis, and Washington had racially integrated their parochial schools years before the *Brown* decision. Ironically, when integration came to Washington's *public schools,* Senator George McGovern and Supreme Court Justice Earl Warren enrolled their children in either private or suburban schools. As Alabama's combative governor George Wallace tartly put it, "They are building a new bridge over the Potomac for all the white liberals fleeing to Virginia."[40]

The crime problem simply added another brick in the wall separating socially conservative ethnics from Great Society liberals. Prior to the Warren Court's expansion of civil liberties for violent offenders, as well as the Great Society's provision of free legal aid to criminals, urban police forces served as armies of occupation. The New Left had that much right. Policemen routinely beat confessions out of miscreants—black, hillbilly, and Italian. On the other hand, police officers kept a lid on crime. Those most likely to become victims of violence—the poor—could walk the streets of their neighborhoods without fear of being gunned down by drug dealers. There was a trade-off between civil liberties and safety that urban people had been making since the first Irish cop slammed a South Boston thug onto the cobblestone pavement. To the refined members of the American Civil Liberties Union, this trade-off was no longer acceptable. But then, the ACLU attorneys did not have to live with the consequences of their legal initiatives. Muggers, dope dealers, and gunslingers had not found their way to Brookline.[41]

Great Society liberals made much of their efforts to open up middle-class employment opportunities for blacks. Conservatives countered that the black standard of living had been improving before federal intervention. In the decade before Johnson gave birth to the Great Society, larger numbers of northern blacks were obtaining college degrees. A new black middle class, either self-employed or working in the private sector, was appearing. In the sixties, the federal, state, and municipal governments brushed aside the private sector as the employer of choice for the black middle class. Blacks became social workers and teachers, directed Community Action Programs, and managed public housing projects. Two-thirds of all public-sector employment in the sixties was related to the operation of the welfare state. More than half of these jobs went to blacks. To the average blue-collar Democrat, it appeared as if the Great Society intended to grab larger chunks of his paycheck in order to benefit black welfare recipients. He could discern little difference between the black social worker and the black welfare mother. Big Government was becoming identified as Black Welfare Government.[42]

If the issues dividing ethnics and upper-middle-class liberals had remained confined to Big Government, welfare, and crime, there might have remained some small hope for reconciliation. After all, both groups still embraced many of the tenets of New Deal liberalism; namely, a belief that government should promote equal opportunity for all Americans. Rapprochement, however, was not in the cards. With libertarian sensibilities swelling among liberals and radicals, new protest movements arose out of the bowels of the Black Power movement. Feminism and the legalization of abortion took center stage among the causes of social liberalism in the sixties.[43]

In 1966, secular Jews and Protestants founded the National Organization for Women. NOW was a political pressure group that spoke on behalf of women with careers, not working-class women with low-paying jobs and struggling families. Ninety percent of NOW's members were college graduates, one-third possessed graduate degrees, and a substantial number were lesbians. It would have been difficult to have found a group more alien to the average high-school-educated, married woman. Not surprisingly, NOW's advocacy of abortion deeply offended Catholics and fundamentalists. Although NOW tried to frame abortion rights as an issue pitting women against men, the polling evidence showed the hollowness of its contentions. Throughout the sixties, working-class Protestant women expressed the greatest opposition to the legalization of abortion. Conversely, unchurched men in their twenties were the most fervent advocates of abortion. ("If you can't be with the one you love," Stephen

Stills sang, "Love the one you're with." However, if you get pregnant, that is your problem.)[44]

The most annoyed Catholics established political networks to combat the forces of social liberalism. Phyllis Schlafly, a "housewife" and devout Catholic, concluded that the only hope for social conservatives was to wrest the Republican party away from its liberal East Coast leaders. By her lights, the Democrats had already gone too far to the left to be redeemed. In 1968, a group of religious traditionalists founded Catholics United for the Faith. These conservatives opposed sex education in the schools, embraced the Vatican's opposition to all unnatural forms of birth control, and viewed liberal priests with repulsion. Although Schlafly and Catholics United for Faith spoke for only fifteen thousand or so core activists, their constituencies were already much larger and more politically formidable than the Catholic Left. By focusing on countercultural Masses, liberal journalists once again missed a major development in American religion.[45]

Since the Great Depression, Catholics had seen the national Democratic Party and the federal government as friends. For all of the Republican rhetoric about New Deal socialism and tyrannical Big Government, the Democrats had fairly modest ambitions. Washington created a welfare state, but its beneficiaries were the deserving poor who had been thrown out of work through no fault of their own. Widows received AFDC. (Single women, after all, did not have children out of wedlock and men did not desert their families.) Washington expected businessmen and laborers to contribute to Social Security and unemployment compensation funds. Those who did not work would not collect government checks. Anyone who committed a crime against life and property went to jail. Finally, the federal government regulated labor-management relations, not personal morality. Sexual liberation and abortion rights were not on the plate.

So long as Washington and the Democratic Party remained true to the New Deal, Catholics trusted government to do good. When it came to issues of morality and poverty, communities and churches did what Washington did not and should not do. In Catholic theology, this emphasis upon moral solutions to local problems was called subsidiarity. Schools belonged under the control of parents, not city, state, or federal bureaucrats. Poverty is not abolished by giving the poor checks but by expecting them to work. At the local level, the churches and charitable individuals must teach the poor skills and place them in jobs. The Great Society, the

Warren Court, and the New Left rejected every component of Catholic social instruction and New Deal philosophy. For the first time since 1933, many Catholics came to regard Washington as an unfaithful friend.[46]

Facing growing divisions within the New Deal coalition over welfare, crime, and abortion, Great Society liberals only compounded their problems. President Johnson's escalation of the Vietnam conflict in 1965 opened the way for additional rifts in the Democratic Party. Although Johnson's anti-Communist foreign policy was in keeping with principles set down by Harry Truman after World War II, a new anti-Cold War constituency had appeared. With its base growing on the university campuses and in the white-collar professions, the New Left sought to undermine Cold War liberalism. Johnson made some effort to appease dovish critics by waging a limited war in Southeast Asia and keeping lines of communication open to Hanoi. Since the president would not consider a unilateral withdrawal from Vietnam, his foreign policy only infuriated Democratic doves and radicals. Antiwar protests became larger and more confrontational.

With Johnson unwilling to unleash America's full military might against North Vietnam, ethnics and fundamentalists became disenchanted. Although Southern Baptists and Catholics had vigorously disagreed with one another on issues ranging from Prohibition to labor union recognition, they were united in at least one thing. Both groups were extraordinarily patriotic. During World War II, Catholics and southerners had outdone themselves in supporting the crusade against Germany and Japan. As a proportion of the American population, they shouldered more than their share of the combat burden in the European and Pacific theaters. Further, Catholics were more likely than Protestants and Jews to think that the surrender of Japan did not really mean the war was over. American Catholics believed that the Soviet Union would inevitably become a dangerous foe. Southern Protestants, unlike their northern counterparts, did not lag far behind Catholics in their suspicion of the USSR—even if many fundamentalists and Pentecostals remained fearful of the Vatican.[47]

Although former Vice President Henry Wallace thought well of the Soviet Union, most Democrats appreciated Truman's efforts to restrain Joseph Stalin. Croatian, Polish, and Slovak-American Democrats, whose ancestral homes were now under Communist subjugation, voted against any candidate—regardless of party—who did not promote a strong military defense against the Soviet Union. In 1948, Henry Wallace challenged

Truman, declaring himself the presidential candidate of the leftist Progressive Party. Although Wallace claimed not to know that the American Communist Party provided him with the bulk of his funds and volunteers, it was an open secret.[48]

Euphoric over Wallace's spectacular defeat and quick disappearance from the political scene, Cold War liberals overlooked a few warning signs. Wallace had racked up enough votes in New York City among secular Jews and Anglo-Saxon professionals to deny Truman the state's electoral votes. If there had been more such Wallace voters in other cosmopolitan locales, the Republicans would have captured the White House. In 1948, there were not a sufficient number of college professors, journalists, and secular voters to constitute a bloc capable of inflicting electoral damage upon anti-Communist Democrats.[49]

Liberals expressed greater concern when South Carolina governor Strom Thurmond stalked out of the 1948 Democratic convention. Thurmond and his followers were protesting Truman's modest civil rights concessions to the growing northern-black voting bloc. Even though Thurmond won a few southern states as the Dixiecrat presidential candidate, and later became the first Deep South Republican senator since Reconstruction, Truman held nearly all of the region. The Democratic Party rallied the Catholics, brushed off the Left, threw a few crumbs to northern blacks, and retained the loyalties of most white southerners. As far as Johnson was concerned, what worked in '48 should work in '68.[50]

Johnson's failure to win a quick victory in Vietnam was not the greatest cause of distress among ethnics and southerners. Through the provision of deferments for college students and those who worked in Great Society agencies, 60 percent of draft-age males avoided military service. More than four-fifths of all college students came from the middle and upper classes, and the legal aid lawyers and social workers who flocked to the ghetto often had impeccable pedigrees. During the Vietnam War only one student each from Harvard, Princeton, and Yale died in combat. By 1968, working-class ethnics, like most Americans, had grown weary of the war. Dearborn, Michigan, a lower-middle-class Catholic suburb of Detroit, voted for a resolution against the war. This vote dumbfounded many campus activists since Dearborn had a well-deserved reputation for being hostile toward antiwar students and blacks. Ann Arbor's constituency of conscience should not have been puzzled by its neighbors' disgust with Vietnam. As a result of the 1968 Tet Offensive, Dearborn had lost more of its children in the war than any other community in the nation.[51]

Like their Catholic counterparts, Southern Baptists and Pentecostals were raising their voices against Johnson, the doves, and the campus Left. While large numbers of Presbyterian and Episcopalian clergy wanted an immediate withdrawal from Vietnam, or at least a bombing halt as a prelude to peace negotiations, the majority of fundamentalists and Pentecostals called for a military escalation. North and South, the religious traditionalists were one. In Carbondale, a southern Illinois community largely composed of Pentecostals and Italians, the local newspaper denounced the doves of 1968 as rioters and killers. The majority of folks in the hinterland remained patriotic. They were, however, losing faith in government leaders who seemed unable to defeat Communism overseas and quell domestic unrest. Contrary to the image presented by the media, most students, particularly those from humble backgrounds, were no less critical of the peace protesters.[52]

By 1968, a year of high casualties in both Vietnamese and American cities, John Kennedy's presidency had taken on mythic proportions. Through misty eyes, liberals referred to the early sixties as a golden age of peace and prosperity. Kennedy's election in 1960 had changed the course of American history. Americans wanted the idealism and glamour of the Kennedys, not the cynicism and dreariness of the Nixons. Of course, this was, demographically speaking, nonsense. Kennedy's election by 100,000 votes hardly represented a mandate for ambitious liberal reform. If anything, Nixon's near-victory, and the fact that twenty-two Democrats lost their House seats, indicated how far the Republicans were cutting into the New Deal's constituencies. Kennedy's efforts to reassure Southern Baptists that as president he would not be at the beck and call of the pope scored some points in the South. (Despite his efforts, Boston's most lapsed Catholic still lost Florida, Mississippi, Tennessee, and Virginia.) At the same time middle-class Irish Catholics who believed that Kennedy had distanced himself too far from the church defected to Nixon. Slavs were more sympathetic to Kennedy's religious balancing act, enabling him to carry the electoral vote-rich states of Illinois, Michigan, New York, and Pennsylvania.[53]

President Kennedy avoided engagement with the civil rights movement for as long as possible. His position was understandable. The segregationist wing of the Democratic Party ruled Congress with a magnolia fist. Kennedy needed southern congressional support for his anti-Communist foreign policy initiatives. Domestic policy did not interest him. Tellingly, it had been Vice President Richard Nixon who fought for the 1957 Civil

Rights Act in the Senate, not Kennedy. After the gun smoke cleared in Dallas, all of this would be forgotten. As far as Brookline and Manhattan were concerned, the usurper of Camelot's throne received little credit for the Great Society's welfare and civil rights legislation. Kennedy was the real author, not Lyndon Johnson. Moreover, Kennedy would not have escalated the Vietnam War. Never mind that it was Kennedy who had radically increased the number of American military advisors serving in Vietnam. No wonder Johnson, a man whose oversized ego could be easily bruised, flew into fits of rage at the mention of the Kennedys. Johnson's mistake was to allow the family to get under his skin. At least in this one instance, Nixon was content to stand aside and allow the family to indulge in its self-destructive tendencies.[54]

In 1964, convinced that he was the Second Coming of Franklin Roosevelt, Lyndon Johnson scored impressive victories in Congress and the Electoral College. Knowing well the ways of the un-Reconstructed South, the Texan rounded up congressional support from the liberal Republicans of the North. The Civil Rights Act of 1964 passed with bipartisan support. Considered more closely, however, Johnson's legislative win was almost entirely sectional. *Northern* Democrats and Republicans, not southern Democrats and western Republicans, followed the president. Although Johnson conceded that he might have hurt the Democrats' future prospects in the South, Great Society liberals hoped to make up those possible losses elsewhere. In particular, liberal Democrats looked forward to an ideological and regional split in the Republican Party. If conservatives from the Sunbelt captured the GOP in '64, Republicans like New York governor Nelson Rockefeller would lead GOP liberals into the Democratic camp. Liberal Republicans agreed with Johnson on foreign policy, supported civil rights, and endorsed most of his anti-poverty programs. Their only caveat was that they could run Big Government more efficiently than the Democrats.[55]

To Governor Rockefeller's astonishment, the conservatives not only denied him the presidential nomination in '64, they also repudiated every aspect of country-club Republicanism. Led by Senator Barry Goldwater of Arizona, the conservatives vowed to privatize Social Security, dismantle federal safety regulations in the workplace, wage war on labor unions, and halt the racial integration of public accommodations and schools. Here was a visionary political agenda that succeeded in alienating every constituency in America with the exception of the Chamber of Commerce. Conservatives thought that most Americans were tired of Big Government.

Likewise, they expected to pick up votes from white southerners. Even though Eisenhower and Nixon had done well among minorities, conservatives chose to write off the northern black vote. As Goldwater informed one Georgian audience, "We're not going to get the Negro vote as a bloc in 1964 and 1968, so we ought to go hunting where the ducks are."[56]

Looking to ethnics, Goldwater made cursory attacks on Great Society liberals, whom he accused of promoting crime and pornography. The overwhelming majority of Catholics perceived Goldwater as a defender of libertarian economics, not morality. Besides, the advance of social liberalism had not become sufficiently alarming to spark huge Catholic defections to the GOP. Ethnics saw Goldwater and his Sunbelt fans as little more than greedy Republicans who enjoyed stepping on hard-working folks like themselves. It did not help GOP prospects among northern workers when Ronald Reagan, a former Hollywood actor, stumped for Goldwater. A corporate spokesman and millionaire, Reagan called Social Security "a welfare program." In Reagan's mind, senior citizens and un-wed mothers were parasites who lived off the federal welfare trough.[57]

Johnson won a landslide, which he interpreted as a clarion call for liberal legislation. Reform-minded Democrats picked up congressional seats in the North, usually at the expense of Johnson's Republican allies. With liberal Republicans all but endorsing Johnson, bipartisanship wreaked havoc upon the northern GOP. The surviving congressional Republicans tended to be conservative westerners. More worrisome to Johnson, Goldwater had carried five Deep South states. After 1964, Great Society liberals counted upon making up some of their southern losses with the enthusiastic support of newly registered black voters. They did not expect the conservative white South and West would ever gain enough population to shift power in the Electoral College away from the liberal northeast. Having kept the ethnics in line, while gaining the votes of silk-stocking Republicans, liberals wrote off the GOP. The Democrats should not have been so cocky.

Although Catholics pulled the lever for Johnson in the national election, quite a few had sent a personal message to the national Democratic Party during the primaries: We have *some* concern for social issues. In 1964, presidential primaries were little more than beauty contests. Congressional leaders, union chiefs, and machine bosses generally gave the nod to acceptable Democratic candidates. On the other hand, smart politicians did not entirely ignore the primaries since they gave a rough measurement of rank-and-file disaffection or approval. Dissidents found the primaries useful in expressing their displeasure with the national party. Alabama's George Wallace decided to become the Democratic spoiler in the '64 primaries. Wallace garnered a quarter of the vote in Wisconsin, with much assistance coming from Milwaukee's ethnic precincts. Only liberal Republicans who crossed over to vote for Johnson prevented an embarrassing development in Wisconsin. The situation was the same in Indiana. Hoosier liberals accused Wallace's followers of not being real red-blooded natives. Rather, they were Southern Baptist and Pentecostal migrants who brought Ku Klux Klan politics to Indiana. (Hoosiers did not need transplanted southerners to help them discover the Klan. In the twenties, one-third of the state belonged to the Klan and the organization ran the legislature and governor's office.)[58]

Without a doubt, Wallace played upon ethnics' prejudices and fears. However, the southerner made some excellent opening shots in the early days of America's culture war. His favorite foe was the Fifth Circuit Court's Judge Frank Johnson, who had ordered the racial integration of Alabama's public schools. Even as Judge Johnson integrated Alabama's public schools, he was founding a private academy for his own son. The governor's children went to integrated public schools. Judge Johnson's boy attended school with the wealthy Episcopalians, Unitarians, and liberal Republicans of Montgomery. (In the sixties, Frank Johnson's son obtained a college-student deferment and became a New Left activist. With so many southerners perishing in Vietnam, the judge had few friends outside his segregated country club.) Positioning himself as the spokesman for the working poor, Wallace also aimed barbs at the segregationist Baptist ministers of the South. As Wallace contended, their church-sponsored Christian academies were little different from the school Judge Johnson established. The middle class and the rich could avoid integrated public schools and recreational facilities. Only poor blacks and whites would remain behind to use cash-strapped municipal schools and parks.[59]

In attacking the 1964 Civil Rights Act, Wallace warned that the Equal Employment Opportunity Commission (EEOC) would mandate hiring quotas. Senator Hubert Humphrey of Minnesota and Roy Wilkins of the NAACP denied that the legislation required racial quotas to correct perceived disparities in private and public sector employment. The word *quota* had a special resonance with white ethnics. Many state universities and the Ivy League had long maintained religious admissions quotas to limit or to exclude outright Catholic and Jewish students. Corporations often would promote only a few Catholics and Jews to low-level managerial positions. Moreover, the 1924 immigration restriction law established a national-origins quota explicitly aimed at keeping Eastern European Catholics and Jews out of the country.[60]

As Wallace predicted, civil rights leaders did demand quotas or, as it was euphemistically called, "affirmative action," in college admissions and employment. Those whites most likely to lose out on educational and job opportunities were poor southerners, Catholics, and lower-middle-class Jews. Federal and state agencies, school districts, police departments, and colleges began creating preferential hiring mandates for blacks. Paradoxically, Alabama State University, the cradle of the Montgomery bus boycott, violated all of the anti-discrimination provisions of the 1964 Civil Rights Act. The historically black college usually declined to hire whites and made life miserable for the handful of non-black faculty. According to Great Society liberals and radicals, only racists like George Wallace argued that there was such a thing as discrimination against whites.[61]

President Johnson's dreams of erecting the Great Society and containing Communism in Vietnam had turned to ashes months before the '68 campaign began. During the long hot summer of '67 American race relations hit their nadir. In Newark, New Jersey, the white chaplain of the Essex County Youth House was caught up in pitched battles and looting. Writing to his Home Mission supporters in North Carolina, the minister noted an especially absurd incident. "Women and children were still looting stores," the urban missionary observed, when "one woman sent her son back into a Foodtown to get the right thing—'Wonder Bread,' (which builds twelve different ways.)" Most Newark whites could not relate to nutrition-conscious looters. Shortly after the riot, Newark went from a city that was two-thirds white to one in which blacks and Puerto Ricans were the majority.[62]

Less than a week after the Newark uprising, a Detroit police raid on a blind pig precipitated an even worse riot. Forty-three people died as a result. With the police unable to contain the arsonists and looters, the Michigan National Guard occupied Detroit. The Guard proved no more successful in restoring order, forcing President Johnson to send the 101st Airborne Division into Detroit. One square mile of the city had already gone up in flames by the time the division that had halted Hitler's Ardennes Offensive in 1944 arrived. The white flight out of Detroit accelerated. In 1960, Detroit's population had been 70 percent white. Blacks became a majority within a few years of the riot. (Today, Detroit is 80 percent black.)[63]

Exulting in the spectacle of Catholics fleeing their crime-plagued neighborhoods, a black municipal employee in Cleveland informed a reporter, "It makes me feel good to know we can chase them. Whites don't understand we don't care about being around them either." This black home owner was not atypical in his hatred of working-class whites. Four-fifths of the rioters arrested in Detroit for looting white-owned property had jobs and homes. Many were members of the auto workers union. The only explanation liberals could come up with was that successful blacks, their expectations rising yearly with their incomes, wanted increased political and economic clout. Once Cleveland, Detroit, and Newark became black cities, racial minorities obtained political power. Economic clout, however, did not follow since many employers chose to relocate to the safer suburbs. After 1967, the only large employers of blacks remaining in the northern urban centers tended to be federal, state, and municipal agencies. A problem looming on the horizon was that urban tax bases were shrinking just as municipal payrolls swelled.[64]

A Gallup poll in the early days of 1968 revealed that, for the first time since the Great Depression, most Americans did not rank unemployment and poverty as leading concerns. Instead, Americans said that they were fed up with crime, inflation, and high taxes. (In 1950, 2 percent of annual family income went to pay federal taxes. As the years progressed and government spending rose, nearly a quarter of annual family income went for federal taxes.) Liberals, however, failed to provide an astute response to the electorate's mounting moral and fiscal conservatism. Instead, the President's National Advisory Commission on Civil Disorders blamed social unrest on "white racism." Resurrected from the political dead, Richard Nixon scored Johnson's commission for "blaming everybody for the riots except the perpetrators of the riots." Nixon realized that the majority of Americans had at least one firm belief: people were to take responsibility for their actions. Defending looters was not a smart political strategy. Spending more money on anti-poverty programs, as commission chair Otto Kerner recommended, was even less intelligent. Such a course of action would make liberals look like they were rewarding criminal behavior.[65]

Nixon did not need to tell Johnson any of this. The president knew that the Democrats had to put the Vietnam War behind them and get tough on crime. Unfortunately for Johnson, vocal elements in the radical wing of the Democratic Party were not listening to his counsel. Senator Eugene McCarthy of Minnesota entered the Democratic presidential primary in New Hampshire. Poet-philosopher and peace activist "Clean Gene" lost, but his tally was sufficient enough to alarm Johnson. Paradoxically, doves misinterpreted McCarthy's showing as a sign of their electoral strength. Bobby Kennedy, the younger brother of the martyred president, quickly declared his own candidacy. Only the party regulars understood that the insurgents had gotten the New Hampshire results wrong. Three-fifths of McCarthy's votes came from hawks and Republicans who were upset with Johnson. They wanted an escalation of the war and an end to liberal reform. Going blithely on his way to the Indiana and California primaries, Bobby Kennedy promised to end the war and extend the writ of the welfare state.

While McCarthy and Kennedy traded barbs, Johnson, having withdrawn from the race, gave Vice President Hubert Humphrey the nod. Humphrey may have won only 1 percent of the party's primary vote, but he had the support of organized labor, the big-city mayors, and the majority of Democratic congressmen. With Bobby Kennedy gunned down in California and the disorganized McCarthy campaign lost in its own existential universe, Humphrey easily snagged the Democratic nomination. The televised clashes between antiwar protesters and police officers at the Chicago convention, however, underlined the hollowness of Humphrey's victory. A party that promised to end social unrest yet could not maintain order at its own convention did not inspire faith in the electorate. Stranger still, having decisively proved in Chicago that Humphrey should not be placed anywhere near hostile students, the vice president made it a point to campaign on college campuses. The results were predictable. Going into the fall campaign, Nixon led Humphrey by fifteen points.

Nixon's campaign was, depending upon whom you asked, either brilliantly evasive or evasively brilliant. Having spent his post-1960 exile cultivating liberal and conservative Republicans, Nixon had little problem securing key endorsements and breezing through the party primaries. A late challenge by California Governor Ronald Reagan proved ineffectual. Although conservative activists liked Reagan's anti–Big Government rhetoric, most Republicans feared his earlier attacks on Social Security would once again alienate disaffected ethnics. Nixon, on the other hand, made distinctions between Great Society and New Deal programs, with the former embodying all the evils of contemporary liberalism and the latter representing truth, justice, and the American Way. (It was a shrewd position to take. Forty percent of Nixon's votes in the general election would come from people who had voted Democratic in '64.) On the issue of Vietnam, Nixon told voters he would somehow end the war. Striving to be a hip, with-it Republican, Nixon appeared on the satirical television show "Laugh-In." Nixon's line, "Sock it to me," was one that liberals could endorse.[66]

Great Society liberals and radicals denounced Nixon for using racial code words. According to them, Nixon was making white southerners and ethnics feel morally justified in their racism. Whether or not calling the Democratic Party's largest bloc of voters bigots for responding to denunciations of violence, illegitimacy, and welfare, was a wise strategy, it was inaccurate. Social concerns are valid issues, particularly if your community is the one being mugged by criminals and Washington bureaucrats. For his part, Nixon detested upper-middle-class white liberals, inner-city rioters, and dovish Jews. He hated all liberals and leftists equally. He made no effort to conceal that. On the other hand, like many Anglo-Saxon Republicans, Nixon felt ill at ease around blacks and Jews. Once they proved their loyalty, however, Nixon had no compulsion against deploying black and Jewish Republicans against the Left.

For all of Nixon's efforts, he defeated Humphrey by 1 percentage point in the popular vote. The AFL-CIO rallied enough of its rank and file behind Humphrey to tighten up the race but ultimately fell short. To organized labor's chagrin, it was Independent presidential candidate George Wallace who cut into the Democratic tally. In South Philadelphia, the home of "Rocky Balboa," Wallace garnered 12 percent of the vote, enough to make Humphrey the first Democrat in forty years to lose the district. South Philly had been the scene of increased muggings and militant black demonstrations. Ignoring political directives from the AFL-CIO, New Jersey and Illinois UAW locals gave Wallace more than 80 percent of their vote. In the crucible of industrial unionism and the New Deal, Pittsburgh steel workers served as Wallace volunteers. Those ethnic precincts in Buffalo that bordered upon black neighborhoods or had seen radical student communes sprout up turned out for Nixon or Wallace. The southerner also picked up ethnic votes in Cleveland and from the Appalachians who had migrated to Akron and Columbus. (As a consequence, Ohio went to Nixon.) Given this situation, it was understandable that Humphrey did not make the Gallup poll's list of most admired men. Wallace, Nixon, and Pope Paul VI did.[67]

Wallace cut most deeply into the Democratic Party's southern front. The governor carried Alabama, Georgia, Louisiana, Mississippi, and Arkansas. *Wallace ran second to Nixon* in Tennessee, North Carolina, and South Carolina. The governor scored best in the southern precincts that favored closing down honky-tonks and blind pigs. In the blue-collar suburbs of Richmond, Wallace did well among white voters who opposed welfare and tax levies to support community colleges. Such people felt that welfare benefited the lazy and that their children would never attend college. So why fund higher education? Even though Wallace had tweaked Protestant churches for establishing segregated academies, many Baptists did not hold it against him. Wallace received nearly half of the Southern Baptist vote. Indeed, the governor did best among Baptists and Methodists and scored poorly with Episcopalians and Jews. In a development that foreshadowed the shape of things to come for the Democrats, Wallace strongly appealed to working-class voters under the age of thirty who were not going to follow their parents into the party of liberalism. Worse, just 35 percent of whites voted for Humphrey, compared to 97 percent of blacks. Racial and cultural polarization spelled disaster for the Democratic Party.[68]

Nixon's campaign strategists learned first hand what a potent electoral force could be harnessed by embracing social conservatism. To secure a Republican presidential majority in '72, the GOP had to win Wallace's ethnic and southern base. Not all the conservative faithful, however, viewed Wallace as a desirable role model. William F. Buckley, like other fiscal conservatives, found the governor's economic populism distasteful. As a state legislator in the forties and fifties, Wallace had authored a bill to provide free tuition to Alabama widows and orphans. Thanks to this legislation, forty thousand people in his state, one-quarter of them black, received college diplomas. Wallace was also instrumental in establishing six new technical schools for members of both races. As governor, Wallace raised taxes on Birmingham and Montgomery's elite to finance hospitals, roads, and schools that benefited working-class blacks and whites. The segregationist governor did more to advance the material conditions of poor Alabama blacks than Judge Frank Johnson, the Warren Court, and Great Society liberals were willing to admit. Buckley knew a crafty tax-and-spend populist when he saw one. The challenge for the GOP was to divorce social conservatism from economic populism. Vilifying Big Government and the Democratic Party as promoters of immorality would do the trick. Luckily for Nixon, liberal reformers would provide vital assistance to the GOP.[69]

CHAPTER TWO

Deluge '72

For a ten-year-old political junkie growing up in Miami, 1972 was an exciting year: both major parties held their national conventions in that city. The Republican National Convention gave television viewers the impression of a coronation; the Democrats yet again provided excitement. As many reporters noted, the dissidents of '68 were now in charge of the Democratic Party. The Democratic convention was a loud, raucous affair. Delegates were so wired that intellectual debates and floor demonstrations delayed George McGovern's acceptance speech until 2:30 in the morning. Glued to the television set, cherub-faced Ralph Reed could not help but anticipate that the fall campaign would pit Richard Nixon's well-oiled machine against liberals who would rather be ideologically pure than have a Democrat in the White House. If only Reed knew how near to disaster the Nixon campaign had been.[1]

Nixon's efforts to be the law-and-order president had misfired from the start. His inauguration was the first in American history to be disrupted by antiwar protests. Club-wielding cops and bottle-throwing militants did not make for reassuring television. When gun-toting black radicals seized a building at Cornell University and threatened white students and faculty in 1969, Nixon's pledge to restore order to the nation's campuses rang hollow. The slaying of four students at Kent State University a year later did not enhance Nixon's reputation. Most Americans thought that the Ohio National Guard had done the right thing, but they also criticized Nixon for escalating campus protests by invading Cambodia. The electorate did not like peace demonstrators or the Indochinese war. Voters wanted Nixon to end the Vietnamese conflict without withdrawing in defeat or committing the necessary military resources to win. Instead of becoming enraged at peace activists, the president might more honestly have told the American people that their expectations were idiotic. Only one incumbent president, however, has ever blamed voters for being the architects of their own frustrations. And Jimmy Carter did not win a second term.[2]

Since Nixon had taken office, assaults on public school teachers had increased 85 percent. The number of weapons confiscated in the classroom rose by half. Teen pregnancy also ballooned. According to a series of secret polls conducted for Nixon by Republican consultant Bob Teeter in late '71 and early '72, the GOP could lose the White House. Beyond the Vietnam War, social issues were killing Nixon. He received low ratings for his efforts to combat drugs and crime. Additionally, two-thirds of the voters surveyed held him responsible for failing to reform welfare and cut taxes. Catholics seemed likely to return to their political home. Teeter bluntly noted that blue-collar Catholics were a group "that has disliked Republicans fairly intensely for a long time." With crime rates and the cost of living rising, Nixon exercised little appeal to ethnics and working-class Americans. Nixon could not even count upon white southerners. His best hope for reelection was that the Democratic Party would bypass Senator Edmund Muskie of Maine and nominate a strident social liberal.[3]

The president made serious efforts to shore up his southern front. He directed Solicitor General Robert Bork to delay court-ordered school busing. Liberal federal judges had hoped to integrate public education by forcing white suburban students to attend black inner-city schools. Busing affected Richmond no less than Detroit and, therefore, was an issue that united ethnics and southerners. Nixon further directed the former Yale professor to find conservative southern judges whom he could nominate to the Supreme Court. Northern liberals like Teddy Kennedy rejected his nominees and thereby angered the white South. Some conservatives wondered whether Nixon had intended this result, being more interested in symbolic gestures than reversing the liberal course of the federal judiciary. Even among his Republican brethren, Nixon could not overcome his image as a shifty used-car salesman. If nothing else, Nixon had the self-awareness to appreciate that he had not won the presidency because people loved and trusted him.[4]

Looking to build a base among religious conservatives, Nixon cultivated ties to Billy Graham. Although his friendship with Graham dated to the fifties, Nixon had not previously sought political advantage by appearing with the North Carolina Baptist. Graham, who had been a confidant of sorts of Dwight Eisenhower and Lyndon Johnson, delivered an impas-

sioned invocation at Nixon's inauguration and made frequent public appearances with the wily politician. If President Kennedy had spent as
much time with a Catholic bishop as Nixon spent with Graham, dark
tales of Vatican influence would have swept the nation. Fortunately for
the duo, the Protestant double-standard remained alive and well. Among
conservatives, William F. Buckley was the rare commentator who found
Graham's relationship with Nixon troubling. Buckley took offense at Graham's hints that "God is a middle-class Republican." He believed that
politics—even conservative politics—could easily sully God's church.
The secular could not be made holy. Buckley felt that religious activists
such as Graham should be more careful in approaching the political
arena.[5]

Buckley suffered from the American Catholic syndrome. Belonging to
a minority that had experienced religious discrimination for more than a
century, Buckley felt the need to keep some distance between the Catholic
Church and a polity that reflected the values of the Protestant majority.
Conservative Protestants had an entirely different mind-set. They had
taken their ownership of the federal government to be the natural order
of American politics. Complacency gave way to militancy when the secular left appeared on the scene to challenge Protestant traditionalists for
control of the nation's culture and politics. An enormously complex man,
Billy Graham possessed a sense of morality that led him to embrace both
Martin Luther King, Jr., and Richard Nixon. With King dead and the civil
rights movement having moved in a secular direction, Graham had only
Nixon. The evangelist persuaded himself that his friend was the Defender
of the Faith. Buckley, on the other hand, remained a Nixon agnostic.[6]

If the new cultural order led Graham to cleave more closely to Nixon,
it knocked the old-style southern politicians off their feet. Virginia blacks
had wasted no time in registering to vote and, in alliance with Washington's liberal suburbanites, sending Senator A. Willis Robertson packing.
The days of segregationist appeals were at an end. Of course, Virginian
conservatives could legitimately attack white liberals who refused to send
their children to school with Washington's poor blacks. Then again, just
as blacks were asserting their political power in the District of Columbia,
middle-class minorities moved into the Virginia and Maryland suburbs.
The race issue that had so long warped the politics of the South was being
supplemented by class considerations. With middle-class minorities expressing their desire not to live next door to poor blacks and "white

trash," Virginia politics required more tap dancing than had been the case in the past.

Ironically, where blacks had struggled to win the right to vote, poor southern whites saw that plum dropped in their laps. For every two blacks who registered to vote, seven new white voters showed up at the polls in the sixties and seventies. While blacks entered the ranks of the southern Democratic Party, a larger number of formerly disfranchised whites voted a straight Republican ticket. Even though southern blacks and whites often shared a life of poverty, many could not see themselves belonging to the same party. Racial grievances were too deep to be uprooted overnight. Moreover, how could Dixie's blacks and whites ever reconcile their sharply contrasting views of Big Government? Class solidarity would be one way to unite the races. However, that had never been the southern way. Working-class southerners were like scabby alley cats fighting over who would lick clean the bottom of the garbage can.[7]

Many impoverished blacks did not even bother to vote. For one black who toiled on a Louisiana sugarcane plantation, electoral politics were irrelevant. To him, the civil rights revolution was something he had seen on television. In the larger scheme of things, Martin Luther King, Jr., had simply given him the abstract right to dine at restaurants and stay at hotels that were beyond his financial means:

I doesn't vote because sometimes you votes for the right man and sometimes you votes for the wrong one. And whoever gets in isn't going to care about me anyway, so what difference does it make?

I tell you the truth. I think what that Martin Luther King did was good. That's for sure. But it never made much difference to me.[8]

Not everyone experienced such feelings of political estrangement. There were southerners who became politically engaged in the aftermath of the sixties rebellion. Jerry Falwell saw about him a nation rapidly going to hell in a handbasket. Even Lynchburg, a place considered so far off the beaten path that the Yankees had not bothered burning it to the ground, was experiencing an economic boom and influx of cosmopolitan outsiders. Like another religious visionary, Falwell announced his intent to launch a Reformation. Instead of founding a new religion, the Virginian established "God's University." In 1971, Lynchburg Baptist College, with 124 students, opened for business. Rejecting the secular culture of the contemporary college, and seeking to prepare young social conservatives for careers in politics, teaching, and journalism, Falwell posted his own

theses. As he noted in retrospect, few paid attention to his press conference at which Lynchburg (later Liberty) Baptist enlisted in the culture
war:

I used words like "unashamedly Christian"—academic excellence—young
champions for Christ who will change the world . . . commitment to an inerrant
Bible—no compromise of theological integrity—no tenure—a strong behavioral
and honor code, dress code, and curfews—no immorality, alcohol, or drugs
allowed—respect for authority—devotion to America—commitment to political
conservatism, capitalism, and free enterprise," and other concepts and ideas
which must have sounded off the wall to the media in attendance, especially in
the midst of the "rebellious, counterculture youth generation" back in 1971.[9]

Falwell represented just one tendency in America's mounting moral
revolt. In 1969, Uprising for Decency, a southwestern anti-pornography
organization, came into existence. That same year, the Midwestern Inter-
denominational Citizens' Council for Decency mobilized for action.
While the national media devoted much ink to the 1969 peace march on
Washington, they overlooked countless grassroots protests against adult
bookstores and theaters. Many of the moral crusaders were small-town,
lower-middle-class Protestants. To a person, they viewed federal judges as
partisans of immorality. All of the way up to the Supreme Court, liberal
judges prohibited children from praying in the public schools and, at the
same time, overturned local ordinances against pornography. At the root
of the problem, the smut opponents argued, were radical college students
and professors who thought that pornography was constitutionally protected free speech. Liberals had quite simply debased American culture.[10]

The opponents of skin flicks and campus radicalism were Nixon's kind
of people. Seeing an opportunity to score some political points, the president touted the work of the Commission on Obscenity and Pornography
(Johnson had originally appointed the commission). Beyond that, the
White House did little. In 1970, to Nixon's embarrassment, the presidential commission concluded that pornography was "therapeutic" and
urged the repeal of all local obscenity laws. In a letter to a North Carolinian smut foe written a year after the commission report, Rev. Nelson Bell
opined that he saw nothing harmless about *Playboy* magazines and peep
shows: "Pornography is moral sewage designed to corrupt and subvert
people—particularly the youth—and its end result is a debauching of the
minds and bodies of those who come under its influence." Bell assured
his correspondent that son-in-law Billy Graham supported her efforts. He

did not reassure her that Graham's friend in the Oval Office was on their side.[11]

While social conservatives mounted an unsuccessful assault on pornographers, another crusade was in the offing. New York had legalized abortion in 1970. (By 1972, New York doctors had performed 270,000 abortions.) In Texas, liberals had persuaded a federal court to declare all state laws that banned abortion to be unconstitutional. Appeals were wending their way to the Supreme Court. (The justices ruled on *Roe v. Wade* in 1973.) Those supporting abortion made any number of arguments on behalf of their cause. If a family could not afford to have any more children, then the option to have an abortion should be available. Similarly, unmarried women on welfare might find their lives easier if they did not have to raise additional children in poverty. On the other hand, if single women chose to bear more children, then the federal government must increase their AFDC payments. Social liberals missed a defect in their argument that would cost them politically among the citizenry. Married, working-class mothers who did not terminate their pregnancies were generally not eligible for welfare to support their children.[12]

As a group, the abortion activists bore little resemblance to the nation at large. The highly educated white male and, to a somewhat lesser extent, white female, promoted the legalization of abortion. Eighty-two percent of Jews supported abortion on demand for reasons ranging from protecting the health of the mother to the desire to end an inconvenient pregnancy. Although many Episcopalians and Presbyterians approved of abortion, overall only one-third of Protestants supported abortion on demand. Conversely, those who regularly attended church, particularly Catholics and Baptists, regarded the fetus as a living child. Abortion was murder. To social liberals, the fetus was just a collection of tissue. Life did not begin at conception. Further, women should have the right to do with their bodies as they pleased. If women desired to terminate a pregnancy, then local communities and churches had no legal right to interfere. State-based efforts to maintain the prohibition against abortion were akin to attempts by southern segregationists to deny blacks their human rights.[13]

In 1971, the Catholic bishops of Texas addressed their parishioners on the abortion issue. The Texas bishops deplored the federal court decision that overturned state statutes against abortion. At the same time, they recognized that social liberalism, in its championship of individual rights, exercised enormous appeal among activist judges. The Texans also realized that they had not been sufficiently organized and politically astute enough to stop the *Roe v. Wade* case in its tracks:

... religious voices are being drowned out by an abortion lobby which is single-minded, well-organized, and exceedingly skilled at making the most of the civil and political arguments which carry greater weight in courts and legislatures than abstract moral arguments stressing the respect to be paid to human life. By virtue of their inability to agree on substantive human goods, pluralistic societies are forced to settle issues in terms of maximum individual choice. Sadly, once the abortion debate was successfully cast in terms of individual freedom the political and legal outcome was predictable. Little heed was thereafter given to those who urged the necessity of recognizing that there are certain proper and necessary limitations on the freedom of individuals in society, and that the prime reason for existence of the state is the protection of life against forces that cheapen or destroy it. Seemingly forgotten was the fact that two lives are involved in every abortion.[14]

Although the Catholic bishops in Massachusetts joined their Sunbelt brothers in condemning abortion, Senator Teddy Kennedy sidestepped the issue. His response was that, as a Catholic, he personally thought abortion wrong, but, as a member of the civil government, he had to obey the strictures of the federal courts. Republican liberals were less evasive than Kennedy. New York's Nelson Rockefeller enthusiastically supported abortion. Sensing that Republican and Democratic liberals would never take their moral and economic concerns seriously, Father Geno Baroni, a child of the Pennsylvania coalfields, exhorted white ethnics to become a third force in American politics. Catholics should stand apart from opportunistic Republicans and elitist social liberals.[15]

A highly skilled publicist, Baroni attracted to his cause some exceptional Catholic intellectuals who believed that morality and justice could not be divorced. In their minds, social and economic libertarianism sprang from selfishness. There was no thought given to the people least able to defend themselves—unborn children and struggling workers. Baroni's greatest disciple was Michael Novak. The son of humble Slovaks from Johnstown, Pennsylvania, Novak had grown up during the Great Depression. When he was four years old, the Bethlehem Steel Corporation brutally suppressed a strike for union recognition. The union officers and organizers were all pious Catholics. No stranger to social injustice, Novak had little sympathy for William F. Buckley's anti-New Deal politics. To this former seminary student, Buckley's "Anglo-Saxon" style and privileged background made him ill-suited to speak to working-class Catholics. As Novak confessed in later years, "Like many young Catholics and Jews,

I had imbibed from an early age a set of suspicions concerning big business, capitalism, Marlboro man individualism, and Anglo-Saxon ethnic superiority." Buckley seemed to be one of *them* rather than one of us.[16]

In the sixties, Novak became a reporter for the liberal Catholic magazine *Commonweal*, promoted the antiwar cause through the Catholic Peace Fellowship, and taught religion at Stanford. Dismayed by the mounting violence of the campus Left, and disturbed by what he saw as an anti-Catholic bias in the news media, Novak reached his breaking point during the 1972 presidential campaign. When college professors and students complained about Nixon's "Silent Majority" of hawkish ethnics, Novak became exasperated. "Antipersonnel bombs were not invented by men on a construction gang," he replied. "Guys on beer trucks did not dream up napalm. Ph.D.'s from universities, who abhor bloodshed, thought them up." His experiences as an advisor to vice-presidential candidate Sargent Shriver led to Novak's disavowal of the Democratic Party. Novak could not endorse abortion and school busing. (He eventually joined the staff of the American Enterprise Institute, a neoconservative think tank headquartered in Washington.)[17]

At least one Catholic in the Nixon White House saw an opportunity to build a Republican majority with the help of social conservatives. Born into a middle-class family of devout Catholics in 1938 and raised in the hothouse atmosphere of Cold War Washington, Patrick Buchanan suckled on religion and politics with equal vigor. To Buchanan, the decade of the fifties was the "Golden Age of American Catholicism," and his Jesuit teachers were "the Pope's Marines," doing battle with Communists and juvenile delinquents. Protestants and Jews largely did not exist in Buchanan's physical and mental worlds. His heroes tended to be Irish Catholics who rejected New Deal liberalism: Wisconsin Senator Joseph McCarthy and Father Charles Coughlin, a controversial depression-era radio personality. (Buchanan did, however, have a high regard for General Douglas MacArthur, a Protestant conservative who had urged President Truman to escalate the Korean War by attacking China.) Buchanan served Nixon as a low-level speech writer and idea man. He needed no cajoling from the president to savage antiwar liberals. His brother fought with the 101st Airborne in Vietnam. (An arthritic knee placed the former Army ROTC cadet on 4F status—unfit for military duty. Unlike many other young Republicans, Pat Buchanan *wanted* to fight.)[18]

The feisty conservative urged Nixon to ignore the antiwar movement, civil rights, and the Catholic Left. Most Catholics, Buchanan contended, were concerned with social issues: abortion, crime, and pornography. If the Republicans appeared to be de-escalating the Vietnam War, then the liberals did not have a chance to win. Catholics, like other Americans, were tired of the war and suspected peace activists of being un-American. To secure a landslide reelection, Buchanan realized, Nixon had to win Wallace voters to his side and distance himself from the Republican Party label. As Buchanan later noted, what made Wallace such a force in American politics was that he had been "the only vehicle through which working-class Democrats could cast a vote against the increasingly leftist policies of their national party—without voting for a Republican." Of course, attracting the majority of Wallace voters, Buchanan admitted to Nixon, meant placing even more distance between the White House and the civil rights establishment. "The second era of Reconstruction is over," he told Nixon, "the ship of integration is going down; it is not our ship; it belongs to national liberalism—we cannot salvage it; and we ought not to be aboard."[19]

Buchanan's race strategy was misguided. A law-and-order constituency existed among blacks and Hispanics that Nixon could have cultivated. In 1970, three of four Harlem blacks favored a minimum prison sentence of ten years for heroin pushers. Sixty-five percent would have sent marijuana dealers to jail for the same length of time. Meanwhile, hundreds of Pentecostal churches in Brooklyn mobilized their Puerto Rican flocks to combat crime. Buchanan made the mistake of thinking that Manhattan liberals and Black Panthers were the spokesmen of the urban poor. In reality, most minorities did not regard dope dealers as the innocent victims of a racist legal system. Inner-city blacks and Hispanics saw neighborhood drug pushers as the violent emissaries of a white organized-crime syndicate that seemed beyond the reach of the legal system. An aggressive posture toward the drug lords, as well as the street dealers, could have won votes for the GOP and defused racial tensions between urban minorities and white police officers.[20]

If off-base in his approach toward racial minorities, Buchanan did know how to deal with white liberals. As Buchanan argued, why not encourage gays, black militants, and Ivy League SDSers to make a donation to Nixon's New Hampshire primary challenger, Representative Pete McCloskey of California? "When the check is cashed," Buchanan advised, "that fact should be brought to the attention of the voters of New Hampshire by the Manchester *Union Leader*." McCloskey, however, was not the most serious threat to Nixon. In Buchanan's eyes, the nomination of

Senator Muskie would prove disastrous. "Muskie," he noted, "is a figure ideally situated to unite the warring factions of his party, and if they are united that is bad news for us." Conservatives could not hurt Muskie in the New Hampshire primary, Buchanan observed. Instead, "our interests dictate that George McGovern . . . be given as much assistance, publicity-wise and otherwise, as we can muster. Statements by [Nixon] people, on background and off the record, that McGovern's organization may surprise everyone, that Muskie may be in trouble—in addition to heated infighting among Democrats—are to be encouraged, in any way possible."[21]

To Buchanan's subsequent astonishment, other more influential Nixon staffers took "any way possible" to mean by any illegal way possible. The Committee to Re-Elect the President, known rather tellingly as CREEP, engaged in dirty campaign tricks that ranged from the humorous to the felonious. In Florida, during that state's Democratic primary, the White House frat boys arranged for a young woman to race through a retirement community clad only in a Muskie for President banner. Meanwhile, CREEP's personnel broke into the Washington headquarters of the Democratic National Committee to plant listening devices. (CREEP's operatives specialized in tracking down the sources of news leaks in the White House. Hence their nickname, "the White House plumbers.") Still other staffers, learning that John Lennon might picket the Republican National Convention, placed the singer and his wife under FBI surveillance. All the FBI was able to ascertain was that Yoko Ono "can't even remain on key."[22]

Although the escapades of the Nixon White House ultimately toppled the administration and brought grief to the GOP, the irony was that the Democrats required no assistance in destroying themselves. Teddy Kennedy, whose name, wealth, and profile made him a natural presidential candidate in '72, had taken himself out the running. A late-night automobile plunge off a Chappaquiddick, Massachusetts, bridge and the unseemly death of his female passenger ended his presidential ambitions in one fell swoop. George Wallace, returned to the Democratic fold, might have won the party's nomination. His attacks on court-ordered busing gave him the Maryland and Michigan primaries. Overall, Wallace led McGovern by one million votes in the primaries, even though McGovern claimed more delegates. However, an assassination attempt that left him paralyzed removed him from the national political scene. (Just to make sure Wallace remained out of the picture, Billy Graham urged the southerner not to run an independent campaign in the fall that would hurt Nixon's reelection.) Muskie, or even Hubert Humphrey, appeared strong. Both had the support of the party regulars. Only when it was too late, however, did Humphrey and his '68 running mate realize that the rules of the game had been changed when they were not looking.[23]

Following the Democrats' embarrassing Chicago convention, South Dakota senator George McGovern had led an effort to reform the party's method of picking presidential candidates. The senator increased the number of primaries, reduced the power of the unions and party bosses, and imposed gender and racial quotas on the selection of delegates. While primaries appeared to place the nomination machinery directly into the hands of ordinary people, the opposite proved true. Most working-class Democrats paid little attention to primaries. They had labor leaders and machine bosses to take care of the mundane business of choosing candidates. The typical voter did not follow campaigns until the general election. Those most likely to vote in a primary were middle class, college educated, and motivated by a cherished cause, whether it was ending the Vietnam War or legalizing abortion. At the same time, less affluent but more conservative activists might show up at the polls to advance their agenda. Given low turnout, the Democratic primaries were perfect for any candidate who represented the ideological extremes of his party: McGovern or Wallace. Moderates like Muskie and Humphrey had few friends among activist primary voters. Since Nixon's nomination was a foregone conclusion, the GOP's parallel efforts to enhance the role of its primaries would not wreck havoc until the '76 election.[24]

McGovern's supporters had a limited understanding of the average American. One liberal professor of religion reasoned that "American national self-respect, if it had any value at all, was certainly not fragile and could easily survive a quick withdrawal from a mistaken war." The professor later admitted his error in judgment. Most Americans did feel that "national as well as personal self-respect was not only fragile but imperiled." In Milwaukee, the Christian Family Movement, which had championed school busing in the sixties, formed the core of McGovern's volunteers in '72. Ethnics did not appreciate them, or their candidate. (Milwaukee's conservative Catholics soon created a national organization to combat the Religious Left and the liberal media: the Catholic League for Religious and Civil Rights.) Public opinion polls indicated that churchgoing Catholics found Nixon less offensive than McGovern.[25]

Angered by the presence of so many blue-collar social conservatives in the Catholic Church, Monsignor Charles Owen Rice of Pittsburgh argued that progressives must purge the regressive majority:

The rank and file are a problem, not only because they do not appreciate the outspoken and rebellious young, but because they tend to be racially bigoted and militaristic. One is tempted to say that we must push ahead regardless of cost, even if the cost should turn out to be a good proportion of the rank and file; after all Catholicism has not been making much of an impression on them nor influencing their lives in the most important areas of conduct. However, one has to have compassion for all, even the bigoted ordinary Catholic with his narrow outlook. He himself is exploited and his family endangered from above and below; he needs understanding and help, although he cannot be allowed to run the show. We have to reassure these people, but never hide the truth or discard principles.[26]

Rice had come a long way from the thirties when he had helped build the steelworkers union and fought Communism in the CIO. Repudiating his anti-Communist beliefs in the sixties, Rice became a radical peace activist. Significantly, most of his antiwar organizing took place at the University of Pittsburgh and Carnegie Mellon, not at the city's Catholic college, Duquesne University. When Rice ran as a peace and Black Power candidate for the city council in 1971, he scored best in Pittsburgh's secular university and Jewish precincts. The priest trailed miserably in Catholic and working-class neighborhoods.[27]

Like Monsignor Rice, the liberal evangelicals who enlisted in the Mc-Govern campaign found that they were swimming against the tide. In 1972, an organization called Evangelicals for McGovern appeared on the scene. Despite having only 358 contributors, the liberal Protestant group boldly announced that "Billy Graham does not speak for all of the nation's evangelicals." Eschewing matters like pornography and drug addiction, Evangelicals for McGovern argued that the real moral issues in the presidential race were "racism, poverty, and the grossly unjust distribution of wealth here and abroad." Upon receiving campaign literature from Evangelicals for McGovern, a professor of religion at Maryland's Washington Bible College expressed his dismay. He rebuked the religious liberals, contending that the McGovern campaign was profane and sacrilegious:

Our faculty members, students, and many others have received copies of advertising material which is being used in the McGovern-Shriver campaign with the title, "How in the Hell can you vote for Nixon?"

In this area, and possibly in other areas as well, one of the McGovern-Shriver campaign songs is set to the tune of "Jesus loves me, this I know," and goes like this, "Nixon bugs me, this I know; Martha Mitchell [wife of CREEP chair John Mitchell] tells me so."[28]

In response, a supporter of Evangelicals for McGovern argued that although profanity was deplorable, distinctions had to be made between "social morality and personal morality." Character, or personal morality, was far less significant than the candidate's politics. He defended McGovern "because his position on social questions such as poverty and militarism to me is closer to Christian standards than that of President Nixon." A history professor and evangelical echoed his colleague's response. Character aside, "Mr. Nixon is hardly the man who ought to command such uncritical backing by my brethren," the historian wrote. "I am particularly outraged at his shameless exploitation of evangelicals in general and Mr. Graham in particular. I have spoken out in other places about the dangers of the cozy relationships that exist between American evangelicals and political conservatism."[29]

Although their conservative counterparts caused them no little amount of frustration, the liberal evangelicals did speak some things that Graham and Falwell would have endorsed. Evangelicals for McGovern complained that the secular news media trivialized, or ignored, anyone who approached politics with a religiously informed set of values. According to the Christian liberals, at least one network news personality flatly told them that moral issues did not concern the electorate in '72. Instead, American voters were interested in only the economy and foreign policy. It never occurred to the secular media that morality, economics, and diplomacy might bear some relationship to one another.[30]

To an extent it was understandable that the secular media, as well as religious conservatives, paid little attention to McGovern's Christianity. His religious beliefs were too complicated to be conveyed in a television sound bite. The son of a Methodist minister, McGovern had forsaken his father's fundamentalism. Even before he received a doctorate in history from Northwestern University, McGovern scoffed at the idea of biblical inerrancy. One had to approach the Bible as an allegorical work of literature rather than as a historical document. During the '72 campaign, McGovern appeared at Wheaton College in Illinois, where he explained his religious beliefs: "In our family, there was no drinking, smoking, dancing or card-playing. . . . In all candor, I regard that kind of strict legalism as somewhat beside the point today and as not a necessary or totally positive part of a Christian upbringing." (No one could fault McGovern for being overly cautious. Wheaton College was Billy Graham's alma mater.) Mc-Govern then informed his audience that the true Christian issues in America revolved around racism, the Vietnam War, and poverty. A president with the correct moral outlook, McGovern insisted, could eradicate social injustice and create a secular paradise. Fundamentalists and Catholics needed no more confirmation that McGovern was unworthy of their support.[31]

In truth, the vast majority of McGovern supporters did not want their candidate identifying with any kind of Christian belief. Far from linking McGovern to the Social Gospel reformers of the early twentieth century, as evangelical liberals attempted to do in their literature, his secular troops looked to the campus-based Left. The cultural agenda of the New Left, not the economic objectives of the Social Gospel, informed the beliefs of McGovern's champions. They wanted a government that would immediately withdraw from Vietnam while promoting abortion, busing, gay rights, and racial hiring quotas. Antiwar Democrats, in their quest to build an ideologically inclusive movement, had given the New Left entree into the party. Having mobilized feminists, abortion-rights activists, and other cultural radicals behind McGovern in the Democratic primaries, the New Left expected to shape the party's direction.[32]

The McGovern delegates to the Democratic National Convention generally came from the ranks of the highly educated professional class. (In contrast, just 29 percent of the electorate had ever set foot inside a college classroom, let alone obtained a degree.) McGovern's people were also profoundly liberal in their attitudes toward social issues. Two of three McGovern delegates favored busing, compared to 15 percent of blue-collar and middle-class Democrats. Three of four believed that the constitutional rights of criminals had to be given precedence over cries for law and order. After all, poverty and racial discrimination, not immoral behavior, bred crime. Only 36 percent of the party's traditional constituencies saw things this way. Fifty-seven percent of McGovern's delegates also dismissed any criticism of federal welfare programs, arguing that America had to abolish poverty by any means at hand. With nearly a quarter of McGovern's California delegation collecting welfare, their emphasis upon expanded anti-poverty programs was understandable. Working-class Democrats might have wondered, though, how welfare recipients could set aside time for campaigning but not for finding a job.[33]

To heap insult upon injury, the McGovern staff denied Chicago mayor Richard Daley and AFL-CIO president George Meany a role in the convention. Rev. Jesse Jackson took Daley's place at the Miami convention, and Gloria Steinem, a leader of the National Organization for Women, "replaced" Meany as power broker. Thus a black militant and an abortion-rights crusader replaced two socially conservative Catholic party leaders. Strangely, the McGovern people thought that the humiliated Daley and Meany would have little choice but to support their candidate and platform. It was a miscalculation of epic proportions. Although the percentage of social liberals had swollen in the sixties with the expansion of the professions, there were not enough secular lawyers, humanities professors, and media personnel to win a general election. (Nineteen percent of the electorate was made up of professionals, compared to 16 percent in 1964.) McGovern believed his ability to win the Democratic primaries would translate into a general election triumph. Ironically, McGovern lacked a sense of history. No Democrat since Roosevelt had secured the White House without Catholics and workers.[34]

Underscoring its contempt for working-class Democrats, the McGovern campaign refused to give union officials any passes to the convention floor and gallery. At the same time, long-haired writers from the countercultural press moved about freely. Benefiting from rigid quotas to select delegates, feminists and blacks were well represented. Organized labor and big-city ethnics did not fare as well. This state of affairs might have been excused by the inexperience of McGovern's campaign manager, Gary Hart, a thirty-three-year-old Colorado attorney. Hart, however, shared with McGovern activists a suspicion of labor leaders and ethnics, viewing them as racists as well as anti-Communist extremists. Hart expressed no little amount of class snobbery and nativism by observing that many anti-Communists had funny, non-American (meaning Slavic) surnames. Although raised in the fundamentalist Church of the Nazarene, Hart had abandoned his religion (along with his birth name, Hartpence) by the time he entered Yale Law School. He had an "open marriage" and developed close friendships with Hollywood's sexy set, among them the actor Warren Beatty. Like many secular liberals, Hart was a man who thought he had transcended history and the moral hang-ups of a dead God.[35]

McGovern's campaign rhetoric, overheated in the primaries, became more shrill in the general election, where smart candidates usually moved to capture the political center. For the first time in his career, Nixon faced an opponent who came more easily unglued than himself. Nixon wisely kept above the fray, appearing presidential. Simultaneously, he eliminated

Vietnam as a campaign issue. Nixon's rapprochement with China and détente with the Soviet Union effectively isolated North Vietnam from its military benefactors. With enough pressure from the U.S. Air Force, it was only a matter of time before Hanoi agreed to a truce that would make it appear as if Nixon had concluded the war on a victorious note. McGovern apparently thought he understood the North Vietnamese regime, having met with its diplomatic representatives in 1971. North Vietnam should make peace with the antiwar liberals who had sympathized with their plight, not with the bellicose Nixon.[36]

Clutching at straws, McGovern attempted to make the bugging of the Democratic National Committee's headquarters in the Watergate Hotel a campaign issue. The Watergate affair, he argued, was reminiscent of the tactics deployed by Hitler against his opponents. Taken with his Hitler analogy, McGovern then compared the president's Vietnam policy to the Nazis' extermination of the Jews. Although his strident rhetoric resonated with CBS Evening News and the *New York Times,* most Americans were not impressed. In contrast to liberal reporters, working-class voters were not shedding tears in response to McGovern's "profound decency." With an insight that could have applied just as well to himself, Nixon privately recorded the epitaph of the antiwar movement and its media champions: "I think as the war recedes as an issue, some of these people are going to be lost souls. They basically are haters, they are frustrated, they are alienated—they don't know what to do with their lives."[37]

To Nixon's delight, conservative Democrats were mobilizing against McGovern. During the Democratic primaries Humphrey had ridiculed his opponent's plans to raise taxes on the middle class in order to finance more anti-poverty programs. In Florida, the man who had once championed the Great Society brazenly courted the backlash vote against Big Government. Humphrey's campaign advertisements pledged that he would "stop the flow of your tax dollars to those who chisel their way onto the welfare rolls through fraud." An unconvincing foe of Big Government, Humphrey could not beat George Wallace in the South. Once Wallace was out of the race, however, the Minnesota senator hoped conservative Democrats would throw their support to him. In California, Humphrey denounced McGovern's proposal to give every welfare recipient an additional thousand dollars. "I'll be damned if I'm giving everybody in the country a thousand-dollar bill," Humphrey fumed. "People in this country want jobs, not handouts." Humphrey did not realize that the share of conservatives voting in California's Democratic primary had been steadily shrinking since the sixties. Traditional Sunbelt Democrats wanted Wallace or Muskie, not Lyndon Johnson's junior partner.[38]

Trying to rally Nebraska's considerable bloc of Irish Catholic voters to Humphrey's banner, conservative Democrats decried McGovern as the candidate of amnesty (for draft dodgers), acid, and abortion. Impressed, CREEP adopted "amnesty, acid, and abortion" as its own attack slogan. (McGovern hoped to sidestep the abortion controversy, claiming that he opposed legalization even as his supporters promoted it in the Democratic platform. In reality McGovern had once arranged for his rebellious daughter to terminate her politically embarrassing pregnancy.) Governor Jimmy Carter of Georgia publicly stated that McGovern was too radical, as well as too inept, to be president. Unlike McGovern, Carter was seemingly an unabashed social conservative. Following the Kent State slayings, Carter vowed to send the National Guard to any restless campus "with live ammunition and with orders to shoot to kill." Two years later, he called for a constitutional amendment to ban school busing. Social liberals viewed the southern partisan of the anyone-but-McGovern-movement as a cornpone version of Governor Ronald Reagan. In turn, Carter accused McGovern Democrats of willfully ignoring southern concerns and moral values.[39]

Like Carter, Mayor Richard Daley let it be known that McGovern was a difficult, if not impossible, candidate to support. His disgust with McGovern predated his snubbing at the Miami convention. At the hearings held by the McGovern Commission on Delegate Selection, antiwar activist David Mixner insisted that Daley be forced to apologize for his actions at the '68 convention. Bowing to Mixner's demands, McGovern confronted Daley and denounced the Chicago police force for provoking violence. Outraged, Daley stalked out of the hearings. Mixner and other Boomers did not rest until Daley had been read out of the party. "No longer would the power of the bosses prevail over the vote of the American people," Mixner gloated, conveniently overlooking the fact that the American people generally preferred party bosses over gay countercultural enthusiasts.[40]

Following Daley's example, the AFL-CIO informed the press that organized labor could not endorse McGovern. George Meany personally told Nixon that he would not vote for either presidential candidate. In a post-convention speech, Meany, after denouncing the McGovern crew as upper-class elitists, offered his opinion of the social liberals:

We listened for three days to speakers who were approved to speak by the powers-that-be at that convention. We listened to the gay lib people—you know, the people who want to legalize marriages between boys and boys and legalize marriages between girls and girls. . . . We heard from the abortionists, and we heard from the people who looked like Jacks, acted like Jills, and had the odors of johns about them.

If Meany sounded a lot like the fictional bigot Archie Bunker on the CBS series *All in the Family,* he spoke for many social conservatives who did not like chic liberals or Republican businessmen. (Unlike Meany, however, Archie Bunker never would have held a press conference at which he expressed longing for an old-fashioned socialist candidate.)[41]

At the outset of his campaign McGovern had turned his back on the New Deal coalition, vowing to build an insurgent political movement "around the poor and the minorities and the young people and the antiwar movement." Pursuing his vision with missionary zeal, he very nearly lost the Democratic Party's most reliable constituency: Jews. In the Orthodox precincts of Brooklyn and Philadelphia, Jewish voices were raised against crime, drugged-out hippies, and racial quotas. Philadelphia's 1969 mayoral race saw Republican Frank Rizzo, a flamboyant police commissioner, receive half the Jewish vote. During the Democratic Party primaries, McGovern had swept affluent, secular Jewish neighborhoods in Beverly Hills and Cleveland's Shaker Heights. However, Humphrey had scored well in California and Ohio among religiously observant Jews. Trying to put some distance between himself and his New Left foot soldiers, McGovern reassured the American Jewish Committee that he was sympathetic to Israel and was not wedded to hiring quotas. In 1968, Humphrey had captured 97 percent of the Jewish vote. McGovern's tally would be 27 percentage points below that.[42]

Catholic intellectuals articulated a damning indictment of social liberalism. To Father Andrew Greeley, a syndicated newspaper columnist, and Jeane Kirkpatrick, a Georgetown political science professor, McGovern's followers were members of a New Class that was fundamentally hostile to the moral values of the average American. In Kirkpatrick's mind, McGovern's band of college professors, journalists, and lawyers was a threat to democracy. "The political temptation of the New Class," she observed after the '72 election, "lies in believing that their intelligence and exemplary motives equip them to reorder the institutions, the lives, and even the characters of almost everyone—this is the totalitarian temptation." No more kind, Father Greeley turned his fire on Catholic liberals like Monsignor Rice and author Garry Wills. "The American Catholic community," Greeley lamented, "has finally succeeded in producing an intelligentsia so taken with itself that it either does not know anything about the Catholic community as a whole or simply thinks that the masses are too dull to bother with."[43]

The elitism and self-righteousness of the McGovern movement alienated more than socially conservative intellectuals. At Georgetown University, a Vietnam veteran named James Webb encountered an extremely hostile law professor. The antiwar professor deliberately included Webb's name in a final exam question that had him shipping home pieces of jade inside the bodies of fallen comrades. The liberal academic would never ridicule blacks or gays, but he believed Vietnam combat veterans—baby killers all—were fair game. Webb, an Annapolis graduate who would someday serve as President Reagan's navy secretary, developed an abiding distrust of liberals.[44]

Webb was not alone in his disenchantment with McGovern and the New Class. Peggy Noonan attended her first antiwar demonstration in 1971. On the bus ride to Washington, she listened to the protesters:

There was contempt for the nineteen-year-old boys who were carrying guns in the war or in the [National] Guard. It was understood that they were uneducated, and somewhat crude. There was contempt for America:

—What can you expect of a culture that raises John Wayne [a conservative Hollywood actor] to the status of hero?

—We were founded on violence and will meet our undoing in violence.

—We're at the collective mercy of a bunch of insecure males who have a phallic fascination with guns.

—We're a racist, genocidal nation with an imperialistic lust for land that isn't ours, and . . . and . . .

And get me off this bus! I looked around, and I saw those mouths moving and shrank in my seat. What am I doing with these people? What am I doing with these intellectuals or whatever they are, what am I doing with this—this contemptuous elite?[45]

Patrick Buchanan had mapped out a campaign strategy designed to "portray McGovern as the pet radical of Eastern liberalism, the darling of the *New York Times,* the hero of the Berkeley Hill Jet Set, Mr. Radical Chic." CREEP, however, did not have to go out of its way to make McGovern look bad to social conservatives. McGovern and Hart did just fine on their own. When the campaign concluded and the votes were counted, Nixon had won 61 percent of the popular vote. Among evangelicals, Nixon captured 80 percent of their vote, beating McGovern thirteen million votes to three million. McGovern lost the Catholic and working-class vote, with Nixon capturing 60 percent of the ethnic and blue-collar electorate. In Buffalo's working-class suburbs, conservative congressman Jack Kemp won a stunning reelection, garnering a 90,000-vote victory margin in an area where the Democrats had a registration edge of 25,000. Two years earlier, Kemp had won with just 6,000 votes. Socially conservative Catholics and workers liked the former Buffalo Bills football player—far more than they cared for Nixon, actually.[46]

There was some good news for liberals. McGovern was the first Democrat in living memory to win the majority of upper-middle-class, college-educated voters—the core of the New Class. Harvard law students supported McGovern 698 to 131; just four of their thirty-eight professors voted for Nixon. Such results were repeated at Yale, where bright law students like Hillary Rodham wanted to assist the Democratic Congress in investigating the Watergate affair. Reporters for the national networks and prestige press were no more fond of Nixon. Eighty percent of the media elite voted for McGovern. Not surprisingly, most high-profile journalists did not come from the conservative South, and 86 percent did not usually go to church or temple. It was a rare newspaper columnist, like Chicago's Greeley or Mike Royko, who articulated the fears of blue-collar ethnics. Working-class Americans were too far removed the offices of the *New York Times* and the Brookline homes of Harvard law professors to receive serious attention from the McGovern partisans.[47]

Despite their small numbers, the cultural liberals in the New Class had the money, media influence, and social position to carry on a twilight struggle against conservatism. At the same time, there were free-market libertarians among the New Class who had the means to wage war on the New Deal economic order. Conservative intellectuals tended to overlook the fact that the New Class had many libertarians who were just as hostile to moral crusades as the Left. (The fame of such libertarians, however, did not spread until the eighties, when David Stockman and Phil Gramm championed the Reagan Revolution.)

During the Democratic primaries and in the general election, McGovern had tapped into a tremendous source of campaign funds: Hollywood. Directors and producers funneled millions of dollars into McGovern's coffers while entertainers sponsored rock concerts and made public appearances. Paul Newman and Shirley MacLaine, among other "Left Coast" actors, had long participated in antiwar and civil rights protests. With no less vim, these performers gave their all for McGovern. Warren Beatty became an unofficial advisor to Gary Hart; his sister, Shirley MacLaine, served as a California delegate to the Democratic National

Convention. MacLaine drew great media attention as an outspoken advocate of abortion. From television producer Norman Lear, creator of *All in the Family* which mocked working-class whites, to Jane Fonda, who had posed for a photograph astride a North Vietnamese anti-aircraft gun, the Democratic Party had a new, culturally powerful constituency. Bob Hope was the only major star to make a large contribution to the Nixon campaign.[48]

In one of the worst blunders of his presidency, Nixon had made little effort to gain GOP seats in Congress during the '72 election. Democrats remained securely in charge of the House and Senate. Moreover, Democrats were gun shy and extremely wary of Nixon's domestic and foreign policy initiatives. Congressional Democrats would not have sanctioned Nixon's secret agreement with the South Vietnamese government. In the event of a massive attack by Hanoi, Nixon had promised that America would come to South Vietnam's defense. The Democrats were also sufficiently annoyed by the Watergate wiretapping to organize special investigative hearings. All of this did not, however, mean that congressional Democrats were fans of McGovern's. Only a handful had been selected as delegates to the Democratic convention. (The few female and black members of the House were more likely to be chosen as delegates than the white men who dominated Congress.) Brookline and its similarly affluent suburban neighbors might elect antiwar liberals to public office, but the South and the industrial heartland did not.[49]

At the same time, Nixon faced sharp critics from the conservative wing of the GOP. Buckley and other anti-Communist activists had been appalled by the president's diplomatic overtures to China and the Soviet Union. So far as the Republican Right was concerned, arms-reduction talks and opening up trade with China bordered on treason. (Privately, Nixon said that William F. Buckley and his brother, Senator James Buckley of New York, were "nuts.") Conservative Democrats like Jeane Kirkpatrick and Senator Henry "Scoop" Jackson of Washington concurred with the Republican hawks. To make conservatives even more irate, Nixon had outdone Lyndon Johnson as a champion of Big Government. Nixon went along with Congress in the establishment of federal agencies to regulate pollution and workplace safety. Many corporation executives, particularly those in the Sunbelt, regarded the Environmental Protection Agency and the Occupational Safety and Health Act as socialistic. In a rare understatement, Buchanan mused that Nixon was "the least ideological statesman I ever encountered."[50]

The Nixon administration further irked conservatives by mandating quotas in federal hiring and university employment. While opening up a future of reverse discrimination to young working-class white men, Nixon bought off the senior citizens and earned the good graces of the aging World War II generation. All Nixon had to do was increase Social Security spending by 55 percent and expand entitlement programs across the board. Fiscal responsibility might have been a wise policy to pursue in the long term, but it was suicidal politics. Moreover, while Nixon talked tough on affirmative action, busing, and pornography, he had no intention of providing America with moral leadership, curbing the liberal excesses of the federal judiciary, and cutting taxes. He ducked the abortion issue as well. Since there was no credible alternative in the presidential election, ethnics and southerners had to content themselves with Nixon's empty rhetoric.[51]

Although the GOP established the National Republican Heritage Groups Council in 1971 to compete for the white ethnic vote, it was a sham organization. Most Republicans did not want to deal seriously with controversial issues like abortion, urban decay, and stagnant wages. Moreover, the ethnic leadership of the Heritage Groups Council included individuals known for their anti-Communist foreign policy views, not their sensitivity to domestic matters. Co-chair Anna Chennault, the Chinese widow of General Claire Chennault, had better contacts with the Central Intelligence Agency than with Michael Novak's beer-truck drivers.[52]

Where liberals accused Nixon of shrewdly promoting affirmative action in order to drive a wedge between black and Jewish Democrats, most conservatives saw treachery. In North Carolina, Jesse Helms won a Senate seat as a conservative Republican. Beyond castigating "restless Negroes," Helms had spent years sounding off about liberal college students who spent "riotous weekends at beaches in Florida . . . where orgies and mayhem are highly advertised." A media entrepreneur, as well as a polemicist, Helms spoke on seventy radio stations and wrote diatribes for fifty southern newspapers. Denying that he was racist, Helms led with his chin, arguing that "crime rates and irresponsibility among Negroes are facts of life which must be faced." Helms also attacked Social Security, labor unions, Medicare, and détente with China and the Soviet Union. The senator would quickly make his presence felt in the national Republican Party. Nixon might have won a landslide by assaulting McGovern-style liberalism, but conservatives would not stand by him if the going got rough.[53]

CHAPTER THREE

J. C. Saves in '76

Never before had a president gone before the people to reassure them that he was "not a crook." Unfortunately for Richard Nixon, few Americans believed him. White House personnel, whether in court or before a congressional investigating committee, ratted each other out. In the course of the Watergate hearings, Americans learned that Nixon had secretly taped his meetings with various staffers. In what became known as the "smoking gun" of the scandal, the tapes revealed that Nixon had actively participated in the cover-up of the Watergate break-in. Clinging tenaciously to office, Nixon stonewalled the courts and directed Solicitor General Robert Bork to fire the Watergate special prosecutor. Making up in enthusiasm what he lacked in political sense, Bork executed Nixon's orders. (Attorney General Elliot Richardson resigned rather than dismiss the special prosecutor. Unlike the Massachusetts Brahmin, Bork was a team player.)[1]

While conservatives cared little that Nixon had bugged the Democrats' Watergate headquarters, they were disturbed by other moral lapses. To begin with, Spiro Agnew had forfeited the vice presidency in 1973 after pleading no contest to charges that he accepted bribes. Nixon's foul language, captured on tape in all of its teamster-wannabe glory, destroyed his reputation among conservative clergy. Christians who voted for Nixon, Pat Robertson lamented in 1974, had been "the victims of a cruel hoax." Rebuking a fellow member of the clergy, Robertson informed viewers of the Christian Broadcasting Network that "Dr. Billy Graham has been used for political-image building." For his part, Graham confessed to vomiting when he read transcripts of the Nixon tapes. With Nixon's resignation in 1974, and the elevation of House Republican leader Gerald Ford to the presidency, Graham abandoned the political arena.[2]

As a result of the Watergate debacle, coupled with rampant inflation, high unemployment, and a disruptive Arab oil embargo, Democrats captured forty-nine House seats and four governorships. In 1974, Michael Dukakis of Brookline became governor of Massachusetts, and Jerry Brown succeeded Ronald Reagan. Both pledged to make government services less costly and to promote economic growth. Even though the respective governors had been raised in Greek Orthodox and Roman Catholic households, their sensitivity to religious issues was sorely lacking. Neither Brown nor Dukakis questioned the morality of abortion. (Suspecting that Brown was a charlatan at heart, liberal cartoonist Gary Trudeau had the Californian say to cheering supporters, "My programs . . . emerge through the dialectical process. They come, they go; things just happen. I don't have the answers. I have the questions.") Meanwhile, Boston's affluent suburbs sent a radical Catholic priest to the House. In Colorado, McGovern's erstwhile campaign manager, Gary Hart, won a Senate seat.[3]

Amid the celebrations of the Congressional Class of '74, a discouraging trend went largely unnoticed. Working-class whites did not come back to the Democratic Party in droves. Most of the new Democratic House members owed their elections to suburban professionals, not to religiously observant members of the middling classes. Having learned nothing, Senator McGovern blamed his '72 rout on Nixon's dirty tricks and the fact that he had alienated the Left by moving too far to the right (!). McGovern exhorted the Democratic Party to remain uncompromisingly true to its liberal principles. The overwhelming majority of Americans, McGovern believed, supported abortion, affirmative action, busing, and gay liberation. There were only a handful of racists who would vote for Republicans in the future.[4]

Convinced that they could build a presidential majority with just professionals and inner-city blacks, social liberals sowed the seeds of their eventual destruction. In Boston, a liberal federal judge assumed control of the city's public schools. The council of advisors he chose to implement his busing orders included blacks, activist clergy, and corporate leaders— all of whom were residents of the upper-middle-class suburbs. Several hailed from Governor Dukakis's Brookline neighborhood. Those most affected by busing—black and white—had no voice in the education of their children. Working-class blacks and Catholics, their incomes eaten away by inflation, struggled to pay for the burdensome property taxes that financed public education. Little household money remained for parochial or private school tuition. For the working poor, there was no escape from busing and crumbling urban schools. Resentment against this state of affairs cut across racial lines. According to a nationwide 1976 Louis Harris poll, 51 percent of blacks and 81 percent of whites opposed busing. White liberals lamely retorted that blacks who criticized busing did not know any better. If George Wallace had advanced that kind of argument he would have been called a racist.[5]

In 1974, the Rockefeller Foundation gave the Boston branch of the NAACP $100,000 to assist in its busing battles. Michael Novak angrily resigned from the board of directors. "No sweat off the foundation's back," Novak fumed, "let the Boston Irish pay for the sins of slavery." Calling busing "the Vietnam of the 1970s," Novak declared a class war on social liberalism:

Many Americans seem to feel that something important in the busing conflict in Boston is eluding them. They understand well enough naked racism. But stray bits of evidence, flapping in the wind, suggest that something more than racism— and more important than racism—is at stake. For the citizens of South Boston have at least as much contempt for affluent, church-going, liberal white Brahmins as they have animosity against blacks, and perhaps more. If one can read the signs correctly, many whites in beleaguered Boston seem to regard a certain class of blacks as infested with a kind of plague, a plague that may be catching, a "tangle of pathologies," and they seek a form of quarantine. They do not regard all blacks, but they do regard such blacks, as victims. They regard white liberals in their university drawing rooms, paneled bank offices, and editorial chambers as hypocritical and duplicitous: incarnations of a classic type of morality-spewing villain, the new version of the pious Robber Barons of the past.[6]

By the midseventies, Novak was no longer a lonely voice in the wilderness. Evangelicals for Social Action ruefully observed that "conservative religious tide is sweeping the country." (Unlike Novak, liberal evangelicals blamed "institutional racism" for the rise of social conservatism.) In Altoona, Pennsylvania, a member of the local school board spearheaded an effort to bring God back into the classroom. She wanted a constitutional amendment that would overturn the Supreme Court's 1962 ruling against prayer in the public schools *(Engel v. Vitale)*. "The morals of our younger generation have deteriorated at an alarming pace," she contended. "If prayer and Bible reading are once again permitted in our public schools, there would be less corruption, less demonstrating, and more love in this country." With support from the Fundamentalist Ministerial Association of the Altoona Area, this conservative activist also wanted to ban *The Catcher in the Rye* and other "dirty" books from public school libraries.[7]

Where Altoona's Fundamentalist Ministerial Association blamed liberals for debasing American society, other conservatives pointed to the worsening economy. They believed that recent economic trends were damaging the family—the essential building block of a moral society. By 1976, the proportion of wage workers whose income had fallen behind the rate of inflation stood at 43 percent. For the average household, post–World War II earnings peaked in 1973 and declined thereafter. In a historical first for the United States, over half of the women with school-aged children were in the labor force. They worked out of necessity, not because they sought self-discovery and a rewarding career. Consequently, their children received less parental guidance and little religious instruction. Taking the place of parent and church—traditionalists feared—were pot-smoking peers and a hedonistic media culture. Under such economic pressures and cultural influences, families fell apart and the white illegitimacy rate climbed throughout the seventies.[8]

According to social conservatives, many ministers were unwilling to condemn divorce and illegitimacy. Such clerical progressives had accommodated themselves to the secular world and their cosmopolitan flocks. Chicago *Tribune* columnist Andrew Greeley bluntly wrote that the liberal clergy had failed God. Where could teenagers who were thinking about becoming sexually active turn for moral direction? Who could comfort the child of divorce, or provide wholesome recreational activities to children whose parents were still at work when the children came home from school? Greeley's emphatic answer was not the Episcopalian or Presbyterian churches:

If such cultists as Sun Myung Moon [the head of the controversial Unification Church] have so much following it is precisely because so many of the offspring of upper-middle-class Protestantism have discovered that the local church doesn't stand for anything at all, except what the local pastor picks up from the *New York Times* Op-Ed page, *The Christian Century*, or the *New York Review of Books*.[9]

Conservative clergy and laity sought to fill this moral void. Acting independently of the Altoona fundamentalists, John Cardinal Krol of Philadelphia called for moral instruction in the public schools. Cardinal Krol informed the news media that "every student has the right to hear about God, about religion, and about moral values in the normal course of his or her studies." With nearly twelve million of the fifteen million Catholic students attending secular schools, Krol believed that subjects like abortion, euthanasia, and birth control should be avoided or "treated with extreme sensitivity." Philadelphia's cardinal expressed contempt for atheists and liberal Jews who attacked "the right of Catholic parents to their share of the educational tax dollars for secular subjects." Secular Jews and WASPs, Krol argued, "exude hatred, resort to lies, distortions of fact, and forms of sarcasm that one can only be described as hateful." Krol denied that his sentiments were anti-Semitic. He just did not like social liberals, regardless of their cultural origins.[10]

More circumspect, Timothy Cardinal Manning of Los Angeles identified an ethnically generic "pagan culture" as the enemy of God. Abortion, divorce, pornography, and a militantly secular public school establishment, he contended, were destroying the family. Other Catholics echoed Manning's words, while noting that there was an additional threat to the well-being of the Christian family: the proposed Equal Rights Amendment (ERA). Championed by NOW and the National Education Association, the ERA was supposed to provide a constitutional guarantee of equality between the sexes. Conservative Catholic lay persons like Phyllis Schlafly, however, discerned something more sinister. Social conservatives argued that the ERA would lead to gay marriages and unisex restrooms. Moreover, the ERA would undercut long-standing legislative efforts to compel irresponsible men to support their families. Whether or not the first two items were true, ERA opponents were on to something in their last point. Fully equal women, by NOW's own logic, did not need child support and alimony. If that was not the intention of ERA's feminist supporters, certainly conniving divorce attorneys would put such a reading on the amendment if it were ratified by thirty-eight of the fifty state legislatures.[11]

For the first time in American history, a large number of Catholics and Protestants found themselves on the same side of a cultural conflict. Together they worked against the ERA in Florida, Illinois, North Carolina, and Texas. In 1975, twenty-five hundred ERA opponents in Texas appeared at the state legislature to urge representatives to rescind their earlier endorsement of the amendment. Catholics, fundamentalists, and Pentecostals lined up against their liberal foes. Ninety-eight percent of the anti-ERA women were active church members. None were Jewish. The conservative activists emphasized that they approached the legislature as concerned individuals and Texans, not as members of a national—that is to say, un-Texan—organization like NOW. In contrast to NOW, the ERA opponents who came to testify had a list of tips on how to behave in front of a legislative committee. Among their directions was to "be lady-like and courteous, no matter what," and, when finished, to "thank the committee and exit like Loretta Young." For feminists raised on sexually aggressive Jane Fonda movies, the demure Loretta Young style was not an option.[12]

The legalization of abortion proved even more important than the ERA battle in cementing the alliance between Catholics and fundamentalists. In 1973, the Supreme Court, with a less than firm majority, decided to resolve the abortion controversy once and for all. As an earlier Court had done on the issue of slavery, the justices inserted themselves into a debate that had polarized the nation—and set the stage for a civil war. Although New York had legalized abortion before the *Roe v. Wade* ruling, the legislature subsequently voted to rescind its action. Only Governor Nelson Rockefeller's veto had kept abortion legal. (Because Ford had picked Rockefeller as his vice president, social conservatives were directing their ire at the White House, as well as the Supreme Court.) In 1972, Michigan and North Dakota voters shot down ballot initiatives to legalize abortion.[13]

Although Planned Parenthood published polling data proving that the majority of Americans favored abortion, its methods were flawed. When polling questions were more specifically worded, the responses showed that most Americans opposed *discretionary* abortion. Few believed abortion should be legal past the first trimester of a woman's pregnancy. At best, a plurality supported abortion in the event of rape or incest, and to save the life of the mother. NOW and Planned Parenthood wanted abortion on demand—and as late as the third trimester of pregnancy. Few Americans took such a radical position. In 1975, a year in which doctors performed one million abortions, 70 percent of *women* opposed the termination of a pregnancy after the first trimester. As had been true in the sixties, men were more sympathetic to abortion than women. The feminist claim that men wanted to keep women barefoot and pregnant contributed nothing to the debate. Abortion was just as much a religious and class issue as a gender issue. The less religion and the more wealth one had, the likelier one was to support abortion.[14]

In 1968, Catholics had taken the lead in opposing abortion, founding the National Right to Life Committee. Its lobbying efforts were modest. The *Roe* decision, however, invigorated the organization and inspired conservative Protestants to take a greater role in resisting abortion. The three-million-member Missouri Synod of the Lutheran Church enlisted in the battle against *Roe*. Founded by German immigrants in the 1840s, the Missouri Synod broke away from its Lutheran kin a century later. While liberal Lutherans championed abortion and gay rights in the seventies, the Missouri Synod clung to the old-time social orthodoxy. (Despite losing one-third of its flock, the Lutheran Church believed it was better to be ideologically pure than to be great in number.) Seeking legal protection for the unborn, representatives of the Missouri Synod testified before the House Judiciary Subcommittee on Civil and Constitutional Rights in 1976. Taking a stance that would have had Martin Luther spinning in his grave, the conservative Lutherans condemned liberal journalists and politicians for bashing their Catholic brethren. Social liberals, the Missouri Synod stated, were indulging themselves in religious prejudice.[15]

Missouri Synod minister Eugene Linse informed Congress that Christians would no longer remain silent on abortion and other moral issues. The Constitution belonged to the religiously devout just as much as it did to Planned Parenthood and NOW:

I have heard it stated that to enact proposals prohibiting abortion, except in limited and medical emergency situations, into law or into a constitutional amendment is itself a violation of the guarantees of freedom of religion, that is, the freedom to follow the dictates of one's conscience, protected in the First Amendment. That, in my judgment, is an argument involving a distortion of the first magnitude. In addition, moreover, to argue that those who have religious convictions should remain silent lest they foist their views on those who disagree with them, is a classical denial of the freedom of dissent and the freedom to petition for redress of grievances, both protected by the same First Amendment.[16]

Missouri Synod Lutherans and Catholics quickly discovered that many politicians, Democrat and Republican alike, did not want to deal with divisive social issues. This seemed to be particularly the case if there were more campaign contributions to be found in liberal Hollywood and Manhattan than in stodgy South Boston and St. Louis. Moreover, as Catholic activists in the New York chapter of Right to Life observed, sympathetic politicians had a knack for pulling disappearing acts when push came to shove. "My heart was with you," a New York assemblyman told prolifers during a 1970 legislative debate on legalizing abortion. "But I would surely have been defeated unless I voted for abortion. . . . I know you are fair and will look at my entire record. You are too mature and too intelligent to vote against a man on just one issue." Six years later it was evident that some voters would try to defeat a candidate solely on the basis of "just one issue."[17]

Coming out of the liberal wing of the GOP, Gerald Ford wanted to keep social and economic conservatives at arm's length. He accepted Big

Government as a fact of life, although some federal programs, he felt, might be slightly reduced so long as such initiatives did not offend any powerful political constituency. As far as moral issues were concerned, President Ford appeared content to have his wife, Betty, speak for him. In an interview on the CBS newsmagazine show *Sixty Minutes*, Betty Ford said that premarital sex might reduce the divorce rate, compared marijuana smoking to drinking "your first beer," and praised *Roe v. Wade* for bringing abortion "out of the backwoods" and putting "it in the hospitals where it belongs." Conservatives did not find Betty Ford's candor refreshing. (A divorcee and onetime performer of modern dance, Mrs. Ford would never be a favorite of social conservatives.)[18]

The Ford administration's dealings with moral traditionalists were breathtakingly cynical. Irving Kristol, editor of the neoconservative journal the *Public Interest*, summed up the attitude of many in the GOP who were more comfortable discussing foreign policy and free-market economics than social issues. As Kristol wrote to presidential advisor Bob Goldwin, a fellow neoconservative, "This letter concerns itself with abortion, of all things. . . . In a heterogeneous society such as ours, it's folly to try to dictate to the citizenry a national policy on such a controversial moral issue." However, since abortion was one of the many social issues that ripped apart the Democratic coalition, Ford should *appear* to be doing something about it without actually doing much of anything. Ford's campaign strategists concurred with Kristol. Not surprisingly, Southern Baptists never entirely trusted Jewish neoconservatives like Kristol and Goldwin. Likewise, urbane Jewish neoconservatives felt uneasy around right-wing populists and Christian moralists.[19]

When leaders of the Coalition for Life—representing twelve hundred anti-abortion groups—sought a meeting with Ford in 1974, his appointments secretary replied that the president was too busy to see them. Privately, Ford's advisors told him to avoid such people at all costs. In turn, the Coalition for Life wondered how the extremely active president found time to host representatives from NOW. "Sooner or later," Coalition for Life director Randy Engel wrote to a presidential assistant, "[Ford] will have to face [America's] many moral problems." Engel criticized the federal government for providing grants to Planned Parenthood and allowing welfare recipients to use their Medicaid benefits to pay for abortions. (Half of the abortions performed in 1976 were covered by Medicaid.) While Ford's representatives told Engel that the poor had a right to such federal funds, the administration, in a move worthy of Machiavelli, ordered Robert Bork to file a brief with the Supreme Court against Medicaid-sponsored abortions.[20]

As Bork argued in *Beal v. Doe* (1976), "the fact that a woman has a qualified right to an abortion does not imply a correlative constitutional right to free treatment. . . . The Equal Protection Clause does not affirmatively require a state to cover the costs incurred by indigents in undergoing such procedures." Bork undertook his task with missionary zeal. However, the Ford administration had little expectation that Bork's legal reasoning would prevail. While Bork crossed swords with the Supreme Court, the president opened a second front, arguing that it should be left up to the individual states to decide if they wanted abortion. Rather than have the White House get directly involved in the controversy, Ford believed, it would be far better if a constitutional Right to Life Amendment went before the states for ratification. Plainly, Ford hoped to appease prolifers with symbolic gestures while winking at GOP liberals. In the event that liberal Republicans became upset, Bork, not Ford, would take the hit. (Bork's arguments before the Supreme Court ultimately won the day, thereby placing him on NOW's and Planned Parenthood's enemies list.)[21]

Although many of Ford's staff people were nonplussed about the abortion issue, others were clearly panicking. At least one aide urged the president to muzzle his wife, pointing out that every time the *New York Times* and the *Washington Post* praised Betty, Ford lost Catholic and blue-collar support. Another advisor noted, "The abortion issue can provide President Ford with the means by which he can make the necessary inroads into the traditionally Catholic Democratic constituency, as well as the equally Democratic Southern fundamentalist one, votes that provided the margins that elected both [Dwight] Eisenhower and Nixon." Ford paid some attention to his worried advisors, choosing to meet personally with representatives from the National Conference of Catholic Bishops rather than—as he had done with Protestant prolifers—passing them along to low-level assistants. Still, the president promised nothing to the bishops' prolife spokesman, Joseph Cardinal Bernardin of Cincinnati. Meanwhile, Betty reiterated her support for abortion.[22]

A year later, with a presidential election approaching, Ford met a second time with the Catholic bishops. This time, Ford said he would exhort the state legislatures to ratify a Right to Life Amendment. Ford followed up this meeting with a letter to Cardinal Bernardin emphasizing that "the government has a responsibility to protect life—and indeed to provide legal guarantees for the weak and unprotected." Ford later whipped up delegates at a Catholic Eucharistic Congress, denouncing liberals for harboring an "irreverence for life." The president sought further political advantage by coyly suggesting that Democratic Party elites were hostile to the moral values of decent, ordinary Americans. For all of Ford's efforts, however, the Yale-educated Episcopalian had difficulty in persuading the majority of Catholics of his sincerity.[23]

Catholic opposition to busing and racial quotas posed even greater problems to Ford. In 1975, Novak and several prominent academics and Catholic politicians met with Ford to discuss the concerns of white ethnics. Even as they met, Novak recounted, "the president betrayed us." Ford withdrew administration support for the Ethnic Heritage Act. (This legislation funded Eastern European folk festivals and white ethnic studies at the college level.) Additionally, the president's advisors warned him not to address matters such as illegitimacy, busing, crime, "reverse discrimination court decisions," and welfare since liberal Republicans did not want to appear racist. One White House aide informed Novak that any gesture of friendship Ford made to big-city Catholics could be only interpreted as anti-black. Novak was astounded.[24]

If the White House thought Catholics were prickly, Ford's staffers found fundamentalists and Pentecostals utterly baffling. During his short tenure as vice president, Ford once received a letter from the pastor of a fundamentalist church in Tennessee. The minister was writing on behalf of his flock, which wanted to know if Ford was a Christian. After all, "Our people are suspicious by nature, if you know mountain folks," the southerner wrote, "and they are even more so about government." Ford replied that he was an Episcopalian, not understanding that southern fundamentalists might have a hard time considering that to be solid evidence of Christian faith.[25]

In 1976, President Ford addressed four thousand delegates at a joint convocation of the National Association of Evangelicals and the National Religious Broadcasters. He confined himself to some vague statements about why God was good. After Ford departed, activists counseled evangelicals to move out "from the pews to polls" and elect real Christians. When one minister noted that the "moral cesspools of America are overflowing," conservatives had to wonder why the president—good Christian that he was—had not been out cleaning the national sewer system.[26]

Ford's appearances before religious organizations like the National Association of Evangelicals and the Southern Baptist Convention were carefully programmed to ensure that he did not say anything offensive to liberals or conservatives. Actually, the president knew next to nothing about Southern Baptists, while Pentecostals remained even further beyond his ken than Catholics. Invited to speak to CBN's viewers, Ford sent a taped message eleven sentences long. His advisors had to apprise Ford of the fact that the son of a former Virginia senator owned CBN. Beyond Ford's brief message, his staffers seemed uninterested in developing a relationship with Pentecostals. They should have done some additional research. By 1976, CBN aired programs on 1,200 cable systems with a potential audience of 110 million. CBN's first nationwide special, "It's Time to Pray, America," broadcast in honor of the Bicentennial, was shown on 228 television stations. An election-year invitation from Rev. Jerry Falwell to talk to the 15,000 members of the Thomas Road Baptist Church elicited a thirteen-sentence taped message. Clearly, Ford had little to say to southerners and social conservatives.[27]

Conservatives also had little to say to Ford. In 1975, the American Conservative Union and the Young Americans for Freedom sought to promote Ronald Reagan as a third-party presidential candidate. Richard Viguerie, a former fund-raiser for George Wallace, liked the idea and pledged to build a formidable direct-mail operation to finance a conservative party. Senator Jesse Helms could see the sense in establishing such a new party, but hoped that Reagan could receive the GOP nomination. All Ford and Vice President Rockefeller had to do, Helms argued, was to step aside and allow real Republicans to run the White House. One-time Nixon campaign strategist Kevin Phillips considered liberal Republicans obstacles to economic and moral reform. Pat Buchanan, having left the Ford administration, lamented that the president had no "vision for the future." Ford was a rudderless politician "much less interested in altering the composition, or influencing the direction of the Supreme Court, than in having his nominees acceptable to everyone." The president, Buchanan concluded, was guilty "of committing liberalism," and, therefore, should be sentenced to an early retirement.[28]

Ford had identified Reagan as a threat almost from the day he became president. To stave off a primary challenge, the Fords visited Ronald and Nancy Reagan in California. They must have discussed politics in very general terms, for Ford said he had an enjoyable time. When Reagan wrote to Ford in 1974 about adopting California's welfare reforms on a national level, the president expressed only polite interest. Meanwhile, the

White House sent its operatives into action, collecting intelligence on the erstwhile actor. Ford's people tried to learn which of Reagan's advisors could be bought off with White House jobs. They concluded that Mike Deaver was the only prospect since he had "a socially ambitious wife." The rest were dedicated conservatives, with at least one of them on the Coors payroll and "loaned" to Reagan. California Assemblyman Pete Wilson did his part, sending a report to Ford detailing why Reagan's claims to being a welfare reformer and tax cutter were fraudulent. Reagan, Wilson felt, should be disqualified "from holding any leadership position."[29]

Reagan signaled several months before the primaries that he intended to take no prisoners. The Oklahoma Citizens for Reagan mailed a bitter fund-raising letter to Republicans. According to the Reaganites, Ford and Nixon were just as responsible as Kennedy and Johnson for the growth of the welfare state and the Communist conquest of South Vietnam:

We are opposed by the powerful forces which have brought us the welfare way of life, the largest federal budget deficits ever proposed or enacted, total amnesty for draft dodgers and deserters, a weak foreign policy, our first defeat in war . . . the list goes on and on. What might we see next? Giving away the Panama Canal? Clothing stamps with abuses as wild as in the food stamp program? Gun registration, possibly confiscation? Ever increasing federal deficits? These programs are all proposed! Where will it end?

Disgusted, Oklahoma Senator Henry Bellmon warned moderate Republicans that the conservatives were intent upon destroying Ford, even if it led to the Democrats capturing the White House.[30]

At first, Reagan floundered in the primaries and Ford used every advantage of incumbency he could muster. When all appeared lost, Helms came to the rescue, rallying North Carolina behind Reagan. His fortunes turned around, Reagan marched triumphantly through the South, winning three-quarters of the region's delegates. The West proved even friendlier to Reagan, with the Californian garnering four-fifths of the delegates. Ford's staffers were stunned. Working-class whites who once could have been counted upon to stay away from GOP primaries flocked to Reagan. In private polls that the Ford staff kept very quiet, the president learned that just 1 percent of black Republicans had voted for Reagan. Although their numbers were not large, blacks made enough difference in the Kentucky and Tennessee primaries to give Ford two rare wins in the South. Whatever southern votes Ford received came from blacks and liberal white Republicans. (Jody Powell, the press secretary to Georgia governor Jimmy Carter, provided the best description of the southern

GOP before the Age of Reagan. According to Powell, Dixie's white Republicans were backwoods Baptists who moved to the Atlanta suburbs, joined the Episcopalian Church, found a good country club, and "learned to tell jokes about rednecks as well as blacks.")[31]

Although the Midwest and the Northeast provided him with the slim eighty-delegate margin he needed to win the GOP nomination, Ford still experienced difficulties. Once again, blacks, this time in Chicago and Detroit, proved crucial to Ford's Illinois and Michigan victories. Larger numbers of Catholic Democrats, like their Protestant counterparts in the Sunbelt, voted for Reagan so long as the primaries were not restricted to registered Republicans. Moreover, prolife groups were not bashful about standing outside Catholic churches to "educate" parishioners about which GOP candidate was truly opposed to abortion. Ford hit back, asserting (accurately) that welfare rolls and government employment grew sharply in California during Reagan's tenure as governor. He also reminded blue-collar ethnics that Reagan had recently suggested making Social Security a voluntary program. (Once voluntary, there would be no Social Security.) In an aside to liberal white and black Republicans, Ford charged that Reagan's attacks on welfare were racially motivated. By way of evidence, Ford pointed out that Reagan often made reference to a black "Welfare Queen" in Chicago whom he accused of defrauding the federal government of $150,000. (To be fair to Reagan, he never identified the woman's race. However, that did not deter liberal Republicans from contending that "Welfare Queen" was a code word for black. Newly sensitized, perhaps hypersensitized to the issue of race, moderate Republicans had become just as skittish as liberal Democrats. It appeared as if the Left had successfully placed any discussion of welfare reform out of bounds.)[32]

Luckily for Ford, many social conservatives continued to vote in the Democratic primaries. In 1976, two-thirds of the voters who identified themselves as conservatives were either Democrats or independents. Even if three-quarters of the country's liberals were Democrats, a large share of traditionalists remained loyal to the party of Roosevelt—at least for one more presidential election. Throughout the primaries and into the GOP National Convention, where Reagan continued to dispute Ford's leadership, liberal Republicans called the Sunbelt politician hopeless. "Reagan's constituency," they claimed, "is much too narrow . . . he cannot defeat any candidate the Democrats put up." This was not true. If Republicans remained the party of northeastern and midwestern Protestant liberals, then, of course, a conservative could not win. However, if the GOP broadened its appeal to attract white southerners and northern Catholics, playing up social issues and fueling resentment of taxes and Big Government, a conservative electoral majority could be forged. However, Republican liberals did not want the GOP to retain the White House and take Congress if it meant opposing abortion, quotas, and welfare.[33]

Aced out of the nomination, conservatives forced Ford to dump Rockefeller from the ticket and tried to have their way with the Republican Party platform. Helms, the Senate sponsor of a Right to Life Amendment, insisted that the GOP take the only correct posture on abortion. Assisting the prolife conservatives were activists like Bishop James Malone of Youngstown, Ohio. Malone movingly testified before the GOP platform committee against abortion. However, conservatives paid little heed to the rest of his message. Speaking for the nation's bishops, Malone contended that stagnant wages and the lack of affordable health insurance were just as detrimental to the family as abortion. So far as the libertarians were concerned, Catholic prolifers seemed a little too New Dealish for their tastes.[34]

Conservatives also wanted the GOP to reject the ERA. To their consternation, Betty Ford led a narrowly successful counterattack. Her foes insisted that they supported equal rights for women but had to oppose the ERA due to the radical cultural agenda hidden beneath the amendment's innocuous language. ERA opponents clashed with liberal Republicans, calling them "petulant" and out of touch with the will of the people. Surveying the scene, Ford decided that rather than running on the Republican platform in the general election, he would run away from it.[35]

"Hi! I'm Jimmy Carter, a peanut farmer. Do you accept Jesus Christ as your personal savior?" Thus did Pennsylvanians get their first glimpse of the toothy Georgian. Having lost his first gubernatorial bid in 1966, Carter had a religious awakening that prompted him to do missionary work in benighted Pennsylvania. Many people found the smiling evangelical who knocked on their doors to be either charming or disturbing. Little could they know that Carter would be back—the next time running for president.[36]

President Jimmy Carter? On the face of it, the notion that a one-term governor from Georgia, whose chief (not to mention false) claim to greatness was that he had reduced the state payroll, seemed ludicrous. Yet a few developments conspired to make Carter the Democratic presidential nominee. The 1969 Chappaquiddick incident remained too vivid to permit Teddy Kennedy a '76 run. With the best-known candidate out of the way, twelve senators, governors, and House members of lesser renown entered the Democratic primaries. Eight were social liberals and at least two of the four conservatives had limited appeal. "Scoop" Jackson, with great support from Jews who appreciated his Zionist sympathies, could win New York but little else. In the South, Carter faced off against George Wallace, assuring white voters that he was a traditionalist like Wallace but with an important difference—the Georgian could win the White House. To southern and northern blacks, Carter pledged his undying friendship. Martin Luther King, Sr., and other civil rights activists accompanied Carter on the campaign trail, making sure blacks understood that this man was no redneck southerner.[37]

Carter had the best of all possible worlds. Liberals, who made up the majority of voters in the Democratic primaries, failed to close ranks. In Massachusetts, they split their votes among several candidates. At the same time, Jackson and George Wallace shared the blue-collar anti-busing vote. Carter won black Boston. With less than a quarter of the vote, Jackson's victory was hollow. In Pennsylvania, AFL-CIO leaders were friendly to Senator Jackson. Unfortunately for the Washington senator, the union rank and file stayed at home, wishing Hubert Humphrey had entered the race. Philadelphia blacks gave Carter a major win in the industrial North. The same held true in Michigan, with black Detroit putting Carter over the top. Overall, Carter won just 40 percent of the primary vote. Churchgoing blacks, Southern Baptists, and Pentecostals formed the core of Carter's supporters. (Carter received little support from blacks and whites who did not regularly attend religious services.) Hoping to attract more social conservatives to his cause, Carter was no Ford—he sought out Pat Robertson for an endorsement. Robertson obliged. Liberal Democrats (as well as President Ford) should have looked a little more closely at all of those Pentecostal churches blanketing black neighborhoods in Boston, Detroit, and Philadelphia.[38]

Both McGovern liberals and northern New Deal Democrats were upset. A conservative southern Democrat, a man whose ancestors owned slaves no less, had separated them from their black allies. *Washington Post* reporter Jules Witcover ridiculed Carter as a "peanut-farmer Billy Graham," publicly venting his contempt for America's fifty million evangelicals and charismatics. Carter campaign strategist Hamilton Jordan was not surprised by Witcover's attacks. Jordan had believed from the outset of the primaries that Carter would have to run against the "Eastern liberal news establishment which had tremendous influence in this country all out of proportion to its actual audience." Meanwhile Humphrey sputtered that if voters closed their eyes and listened to Carter's criticism of the liberal news media and Big Government, they might think Ronald Reagan was speaking with a mush-mouthed accent. Ronald Reagan, though, would never have said that he wanted the federal government to be "as good and honest and decent and truthful and fair and competent and idealistic and compassionate, and as filled with love as are the American people." Reagan wanted Big Government disposed of, not healed.[39]

Like John F. Kennedy, Carter's religious background both helped and hindered him in the general election. On the positive side of the balance sheet, his Baptist faith—more freely expressed and deeply held than Kennedy's Catholicism—served him well among a growing segment of the electorate. William Rusher, the publisher of the *National Review,* spoke approvingly of Carter's religiosity, making him the first Democrat ever to receive a kind word from the waspish commentator. (Oozing insincerity from every pore, Senator Birch Bayh, one of the liberal contenders for the Democratic presidential nomination, said during the primaries that he felt "closer to God" by living in Indiana. Rusher had to ask why, "in that case, he was trying so hard to take up residence on Pennsylvania Avenue.")[40]

In Jimmy Carter, many Southern Baptist clergy initially thought they had found a man who would redeem the nation. After all, the Democratic presidential nominee proudly identified himself as a "born-again Christian," his sister, Ruth Stapleton, was a faith-healing evangelist, and his son Jeff was a divinity student. Carter was not, however, a typical Southern Baptist. He did not believe everything in the Bible should be taken literally. At the same time, he clung to one traditional Baptist belief that many conservative ministers were in the process of abandoning—keeping the church separated from the corrupting influences of political office. As Carter argued, a religious sect that tried to make laws for civil society could find itself co-opted by the secular state. In essence, Carter believed in personal morality but would never allow his religious beliefs to influence judicial appointments and social policy. Since the Supreme Court had legalized abortion, Carter did not feel that it would be proper for him, if the occasion ever arose, to appoint prolife judges to the bench. Although Carter opposed abortion, and had doubts about the ERA—

which his wife and advisor Rosalynn did not share—as president he would not disturb the liberal status quo. So far as religion went, Carter was not that much different from George McGovern. Both viewed themselves as instruments of America's salvation.[41]

Protestant social conservatives should have had some advance inkling that Carter wanted their votes, not their advice. When the editor of the liberal *Christian Century* magazine ended up as Illinois state chair of the Carter campaign, fundamentalists ought to have concluded that something was amiss. They might also have read Carter's interview with a reporter who wrote for various progressive Catholic journals. Carter praised family planning and, so far as banning abortion went, reiterated his belief that a president "has no role to play in the constitutional amendment process." Then again, Southern Baptists, if they wanted the best insight into the tenets of Carter's Christian faith, could have read his freewheeling interviews in *Playboy* and the *New York Times Magazine.*[42]

In a ploy to reassure the Democratic Party's left wing that he was no holy roller, Carter played swinger in the premiere magazines of social liberalism. The presidential nominee informed *Playboy*'s readers that "Christ says don't consider yourself better than someone else because one guy screws a whole bunch of women while the other guy is loyal to his wife." Carter then admitted to having lusted in his heart after other women. If one followed a strict interpretation of the Ten Commandments, Carter argued, then he was guilty of committing adultery. In a racy *New York Times Magazine* interview, Carter used the "f-word" to refer to sexual intercourse. (Republican vice-presidential candidate Bob Dole told an Ohio audience that Carter "has been giving a great many interviews lately, and some I haven't read. Others are still looking at the pictures.")[43]

Bailey Smith, a leader of the Southern Baptist Convention and a Carter supporter, rebuked the Georgian. "We're totally against pornography," Smith said. "And, well, 'screw' is not a good Baptist word." Another Carter backer, the reverend W. A. Criswell, representing the largest Baptist church in America, switched his allegiance to Ford. "There are other public media through which we can discuss the moral issues of life and government than the pages of a salacious, pornographic magazine," the Dallas Baptist stormed. Equally outraged, Falwell vowed to do everything within his power to deny Virginia to Carter in the general election. More disappointed than angry, Pat Robertson reluctantly followed Criswell, Falwell, and Smith into the Ford camp. He would not, however, campaign for Ford. Robertson believed that neither political party offered much to social conservatives other than empty symbolic gestures and the all too frequent act of betrayal.[44]

Rev. Harold Lindsell, editor of the evangelical magazine *Christianity Today,* concurred with Robertson. Both nominees were "mediocre candidates." In many ways, though, Carter was the worse "of two lesser candidates." Among Carter's offenses, according to Lindsell, was his deliberate misinterpretation of Christ's words. Contrary to Carter, Jesus condemned adulterers and expected his followers to do likewise. A moral society could not tolerate the wicked any more than it should put up with politicians who gave interviews to *Playboy* and used "scatological language." Responding to Carter's defenders in the news media, Lindsell insisted that "any analysis of a candidate running for public office must take into account his personal life and his language, as well as his gifts and abilities for occupying the office to which he aspires." On that basis, Carter was unfit to be president.[45]

The response to Lindsell's editorials and sermons underscored just how badly divided white Protestants were about Carter's character. One female correspondent from Virginia praised Lindsell's stance and assailed Carter. "It seems to me all he did was advertise for this magazine [*Playboy*] that we would not allow in our homes, and if he wins one soul for Christ through this interview, I sure would like to know about it." Others criticized Lindsell. A liberal Baptist from Maryland informed the minister that he resented "very much the interference of religion into political matters. . . . It seems to me that your attack was in the same vein as the Catholic bishops who have tried to inject the abortion issue into the political scene." Similarly, a theologically liberal Presbyterian from the Washington suburbs castigated Lindsell's "foolish criticism," hypocrisy, and stupidity. "I don't hear evangelicals sounding off about divorce anymore—Mrs. Ford, [Robert] Dole, [Ronald] Reagan [The three were on their second marriages in 1976.]. . . . Please do not make the mistake of thinking that most Christians are as narrow or one dimensional as your comments indicate that you are."[46]

If white Protestants found Carter's general election campaign divisive, Catholics remained leery of the governor. Carter responded to such suspicions with several contradictory tactics. In seeking to rally Dixie, Carter's staff would tell fundamentalist and Pentecostal groups that social liberals and northern Catholics were prejudiced against Southern Baptists. (New York's favorite Irish Catholic journalist and pub connoisseur,

Jimmy Breslin, admitted that he could never vote for a Southern Baptist. Then again, one Irishman did not make a Vatican horde.) Even as Carter obliquely conjured up horrifying images of scheming bishops and Manhattan trendsetters, he hoped to play to the prejudices of ethnics. The southerner praised the moral cohesion of white-ethnic neighborhoods and reassured Catholics that he would not promote open housing for blacks. "I see nothing wrong with ethnic purity being maintained." Carter said. "I would not force a racial integration of a neighborhood by government action." When Jesse Jackson cried foul, Carter's black supporters let it be known that the governor did not really mean what he had told Catholics.[47]

Father Greeley and Michael Novak, among other Catholic intellectuals, hurled brickbats at Carter. They detected in Carter an anti-Catholic bias, as well as an inclination to deliver to the civil rights establishment whatever it wanted, no matter how detrimental it was to the interests of working-class ethnics. "It is the urban ethnics who must pick up the tab for every major social change going on in this society," Greeley wrote. "But that's all right, because they're guilty and inferior anyway." Echoing Greeley, but expressing even greater loathing of Carter, Novak thundered:

On the issue of whites and blacks in the major cities of the North and North Central states, Carter is plainly owned by blacks, as in Detroit. His candidacy may be healing in the South, but divisive in the North. He may be "laying down the burden of race" in the South. It looks as though his scapegoats in the North will be the Catholics who live in the inner cities and the inner ring of suburbs around the cities.

Carter is no Robert Kennedy, nor even a Hubert Humphrey, uniting both the whites and blacks of Gary, and Pittsburgh, and Chicago, under one set of symbols and policies. On the contrary, Carter reinforces the perceptions that the Democrats are interested in "affirmative discrimination" against working-class and white-collar Catholics.[48]

Novak's mentor, Father Geno Baroni, was calmer than his peers, believing that a more culturally sensitive Carter could build a black-Catholic alliance. Calling on a Carter supporter, Baroni chastised the campaign for implying that most Catholics were bigots. "Urban ethnics," Baroni fumed, "hate the idea that they are red-necked racists." Baroni soon joined Carter's general election campaign. Seeking to improve Carter's image among white ethnics, Baroni persuaded him to visit Pittsburgh's Polish Hill neighborhood. The priest felt Carter would attract better Catholic media coverage by shaking hands with Polish-American butchers and smiling parochial school students, than by speaking downtown to an audience of city and county employees whose union demanded warm bodies for campaign events. In this instance, Baroni showed real political savvy.[49]

Despite his best efforts, Father Baroni could not save Carter from the left wing of the Democratic Party. Having been caught flat-footed in the primaries, social liberals were well prepared for the Democratic National Convention. Liberal activists intended to write the Democratic platform and steer Carter toward an acceptable running mate. In this case, the preferred vice-presidential candidate was Senator Walter Mondale of Minnesota. Although a protégé of Hubert Humphrey's, Mondale had adapted himself to the McGovern wing of the party. In 1973, Mondale earned NOW's friendship by sponsoring Senate hearings intended to promote feminist programs in the universities. Unfortunately for the Carter-Mondale ticket, being too closely identified with NOW caused some discomfort. On July 4, 1976, the president of NOW joined thirty thousand radicals in Philadelphia for an anti-Bicentennial march. Feminists, gays, and black militants lambasted America as racist and genocidal. NOW's actions undercut Carter's efforts to depict himself as more socially conservative than McGovern.[50]

NOW and the NEA, with a few hundred convention delegates between them, insisted that the Democratic platform endorse abortion, busing, criminal rights, and the ERA. The Congressional Black Caucus joined in, exacting from Carter pledges to impose more racial hiring quotas, appropriate larger amounts of federal tax dollars to the cities, and avoid serious welfare reform. Carter complied but hedged his bets wherever he could. To the electorate at large, Carter spoke movingly about the injustice of racial discrimination, avoiding any mention of quotas. Indeed, Carter gave the impression that he was not sympathetic to the idea of preferential treatment for blacks. After all, with the passage of the 1964 Civil Rights Act, the nation had moved beyond the "constant preoccupation with the racial aspect of almost every question." Carter's official statement on the matter of rising crime rates was nine sentences long. Following the path blazed by the architects of the Great Society, Carter blamed the rising crime rate on the lack of good jobs. Unlike the Great Society liberals, Carter said he would happily imprison those same putative victims of inner-city unemployment.[51]

To mollify the moralists in his party, Carter made a somewhat longer than usual statement on the American family. Where he emphasized before black church audiences that the lack of public-sector jobs bred urban crime, Carter seemed to be telling working-class whites that divorce, illegitimacy, and sexual promiscuity contributed to anti-social behavior. But then he retreated from the full implication of his remarks, once again emphasizing joblessness as the chief cause of social decay. Taking a swipe at Ford, Carter asserted that the 20 percent unemployment rate in the automobile manufacturing town of Flint, Michigan, had led to startling rises in alcoholism, drug consumption, and child abuse. Carter's general election strategy was unmistakable. At all costs, he had to direct attention from social issues. Only by focusing on double-digit inflation and an 8 percent national unemployment rate, and accusing the GOP of plotting to abolish Social Security and Medicare could the New Deal coalition be reunited. For good measure, Carter got some mileage from the Watergate scandal, implying that Ford had agreed to pardon Nixon in exchange for the keys to the White House. All in all, Carter had the right idea. Whether he could be successful, however, was unclear.[52]

Certainly, the Catholic bishops did not cut Carter any slack on the abortion issue. To open a dialogue with the bishops, Father Baroni urged Carter to meet with Cardinal Bernardin. Carter's staffers told him that he would only make matters worse. Carter forged ahead. As feared, his session with the bishops was disastrous. Placed on the defensive, Carter denied having had anything to do with the drafting of the prochoice plank in the Democratic Party platform. But the bishops knew that Carter's staff had helped write it. (They also knew that as governor of Georgia, Carter had advocated voluntary abortions and sterilization.) Confronted with his inconsistent statements, Carter reverted to his standard attack on Republican inflation, Republican unemployment, and Republican corruption. Taken aback by Carter's performance, Bernardin immediately held a press conference. The cardinal contended that the Democrats' "abortion plank is irresponsible." Moreover, Bernardin said in reference to Carter,

it has become rather commonplace of late for some elected officials and candidates for public office to allege personal opposition to abortion and personal disagreement with the Supreme Court's abortion rulings—but to couple this with opposition to amending the Constitution to correct the situation they say they oppose.

I do not think many Americans find this either persuasive or responsible.[53]

Carter could only hope that the Catholic laity paid greater attention to its pocketbook than to the bishops. After all, Teddy Kennedy's position on abortion differed little from Carter's, and the Massachusetts senator appeared to have little difficulty in getting reelected. The problem with that line of reasoning, though, was that Kennedy relied less on Catholics and more on the Bay State's large population of blacks, Jews, and suburban professionals to keep him in office. It was such voters, not Catholics, who gave the state its nickname, "The People's Republic of Massachusetts." In the Massachusetts, New York, and New Jersey primaries Carter had won few working-class Catholic votes. Carter could not blame that development on the fact that Catholics disliked candidates who wore their Protestantism on their sleeves (though Carter did just that). After all, Catholics in Connecticut and Michigan lent enthusiastic support to Arizona's *Mormon* congressman, Morris Udall. Even after the primaries and the Democratic convention, many Catholics kept their distance from Carter. Just as worrisome, Carter could not, like Kennedy, count upon social liberals and Jews to compensate for the loss of white ethnics.[54]

The Georgian's difficulties with Jews and social liberals were enormous. During the New York primary, Carter had flippantly remarked that "Scoop" Jackson would get the Jews, and he would get the Christians. While an accurate assessment of the situation, Carter should not have articulated every thought that came to mind. Even Jews who loathed McGovern did not consider Carter to be much of an improvement, even if the Baptist did say that he liked Israel. (For all they knew, Carter might have meant that he liked the idea of Jews living in Israel, as opposed to Long Island.) Giving an interview to *Playboy* did not reassure many Jews that Carter was a mensch among evangelicals. As for college-educated suburbanites, Carter had won few over when he argued that "McGovern's biggest mistake [was to] make the Vietnam War an issue." For white-collar liberals, whose political passions had been aroused by the peace movement, George McGovern remained a revered prophet.[55]

Carter compounded his problems with social liberals by aggressively cultivating their arch enemies Mayor Richard Daley and the AFL-CIO's "voter education" leader Alex Barkan. The Democratic nominee coolly calculated that if the Daley machine and organized labor mobilized their followers on his behalf, he could afford a few defections in the white-collar suburbs. (Carter did buy off one sizable bloc of social liberals, promising the nearly two million members of the NEA that he would create a financially munificent department of education if elected president.) Courted with an ardor he had not seen since '68, Daley anointed Carter as America's moral leader:

He's got a religious tone in what he says and maybe we should have a little more religion in our community. . . . The man talks about true values. Why shouldn't we be sold on him? All of us recognize the violent and filthy movies and the newspapers with all the mistresses on the first page stripped down to the waist. What are the kids going to do in the society that see that all around?[56]

Daley's enthusiasm for Carter was partly misplaced. Where the Chicago party boss saw a moral tribune of the people, other voters could reasonably ask: What will Carter do to help the family—other than declare that promiscuity is bad? Carter had given his answer to that question during the Massachusetts primary. The Georgian promised to eliminate the home mortgage interest deduction in order to balance the federal budget. If Carter followed such a course of action, working-class families would lose their only major tax break. Moreover, a great many families were able to buy a home only because of the mortgage interest deduction. Organized labor chose not to tell the rank and file about Carter's proposed assault on homeowners. Instead, Barkan roused the troops, spent millions in the general election to defeat Ford, and focused labor's attention on unemployment and inflation. "We stay away from divisive issues like abortion, busing, crime, and mortgage interest deductions," Barkan boasted to reporters. Not even Ronald Reagan, the champion of the open shop, suggested balancing the budget on the backs of working-class homeowners. Instead, Reagan preferred sticking it to the politically unpopular recipients of federal aid: welfare mothers, college students, and big-city mayors.[57]

As Carter's problems with social liberals, blue-collar voters, Catholics, and Southern Baptists loomed larger, Ford began to get his act together. It is worth recalling that Ford was America's first unelected president. Moreover, prior to 1976, the Grand Rapids congressman had never even run a statewide—let alone a national—campaign. By pardoning Nixon for his role in the Watergate cover-up, Ford had angered many Americans who wanted the disgraced politician punished—not sent to a sun-soaked retirement in California. To make matters worse, the former football player was incredibly clumsy off the playing field. His pratfalls became legendary, giving young comedian Chevy Chase of *Saturday Night Live* his big break on television. In one skit, Chase, playing President Ford, heard the Oval Office phone ring. Not paying attention to what he was doing, Chase picked up a stapler instead of the phone—with predictable results. What made the skit even more bizarre was that the man playing Ford's press secretary *really was his press secretary*. In August, having barely survived a challenge from the GOP Right, and with unemployment and inflation soaring, the polls showed Ford trailing Carter by thirty-three points.

Ford did not lack for advice. Pat Buchanan, whose newspaper columns had angered many in the administration, urged his onetime employer not to concede the moral issues to the Baptist Sunday school teacher. Rather, Ford should single out Mondale for being "the leading champion of forced busing in the U.S. Senate" and ridicule Democratic legislators for serving in the "*Playboy* Congress." Buchanan was making more than just a sly reference to Carter's *Playboy* interview. The mistress of one Democratic congressional leader had recently bared all to *Playboy*. Although only 15 percent of the public expressed "great confidence" in Congress, most Americans could still be shocked by the fact that congressional staffers were sometimes hired for reasons other than their typing skills. Gary Trudeau was not surprised by the behavior of politicians. In one "Doonesbury" series, an investigating committee asks a congressman's sexy secretary to recite the alphabet. Perplexed, she replies, "The alphabet? *All of it?*"[58]

Few White House staffers agreed with Buchanan. They implored the president to run to the left of Carter on the social issues and to make Betty the centerpiece of his campaign. Such advisors viewed Carter's moral beliefs—softened though they had become for the November election—as

something that could contribute significantly to his defeat. The image of a "holier than thou" re-born Christian imposing his personal brand of morality on the nation will "wear thin" in an intense campaign with great numbers of Americans. Many Eastern liberals, Jews, and, Roman Catholics already are concerned over the heavy religious tone found in his remarks and speeches.[59]

To execute this winning strategy, Ford's advisors concluded, the president had to concede the South to Carter. It was not simply that Ford had little chance to defeat Carter in his home region. Instead, the Ford campaign did not want anything to do with the most socially conservative bloc of voters in the country. The White House believed that the Brahmins, Jews, and social liberals who gave Ford the GOP nomination could carry him to victory in November. The only concession to reality Ford's staffers made was to try to attract the northern Catholics who had voted for Reagan in the primaries. By endorsing the Right-to-Life Amendment that Helms was sponsoring in the Senate, Ford hoped to net Catholic support. It did not matter that the GOP liberals regarded Helm's abortion initiative as a joke. (A Democratic candidate for Congress from Tennessee, however, took the Helms amendment very seriously. Al Gore, Jr., identified himself as an evangelical who believed that life began at conception. Meanwhile, Jesse Jackson decried Medicaid-funded abortions as a form of racial genocide because most were performed on blacks.)[60]

In a remarkable turnabout for Ford, Carter's commanding lead eroded daily. As predicted, Carter did carry the South—with the exception of Falwell and Robertson's Virginia. Carter's support among Pentecostals and fundamentalists melted away in the wake of the *Playboy* interview and the selection of Mondale as his running mate. By election day, Carter actually *lost* the white southern vote to Ford—46 percent to 54 percent. However, Carter ran ten percentage points better than McGovern had in the South among whites. Coupled with dramatic rises in the southern minority turnout, in addition to Carter's capture of nine in ten black votes, he carried the region. Of course, for all of Carter's efforts to run as a social conservative, if he had alienated just a few more Southern Baptists he could have written off Dixie *and* the White House.[61]

The Carter campaign also claimed credit for bringing the Catholic vote home. In Philadelphia, Carter avoided prolife pickets by moving a political rally from a Catholic parish to a liberal Lutheran church. Although he consistently ducked prolife protesters, Carter muddied the waters sufficiently enough to lead many Catholics to believe that he supported a constitutional ban on abortion. (Amazed, the reporters covering Carter composed a special song set to the tune of "Jesus Loves Me." As they sang on the press plane, "Jimmy loves me, yes, I know, Jody Powell tells me so. In Catholic groups he comes on strong, unborn babes to him belong.") Cardinal Bernardin and the bishops were too circumspect to inform the laity that Carter was less than truthful. Besides, with the unemployment rate and the cost of living rising among wage earners— many of whom were Catholic—the bishops were not about to endorse GOP economics any more than they were prepared to bless liberal social policies. Consequently, Carter received 54 percent of the Catholic vote. Once again, Carter improved upon McGovern's showing among Catholics, yet fell twenty percentage points short of bringing about an electoral restoration.[62]

Among Jews and college-educated liberals, Carter did worse than McGovern. Carter received almost two-thirds of the Jewish vote. To a number of Jewish voters, Carter was either too much of a liberal or not enough of one. Even Jews who supported Carter in '76 were not strongly committed to him. At the same time, the California, Massachusetts, and New York suburbs that had the highest proportion of New Class voters punished Carter for his apparent social conservatism. The upper-income "McGovern counties" found Ford to be more ideologically acceptable than Carter. In what had become a political truism since '68, whenever a presidential candidate did poorly in affluent precincts, he scored well in white working-class neighborhoods. Carter's twenty-one percentage-point gain over McGovern in the blue-collar precincts more than made up for the loss of upper-middle-class social liberals. Carter had organized labor, and a poor economy, to thank for his decisive win among workers. (Or, as George Meany observed, "Carter's biggest asset is that the vast majority of the American people have no respect for Ford. He has no class; he's a fumbler. He comes through as a symbol of mediocrity.")[63]

Viewing himself as a resurrected Roosevelt, Carter had kicked off his fall campaign at FDR's vacation home in Warm Springs, Georgia. Usually, a Democratic presidential candidate launched the fall election season by marching in the Detroit Labor Day parade. Michigan, however, was Ford's home state and Carter felt more at ease in the Southland. Since Carter knew that the union vote was in his pocket, he had the luxury of being able to place some distance between himself and a city that many white southerners did not regard as quite American. (Detroit served as the headquarters of the UAW, spawned liberal Republicans like former Michigan governor and automobile executive George Romney, and had earned the nickname "Murder City.")[64]

Buoyed by Carter's victory, his staffers crowed that they had reconstituted the New Deal electoral coalition. Blacks, white southerners, workers, Catholics, and Jews had all voted for Carter. Then again, members of those groups also voted for Ford—some, like white southerners and Catholics, almost evenly dividing their vote between the two presidential candidates. Carter beat Ford by just two percentage points, hardly a landslide worthy of FDR or LBJ. Carter faced a country that, regardless of its religious faith or lack thereof, placed little confidence in the public schools, labor unions, the Supreme Court, Congress, big business, and the media. The major economic, government, and social institutions of the country did not inspire trust. Carter—much like Reagan—played to the voters' scorn for professional politicians and Washington bureaucrats. One of the potential shortcomings of Carter's strategy, though, was that he needed the help of the very constituency groups that he had implicitly defined as being part of the problem. NOW, the NEA, and the 700,000 members of the American Federation of State, County, and Municipal Employees (AFSCME), regarded Carter's denunciations of Big Government, the growing federal deficit, and the moral decay of society as campaign ploys, not as his closely held personal feelings. But, with Carter, who really knew?[65]

Other difficulties loomed for the president-elect. Since Carter had no electoral coattails, and in many congressional districts ran behind the local Democratic candidate, both the party's traditionalists and suburban liberals felt that they owed him little loyalty. Party politics aside, Carter had been elected to combat inflation and unemployment, reduce the deficit and the federal tax burden, scale back Big Government, and make America economically competitive. At the same time, Carter had been elected to expand federal aid to the Snowbelt cities, increase the cost-of-living adjustments for Social Security recipients, expand the Medicaid-Medicare health insurance programs, improve the quality of American public education, impose more environmental and safety regulations upon industry, and create additional public-sector employment. And, depending upon whether one asked a southern white or black, a Catholic or a Jew, Carter had been elected to expand/eliminate racial hiring quotas, ban/defend abortion, and halt/champion busing. Then again, Ford had promised all these things as well. A foolish consistency, as a wise man said, is the hobgoblin of little minds.

Having sat out the '76 presidential election, Billy Graham wrote a prescient condolence letter to Ford:

I am sure that God in His wisdom has spared you from having to carry the terrible burdens that are going to fall on this country in the next four years. The storm clouds seem to be gathering on every front. I am convinced that only God can see us through, no matter who is president.[66]

CHAPTER FOUR

The Great Awakening

1980

Jimmy Carter knew that a successful president had to maintain the peace, promote economic growth, and avoid entanglement in moral issues. Voters might forgive a recession—provided that it was over at least a year before the next presidential election. Most of the electorate could even tolerate a few missteps overseas. So long as American lives were not threatened, few cared whether dictators in some far-off (or nearby) land tortured their own people. And with the social issues, Carter needed liberal Democrats who knew enough not to attack the moral values of religious-minded voters. Nothing ended up going Carter's way. Religious conservatives mobilized against the partisans of social liberalism, the economy soured, and developments abroad humiliated the American people.

Surveying Carter's foreign policy advisors, Bob Tyrrell, the biting editor of the *American Spectator,* observed that the president had hired "every McGovernite not then employed by a rock band." United Nations ambassador Andrew Young called Israel a racist nation and defended Communists' military intervention in Angola. "I don't believe that Cuba is in Africa because it was ordered there by the Russians," the black activist argued. "I believe that Cuba is in Africa because it really has a shared sense of colonial oppression and domination." Outlining his foreign policy objectives in 1977, Carter informed a commencement audience at the University of Notre Dame that anti-Communism was a discredited policy of the past. "We are now free of that inordinate fear of Communism which," Carter told his stunned Catholic audience, "once led us to embrace any dictator who joined us in our fear."[1]

In the three years following Carter's Notre Dame address, the Soviet Union expanded its nuclear arsenal, acquired military bases in Africa and Southeast Asia, invaded Afghanistan, and supplied weapons to Marxist guerrillas in Nicaragua. Meanwhile, Cambodian Communists exterminated two million of their fellow citizens. As American prestige fell, terrorist groups, many of which were armed and trained by the Soviets, stepped up their assaults on various democracies. In 1971, the West endured seventeen terrorist bombings and assassinations. By 1980, the number of terrorist incidents in the West rose to 1,169. In Iran, Islamic fundamentalists overthrew the shah and seized the American embassy. For 444 days, fifty-two Americans were prisoners of a regime that had, by the rules of international law, committed an act of war against the United States. From Tehran to the killing fields of Cambodia, America was a laughingstock.[2]

Two Cold War Democrats diagnosed the problem with Carter's foreign policy. Zbigniew Brzezinski of the National Security Council considered the Vietnam War to have been "the Waterloo of the WASP elite." According to Brzezinski, the dazed and confused Ivy Leaguers in the State Department no longer had the will to project American military power overseas. Their lack of resolve invited aggression. In the same vein, Jeane Kirkpatrick declared Carter did not understand that the shah and his ilk were pussycats compared to the totalitarians waiting in the wings. Pro-American dictators, Kirkpatrick allowed, may kill a few hundred dissidents every now and then, but they did not usually bother other countries. Islamic clerics and Communists, on the other hand, slaughtered their subjects by the thousands and waged wars of conquest against their neighbors. America, to paraphrase country-western singer Tammy Wynette, must stand by its despots.[3]

Clear-eyed analysts that they were, Brzezinski and Kirkpatrick should have been a little less fixated on Soviet imperialism and more concerned about America's friends. Japan, for example, generously subsidized its export industries. Every inexpensive Toyota that entered the United States cost Americans good jobs and left devastated communities in its wake. Instead of updating their plants, companies like U.S. Steel invested in more promising fields. The Big Three automakers continued to produce costly, gas-guzzling rust-buckets. When Chrysler went bankrupt, Congress bailed out the corporation. As part of the Chrysler deal, Carter added the K-Car to the government fleet. Federal workers discovered that K-Cars often stalled going uphill when the air conditioning was on. However, this did not loom as too large a problem since the K-Car's air conditioner, like its radio, seldom worked.

There were more reasons for the nation's economic woes than just cheap imports and the incompetence of American manufacturing. In 1945, America had had the only functioning economy in the world. Lacking any industrial competitors, the United States had enjoyed an unprecedented period of prosperity. By the sixties, refurbished industries had risen from the ashes of Europe and Asia. While America devoted much of its technological expertise to containing revolutionary Communism, the Germans and Japanese were making more, and often better, consumer goods. Then came the Vietnam War and three presidents who were unwilling to reduce federal social spending to pay for their adventure. Thus began the first round of the Great Inflation. To make matters worse, the Arab oil-exporting countries punished America for its support of Israel.

The federal government exacerbated America's economic problems. Layer after layer of regulations (100,000 pages worth), added to the cost of doing business. By 1979, businesses were spending $100 billion a year to comply with the strictures of OSHA, the EPA, and other agencies. While some of the regulations made sense, others were questionable. At one point, Washington halted a major construction project because it threatened the habitat of an endangered fish. The snail darter, as it later developed, was hardly on the brink of extinction. Deprived of their union wages, construction workers were displeased with the man they had elected president. Such workers should have directed their anger at the Democratic Congress as well. When apprised of the fact that his clean air bill would raise manufacturing costs and thereby force the Big Three to fire thousands of people in Michigan, Senator Edmund Muskie replied, "There aren't any auto works in Maine." Having shelved his presidential ambitions, Muskie no longer courted organized labor.[4]

Muskie's parochialism aside, the economic statistics told an alarming tale. In 1976, Carter had criticized Ford for tolerating high levels of inflation. As president, Carter saw inflation reach 18 percent—more than three times the figure under Ford. Inflation artificially raised the value of real estate. As a consequence, property tax assessments soared. Californians, for instance, saw their property taxes rise 120 percent in four years. (The state's irate residents promptly passed a ballot initiative to roll back property taxes.) Round two of the Great Inflation also led to tax-bracket creep. While wages rose in the seventies, their real value fell. The IRS, however, did not adjust rates accordingly. Where just 5 percent of Americans paid the highest marginal tax rates in the sixties, by 1980 half of the working population found itself in the Rockefeller stratosphere.[5]

Like inflation and taxes, unemployment spun out of control. Ten percent of the workers in Toledo and Youngstown were thrown out of work. As a presidential candidate, Carter had decried the 20 percent unemployment rate in Flint. After Carter's four years in office, a quarter of Flint's workers were jobless. Meanwhile, the prime interest rate soared to 21 percent, locking most young people out of the housing market. Gasoline prices rose 52 percent in 1979, thanks to a deliberate reduction in Arab oil production. The Big Three's gas suckers became even less appealing to the public. Not surprisingly, six of ten Americans believed that their children would never enjoy a decent standard of living. Their fears had some foundation. Unlike previous recessions where people returned to work once the economy recovered, many industrial jobs were gone forever. In Michigan, a quarter of a million automobile jobs vanished between 1979 and 1982. The Class of 1980 was the first not to make the trek to the assembly line.[6]

Politicians had spent years bargaining with the devil, not expecting that the day of reckoning was nigh. Entitlement spending had risen three times faster than wages in the seventies, with fifty million Americans collecting $200 billion. In 1979, a family on welfare received AFDC and subsidies for food, rent, and utilities that placed them $1,500 above the median household income. It made more sense for the poor to go on welfare than to continue working. By the time Carter entered the White House, the federal government was spending a third of the nation's Gross National Product. Washington could cover its entitlement obligations only by deficit spending and raising the regressive Social Security payroll taxes on younger workers. These were the very people who could least afford to see their incomes diminished. Given the all-consuming needs of the welfare state, the president and the Democratic Congress were not about to have the IRS seriously adjust the tax brackets. Washington wanted every penny it could snag.[7]

Social Security posed a great danger to the fiscal health of the country. In 1940, Social Security had been a $35 million program ($350 million in 1997 dollars) with 220,000 recipients. By 1977, Social Security gave $100 billion to thirty-three million individuals. Since most Americans in 1940 did not live to sixty-five, few ever collected their pensions. Life expectancy, however, increased after 1940, swelling the ranks of retirees. In the sixties, President Johnson set aside the original formula by which recipients received roughly what they had contributed. The Great Society established a payment floor that reduced the proportion of elderly who lived at the poverty line—from 25 percent to 5 percent. (At the same time, the proportion of young Americans who lived in poverty went from 5 percent to 25 percent. There was a relationship here that few Great Society liberals cared to explore.) In the seventies, congressional Democrats attached cost of living allowances to Social Security, ensuring that pensions stayed above the inflation rate.[8]

So far as members of the World War II generation were concerned, inflation raised their incomes and enhanced the value of their homes. Escalating property taxes did not usually bother seniors because many states offered rebates to the elderly. When the steel and auto corporations announced layoffs, middle-aged workers did not worry. The union protected their seniority privileges, negotiated generous cost-of-living adjustments for them, expanded their health care benefits, and secured corporate pensions to supplement their Social Security. When employers told the unions that without concessions few young people could be hired, they refused to listen. The aging rank and file never understood why so many blue-collar members of the Class of '80 scorned organized labor. Once retired, some seniors went to Arizona and Florida, others remained behind in industrial ghost towns like Johnstown, Pennsylvania, which was in the process of losing half of its population.

Not since World War II had so many *white* people migrated in search of work. In the late seventies, 1.5 million Americans moved to the Sunbelt. (As the saying went in Michigan, "Will the last person leaving the state please turn out the lights?") Arizona, Florida, and Texas experienced enormous residential gains while the populations of New York, Ohio, and Pennsylvania stagnated or declined. The Sunbelt's economy expanded, offering work in agribusiness, aerospace, and computers. Jobs that required college degrees paid excellent salaries. Unskilled laborers, however, did not prosper in the Sunbelt as they once had in Michigan auto plants. On the other hand, a low-wage, non-union job in Texas was better than unemployment in Michigan. Besides, who cared whether or not there was union representation? The UAW had made it clear that it did not want youngsters milling around the Oldsmobile gates looking for work.[9]

By 1980, six of the ten greatest American urban centers were in the Sunbelt. New York, once the nation's largest city, lost one million people in the seventies. The 1980 U.S. Census revealed that a slim majority of citizens lived in the South and West. Congressional redistricting soon gave the Sunbelt half of the seats in the House. A new American economy and politics were coming of age. Conservative commentator Kevin Phillips concluded that a politician who celebrated the free market, supported the high-tech frontier, and reconciled Southern Baptists and Sunbelt libertarians could readily capture the White House.[10]

Against this backdrop of economic dislocation and the growing clout of the conservative Sunbelt, social liberals raised their political profile. Eleanor Smeal and Gloria Steinem of NOW demanded that the Carter administration provide federal funds for abortion. When Carter demurred, feminists chained themselves to the White House fence. (Press Secretary Jody Powell hoped that Smeal and Steinem would take a cue from Vietnam's Buddhist monks, whose idea of protest in the sixties had been to set fire to themselves.) Former New York representative and antiwar activist Bella Abzug ridiculed the "white-male dominated White House." Other feminists attacked Carter for employing too many Catholics whose religious beliefs marked them as sexists and enemies of abortion. Indeed, one feminist sociologist claimed that Christians—especially Catholics—were congenital reactionaries who disguised their politics in order to infiltrate progressive organizations. For her part, Steinem looked forward to the day when "we will, I hope, raise our children to believe in human potential, not God."[11]

Feminist writer Barbara Ehrenreich referred to opponents of abortion as "jeering right-to-lifers." Homemakers, according to NOW, were "domestic drudges" and the "lowest order of humanity." Anyone who worried about the economic prospects of the traditional family was a sexist, racist, uneducated reactionary. (Radical feminists ignored the fact that greater numbers of fundamentalists were going to college. What really irked them was the fact that fundamentalists, unlike every other group that went to college, did not become more liberal. To the Left, being educated had nothing to do with schooling and everything to do with whether the individual embraced the proper political position.) In 1977, with a $5 million grant from Congress, Abzug and Steinem helped organize the National Women's Conference. Two thousand delegates gathered in Houston to denounce "white-male racism" and pass resolutions in support of lesbian liberation. A handful of conservative delegates from the South, tired of being denounced as Ku Klux Klan troopers, stalked out of the conference. The television networks did not permit their cameras to linger on placards that read "The Pope Has Clitoris Envy—He Wears Skirts, Doesn't He?"[12]

While the events in Houston disturbed conservative Democrats, they were nothing compared to what was taking place on the Left Coast. By the late seventies, San Francisco had become a counterculture carnival. One hundred thousand gays, mostly college-educated professionals in their twenties and thirties, had settled in San Francisco. With ninety gay bars and a variety of bathhouses set up for anonymous sex, the city became a major tourist stop for homosexuals. (According to a 1978 Kinsey Institute study, 40 percent of Bay Area gays had been with five hundred sex partners. At the end of the decade, two of every three San Francisco homosexuals had contracted a venereal disease.) In the 1978 Gay Freedom Day Parade, three hundred thousand gays and lesbians marched through the San Francisco streets. Some men dressed up as nuns, mocking the Catholic Church, which condemned gay sex. Others poked fun at California's Pentecostals by putting on "Okie" clothing. San Francisco's homosexuals had cause to celebrate. They were a formidable force in local Democratic politics, and their success inspired homosexuals in other communities to demand, among other things, the legal recognition of same-sex marriages. Meanwhile, sympathetic gay characters appeared on television shows like *Barney Miller* and the Village People brought disco music out of the closet and onto the "Top Forty" playlist. It seemed as if gays were everywhere—but especially in the Democratic Party.[13]

If gays and feminists were not troublesome enough, Carter also had to contend with vocal blacks. Although Carter met regularly with the Congressional Black Caucus and tried to meet its every demand, its members blasted him for not doing enough to advance affirmative action, busing, and welfare. Their complaints about Carter's lukewarm affirmative action policies were unfounded. Carter had sent memos to his cabinet secretaries directing them to cease hiring white, often Jewish, males. Still, White House hiring quotas, and the fact that Carter had appointed thirty black activists to federal judicial posts, merely whetted the appetite of the civil rights establishment.[14]

Seeking approval from the Congressional Black Caucus, Carter's IRS, the EEOC, and the Department of Health, Education, and Welfare launched a new crusade against racial segregation. The EEOC and the IRS first moved to revoke the tax-exempt status of the South's private religious academies. Liberals contended that such schools promoted racial segregation. As segregationist institutions, the church academies were not charitable organizations and must pay taxes. (In Memphis, twenty-two thousand students enrolled in private academies during the seventies. The city's schools went from 50 percent black to 70 percent. Nationally, more than ten thousand religious academies were founded in this decade.) Southerners argued that the academies enabled students, black and white, to avoid the baleful influence of secular humanism. Religious, not racial, segregation was the issue. If the religious schools lost their tax exemptions, tuition would double. Although George Wallace had once been correct to characterize the academies as middle-class preserves, that situation changed radically in the seventies. Sixty percent of the pupils at the southern academies came from working-class and lower-middle-class backgrounds. Their parents could not afford to see their tuition bills double. Having been audited himself, Jerry Falwell groused that the IRS had made it "easier to open a massage parlor than to open a Christian school."[15]

HEW Secretary Joseph Califano also waged war on Dixie. Appointed to Carter's cabinet as a concession to the Left, the unrepentant Great Society liberal went after the university system of North Carolina. Alienating Democrats across the South, Califano threatened to seize control of North Carolina's colleges. He wanted more white students to attend college with blacks. To achieve that goal, Califano ordered colleges with large white enrollments to eliminate several majors, which would then be offered only at schools with heavily black student populations. Additionally, Califano expected the North Carolina legislature to spend larger sums of money on black education. This was social engineering at its worst, with Washington bureaucrats scanning the course offerings and enrollments at North Carolina universities to make sure that they met Califano's requirements.[16]

A stalwart defender of "numerical goals as benchmarks of progress," Califano laid into the white male professors at the City University of New York. In a squeeze play pitting City University's marginal students and blasé administrators against the faculty, Califano embraced lowered admissions and academic standards. Identifying the Jewish faculty as the most vociferous opponents of dumbing down the curriculum, Califano implied that academic standards were racist. In the wake of his assault on City University, tensions between black students and Jewish faculty worsened. (Even before Califano's speech, City University's administrators had annoyed Jewish professors by seeking to "diversify its faculty." By that, they meant City University would avoid hiring any more Jewish males.)[17]

City University, which had produced eight Nobel Prize recipients, had no choice but to teach eighth-grade math. In an era of economic stagnation and a shrinking pool of traditional students, college administrators needed warm bodies and the federal tuition grants that came with them, standards be damned. Knowing firsthand that the academic job market offered dismal employment prospects for white males, most professors went along with the new order. They did not want to be stripped of tenure because of their "racist" belief that miserable students, regardless of color, should be failed. From the UCLA School of Law to Brandeis, where a representative of NOW ensured university compliance with federal affirmative action directives, preferential admissions and hiring quotas, as well as debased standards, became the norm.[18]

In 1974, Allan Bakke filed a discrimination suit against the University of California at Davis. Bakke had been denied admission to the medical school, but blacks with inferior grades and test scores had been accepted. His case reached the Supreme Court three years later. Califano leapt into action, composing a legal brief supporting the university's admissions policy. He also ridiculed Bakke, calling him a white-male engineer who was not bright enough to be admitted to any decent medical school. The ACLU, the NAACP, and the NEA, among other liberal organizations, devoted their considerable funds to crushing Bakke. There were a few twists to *The Regents of the University of California v. Bakke.* To begin with, Bakke had more practical medical learning than Califano wished to concede. He had served as a combat medic in Vietnam. Bakke was also Jewish.[19]

The symbolism was riveting. A decorated veteran denied admission to medical school by liberals who had opposed the Vietnam War. A Jew unable to pursue his dreams because of a quota system. In 1978, the Supreme Court ordered Bakke to be let into the Davis Medical School, but ruled five to four that admissions "goals" were acceptable. Justice Thurgood Marshall, the black attorney who had argued the Brown case before the Court years before, contended that America was such a pervasively racist society that quotas were necessary. To his colleagues on the Court, Marshall chuckled that it was now the white man's turn to suffer. Even though Bakke lost the war against quotas, and in spite of the fact that the Justice Department had filed suit against fifty-one city, county, and state governments for not hiring enough minorities, black activists continued to criticize Carter. They wanted quotas imposed on all employers in the country.[20]

Only a handful of black conservatives questioned the wisdom of quotas. Clarence Thomas, a poor Baby Boomer who had been admitted to the Yale Law School under its special program to recruit talented blacks, posed a troubling question that few liberals wanted to hear: "Would you go to a black lawyer if you felt he was there just because he was black? Would you have your car or stereo repaired by someone if you felt he had the job just because of race and was not really qualified?" One had to wonder why the blacks admitted to the medical school under the quota system still could not, after four years of preferential treatment in their undergraduate programs, make the grade. How long would such students receive preferential treatment—forever? And what of the bright minorities who earned their credentials? Would they also, as conservative black economist Thomas Sowell feared, be suspect in the eyes of whites? Even resented? Unwilling to deal with such questions, social liberals called Thomas and Sowell "Uncle Toms."[21]

Like many social liberals, Marshall and Califano ignored a host of recent developments in American race relations that would have placed the affirmative action controversy in its proper context. To begin with, if America was so racist, why did 97 percent of whites tell pollsters that they believed blacks should have equal job and educational opportunities? (Two of three whites in 1980 *opposed quotas, not equal opportunity.*) By the seventies, the income of black college graduates was 9 percent above that of white college graduates; the number of blacks employed in private-sector, white-collar jobs increased 222 percent; and two-thirds of all blacks were middle class. In the same decade, the rate of black suburban growth surpassed that of whites. Affirmative action might have been responsible for some of this progress but, as Sowell said, that did not given sufficient credit to blacks who worked hard to achieve their improved status.[22]

In their efforts to champion affirmative action, social liberals failed to deal with class and moral issues. Black families that remained together prospered and their children did not become criminals. Fatherless families, black and white, however, remained mired in poverty and their children did poorly in school—if they graduated at all. In 1980, the illegitimacy rate among blacks was 55 percent, double the figure in 1965 when the Great Society launched the War on Poverty. The white illegitimacy rate was 11 percent, but in decaying steel towns such as Portsmouth, Ohio, a quarter of all white births were to single welfare mothers. High school graduation rates fell and violent crime increased.[23]

Preferential admission to medical school did little to assist impoverished blacks. Affirmative action was a middle-class entitlement and, much to consternation of the civil rights establishment, three-quarters of the people benefiting from hiring quotas were *white females.* In the slums that the black middle class had left behind, violent crime rose 367 percent, with more than a million assaults, murders, and rapes committed in the seventies. Nearly two-thirds of the nation's muggers and four of ten rapists were members of the black underclass. By 1980, eight times as many blacks as whites were in prison. A racist judicial system could not be blamed. In "progressive" Iowa, incarcerated blacks outnumbered whites twenty-one to one. The ratio in "reactionary" Mississippi was three blacks jailed for every white. (The ratios are even more startling when one recalls that blacks were a third of Mississippi's population, compared to 2 percent in Iowa.) Middle-class blacks feared that they would be judged by the behavior of the minority underclass.[24]

Weary of black and feminist militants, Carter and Jody Powell also grew impatient with the media. On one occasion, Carter's press secretary seethed as reporters refused to stand for the playing of the National Anthem. According to Powell, Carter made the press uncomfortable because the president, unlike the reporters, was a moral man. Columnists who ridiculed Carter reminded Powell of "the kind of people who view the bloody conflict from afar and then—when the fighting is done and the warriors have departed—come down from the hills to shoot the wounded." Powell claimed that a Boston *Globe* reporter privately called Carter "a redneck, Baptist, Bible thumper." Both Powell and the president loathed the *Washington Post.* (White House officials also despised the *New York Times,* regarding it as a Zionist propaganda rag that skewered anyone who dared to make diplomatic overtures to the Arabs.) Remarkably, the television networks and newspapers that Carter hated the most were the very ones Richard Nixon had believed were out to get him.[25]

Carter's view of the news media was not excessively paranoid. Since 1972, when 80 percent of reporters voted for McGovern, the media had become *even more liberal.* A new generation of Boomer journalists, radicalized by the antiwar movement and Watergate, entered the profession. In terms of breeding, income, and schooling, the Boomer reporters were the most elite in the history of American journalism. Half claimed no religious affiliation. Three-quarters of the Boomer media elite approved of homosexuality, 82 percent endorsed abortion on demand, and half saw nothing wrong with adultery. When they did stories on welfare three-quarters of Boomer journalists went to liberal organizations for information. As journalists, the Boomers disdained "racist" opponents of affirmative action and busing. As private individuals, Boomer reporters sent their children to private or suburban schools and supported hiring quotas so long as they did not affect their own careers.[26]

Boomer journalists, blacks, and feminists, however, were not the president's only critics. The Democratic Congress proved to be an immense thorn in Carter's flesh. In 1969, southern Democrats chaired ten of the sixteen most important Senate committees. Since then, liberals had mounted a coup d'état. By 1979, just three conservative southern chairmen survived. Teddy Kennedy, the most liberal member of the Senate, presided over the powerful Judiciary Committee. Congressional Democrats jealously guarded their prerogatives, writing Carter off as a rube even before he took the oath of office. House Speaker Thomas "Tip" O'Neill of Massachusetts set down the ground rules immediately after the 1976 election. Under no circumstances was Carter to bypass Congress and appeal directly to the American people for the passage of legislation. When Carter made the mistake of suggesting that Social Security reforms were necessary, O'Neill and Kennedy savaged him. Carter's efforts to reduce the number of congressional pork-barrel projects earned him more ill will. One House liberal fumed that Carter's staffers "think we're just a pack of crooked whores." By 1979, House and Senate liberals urged Kennedy to challenge Carter for the presidential nomination.[27]

His public approval ratings having plummeted so low that Nixon looked good in comparison, Carter seemed vulnerable to a challenge from Kennedy. (So reduced in stature was Carter by 1979, that when he horned his way into the Pittsburgh Pirates' locker room to bask in their World Series victory, the players and the press ignored him.) His dismissal of Califano in 1979—late though it was—mollified a few southerners but angered liberals. Moreover, Carter's nationally televised speech in the summer of '79 further damaged his political prospects. Unlike his predecessors in office, Carter argued that America's problems could be blamed on an apathetic, lazy, pessimistic, and spendthrift public:

For the first time in the history of our country a majority of our people believe that the next five years will be worse than the past five years. Two-thirds of our people do not even vote. The productivity of American workers is actually dropping and the willingness of Americans to save for the future has fallen below that of all other people in the Western world.

... [W]e've got to stop crying and start sweating. ... [28]

Kennedy's candidacy galvanized liberals. The Boston *Globe* contended that a candidate's character, marital fidelity, and sobriety were irrelevant.

After all, John Kennedy had been a philanderer and a great president; Nixon had been a faithful husband and a corrupt leader. Harvard historian Arthur Schlesinger, Jr., claimed that the senator had grown because of his suffering over the Chappaquiddick incident. Indeed, Teddy Kennedy was much like Franklin Roosevelt. "Ever since Chappaquiddick," Schlesinger asserted, "[Kennedy had] been spending his life trying to redeem himself for those hours of panic. He has become ever more serious, more senatorial, more devoted to the public good. I think this ceaseless effort at self-redemption may be for Teddy Kennedy what polio was for FDR." In sophistry, Schlesinger had few peers.[29]

Unfortunately for Kennedy, not many voters took their cues from liberal journalists and academics. Working-class Catholics, disgusted with Kennedy's moral lapses and support for abortion, repudiated him in New England and Iowa. Although he took New York, Carter's staff had already concluded that the state was hopeless. Among all Democratic primary voters, New York City's residents were, according to White House polls, the least concerned about a candidate's morals. Moreover, the state had an amazingly large public employee payroll. Just *one* New York local of the American Federation of State, County, and Municipal Employees enrolled 225,000 members. New York's legion of public workers glowed when Kennedy promised to expand government employment. (Kennedy did not worry about mounting deficits and taxes.) To keep AFSCME in line, Carter said he would increase federal spending on public-sector jobs. In the rest of the country, with the notable exception of Hollywood, Carter turned back Kennedy's challenge.[30]

Beyond the hammering the senator took for his character flaws and the implication that he was giving comfort to the Iranians who were holding Americans hostage, Kennedy's own incompetence helped do him in. Offered a chance to discuss his candidacy on network television, the senator could give no reason as to why he wanted to be president—other than that he had an ancestral claim to the office. If forced to speak without a script, Kennedy stumbled and often sounded like this: "I will speak to it and outline—I mean, I mentioned that—and—but I mean—that I think is the best example." (Governor Reagan, whom liberal journalists accused of being a pre-programmed chuckle head, had no problem speaking off the cuff. Of course, his anecdotes might be irrelevant to the issue at hand, or just plain goofy—trees cause more air pollution than industry—but Reagan at least sounded assured. Kennedy gave voters the appearance of being deep in his cups.)[31]

The nomination Carter won in 1980 was not worth much. Three-quarters of all the criticism hurled at the president during the election season came from Kennedy and the Left. Consequently, the GOP could afford to ignore Carter as he bled from Kennedy's knifing. Worse, Carter's position in his own party was so weak that he had no choice but to make crippling concessions to his enemies. Kennedy insisted that his aide Stephen Breyer be appointed to a federal judgeship. Regarding Breyer as a political hack, White House staffers rationalized that it was not as if Carter was putting him on the Supreme Court.[32]

More serious was Kennedy's dictation of the party platform. Carter's policy of relative fiscal and social moderation went out the window. NOW, whose two hundred delegates supported Kennedy, successfully demanded that any Democratic candidate opposed to the ERA be denied party funds. The NEA, claiming five hundred delegates, expected the president to support gay affirmative action and provide Medicaid funds for abortions. (Why an organization representing the nation's school teachers should involve itself in the abortion issue and gay liberation was never adequately explained. Of course, Carter was not about to question a group whose representatives accounted for a sixth of the convention delegates. That was why the NEA had recently received its "own" cabinet-level Department of Education.) The seventy-seven openly gay delegates spent $100,000 to lobby the platform committee. Responsive to their desires, Kennedy compelled the party to recognize sexual orientation as a civil rights matter.[33]

Kennedy's platform victory ensured that conservative Democrats had no role in shaping the party's policies. Carter's primary wins in '76 and '80 had not routed the McGovernites. Social liberals believed that the country was moving left and that only Carter's incompetent, conservative presidency hurt the party. For all of their Ivy League pedigrees and experience as activists, liberals possessed an abysmal knowledge of politics. The winds had been blowing rightward since the sixties, yet liberals never adapted. Their failure at the polls was always the fault of someone else. In 1972, Nixon had stolen the presidential election. Four years later, a Republican disguised as a Democrat fooled the party into nominating him for President. Liberals dismissed all evidence that contradicted their prejudices. That was a formula for disaster.

In 1974, at the very moment when liberals toppled a Republican president, events in a West Virginia coal-mining community pointed to the final breakdown of the New Deal coalition. Concerned parents and fundamentalist ministers, heirs to the party of Roosevelt, objected to public school texts that seemed to teach moral relativism. The ACLU and the NEA lined up to quash the Kanawha County revolt. Instead of retreating, West Virginia's social conservatives fought back, receiving political support from fundamentalist ministers across the country. As Kanawha simmered, religious traditionalists engaged the IRS in battle. White Pentecostals, who had yet to throw themselves fully into the political ring, now felt that there was no alternative but to engage the secular world. They felt besieged by an aggressive, immoral government.[34]

The Heritage Foundation, established in 1973 by activists who thought Nixon a dangerous leftist, provided legal advice to the religious academies and the Kanawha fundamentalists. Pat Robertson also joined battle, informing his thirty-seven million viewers of the issues involved. In the meantime, Southern Baptists assured Yankees that the spirit of racial segregation did not reside in their academies. The one thousand students enrolled at the Arlington, Virginia, Baptist school were taught to place "God and His Holy Word at the center" of their education. Parents were exhorted "to win your child to Jesus Christ as his personal Savior, and then to train him up for Christian service." The Arlington academy did not instruct white children to become racists. A paucity of blacks in the southern religious academies did not necessarily translate into an intention to maintain segregated school facilities. Catholic educators, who operated the most racially integrated private school system in the country, took the fundamentalists and Pentecostals at their word. To America's Catholic and Protestant faithful, the problem was not racism but secular interference in religious matters.[35]

Homosexual advocacy, as social conservatives described it, caused further alarm. Arkansas fundamentalists objected to Governor Bill Clinton's sex education program for the public schools. Their blood roiled when they read passages like this from the Clinton sex education guidelines: "At some time or other, it occurs to most boys to try to put their own penises into their mouths." In Dallas, Rev. James Robison, a Boomer Baptist, had his television pulpit taken away when he criticized the gay lifestyle. A protest march by twelve thousand riled Texans persuaded the station to bring him back. Meanwhile in Miami, a former Miss America, Anita Bryant, fought a ballot initiative that would have granted affirmative action claims to gays. According to the Oklahoma native, "Homosexuals do not suffer discrimination when they keep their perversions in the privacy of their homes." Bryant did not mind gays "so long as they do not flaunt their homosexuality and try to establish role models for the impressionable young people—our children."[36]

Rushing to Bryant's side, Jerry Falwell rallied the faithful who tuned into any one of the four hundred television stations that carried his show, *The Old Time Gospel Hour.* Inspired by Bryant's example, Arkansas, California, and Oklahoma legislators sought to prevent gays from being hired as public-school teachers. Rev. Harold Lindsell of *Christianity Today* also entered the lists, insisting that there was no such thing as a Christian homosexual. In turn, San Francisco Democrats compared Bryant to Hitler and charged that fundamentalists were plotting a Nazi-style holocaust. More seriously, gays boycotted any product that Bryant endorsed. Free-market economics dictated what followed. She lost her commercial endorsements after advertisers concluded that gays were a more desirable market demographic than Baptists. Shunned by secular society, Bryant, like Pat Boone before her, would have to make a living in the Christian counterculture. Religious apartheid though it was, Christian entertainers and writers could earn a living in the fundamentalist and Pentecostal counterculture. However, they would never have their books and stage shows reviewed by the *New Yorker.* And, so the liberal shibboleth went, if it was not in the *New Yorker,* it did not matter.[37]

As with gay rights, the abortion controversy cast a pall over American politics. In the 1978 congressional elections, three senators and twenty-three representatives who supported abortion and the ERA lost their seats. The *New York Times* and Planned Parenthood minimized the extent of the political damage—mainly by cheering the reelection of Patricia Schroeder, a prochoice feminist. One triumphant House member from the Colorado resort and university communities, however, did not make for a liberal resurrection. Indeed, prior to the midterm elections, when the number of social liberals in Congress reached its zenith, the House still voted by a large margin for the so-called Hyde Amendment. Named for Republican Henry Hyde of Illinois, a pious Catholic, the amendment prohibited federal funding for abortions. Conservative Democrats crossed the aisle to support the minority party's initiative. At the same time, GOP liberals, and libertarians like David Stockman of Michigan, voted against any restriction of abortion rights. When it came to moral issues, party labels were becoming less meaningful.[38]

The '78 elections underscored the fact that conservative voters did not regard abortion and the ERA as separate issues. This was understandable since social liberals took the same view. The National Abortion Rights Action League (NARAL) endorsed the ERA, believing that the amendment would enshrine unrestricted abortion rights in the Constitution. The *Roe* decision, NARAL felt, permitted too many limitations on abortion. Phyllis Schlafly pointed out that the ACLU had recently argued that "the denial of taxpayer funds to pay for abortions is 'sex discrimination' within the meaning of the Equal Rights Amendment." Abortion on demand, not to mention gay liberation, Catholic conservatives warned, animated the ERA movement. Prolife Catholic feminists demurred, charging that both NARAL and Schlafly had distorted the intent of the ERA. One feminist Catholic admitted to feeling uncomfortable among Schlafly's followers. On the other hand, social liberals were downright hostile toward anyone who diverged from the party line. At a Washington ERA rally, the ACLU, NOW, and Planned Parenthood prohibited Catholic feminists from passing out prolife literature. The ACLU, prolife feminists concluded, did not believe that the constitutional right to free speech extended to religious activists.[39]

By 1978, when congressional liberals extended the ratification deadline of the ERA, lifestyle politics was badly dividing church activists. The ERA, abortion, and the defense of the traditional family had become just as emotionally wrenching as the Vietnam War. At a Chicago gathering of America's Catholic bishops in 1978, liberal nuns and laity clashed with anti-ERA activists. The National Assembly of [Catholic] Religious Women insisted that the ERA would not harm the family. Indeed, the ERA "would help provide equal pay for ever larger numbers of women who are heads of families." Besides, the Supreme Court had settled the abortion issue in 1973 so there was no sense for the church to continue its prolife agitation. Nuns from Columbus, Ohio, to New Orleans quickly resigned from the church organization, rejecting the Religious Women's "tendency to come off as anti-life," "use of liberal jargon," and divorcing "the moral from the legal."[40]

At an ecumenical conference of abortion foes in 1980, Catholics United for the Faith assailed the liberal values of the modern age:

As for divorce and abortion, just as we are able to dispose of our spouses if we feel like it, so are we able to do away with our children if we feel like it. There is no God for this new morality, much less any divine law except the pleasures of the moment. Abortion is a form of killing engaged in to evade the consequences of sex. These people do not shrink even at killing in order to carry on the tenets of the sexual revolution, and the stage is then set to allow killing as the solution to other responsibilities. It is by this route that we arrive at the justification of legalized euthanasia.[41]

Catholic liberals were quick to counter that the prolife movement served as a protective fig leaf for right-wing reactionaries who were intent upon persecuting the poor. The Religious Left, however, discovered that only a handful of churchgoers shared its worldview. When the Association of Chicago Priests sent letters to the Illinois legislature on behalf of the ERA, a Protestant legislator chided the group: "I cannot believe in my heart that any degree of prayer or true beliefs in Christian tenets would lead you to the conclusion that we should support an amendment that tears apart the family which all Biblical teachings tells us to sustain. I would hope you would review your personal position on this matter."[42]

In Florida, Catholics and evangelicals overcame long odds to defeat the ERA. The Carters, Vice President Mondale, and Betty Ford made appearances in the state on behalf of the amendment. NOW and the NEA poured volunteers and cash into the ratification campaign. As the seventies came to an end, however, pro-ERA Democrats disappeared from the Florida legislature. Conservative Republicans gained sufficient numbers to shoot down the amendment. Although feminists accused male preachers of undermining their cause in Florida (as well as in Illinois), the truth was quite different. Evangelical women—not men—played the leading role in turning aside the ERA. Church women would not endorse any cause they associated with abortion, no-fault divorce, and gay marriage. (They did *not*, however, reject the notion of equal pay for equal work. Given the state of "the Carter economy," many evangelical women had to find jobs outside the home.) The ERA's champions—who were mostly single or divorced—thought they were leading their gender in a battle against male oppression. Instead, feminists found most married women arrayed against them. Radical feminists concluded that the women who opposed the ERA and abortion suffered from a false political consciousness—one rooted in religious superstitions.[43]

During the '76 election, Carter had promised evangelicals that he would sponsor a White House conference on the American family. Nearly four years passed before he made good on his word. The conference, however, did not live up to evangelicals' expectations. To begin with, liberals contended that the definition of family had to be more inclusive. As a result of the sexual revolution, there were many kinds of families in America. Some families did not have fathers, others were composed of unmarried couples and of gay partners. Consequently, the White House Conference on the Family became the White House Conference on *Families*. Social conservatives grew more disturbed when the White House kept Phyllis Schlafly out of the proceedings yet invited liberals like Marian Wright Edelman of the Children's Defense Fund to participate. Conference chair Jim Guy Tucker, a former Arkansas representative and sometime-ally of Governor Clinton, dismissed conservative quibbles with a patronizing smile. Just because Edelman was a close friend of Hillary Rodham Clinton did not mean that the welfare-rights activist received any special consideration.[44]

NOW and NARAL mobilized their membership, dominating the New York delegation while exercising enormous influence in states outside Dixie. Of the 1,500 conference delegates, just 250 were moral traditionalists. The conference that Carter had organized to improve his reputation among social conservatives ended up endorsing the ERA, abortion on demand, and gay rights. Connie Marshner, a former member of the South Carolina Young Americans for Freedom and editor of the *Family Protection Report*, staged a walkout of the conference. The Boomer conservative, who believed that federal family planning programs promoted homosexuality, pornography, and promiscuity, had nothing good to say about the conference either. "Families," Marshner stated, "consist of people related by heterosexual marriage, blood, and adoption. Families are not religious cults, families are not Manson families, families are not heterosexual or homosexual liaisons outside of marriage." Gays, who did not appreciate being lumped together with mass murderer Charlie Manson, bade Marshner "good riddance."[45]

The Carter administration had (yet again) spun lead from straw. Even the religious liberals who had campaigned for McGovern in '72 accused the president of promoting "sinful lifestyles." Democratic Governor Fob James announced that Alabama would boycott "such conferences which do not establish traditional Judeo-Christian values concerning the family, the foundation of our nation under God." The Indiana legislature, as well as an Orthodox Jewish group, followed suit, charging that the conference was dominated "by those opposing traditional religious and family values." In Arkansas, fundamentalists held prayer meetings to protest the conference. They also laid plans to deal with their boyish governor. Hoping to mend political fences, Carter invited Falwell, Oral Roberts, and other troubled church leaders to the White House. Far from reassuring the ministers, however, they concluded that the president led an "un-

Christian" administration. With the political currents running strongly against the Democrats, Carter and Clinton were in for some perilous white water.[46]

Convinced that America was in mortal danger, Howard Phillips, Edward McAteer, and Paul Weyrich asked Falwell to head a new political organization, the Moral Majority. The social activists were a diverse lot. In the Nixon administration, Phillips's mission had been to dismantle Johnson's Office of Economic Opportunity. Upon leaving the White House, Phillips established the Conservative Caucus, which coordinated protests against busing and taxes in 150 congressional districts. Phillips came from a background of government service and was a practicing Jew; McAteer hailed from the world of business and Protestant fundamentalism. A former Colgate-Palmolive executive, McAteer founded the Religious Roundtable. His followers were mostly Sunbelt clergy who wanted the Religious Roundtable to become a theological counterweight to the liberal National Conference of Churches.[47]

Weyrich was the odd duck of conservative activism. The son of working-class, Eastern Rite Catholics, Weyrich had helped give birth to the Heritage Foundation. Unlike many of his colleagues in the New Right, however, Weyrich did not sing the praises of the free market. "Laissez-faire is not enough, there has to be some higher value in society," Weyrich argued. "There can be no such thing as an entirely free market. The market has to be responsive to social responsibility." Richard DeVos, the president of the Amway Corporation and a Heritage Foundation benefactor, did not agree. According to DeVos, the free market was a moral entity that required no social regulation. As DeVos viewed the order of the universe, when businessmen bought luxury cars, mansions, and yachts they were doing God's work on the earth. Their conspicuous consumption created jobs. Meanwhile, Protestant clergy like McAteer and Falwell regarded federal regulators and labor bosses as thieving atheists. Although Weyrich and other conservative populists denigrated unions and government bureaucrats, they still believed that some businesses might have to be coerced into serving the common good. To them, the market was under the control of corruptible men, not a perfect God.[48]

Carter had only himself to blame for the remarkable coalition of free marketers and social conservatives that came together to defeat him. Robert Billings, the first executive director of the Moral Majority, had led the National Christian Action Coalition against the IRS. Indeed, half of the Moral Majority's state chairs were affiliated with the very Christian academies that Carter's IRS had sought to tax out of existence. When the Moral Majority's supporters turned out for the Republican National Convention in Detroit, they made sure that the party platform denounced the IRS "vendetta" against the Christian schools. Like their black counterparts, white fundamentalists from Austin to Indianapolis registered their flocks to vote. The chair of the Indiana chapter of the Moral Majority, who also served as the minister of the Indianapolis Bible Temple, registered a thousand new voters on just one Sunday. Although most of the nation's three million new fundamentalist and Pentecostal voters joined the GOP, a few hoped to save the soul of the Democratic Party. In Gainesville, Florida, a minister and his flock took over the local Democratic committee. Basking in their victory, the conservative minister boasted that "we're running for everything from dogcatcher to [state] senator."[49]

The Moral Majority's rhetoric was militant, even apocalyptic. "The stage is set," Rev. James Robison informed seventeen thousand evangelicals at a 1980 Dallas political rally, "where we are either going to have a Hitler-style takeover, a dictatorship, Soviet Communist domination or we're going to get right with God in this country. It is time for Christians to crawl out from under their pews." Falwell warned the devout that "we are losing the war against homosexuals." He also decried abortion, the banning of school prayer, and the proliferation of smut. "Many Americans," the Lynchburg Baptist roared, "are sick and tired of the way their government has been run. They are tired of being told that their values and beliefs don't matter and that only those values held by government bureaucrats and liberal preachers are worthy of adoption in the area of public policy." To lower-middle-class Protestants, Mormons, and Catholics who felt that their families were endangered by galloping inflation and moral degeneracy, Falwell and Robison appeared prophetic.[50]

Hoping to exploit the estrangement between white fundamentalists and Carter, Reagan went to Lynchburg and addressed Falwell's flock. He also joined Robison at his Dallas rally. As Reagan coyly observed in Texas, "I know you can't endorse me, but I want you to know that I endorse you and what you are doing." Of course the religious activists could not formally endorse Reagan without attracting the attention of Carter's IRS, but there was no mistaking that social conservatives were in the Republican camp. If the IRS questioned the tax-exempt status claimed by the Moral Majority, conservatives could reply that the Southern Christian Leadership Conference had been campaigning for Carter. Both the SCLC and the Moral Majority claimed exemption from taxes because they were nonpartisan, church-related institutions. Neither organization was being candid. Liberals, however, did not see things that way. According to the Left, there was nothing wrong with black clergy entering the political sphere; *conservative white Christians,* on the other hand, had no business getting into politics.[51]

Desperate, the Carter White House took the low road. During an Ohio State University rally, Andrew Young contended that in Reagan's America "it's going to be all right to kill niggers." In Chicago, Carter admonished voters, "You'll determine whether or not this America will be unified or, if I lose this election, whether Americans might be separated, black from white, Jew from Christian, North from South, rural from urban." Speaking at the Ebenezer Baptist Church in Atlanta, the president pointed out to Martin Luther King, Sr.'s, flock that Reagan and the Ku Klux Klan both championed states' rights. Therefore it followed that anyone who wanted to curtail federal power was a racist. On another occasion Carter and Reagan addressed a Catholic audience at New York's annual Al Smith Dinner. Where an amiable Reagan told Irish jokes, Carter barked that the Moral Majority's supporters were like the anti-Catholic nativists of the twenties. Unfortunately for Carter, his efforts to drive a wedge between Southern Baptists and northern Catholics backfired. Although the Moral Majority remained a largely Protestant organization, many Catholics endorsed its positions on social issues. Just as bad for the president, Reagan finally accepted Carter's dare to debate him on national television. Having seen Carter flounder at a traditional Democratic forum, Reagan realized that he could take him down for the count.[52]

Weak though Carter was, Reagan and the Moral Majority *were* susceptible to attack on the race issue. Reagan had called the 1965 Voting Rights Act "humiliating to the South" and went on vacation in order to avoid addressing a NAACP convention. The Republican presidential nominee made the mistake of thinking that the civil rights establishment spoke for America's minorities, not an entirely accurate assumption. Blacks were among the most frequent viewers of religious broadcasting. Pat Robertson, for instance, had a good-sized minority audience—an understandable development since his talk show, *The 700 Club,* was the first in America to employ a black-male co-host. On issues like abortion and the ERA, blacks were less liberal than whites—even though the Congressional Black Caucus embraced NOW. When Representative Louis Stokes of Cleveland pushed a bill to provide federal funding for abortion on demand, he was not representing the views of his black constituents. Frightened by the widening moral gulf separating ordinary blacks from social liberals, the civil rights establishment played its trump card. The SCLC leadership warned that Reagan planned to reimpose disfranchisement and segregation. Joining the chorus, the Congressional Black Caucus accused conservatives of advocating racist policies.[53]

White social conservatives recognized that they had a problem. As a conservative pollster lamented, "Take a black Southern Baptist lady. It's very hard to tell her, 'You should vote with the fat-cat Republicans.' But if you look at a lot of her attitudes, she should vote conservative, at least on some issues." Paul Weyrich admitted to hostile reporters, "I'm not going to kid you that we have minorities running out our ears. This is not a minority movement." Hoping to change this state of affairs, Jeremiah Denton, Alabama's Republican candidate for the Senate, reached out to southern blacks. Having spent seven years in a Vietnamese POW camp, the conservative Catholic knew something about persecution and suffering. (The Communists tortured Denton and other pilots, including John McCain. Ironically, Hanoi produced more Republican senators than the Heritage Foundation.) Denton campaigned among black church groups and exhorted the Moral Majority to recruit minorities.[54]

Falwell was listening. He joined Jesse Jackson at a black church and apologized for his opposition to civil rights in the sixties. Falwell then went to Lynchburg's blacks and extended his hand in friendship. More dramatically, he invited Jackson to preach at the Thomas Road Baptist Church. As opponents of abortion and gay liberation, Jackson and Falwell should have been allies. Public opinion polls showed that nearly half of America's blacks, compared to a third of whites, held the Moral Majority in high regard. Yet, students of minority voting behavior concluded, blacks remained responsive to racial appeals. The memories of Jim Crow were too fresh to permit a moral-based political realignment among southern blacks. Moreover, while many blacks accepted Falwell's offer of fellowship, they did not trust Reagan. Of course, Reagan had given blacks little reason to think otherwise. Even Reagan's moral conservatism, which most blacks endorsed, appeared suspect. As governor of California, Reagan had signed a permissive abortion bill into law and opposed a ballot initiative to prohibit gays from teaching in the public schools. (Reagan counted Rock Hudson and Barbara Stanwyck among his closeted-gay libertarian friends. Stanwyck believed that government had no business regulating economic or sexual behavior.)[55]

Having lived with blacks for four centuries, southern religious conservatives at least knew what made them tick (or ticked off). Jews, however, tended to be a mystery. They could be allies or they could be the best organized foes of social conservatism. Ideologically speaking, libertarian Jews outnumbered religiously conservative Jews thirteen to one. Secular liberal Jews swamped their counterparts in the Religious Right twenty-one to one. The Moral Majority made a point of identifying founder Howard Phillips as a Jew precisely because there were so few in its ranks. Rev. Bailey Smith, the president of the Southern Baptist Convention, did not advance the cause of interfaith understanding any when he observed at a 1980 rally that "God does not hear the prayer of a Jew." (Standing in the wings, Reagan advisors Ed Meese and Mike Deaver cringed.) Smith's point was that since Jews did not accept Jesus as the Messiah, God had no use for them—or for Buddhists, Hindus, and Hollywood pagans. From a theological perspective, Smith, who was a prominent ally of the Moral Majority, had not said anything startling. Orthodox Jews, after all, believed that Christians had embraced a false Messiah and, therefore, were estranged from God. Two factors made the situation touchy. First, Jews were a small, socially insecure minority. Second, no one had recently attempted to throw Southern Baptists into gas chambers.[56]

Rabbi Alexander Schindler, a liberal political activist from New York, alleged that the "rise of right-wing Christian fundamentalism has been accompanied by the most serious outbreak of anti-Semitism since the outbreak of World War II." In Schindler's mind, the Moral Majority was a fascist movement. Black anti-Semites in the Carter White House and Congress were, presumably, just misunderstood. Television producer Norman Lear put in his two cents' worth. Unwilling to expose himself to attack as a liberal Hollywood Jew, Lear persuaded several left-leaning Protestant ministers to front for him. The Protestant clergy placed newspaper advertisements, which Lear paid for, denouncing the Moral Majority as bigoted and un-American. Lear also quietly produced a television commercial that depicted a working-class stiff who did not care for activist preachers. (Politically correct black and white clergy were exempt from Lear's indictment.)[57]

Of course, there was little foundation for Rabbi Schindler's allegations. Academic studies demonstrated that the Christian Right was no more religiously intolerant than any other group in America, including Jews. (Moreover, comparing the Moral Majority to the Nazi Party showed a remarkable lack of historical knowledge. After all, the first thing the Nazis did when they came to power was to attack *Christians,* closing down church schools and executing the bishop of Berlin.) To make sure that religious Jews did not fear Christian activists, Falwell met with Jewish organizations and championed the Zionist cause. (Christian conservatives regarded the establishment of Israel as the fulfillment of biblical prophecy. In the long run, though, Israel was destined to be destroyed by the Beast, and Jews would either convert to Christianity or burn in hell.) Orthodox Jews turned their backs on Lear and Schindler. They felt more threatened by black anti-Semitism, racial hiring quotas, and urban crime than by the Southern Baptist Convention.[58]

Lear would have been surprised to learn that Pat Robertson shared some of his concerns about the politicization of the church. Robertson had been Weyrich and McAteer's first choice to lead the Moral Majority but the Pentecostal declined. In April of 1980, 500,000 social conservatives took part in a "Washington for Jesus" rally. (This event attracted arguably more people than any of the civil rights and antiwar rallies of the sixties.) Although the evangelist endorsed the spring get-together, he admonished his colleagues to remember that "God is not a right-winger or a left-winger." Clergy like Falwell, Robertson warned, "stand in danger of being used and manipulated" by conservative politicians who had no real interest in America's moral salvation. (Robertson would never forget how Nixon exploited Billy Graham.)[59]

Not only did Robertson not campaign for Reagan in the fall, he pointedly withdrew from the Religious Roundtable. CBN's leader feared that partisan politics detracted from the more important "mission of reaching people for the Lord Jesus Christ, and helping to bring spiritual moral revival in America through all the means of communication at our command." When Robertson founded CBN University in 1977, he hoped its graduate programs would "infiltrate secular society with committed Christians [and] permeate the social fabric with biblical values." The Virginian felt that the best way to re-create America was to start from the bottom. The Moral Majority, in contrast, set its sights on the White House, seeking to impose order from the top down. Robertson rejected the Moral Majority's strategy. Christians, he believed, must first struggle to salvage the culture. Even politicians with the best of intentions could not save a nation that lacked a moral center. A writer in *Charisma,* America's leading Pentecostal magazine, concurred, and then admonished readers not to become enamored with the "Pharisees who seem deter-

mined to inflict on this nation a government run by religious zealots."
Pentecostals would have preferred to have been left alone, undisturbed by
IRS agents, gay activists, and the GOP.[60]

The secular media were unable to pick up on the theological and
ideological differences among social conservatives. Worse, journalists ridiculed Christian conservatives, calling them racists, anti-Semites, and "errand boys of old-line, right-wing extremism." (*New Yorker* writer Frances
FitzGerald added another offense to this list: Falwell's women followers
wore "Charlie's Angels'" hairdos, irrefutable evidence that the Christian
Right had no fashion sense.) Blinded by their hatred of conservatism, the
media could not provide an informed analysis of political developments.
In January of 1980, members of Washington's National Press Club predicted that Carter (or, better yet, Kennedy) would vanquish the probable
Republican presidential nominee, George Bush. Only 29 of the 252 elite
political journalists thought that Reagan might have a chance at winning
the GOP nomination. According to the National Press Club, liberal Yankees like Bush and John Anderson continued to dominate the GOP. Reagan had been rejected in '76 by a party that supported abortion, affirmative action, and the ERA. Conservative claims to the contrary, Americans
wanted more government regulation and did not mind paying higher
taxes. Reagan, the media concluded, was a candidate of the past, while
Bush, with his "splendid resume," was a leader for the future. When
Reagan easily won his party's nomination, the *New York Times* refused to
admit that it had been wrong. Instead, the newspaper crowed that Carter
would rout the "worst candidate" ever to run for president."[61]

Dismayed by the prospect of a Carter-Reagan race, social liberals put
their financial and political resources behind Representative John Anderson of Illinois. Although Anderson failed to win a single GOP primary—
even his home state decisively voted for Reagan—his followers encouraged him to run as an independent. Norman Lear spent $200,000 to
produce Anderson commercials. The ACLU, the National Abortion
Rights Action League, Planned Parenthood, and the Sierra Club also provided Anderson with funds and volunteers. Media personalities did their
part, giving Anderson the most favorable press of any candidate. CBS
Evening News called him "forthright" and "the freshest face" on the
political scene. Some liberal Republicans moved into the Anderson camp,
unwilling to see the GOP become a conservative "Sunbelt club." Other
Republican liberals were afraid to vote for Anderson, instead of Carter,
lest they threw the election to Reagan.[62]

Senator Charles Percy of Illinois castigated the social conservatives. He particularly resented their insistence that Reagan appoint "judges at all levels of the judiciary who respect traditional family values and the sanctity of innocent human life." According to Percy, the prolifers had slammed through "the worst plank that has ever been in a platform." Helen Milliken, the wife of Michigan's liberal Republican governor, and Kansas senator Nancy Kassebaum, were equally put off. To their disgust, the platform committee refused to endorse the ERA. Upset, the liberal co-chair of the Republican National Committee resigned and quickly joined the Anderson campaign. The only concession liberal Republicans received was the selection of Bush as Reagan's running mate. Bush, an ardent champion of the ERA and abortion, however, disappointed many GOP liberals by embracing the conservative economic and social agenda. On the other hand, many social conservatives did not trust Bush, finding his conversion on the road to Damascus a little difficult to swallow. (Interestingly, Bush had scored best in the GOP primaries where he spent the least amount of money introducing himself to the electorate. The less voters knew about Bush the better they liked him.)[63]

The Democratic Party's allies in the media were panicking as the election drew closer. There being no credible way to build Carter up, they focused on tearing Reagan down. The *Washington Post* claimed that Reagan was too old to be president and noted that he had the "turkey-neck of those approaching their seventies." Moreover, the *Post* informed readers, Reagan was not very bright. CBS, ABC, and NBC charged that Reagan was misleading voters on his positions. (Presumably, Carter and Kennedy had never misled the electorate.) The *New York Times* and *Newsweek* depicted Reagan as a grenade-throwing extremist, closet bigot, and enemy of progressive causes. *New Yorker* writer and PBS commentator Elizabeth Drew dismissed Reagan and conservative senatorial candidates like Jeremiah Denton as "nihilistic, counter-reformationists." Reagan, of course, *was* a foe of so-called progressive causes. That was the point of being a *conservative* presidential candidate. Journalists quickly learned, to their chagrin, that voters did not care what they said about Reagan. He seemed more like a kindly uncle or grandfather than a wild-eyed revolutionary. Carter, on the other hand, appeared hysterical and nasty. The media were throwing away any remaining public respect and credibility that they had garnered from the Watergate scandal.[64]

Carter made repeated trips to Ohio, trying to persuade workers that Reagan posed a danger to their very existence. Campaigning in the Cleveland suburb of Parma, the president confronted angry Slavic faces. Apparently, no one had apprised Carter of the fact that his Justice Department had charged the blue-collar community with housing discrimination against blacks. If three generations of working-class ethnics lived in the same neighborhood and sold their homes to one another, then there must be a racist conspiracy to exclude blacks. The possibility that Catholic families might want to remain close to childhood parish and kin was not even worth contemplating.[65]

Hoping to divert their attention from the Justice Department, Carter warned Parma's Democrats that if Reagan were elected unemployment and inflation would mount, factories would close, and interest rates would climb so high that the young could not dream about buying a house. Carter overlooked a slight problem. He had just described the *present.* The best television advertisement that the GOP sponsored depicted an unemployed white Boomer walking through a shuttered factory and saying, "I've got just one question for the Democrats. If you're so good for the working people, how come so many people aren't working?" Thanks to McGovern, the Democrats had already lost their claim to being the party of national defense and the traditional family. By 1980, liberals surrendered their last hold card—the economic issue. Carter made it impossible for Democrats to keep running against Herbert Hoover.[66]

As the election results revealed, Carter did poorly among working-class voters—formerly the Democrats' most reliable supporters. He received barely half of the union vote. (George Meany, having given Carter a grade of C− for his performance as president, dropped dead before the election, leaving the AFL-CIO rudderless.) To the amazement of media pundits, defectors from organized labor went to Reagan—not John Anderson. This development should not have been startling, and not only because of the miserable economy. Reagan reveled in telling labor audiences that he had been the president of a union—the Screen Actors Guild. Moreover, Anderson's legislative record showed him to be far more hostile to unions than Reagan. Anderson scored best among upper-middle-class professionals and liberal Republicans. The independent presidential candidate, who received 7 percent of the vote, swept WASP and Jewish precincts from Cape Cod to San Francisco. In university and high-tech communities like Boulder, Anderson's tallies were two to three times higher than his overall vote.[67]

Seeing an opportunity to cut deeper into the New Deal coalition, Reagan vigorously worked the North's Catholic and Jewish precincts. Unlike

Nixon, who had put forth little personal effort to attract the ethnic vote, Reagan haunted Slavic fraternal halls and neighborhoods. Playing to his blue-collar, law-and-order audience, Reagan blamed Carter for rising crime rates and the state of the economy. Reagan's tactics worked well. He not only bested Carter among Catholics but scored a remarkable 39 percent of the Jewish vote. Three-quarters of the Orthodox Jewish voters in Brooklyn went for Reagan. Carter's quotas, Andrew Young's dislike of Israel, and internal religious divisions over abortion and gay liberation shattered the Jewish voting bloc. (Seventeen percent of Jewish voters supported Anderson. They feared Reagan and regarded Carter as insufficiently liberal.) Carter was the first Democrat in fifty years not to win the majority of Jewish voters. Luckily for congressional Democrats, most of Reagan's Jewish followers split their votes. Socially conservative Jews trusted their local Democratic representatives, if not the national party, to safeguard public morals.[68]

Carter took a horrendous beating in the South. His share of the Southern Baptist vote dropped from 56 percent in 1976 to 34 percent in 1980. Among southern white Protestants, just one-third stood by their native son. Indeed, the greatest electoral swing between '76 and '80 occurred among Carter's own brethren Southern Baptists. Moreover, the southern white voter turnout rose sharply, thanks to the efforts of the Moral Majority. As had been true in '76, nine in ten blacks voted for Carter, but this time around far too many southern whites went Republican to give the president a Dixie sweep. Reagan racked up 70 percent of the southern-white vote. (Anderson was a cipher in the South; neither white nor black social conservatives had any use for him.) In the Sunbelt cities of Anaheim, Dallas, and Phoenix, two of three voters chose Reagan. Carter carried the black industrial centers of the Rustbelt, but their populations had declined to the point where they mattered little in national politics. Lee Atwater, Reagan's rakish South Carolina operative, vividly summed up the situation: "We've got [Carter] bleeding like a stuck pig in his own base."[69]

More than a quarter of GOP liberals voted for either Anderson or Carter; not since Barry Goldwater's disastrous race in '64 had so many Brahmins deserted their party. But they were outnumbered two to one by conservative Democrats who lined up behind Reagan. Wherever Ford had done well in '76, Reagan did poorly. Conversely, in the blue-collar Protestant and Catholic districts that Ford had lost, Reagan scored landslides. Seventy-one percent of the Reagan Democrats, as the media quickly dubbed them, believed that black poverty was the result of illegitimacy and criminal behavior, not white racism. Such voters clung to New Deal programs, but wanted all vestiges of McGovern liberalism eliminated. Reagan Democrats were willing to give the Moral Majority a hearing—at least up to a point. Like Paul Weyrich, they remained leery of the GOP's libertarians. Unwilling to bet the farm on the New Right, many of Reagan's Democratic supporters split their votes, hoping their congressional representatives had enough sense to be socially conservative and economically liberal. In the early sixties split-ticket voters were a rarity. By 1980, a third of the electorate judged candidates on the issues, not their party affiliation.[70]

Up to the final days of the election, the media—relying more on wishful thinking than informed analysis—asserted that the presidential race was close. Moreover, Democrats would easily retain control of Congress. They were wrong on all counts. Reagan defeated Carter by ten percentage points. In Michigan, a state that reporters had predicted might go to Carter in a squeaker, Reagan won by a landslide margin of 250,000 votes. Texas, another "Carter state," went to Reagan by a staggering 700,000 votes. Moreover, Republicans gained thirteen Senate and thirty-three House seats. For the first time since 1952, the Republicans controlled the Senate and prominent liberals like McGovern and Birch Bayh of Indiana were turned out of office. The election results underscored just how deceitful and cynical Carter had been during the campaign. Alabama and Oklahoma fundamentalists who, according to Carter, were anti-Vatican nativists, sent Catholic Republicans to the Senate. Finally, the Republicans, with the cooperation of conservative southern Democrats, had secured working control of the House. Congressional leaders, however, were too busy throwing darts at Carter and denying that Reagan had scored a landslide to notice that development.[71]

Not only had the Republican party recovered from the Watergate debacle, many McGovern liberals, including Bill Clinton, had lost their gubernatorial and legislative seats. The Republicans won the solid support of social conservatives, who made up a quarter of the electorate in 1980. Libertarians represented a quarter of the electorate. (These voters tended to be serious ticket splitters, more interested in a candidate's ideology than party affiliation.) Another 20 percent of the electorate were Democratic and Republican populists who had no use for Big Government and Big Business. Reagan's coalition was not very stable, particularly if and when social conservatives, libertarians, and populists decided that their common enemy—Big Government—paled beside their distrust of one another. Reagan Democrats remained an extremely touchy constituency that opposed any rollback of the New Deal, even if it meant letting Social Security and other entitlement programs run amok. Beyond these considerations, one might have wondered if it were possible for Reagan to increase defense spending, reduce taxes, eliminate the budget deficit, get Big Government off people's backs, and reform Americans' moral conduct. These goals appeared contradictory. But, as Reagan often responded to naysayers and worrywarts, "There you go again."[72]

CHAPTER FIVE

"It's Morning in America"

1984

Pamela Digby Churchill Hayward Harriman of Georgetown and Paris was bored. Although riding after the hounds on her Virginia estate had its moments, "Pammy" wanted a new hobby. In short order she found one— Democratic politics. Drawn by her charming personality and deep purse, Washington's glittering liberals made the Harriman townhouse their second home in 1981. With $12 million in political contributions dangled in front of them, Democratic congressmen were understandably loath to pass up an invitation to a "Pammy" soiree. Amidst scrumptious feasts, delightful hors d'oeuvres, and fine spirits, *Washington Post* reporter Haynes Johnson, Arkansas senator Dale Bumpers, and former defense secretary Clark Clifford denounced Republican greed and incompetence. Clifford dismissed President Ronald Reagan as "an amiable dunce" whose administration would be "a hopeless failure." Senator Bumpers assured colleagues that all the Democrats had to do was wait for the inevitable economic collapse. Then voters would return liberals to power.[1]

Democratic House Speaker Tip O'Neill had already sized Reagan up as a loser. At their first face-to-face meeting, O'Neill played "Don Corleone" to Reagan's "Mr. Rogers." Looking across his desk at the smiling president-elect, the "Don" informed Reagan that the conservative legislative agenda was not going anywhere. Although Reagan may have had a successful partnership with California's Democratic state assembly, O'Neill said, "that was the minor leagues. You're in the big leagues now." Believing it was "sinful that Ronald Reagan ever became president," O'Neill made him an offer that he could not refuse. If Reagan wished to avoid being exposed as an idiot, then he should sit back and do nothing until the Democrats won back the White House in '84. O'Neill had no intention of permitting this "cheerleader for selfishness" to be a successful president.[2]

As O'Neill tried to strong-arm Reagan, a revolt against the House Speaker simmered in Congress. Forty-four southerners expressed dismay with their party's liberal leaders. O'Neill scolded the so-called Boll Weevils for undermining his authority. When Texas Democrat Phil Gramm helped usher Reagan's tax cuts and budget reforms through Congress, the Speaker responded by stripping away his important committee assignments. Gramm switched parties and successfully ran for reelection as a Republican. In 1984, grateful Texans sent the one-time economics professor to the Senate. O'Neill also directed his invective at a group of young backbenchers. Led by Newt Gingrich of Georgia, the "C-Span Boys" played to the cameras on the House floor. Miffed, O'Neill ordered C-Span to pan the empty legislative chamber. Few congressmen, O'Neill gloated, were listening to conservative attacks on Big Government. Unbeknownst to O'Neill, he had fallen into Gingrich's trap. Gingrich *wanted* voters to get the impression that liberals were too busy attending parties to hang around the House discussing crime, taxes, and welfare.[3]

Democrats like O'Neill and Joseph Califano refused to recognize that their policies were not solving America's economic and social problems. The erstwhile HEW secretary would not countenance the idea that Great Society initiatives might have even contributed to the unraveling of the nation's social fabric. Califano pined for a return to the Great Society, claiming that President Johnson had successfully fought poverty and advanced racial justice. If America's welfare rolls and rates of illegitimacy and violent crime exploded in the seventies, then urban unemployment and poorly funded anti-poverty programs were to blame. Liberal policies themselves were not at fault. Voters, liberals insisted, had not endorsed conservatism in the 1980 election. The American people believed in abortion, affirmative action, sexual liberation, and welfare. Folks were upset with the state of the economy, not with America's moral climate. Once the electorate realized that Reagan was worse than Carter, conservatives would be brushed aside.[4]

Many liberals, however, were not about to sit idly by awaiting their restoration. Angry Democrats lashed out at the Right. One essayist in *Harper's* asserted that conservatives "operate in near-total ignorance of intellectual discipline and scholarly integrity." Worse, they were strangers "to the democratic process." Convinced that the Religious Right was undemocratic, at least as they defined the notion, secular liberals poured large sums of money into the Democratic Party's coffers. Such donors, whose wealth gave them enormous influence in party circles, rejected organized religion in any of its ideological manifestations—liberal or conservative. To the Left, it was almost as if Martin Luther King, Jr., and Daniel Berrigan had never been members of the clergy. (Leftist academics, embarrassed by the fact that King was a Baptist minister, dismissed his religious beliefs as little more than window dressing. They depicted King as a secular socialist. White supremacists had been doing the same thing since the fifties for quite different reasons.)[5]

An unrepentant McGovern derided religious traditionalists. Moralists who feared for the future viability of the American family, McGovern contended in 1981, really wanted to put "women back in the kitchen, stripping them of any decision on the question of abortion." Elaborating on his views in *Playboy*, McGovern charged social conservatives with "zealotry, self-righteousness, and vindictiveness." He then characterized the Moral Majority as McCarthyite, Nazi-like, and Stalinist. (Richard Nixon's policies, in contrast, had been merely Nazi-like and McCarthyite. After Reagan's election, McGovern must have felt that his rhetorical repertoire needed to be expanded.) Over the course of the eighties McGovern haunted the nation's college campuses, ridiculing mean-spirited social conservatives and decrying Republican greed and racism. In the meantime conservatives charged that he profited from gentrifying slum property for upscale whites. Reagan's tax cuts did not hurt his financial profile either.[6]

At the heart of the Reagan Revolution, which McGovern loathed (and profited from), was a libertarian zeal to cut taxes and starve Big Government to death. Reagan's director of the Office of Management and Budget, David Stockman, embodied the spirit of libertarian radicalism. Like many younger members of the Reagan administration, Stockman had evaded the Vietnam War through student deferments. He also worked with the Students for a Democratic Society on antiwar organizing. That fact made Stockman a standout among his peers. Conservatives typically joined the Young Americans for Freedom in the sixties, not SDS. (Defense Secretary Caspar Weinberger, a World War II combat veteran, is said to have referred to Stockman as "the blow-dried draft dodger.") In the seventies, Stockman had been the only Michigan representative to oppose the Chrysler bailout, believing that management and labor should be punished for making inferior automobiles.[7]

Stockman resented "the irrational right wing and screaming Moral

Majoritarians." In 1976, the one-time divinity student wrote off Reagan as a mindless Bible thumper. Stockman's staff, in Congress and in the White House, advocated huge defense cuts and argued that the Consumer Protection Agency was an unwarranted interference in the right of corporations to conduct their business in any manner they saw fit. Impressed with his knowledge of the federal budget, as well as with his opposition to government regulation, Reagan overlooked Stockman's antiwar activism and support for abortion. With Stockman's appointment, the White House made it clear that it intended to emphasize an economic, rather than a social, agenda.[8]

Stockman, Buffalo representative Jack Kemp, and White House economic policy advisor Martin Anderson advocated a new kind of fiscal policy. They believed that reducing taxes would make corporations more inclined to invest in new plants. Millions of workers could then be hired and, as the economy expanded, federal tax receipts would actually increase. There would be more than enough federal revenue coming in to pay for Reagan's $1.5 trillion defense buildup. Kemp, sensitive to the fears of his white-ethnic congressional district, insisted that Social Security did not have to be cut in order to balance the budget. As far as Republican elites were concerned, Kemp remained too attached to the New Deal welfare state and his own working-class roots. But then, what could one expect from a person who drove trucks and played football to pay his way through college? Gentlemen had trust funds to take care of their schooling.[9]

"Supply side" economics enjoyed some success. As predicted, the tax cuts ultimately increased federal receipts and capital investment. Libertarians like Martin Anderson also expressed satisfaction at having slashed federal spending on education, job training, and regional development projects by 22 percent. But for all of that, there were some small problems. To gain the support of Sunbelt congressmen—Republicans and Democrats—the Reagan administration made numerous concessions. Federal subsidies to farmers and ranchers rose 252 percent. (Jesse Helms insisted that North Carolina tobacco growers share in the Republican largess.) Farm-state Republicans—chiefly Senate finance chair Bob Dole—joined the Congressional Black Caucus in defending the food stamp program. Thanks to Dole, an additional five million Americans received food stamps and overall spending on anti-poverty programs went up steadily. Meanwhile, Social Security expenditures nearly doubled, and almost half of the nation's non-farm households received some kind of federal benefits. At best, conservatives succeeded only in slowing down the *rate* of spending. Whatever additional revenue the government collected quickly disappeared. Reagan, who had criticized Carter for running $40 billion deficits, added a trillion dollars to America's debt.[10]

Unwilling "to stay the course" as Reagan desired, Dole raised taxes. In a remarkably brainless political move, Dole left the Reagan tax cuts in place for higher-income Americans. Rather than tax the affluent, Dole gave blue-collar citizens a $98 billion bill. The Kansas senator went after waitresses, claiming that they were underreporting their tips. Dole also thought that the interest on individuals' savings accounts merited the attention of the IRS. (White-collar professionals put their money into tax-sheltered mutual funds, not savings accounts, as the working class did.) Congressional Democrats promised Dole that they would cut spending by three dollars for every dollar they raised taxes. He is still waiting for those cuts.[11]

To Kemp's chagrin, Stockman endorsed the Dole tax hike and demanded sharp reductions in Social Security benefits. Foolishly, Stockman rejected an offer of assistance from South Carolina's Democratic senator, Ernest Hollings. The southerner told Stockman that he could put together a bipartisan coalition that would scale back the cost-of-living allowances for Social Security recipients. Little did Hollings know that the budget director opposed undertaking any serious Social Security reforms. Stockman's calls for Social Security cuts were for public consumption. He actually hoped that the program would go bankrupt. Frustrated in his attempts to slash the defense budget and undermine Social Security, Stockman concluded that Kemp and Reagan were closet New Dealers who lacked the courage to cut senior citizens and veterans off at the knees. (Reagan, after all, had voted for FDR *all four times*.) Disgusted, Gingrich wailed that Stockman and Dole were "committed to the traditional GOP attitudes—cheap and negative. It goes back to the ways of the stupid party."[12]

Libertarians soon learned that Dole and Stockman were not their only problems. They complained that Reagan's advisors, notably Mike Deaver and Jim Baker, as well as Vice President George Bush, were thwarting their revolution. Their complaints had merit. Deaver, who had championed the Dole tax hike, routinely intercepted hard-core conservative magazines like the *American Spectator* and *Human Events* before they could reach Reagan. If Reagan did read a *Human Events* article, Deaver and White House staffer Dick Darman provided a rebuttal. White

House counselor Ed Meese believed that liberal Republicans leaked derogatory stories about him and other conservatives to the *Washington Post*. Bob Tyrrell of the *American Spectator* observed that "treacherous" GOP liberals lacked any moral and political principles. His description of the typical Bush Republican was not flattering: "The country-club Republican sees politics as an opportunity to meet people from other states, and occasionally even other countries, and to wear lime slacks with one's blazer—occasionally the slacks are beige, having whales and little ducks on them." Such people, Tyrrell concluded, detest radical change.[13]

Arizona senator Barry Goldwater reserved his wrath for Christian conservatives. "I have seen many news items that referred to the Moral Majority, prolife, and other religious groups as 'the new right' and the 'new conservatism,'" Goldwater snorted. "Well, I have spent quite a number of years carrying the flag of the 'old conservatism.' And I can say with conviction that the religious issues of these groups have little or nothing to do with conservative or liberal politics." Goldwater continued in the same vein, stating that "every good Christian ought to kick [Jerry] Falwell right in the ass." Goldwater's rant subsequently appeared on tens of thousands of political buttons. Given the thrust, and color, of the message, social liberals could hardly resist quoting the father of contemporary conservatism.[14]

Libertarian magazines chided social conservatives for seeking to regulate peoples' sexual behavior and choice of drugs. In the libertarian view, morality should be defined "in terms of a life of excellence, a life of achievement, a life of ambition and accomplishment." Material accomplishment, not a belief in God, made people worthy. Although Bob Tyrrell lamented the fact that fundamentalist Christians and libertarians had little in common, he was not about to subordinate economic freedom to religious dogma. Tyrrell praised William F. Buckley's religious faith precisely because it was "shorn of all those Papal phobias against commerce that have been the economic stumbling block of Catholic countries." Of course, it was Buckley's opposition to the social regulation of capitalism— a stance that had been endorsed by the American Catholic bishops and Pope Pius XI in the thirties—that distressed blue-collar ethnics. To them, Buckley was Catholic only in name, not in heart and mind.[15]

Like the libertarian intellectuals, corporate executives kept religious traditionalists at arm's length. Among the fourteen hundred corporate political action committees that contributed large sums of money to the

GOP, just 14 percent of their leaders had a favorable opinion of the Moral Majority and social conservatives. In general, barely a third of the country's economic conservatives said that they felt close to the Moral Majority. When Budweiser, Coors, Miller, and Strohs gave money to New Right congressional candidates in 1980 and 1982, they were looking to advance the cause of market deregulation, not promote Baptist-style temperance.[16]

Having written *Mandate for Leadership,* the blueprint for the Reagan economic revolution, the Heritage Foundation suddenly became respectable. Its morning prayer breakfasts were discontinued and free-market matters clearly took precedence over abortion, busing, and the ERA. Meese, a fan of the Heritage Foundation and later a board member, explained that the economy and America's military defense had to be placed at the top of the national agenda. The president, he insisted, was not "indifferent to social issues." After all, Reagan, with the Heritage Foundation's advice, appointed half of the federal judiciary. Unlike Carter's judges, Meese boasted, Reagan's appointees were not likely to support affirmative action and the rights of criminal defendants. Robert Bork, Reagan's choice to serve on the United States Court of Appeals (Washington Circuit), was certainly not a social liberal. (In 1984 Bork upheld a Georgia sodomy law, ruling that "we find it impossible to conclude that a right to homosexual conduct is fundamental or implicit in the concept of ordered liberty, unless any and all private sexual behavior falls within those categories, a conclusion we're unwilling to draw.")[17]

Paul Weyrich did not take as generous a view of the Reagan White House. At best, where moral traditionalists had been locked out of the White House by Nixon, Carter, and Ford, "in the Reagan administration we have been let in the back door and we are enjoying the crumbs at the servants' table." Not only had Reagan refused to attend a massive prolife rally in Washington, Weyrich and other social conservatives complained, he had appointed an ERA and abortion rights supporter, Sandra Day O'Connor, to the Supreme Court. Just as troubling, the president had failed to develop ties to ordinary black Americans who felt threatened by drugs and crime. Social issues, Weyrich believed, offered conservatives a chance to bypass the civil rights leadership and bring about racial reconciliation. He also aimed a shot at the GOP's country-club "Tories," as well as the "big corporations [that] are as bad as Big Government. They're in bed together." Goldwater's response was cutting: "Who the hell is the New Right anyway? Who is Paul Weyrich? He's not a leader of the Republican Party."[18]

Cal Thomas, the Moral Majority's vice president for communications, was just as disappointed with the Reagan White House as Weyrich: "If we balance the budget and we still keep murdering a million and a half babies every year, there's no way we can say we're better off than we were four years ago." Tax cuts might make the nation materially strong, but they did nothing to nourish the spirit. Falwell, understanding Thomas's concerns, observed that "Mike Deaver probably couldn't spell 'abortion.'" Still, the Lynchburg minister gave Reagan an "A+"—even if he was grading on a curve. Connie Marshner, the chief critic of Carter's Conference on Families and now a Washington-based religious activist, provided a more ambivalent assessment of the Reagan White House. "There's been a lot of good rhetoric, no question about that," Marshner conceded. "But beyond that, it's very nebulous." Phyllis Schlafly, in contrast, vigorously defended Reagan. She told Weyrich and others that they were providing lethal ammunition to the liberal media. Conservatives, Schlafly argued, had to maintain a united front if there was to be any hope for progress. Although she would not have appreciated the comparison, the civil rights establishment took the same position in answering its internal critics.[19]

If social conservatives thought they were being treated badly by libertarians and White House staffers, Republican regulars were no more kind. Lee Atwater, the GOP's Boomer strategist for the Southland, exhorted Reagan to emphasize economic deregulation and not to worry about lifestyle issues. Not surprisingly, religious conservatives regarded Atwater as an amoral cynic who would do anything to win an election. Indiana's newly elected Republican senator, Dan Quayle, denied that the Moral Majority and other religious groups had been responsible for his victory over liberal stalwart Birch Bayh. Indeed, Quayle said, such people hurt him and the GOP. Placing further distance between himself and the Religious Right, Quayle insisted that he was a Stockman libertarian. (Like Stockman, Quayle avoided the Vietnam War. Unlike Stockman, Quayle had a trust fund to fall back upon if his political career ever came to an abrupt end.) During the 1980 Senate campaign Quayle had sided with the Christian academies against the IRS. Privately, he admitted that the fundamentalists made him uncomfortable. They were too religious and too serious for his country-club tastes.[20]

Quayle's fellow golfer-in-arms, George Bush, chimed in with his own criticism of social conservatives. When urged to become more active in the prolife movement, Bush snapped back, "I am not intimidated by those who suggest I better hew the line. Hell with them." (Bush, for that matter, had no use for Kemp's tax-cutting agenda. Some conservatives wished that Reagan had chosen a *Democratic* running mate in 1980— namely, Senator Sam Nunn of Georgia.) Another liberal Republican assured the *Washington Post* that the White House would give social conservatives "symbolism," not action. Then, using a quote from Michael Corleone in *The Godfather—Part II,* the unidentified aide explained why a few token staff positions had gone to Christian rightists, " 'Hold your friends close, hold your enemies closer.' " What the administration planned to do is "to keep the Moral Majority types so close to us they can't move their arms." Secretary of Education Terrel Bell blasted social conservatives as ignorant racists and "cocksure" ideologues. When Bell delivered his 1983 report on American education, *A Nation at Risk,* he told reporters to ignore Reagan's call for school prayer. Reagan and Meese, Bell claimed, were not interested in curriculum reforms, just television sound bites to appease their reactionary constituency.[21]

While libertarians, social conservatives, and GOP preppies fought among themselves, liberals recovered some lost ground. Since Richard Daley's departure to that great political clubhouse in the sky, Tip O'Neill had taken it upon himself to serve as the Democratic Party's grand tactician. O'Neill's directions to Democrats in the '82 midterm elections were simple: accuse the Republicans of plotting against Social Security and Medicare and blame the GOP for continued high levels of unemployment. Under no circumstances, O'Neill warned, should Democratic candidates discuss the budget deficit. Liberals, he admitted, were "not credible on fiscal responsibility." Instead, Democrats must characterize Republicans as rich country clubbers who had done "nothing for the middle class." O'Neill covered all the bases. At the House Speaker's direction, California representative Tony Coelho threatened corporate political action committees with investigation and legislative retribution unless they gave more money to Democrats. Convinced that the GOP would never secure formal control of the House, Republican businessmen complied. (Coelho's freewheeling ethics eventually forced him to relinquish his seat.)[22]

O'Neill's hardball tactics paid off. Democratic liberals recovered twenty-six House seats—just enough to shut down the Boll Weevil–GOP alliance. Most of their victories, however, took place in the decaying Midwest, not the economically dynamic South. Midwestern retirees and union members did not understand that the Democrats would do little for them. After the election, O'Neill raised the Social Security retirement age, in effect cutting benefits for future recipients. Congressional Democrats knew that Social Security, like Medicare and Medicaid, was doomed in the long run. They would never admit this because the Social Security and Medicare programs were useful in rallying their loyal constituency of seniors against the GOP.[23]

The recession that Democrats blamed on Reagan had begun under Carter. In 1979, Carter's Federal Reserve Board chose to stem inflation by raising interest rates. This was the only Carter policy Reagan endorsed. By creating a shortage of finance capital, Federal Reserve chair Paul Volcker offered inefficient Rustbelt industries the choice between radical restructuring or death. Chrysler, Ford, and General Motors survived by replacing hundreds of thousands of employees with robots and offering overtime to their remaining workers. (Paying time-and-a-half was less costly to the Big Three than hiring new, fully insured, employees.) The unemployment rate in the auto industry rapidly rose to 23 percent. Other companies, like Youngstown Sheet and Tube, vanished. For decades the effluents dumped into Youngstown's Mahoning River had kept it from freezing during bitterly cold winter months. Then, as if by magic, children were ice skating on it. Meanwhile their parents downed a few boilermakers before spending another futile day at the union hall looking for work. Despite mounting poverty in the mill towns of Ohio and Pennsylvania, the steelworkers' leaders gave nearly a million dollars to Democratic candidates in 1982. Union dues were being spent on politicians, not on retraining unemployed workers.[24]

Steelworkers and autoworkers demanded tariff protection against cheaper imports and rejected wage concessions, even though they were the best-paid workers in the world. As one Pennsylvania steelworker put it, "I'd rather be unemployed than a slave." In Milwaukee, union workers voted against a wage freeze at the Schlitz brewery and then went on strike, daring the company to shut down operations. Schlitz obliged. For those workers who had union-protected seniority rights, life was pretty good. *Employed* members of the UAW and the United Steel Workers Union typically made $40,000 a year in wages and benefits. This placed them solidly in the ranks of the middle class. Tellingly, an older UAW member from Ohio did not lament the plight of his jobless neighbors. He boasted to a *New York Times* reporter that "I'm just making a lot more money now" because, with all of the layoffs, there was more overtime available. The thirties-era UAW fight song, "Solidarity Forever," rang hollow by the eighties.[25]

Bob Carr, who won back his Michigan congressional seat in 1982 with the help of the UAW, pledged federal assistance to the autoworkers. Carr, however, did little to help the unemployed. Instead, he focused his efforts on building a power base as chair of the House Transportation Spending Committee. He wrote special legislation undercutting various environmental laws in order to benefit favored construction contractors. Grateful businessmen gave Carr hundreds of thousands of dollars in contributions. In Arkansas, Bill Clinton played populist champion of the working class while assuring Tyson Foods that if he got back the governor's chair he would overlook little things like pollution and employee health and safety. (Clinton had already set his sights on the White House. Once restored to the governor's mansion he wasted no time in snagging an invitation to "Pammy's.") Hillary Rodham Clinton helped out by getting a conservative haircut and projecting a more patriotic image to Arkansas voters. The first lady of Arkansas often could be heard in the early morning hours exhorting laggard state troopers to raise "the f——ing flag."[26]

The union rank and file faced disaster. Few unemployed industrial workers were going to acquire good-paying jobs as computer software engineers. Besides, for every computer-programmer position created in the eighties, there were five low-wage, dead-end jobs spawned in the fast-food industry. Poorly paid janitors outnumbered computer systems analysts four to one. Overall, the number of middle-income jobs fell by 20 percent while low-income employment increased by half. Fully a third of the new jobs created during the 1983 Reagan recovery were part-time and seldom offered health and pension benefits. What liberal critics too often overlooked in their recitation of such grim statistics, though, was the fact that the middle class was shrinking for another reason. If millions of Americans were experiencing downward mobility, millions of others were entering the ranks of the upper middle class. Only by the end of the eighties would underemployed Baby Busters coin a term for this phenomenon: the "Brazilification" of the American economy. In the brave new world of MBAs and McJobs one would either be extremely comfortable or up against the wall.[27]

Lane Kirkland, having taken over the AFL-CIO from George Meany, changed the union's political direction. He first set out to reconcile labor with feminists and gays. In part, Kirkland was responding to the declining fortunes of the auto and steel affiliates. Immediately after World War II 35 percent of work force had been unionized. Most union membership was localized in heavy manufacturing. By the eighties, just 17 percent of America's workers belonged to a union. The smokestack affiliates were decimated. While the socially conservative steel and auto unions lost their clout, the liberal public-sector affiliates doubled their representation. By 1984, unions like AFSCME and the NEA accounted for a third of the AFL-CIO's membership. Moreover, they were the only affiliates that successfully recruited new members in the eighties. Recognizing the enhanced clout of the public-employee unions, Kirkland believed it best to support their social causes. Kirkland also joined NOW's abortion-rights demonstrations, embraced hiring quotas, and developed alliances with gay activists. In exchange, he expected to help select the 1984 Democratic presidential nominee. His choice was Walter Mondale, a candidate who vowed to protect Rustbelt industries from foreign competition. Even better, NOW found Mondale to be acceptable.[28]

Thanks to Kirkland, Mondale defeated one of his most bothersome primary opponents, Senator Gary Hart of Colorado. Hart briefly appeared on the verge of winning the Democratic nomination. Then, Mondale counterattacked, depicting Hart as a younger, hipper version of the dreaded Ronald Reagan. Mondale had a point. On economic issues, Hart was a libertarian. A spokesman for the New Class, Hart looked forward to the day when smokestack industries were supplanted by environmentally correct high-tech boutiques. Fortunately for Mondale, liberal party activists remained neutral or supported him—expecting a payoff at the party convention. Hart's volunteers, in contrast to Mondale's, did not tend to be closely affiliated with NOW or any other liberal organization. Indeed, the Young Urban Professionals, or Yuppies, who backed Hart had little regard for either party. Yuppies valued the free market and a charismatic political style. They also believed in abortion on demand, yet discounted Reagan's prolife statements as "boob bait for the Bubbas." Many of Hart's supporters in the primaries subsequently voted for Reagan.[29]

Although Mondale easily brushed Hart aside, he found Jesse Jackson more troublesome. Few Democrats, let alone Republicans, wanted to deal with the problems confronting the black underclass. Academic leftists and militant activists brought little to the discussion of race and poverty. They leveled the usual charges against the New Right, asserting that "racism was central to its emergence and remains crucial for its overall appeal."

Roger Wilkins—the nephew of civil rights leader Roy Wilkins—claimed that Reagan practiced "smiling racism" in his efforts to "keep the niggers in their place." The president may have said that he was not a racist, Wilkins argued, but Reagan's criticism of inner-city crime and affirmative action proved otherwise. One Mississippi civil rights activist denied that southern blacks were better off now than they had been thirty years before. White southerners were still racists who "see the black population as a cheap, abundant, exploitable labor force, and they intend to keep it that way." Mississippi minorities, he insisted, needed hiring quotas and more federal welfare programs.[30]

Only rarely did a black clergyman or academic break ranks. The Reverend T. J. Jemison, the president of the Northern Baptist Convention, met with Reagan and then told reporters that White House policies were not so much racist as they were misguided. Jemison also obliquely chastised liberals for indiscriminately smearing anyone who disagreed with them. Such militants were discrediting the civil rights cause. Taking a different tack, economist Glenn Loury told activists not to blame whites for their problems. Instead, blacks should recognize that

many of the problems of contemporary black American life lie outside the reach of effective government action, and require for their successful resolution actions that can only be undertaken by the black community itself. These problems involve at their core the values, attitudes, and behaviors of individual blacks. They are exemplified by the staggering statistics on pregnancies among young, unwed black women and the arrest and incarceration rate among black men. Such complicated problems, part cause and part effect of the economic hardship readily observed in the ghettos of America, defy easy explanation. These problems will not go away with the return of economic prosperity, with the election of a liberal Democrat to the presidency, or with the doubling in size of the Congressional Black Caucus.[31]

The social statistics concerning the black underclass were, as Loury said, staggering. By the early eighties, one-quarter of the income of inner-city blacks came from criminal activities, usually drug dealing. (In Reagan's first term the number of deaths from narcotics overdoses in New York City doubled. Middle-class whites tended to kill themselves with cocaine; poor blacks had to content themselves with less expensive heroin.) In 1984, black juveniles—most of whom were fatherless—committed half of the nation's violent crimes. Black teens became sexually active at a younger age than whites and were less inclined to protect themselves against social diseases and pregnancy. Nearly four of every five teenage girls in Washington were unwed welfare mothers. In Chicago's Cabrini-Green public housing project, 89 percent of the teens dropped out of high school. Most belonged to the project's one hundred gang factions. Single women headed 80 percent of Cabrini-Green's households. Men made an appearance only on "Mother's Day"—the first of the month when the welfare checks arrived. Few residents attended church, although girls who did so were less likely to bear children out of wedlock. None of Cabrini-Green's tenants received faculty appointments to the University of Chicago or Northwestern under their affirmative action plans.[32]

As a candidate for the Democratic presidential nomination, Jesse Jackson muted his criticism of abortion and illegitimacy. He also reversed his position on homosexuality, thereby earning the endorsement of San Francisco's Stonewall Gay Democratic Club. Instead of lifestyle issues, Jackson emphasized economic matters. His approach, however, bore little resemblance to one taken by Kirkland and O'Neill. Jackson blamed white racism for destroying the lives of inner-city blacks. When among black reporters, Jackson singled out Jews for special abuse. For years he had called William Singer of Chicago "the little Jew." (In 1972, Singer had helped oust Richard Daley from the Democratic National Convention so that Jackson could take his seat.) Moreover, Jackson did not appear to have any problem with the "poetry" of his militant *black* ally LeRoi Jones (a.k.a. Amiri Baraka): "I got something for you . . . I got the extermination blues, Jew boy."[33]

To Jackson and the black professionals who flocked to his banner, New York City was "Hymietown," a place filled with rapacious Jewish landlords and price-gouging merchants. When Milton Coleman, a black reporter for the *Washington Post,* publicized Jackson's "Hymietown" epithet, Nation of Islam leader Louis Farrakhan warned Coleman that "one day we will punish you with death." Addressing himself to Jackson's Jewish critics, Farrakhan praised Hitler and contended that "you hate us because we dare to say that we are the chosen people of God and can back it up. We are ready to do battle with you wherever you come from on the earth. It is the black people in America that is the chosen people of Almighty God."[34]

Far from repudiating Farrakhan, Jackson's campaign embraced him. The Democratic Party, Jackson volunteers asserted, could do without the support of rich racist Jews. They also complained that the media were singling out Jackson for abuse because he was black. This was not true. Ohio senator John Glenn saw his presidential ambitions thwarted after the *New York Times* reported that he was not a true champion of Israel. Glenn foolishly confided to colleagues that Zionists exercised too much power in Congress and dictated America's Middle Eastern policy. An irate Glenn staffer fumed that the Jewish media had destroyed the senator's candidacy. Jews, according to Glenn's assistant, dominated the "Magnificent Seven": the *New York Times,* the *Washington Post, Time, Newsweek,* ABC, NBC, and CBS.[35]

Coming to Farrakhan's defense, a Jackson campaign organizer asked, "Why should [Jackson] renounce someone who is registering and turning out the vote for him to curry favor with white America when white America is not going to vote for him anyhow?" Lucius Barker, a Jackson delegate and political science professor at the University of Illinois, accused Coleman of betraying his race. At the 1984 Democratic National Convention, three-quarters of the white delegates expressed their distaste for Farrakhan. On the other hand, half of the blacks—many of whom were Jackson delegates—had a good opinion of Farrakhan. Although the Nation of Islam was said to have its greatest following among poor blacks, Jackson's four hundred delegates were solidly middle class. Barker observed—with pride—that whenever Jackson delegates got together for cocktails he felt himself in familiar surroundings—as if he was at an academic conference.[36]

Despite the fact that half of the white civil rights workers who went south in the sixties were Jews, anti-Semitism permeated the ranks of the black middle class. Indeed, public opinion surveys revealed prosperous blacks to be far more anti-Semitic than conservative whites. Black Boomers resented the Jews who occasionally led, and often financed, civil rights organizations like the Urban League and the NAACP. Now that so many blacks had entered the professions, the civil rights struggle shifted ground. Jews, not southern whites, stood in their way, holding down professorships and law-firm partnerships that college-educated blacks felt belonged to them. Most liberals were too timid to cry foul. Mondale sidestepped the Farrakhan controversy, McGovern praised Jackson, and the party platform once again embraced quotas and the expansion of the welfare state. Not a word was said about black anti-Semitism. Then again, white Democrats needed to be pragmatic. Jackson had already registered 700,000 new black voters. In the primaries he had carried three-quarters of the black vote. Besides, Jewish liberals did not want to confront black anti-Semitism lest they divide the Democratic Party.[37]

Jackson's platform demands and hints that he might not campaign for

Mondale made the nominee appear spineless. Matters grew worse when NOW insisted that Mondale select a woman as his running mate. Moreover, the woman had to be either prochoice, or at least not inclined to challenge *Roe*. Mondale hemmed and hawed, insisting that he would choose a candidate based on merit, not gender. Then he caved in. NOW had Representative Geraldine Ferraro of Queens in mind for the number-two slot. In addition to NOW, Ferraro possessed other powerful connections. Ferraro counted Tip O'Neill, corporate lobbyist Anne Wexler, and actress Jane Fonda among her backers. Delighted by Ferraro's nomination, Fonda organized a Hollywood political action committee to help the ticket. Fonda's twentysomething protégés included Rob Lowe and Daphne Zuniga, who later demonstrated her political consistency and acting skills on the television series *Melrose Place*. Feigning enthusiasm—or what Mondale considered to be enthusiasm—the nominee said that Ferraro would attract votes from feminists *and* ethnics. Mondale's political senses were never keen. In his nationally televised acceptance speech, Mondale promised to *raise* taxes. He expected people to appreciate his honesty and vote for him.[38]

Mondale quickly discovered that Ferraro was radioactive. The Democrats had planned to make the "Reagan Sleaze Factor" the centerpiece of their '84 campaign. Since 1981, forty-five members of the Reagan administration had been investigated for various conflict-of-interest matters. Labor Secretary Ray Donovan stood accused of having Mafia ties. (Donovan was cleared of any wrongdoing, but the ordeal irreparably damaged his reputation.) At the outset of the election, Tony Coelho had condemned the "long and growing pattern of ethical misconduct by Reagan administration appointees," and Gary Hart had criticized Republicans for abusing their positions of power.[39]

The "sleaze factor" blew up in Mondale's face. It seemed that Ferraro and her husband, John Zaccaro, had undertaken some creative business arrangements. They were also highly successful in locating tax loopholes. (Ferraro's criticism of Republican greed appeared hypocritical in light of her income tax returns.) No sooner had these tidbits came out than the *Wall Street Journal* and the New York *Post* revealed that her father-in-law once had organized crime ties. More recently, Zaccaro had rented office space to the Gambino crime family for its pornography operations. Ferraro denied every allegation, explained inconvenient facts away, and, full of self-pity, said she was being persecuted by the Right because she was a woman. Boomer reporters took up her cause. William Henry of the Boston *Globe* dismissed the *Wall Street Journal* as "rightist and occasionally loony." Henry's efforts to muddy the waters, however, came to naught. After the election, Zaccaro pled guilty to fraud. In a bizarre sidebar, Ferraro's son was later convicted of dealing cocaine at his exclusive Vermont college.[40]

While Mondale receded into the background, Ferraro moved squarely to the center of the campaign. A smart politician would have dumped Ferraro from the ticket the minute her financial affairs came to light. (Then again, any politician worth his salt would have investigated Ferraro before selecting her as his running mate.) As the "affirmative action candidate," however, Ferraro was untouchable. At best, Mondale could hope that the voters forgot about her—much as they were forgetting about him.

To the dismay of party loyalists, Ferraro seemed to seek out controversy. Her most embarrassing performance came in the debate over religion and abortion. Ferraro argued that there was no contradiction between billing herself to ethnics as a devout Catholic while refusing to embrace church teachings that proscribed abortion. Indeed, Ferraro's support for abortion was much greater than she had let on at the Democratic convention. When questioned about her views on abortion Ferraro changed the subject, deciding that it was time to attack Reagan's morals. "The president walks around calling himself a good Christian," Ferraro snarled, "but I don't for one minute believe it because the policies are so terribly unfair."[41]

Archbishop (later Cardinal) John O'Connor of New York questioned how anyone who called herself a Catholic could be prochoice. Ferraro quickly derided O'Connor, John Cardinal Krol of Philadelphia, Bishop James Malone of Youngstown, and her other church critics as little more than Reagan underlings. She then asserted that the prolife movement was filled with "violent, "narrow-minded," and "mean-spirited" Republicans who were "anti-woman." Archbishop O'Connor pointed out that, unlike the GOP, he supported labor unions. Moreover, the prolife bishops of the U.S. Catholic Conference had criticized White House proposals to eliminate federal welfare programs. While the bishops agreed that America's churches needed to pitch in and do more, no one church had enough volunteers and funds to assume the entire federal welfare obligation. Even corporations, many bishops warned, could not resurrect Youngstown or Detroit on their own. Shifting ground, Ferraro countered that the bishops placed abortion above the economic plight of working families. This was a peculiar accusation coming from someone who had more friends in Planned Parenthood than in the steelworkers union.[42]

Ferraro refused to listen to prolife Catholics. In 1981, Terence Cardinal Cooke of New York, a prolife activist, had testified before Congress. His thoughts deserved some attention. "All of us are concerned about the growing evidence of violence in our nation," Cardinal Cooke observed. "I am convinced that a society is doomed to violence when it allows direct attacks on the most fundamental of all human rights, the right to life itself." Having turned a deaf ear to Cardinal Cooke, Ferraro was not about to give O'Connor a serious hearing. As O'Connor contended:

Life is of one piece. Assaulted in *any* way it is open to assault in a thousand other ways. . . . It was prophesied with *Roe v. Wade*, in 1973, that once we legitimized killing of the unborn, ultimately no life would be safe—"hopelessly" retarded, blind, wheel-chaired, cancer-ridden, elderly, or simply those who eat food, drink water or occupy crowded space! Easy recourse to death to resolve problems related to the unborn constantly leads to easy recourse to death to resolve a host of other problems.[43]

Incensed that moral issues had been injected into a political campaign, Teddy Kennedy and Sydney Schanberg of the *New York Times* attacked O'Connor. The Massachusetts senator decried "blatant sectarian appeals" and insisted that America could not write "every moral command" into law. Perhaps realizing that the abortion controversy presented a no-win situation to Democrats, Kennedy shifted gears. Setting aside matters of evidence, logic, and relevance, Kennedy characterized the Republican Party as a haven for anti-Semites. Anyone who opposed Ferraro and abortion, Kennedy implied, was a religious bigot. (Only white conservatives could be anti-Semites. Black liberals like Jesse Jackson were sacrosanct.) Schanberg took the same route, claiming that social conservatives were "intolerant and divisive." Religious beliefs, or at least *conservative* religious beliefs, Schanberg argued, had no place in a democratic society.[44]

New York governor Mario Cuomo also entered the fray. Among other sins, Cuomo blamed the Catholic bishops for defeating the ERA and politicizing the abortion issue. Although personally opposed to abortion, Cuomo reassured fellow Catholics, elected officials in a secular society could not permit their religious beliefs to shape public policy. If the majority of Americans voted to ban abortion then Catholic politicians would be free to act upon the tenets of their faith. As members of a religious minority, however, Catholics should not impose their prolife beliefs upon others. Reagan fired back, asking, "Why do those who claim to represent the party of compassion feel no compassion whatsoever for the most helpless among us—the unborn?" Charles Colson, a Christian evangelist and former Nixon White House aide, also rejected Cuomo's reasoning: "So God's truth is binding only when ratified by a majority vote." Cuomo, Colson concluded, "reduces Christianity to a religion of personal tastes that has no place in the political arena."[45]

Ralph Reed, the executive director of the National College Republicans, had no more patience for Cuomo's abortion views. The problem with liberals like Cuomo, Reed believed, was their propensity to remain silent on moral issues so as not to be "divisive." By that logic, the abolitionists should have kept quiet about slavery. After all, the anti-slavery movement split several Protestant denominations, destroyed a political party, and set the stage for the Civil War. In truth, Cuomo feared that the abortion issue did resemble the slavery controversy. Banning abortion could lead only to religious schism, civil disorder, and the collapse of the Democratic Party. Though Cuomo regarded himself as a worthy successor to Abraham Lincoln, he more closely resembled James Buchanan—enforcing divisive laws in the vain hope of avoiding division. Archbishop O'Connor was Cuomo's John Brown.[46]

If Cuomo's and Ferraro's only critics had been the Catholic bishops and a few Republicans, they might have won the day. However, that was not the case. The Catholic Church had spent the past decade discussing the ethics of abortion with its parishioners. Many priests even led off Mass by petitioning God to eliminate "the scourge of abortion." While middle-class Catholic liberals might accept *Roe v. Wade* as the immutable law of the land, other members of the church did not. Cuomo's gubernatorial predecessor, Hugh Carey, a Catholic politician with impeccable Democratic credentials, lamented that the liberals were "gloating and gleeful that their party will kill more fetuses than the other party." Eugene McCarthy, once the darling of the Democratic Left, chided Cuomo, arguing that "abortion is a legitimate political issue and far from sectarian, since more than just Catholics oppose it." New York senator Daniel Patrick Moynihan, though a friend of the Mondale campaign, nevertheless lavished praise upon prolife activists: "Of all the groups which appeal for the attention and support of a senator from New York, the one that by far is the most broadly based in the electorate and least self-interested—save as the public confirmation of personal moral beliefs is a matter of self-interest—is the Right to Life movement."[47]

While the abortion controversy ripped apart the Democratic Party, the

GOP wrestled with gay rights. Since the advent of AIDS, sexual politics had become a matter of life and death. Between 1980 and 1984, thousands of gays and heroin addicts—as well as the recipients of blood transfusions—had contracted the lethal disease. Included among the afflicted was libertarian activist Terry Dolan, the closeted leader of the National Conservative Political Action Committee. At first, the disease was known as Gay Related Immune Deficiency. Gays, however, demanded a less "homophobic"-sounding name. (Calling it the Acquired Immunity Deficiency disease left up in the air how most people contracted the virus.) Although unprotected anal sex clearly accounted for most of the five thousand AIDS fatalities, the partisans of the Stonewall Gay Democratic Club denied that their lifestyle put them at risk. By 1984, half of San Francisco's gay population had AIDS, yet activists opposed closing the bathhouses or even posting warning signs. Only a third of the Bay Area's gays informed public health officials and sex researchers that they were using condoms and cutting back on the number of partners with whom they had anal and oral sex.[48]

Many opponents of the gay lifestyle argued that AIDS should be treated as a public health matter rather than a civil rights issue. They tended not to be too concerned if gays lost their jobs and health insurance because of their affliction. Some social conservatives hoped that the disease could be contained within the very populations that had never found favor in traditional society: heroin addicts, homosexuals, prostitutes, Broadway players, dancers, and Hollywood stars. The Reverend W. A. Criswell of the First Baptist Church of Dallas left no doubt as to where he stood on gay rights: "In our lifetime we are scoffing at the word of God . . . and opening up society and culture to the lesbian and sodomite and homosexual . . . and now we have this disastrous judgment . . . the disease and sin of AIDS." In the same vein, newspaper columnist Patrick Buchanan wrote, "The poor homosexuals. They have declared war on nature and now nature is exacting an awful retribution." Jerry Falwell, believing that homosexuality was part of a larger moral failing in America, declared that "AIDS and syphilis and all sexually transmitted diseases are God's judgment upon the total society for embracing what God has condemned: sex outside of marriage." Falwell, though, hastened to add, "I don't believe that state punishment of homosexuals provides any answer whatever. I personally believe that homosexuals should be afforded total civil rights."[49]

Other social conservatives tried to "separate the sin from the sinner," condemning the gay lifestyle but not consigning homosexuals to the pits of hell. The evangelical magazine *Christianity Today* featured stories about fundamentalist and Pentecostal ministers who "are helping gays escape from homosexual lifestyles." To these clergy, San Francisco, New York, and Washington were missionary outposts where Christians went to transform homosexuals into married, monogamous, heterosexuals. In New York, the Catholic Church and O'Connor lobbied against gay rights legislation. At the same time, however, O'Connor opened the city's Catholic hospitals to AIDS-afflicted homosexuals and drug addicts who would never be able to pay for their medical care. ("Homophobic" Catholics never received the recognition they deserved from the liberal media. One wonders how many *New York Times* reporters would have accepted a regular tithing of their salaries to cover the hospitalization costs of AIDS patients?)[50]

O'Connor's chief liberal critic, Mario Cuomo, may have talked a good game about tolerance, but his actions betrayed him. In his 1977 New York City mayoral race, as well as his successful 1982 gubernatorial bid, the Cuomo campaign had cast aspersions upon its Democratic primary opponent, Ed Koch. The governor's "unofficial" campaign slogan in both primaries was "Vote for Cuomo, Not the Homo." A bachelor who supported many homosexual causes, Koch denied that he was gay. O'Connor, who constantly crossed swords with Koch over abortion and gay rights, often had him over for dinner and genuinely enjoyed his company. Cuomo, on the other hand, was not the kind of man who would socialize with people whose politics were not pure enough for his refined intellectual tastes. The wonderful thing about being Mario Cuomo was that he never had to live up to his own exacting standards. O'Connor and Reagan were selfish, mean-spirited bigots who slandered their foes. And Koch was a homo.[51]

Where Ferraro, Cuomo, and Kennedy flung themselves into the culture wars of the eighties, Reagan remained above the fray. (Mondale had been missing in action since the Democratic convention.) Lee Atwater's electoral strategy was a simple blend of patriotism and morality—both of which made boisterous celebrations of the good life go down that much smoother. The Reagan campaign commercials said it all: "It's Morning in America." America's economy was booming—at least for those who adapted. To underscore the administration's devotion to spiritual values, Falwell, Criswell, and Texas evangelist James Robison received invitations to the Republican National Convention in Dallas. At a prayer breakfast held during the convention, Reagan observed, "The truth is, politics and morality are inseparable. And as morality's foundation is religion, religion and politics are necessarily related." Reagan's foreign policy stances were similarly laden with religious import. In 1984, Reagan had gone so far as to tell a cheering audience of Christian broadcasters that Russia was "an evil empire." Reagan, the McGovern liberals sneered, had confused himself with Obi Wan-Kenobi.[52]

Christian conservatives geared up for the '84 election. Rev. LaVerne Butler, the leader of the Kentucky Moral Majority, left little doubt as to which party God endorsed. Butler observed that the respective Democratic and Republican conventions "were as different as a sex orgy and a Sunday School picnic." Another religious conservative informed his flock that if elected president, Mondale would "turn America into Sodom and Gomorrah." Charles Colson, on the other hand, admonished his friends in the Religious Right not to get carried away with "the seductions of power":

Our well-intentioned attempts to influence government can become so entangled with a particular political agenda that it becomes our focus; our goal becomes maintaining political access. When that happens, the Gospel is held hostage to a political agenda, and we become part of the very system we were seeking to change.[53]

Few Christian conservatives heeded Colson's warning. Mondale, after all, had a long history of supporting busing, abortion on demand, and gay affirmative action. Half of the Moral Majority's members were Baptists who required no prompting to work against the Mondale-Ferraro "abortion ticket." They also did not hesitate to cite appropriate biblical verses on the social issues of the day. The Democrats were clearly not measuring up to the standards God had set down in Genesis, Exodus, Leviticus, Numbers, and Deuteronomy. (Like Orthodox Jews, Christian fundamentalists focused their attention on the morally exacting Pentateuch. Pentecostals often cited scripture from the mystical, apocalyptic books Revelation and Daniel. Catholics went for the redemption-minded New Testament Gospels. Jesus offered mankind a new deal; the God of Moses and Daniel sent infidels to their graves. One Bible—many different emphases.) Nationally, the Moral Majority registered two million new voters, dwarfing Jackson's efforts on behalf of the Democratic Party.[54]

Rev. Lamarr Moneyham, the Moral Majority's field director, paid tribute to Jackson's pioneering efforts to register churchgoers : "You know Jesse Jackson was right. He showed us the way. I am indebted to him."

Falwell went further, citing the early civil rights movement as a worthy predecessor of the Moral Majority:

I firmly believe it is a religious duty to be a good citizen, and that it is one's duty as a good citizen to participate in politics. But I can be true neither to my country or my God if I separate my religious convictions from my political views.

This is not "radical" fundamentalist theory. It is the basic belief that drove the Pilgrims to our shores—and the spirit with which the Rev. Martin Luther King, Jr., took his message of racial harmony and equality from the pulpit to the streets.[55]

Ideological differences aside, the Moral Majority and the Left shared a sense of the melodramatic. Moneyham, for example, framed the '84 election in Jacksonian end-of-the-world terms. "If the liberals gain control of the White House and the Senate in the coming election," Moneyham cried, "it will be over for free elections by 1988. Oh, we may vote in 1988, but it will be no contest, for by then the liberals will have curtailed our access to the minds of the American people." On the Left, Norman Lear, the Democratic National Committee, and the ACLU warned that Reagan's reelection would mean the abolition of civil liberties for all Americans. Concentration camps would surely follow. Judy Goldsmith of NOW, in a desperate attempt to link several recent attacks on abortion clinics to the White House, claimed that Reagan's "irresponsible and inflammatory anti-abortion, anti-women rhetoric . . . incites and encourages right-wing terrorists." The radical Christic Institute asserted that Reagan and the Religious Right were preparing for an apocalyptic clash between the United States and the Soviet Union. Even Mondale briefly resurfaced, charging Reagan, and social conservatives in general, with "moral McCarthyism."[56]

Prior to Reagan's appearance at its 1984 convention, B'nai B'rith passed a resolution condemning Christians who sought to restore prayer to the public schools. One B'nai B'rith delegate informed the *Washington Post*, "Sometimes I think [Reagan] wants to make Israel strong so that when he makes the United States into a Christian country, he can send us all over there." Brooklyn's Orthodox Jews, however, did not find Reagan's relationship with the Moral Majority to be particularly disturbing. One twenty-two-year-old Jewish woman waved aside Reagan's critics: "As for Reagan talking about Christianity, why should I care? As a Christian, he has right to speak in the context of his own values."[57]

Paradoxically, several right-wing clergy joined Lear and the ACLU in denouncing the Moral Majority. Rev. Bob Jones of South Carolina—the proprietor of the segregated Bob Jones University—objected to Falwell's recruiting efforts among Catholics and blacks. (Falwell, like Pat Robertson, was no fan of Bob Jones. Still, the Reagan administration expended great effort to defend Bob Jones University from civil rights suits. In his dealings with clergy activists, Reagan, apparently, could not distinguish the saints from the sinners.) Following in Bob Jones's footsteps, Rev. Tim LaHaye, the chair of the American Coalition for Traditional Values (ACTV), denounced Catholicism as a "false religion." When LaHaye exhorted "every Christian, every church, every Christian radio station and television station owner" to support Reagan, he meant that he wanted every *Protestant* to vote Republican.[58]

Sectarian quibbles aside, social conservatives were united behind Reagan. Further, whatever tensions existed among moralists, libertarians, and country-club Republicans did not hinder the GOP. The Mondale campaign was a different matter altogether. Taking a leaf from Carter, Mondale studiously avoided the Detroit Labor Day parade. He did not want the electorate to associate him with the decaying, crime-ridden "Murder City" even though urban areas like Detroit were his only dependable friends. Instead, Mondale headed off to New York on Labor Day, thinking that at least the city's social liberals would turn out for Ferraro. He was wrong. Ferraro and Mondale marched past mostly empty sidewalks. Small knots of AFSCME workers did show up, but many others had headed to the beach. In November, two-thirds of New York City's Italian-American voters went to Reagan. The president racked up impressive tallies in Ferraro's congressional district. Nationally, the much touted "gender gap" that NOW hoped to exploit by placing Ferraro on the ticket never materialized. Although a somewhat greater percentage of men supported Reagan than was the case for women, the president easily won the majority of the so-called women's vote.[59]

As in the '80 election, Reagan whistled Dixie without missing a note. Visiting Nashville's Grand Ole Opry, Reagan told cheering country-western music fans that the liberals would not know how to behave in such an American setting. "They'll just sing the blues," Reagan laughed. (The president intended no racial slight—though the blues was not the kind of music that Okies from Muskogee listened to on the radio.) In contrast to Reagan, Mondale did not enjoy himself in the Southland. During a Democratic rally in Elvis Presley's hometown of Tupelo, Mississippi, a teenage girl questioned Mondale's morality: "You said you cared about the human race, you care about the people and stuff. Well what about abortion? That's killing people?" Mondale winced while the audience cheered the teen. A University of Mississippi student characterized the Democratic Party platform as "pro-abortion, pro-gay rights, and anti-religion," and then told Mondale, "Those may represent America's values, but they don't represent Mississippi's values. Please tell us how you can come to Mississippi as a good Christian and represent such perversions as this?" Mondale pointed out that Reagan was not a paragon of virtue either, but not even a resurrected Elvis could have persuaded Mississippians to give Mondale a break.[60]

Mondale's Tupelo ordeal was repeated throughout Dixie. Southern Democratic leaders anxiously informed the campaign that their constituents were asking them why their party "is against God and religion." In November, Reagan won almost three-quarters of the southern-white vote. (Yet again, nine of every ten southern and northern blacks voted Democratic. Indeed, one-third of Mondale's *entire vote came from blacks.*) Meanwhile, Texas, once a bulwark of the Democratic Party, sent Republican Dick Armey to Congress. A vigorous champion of the free market and bitter foe of the New Deal, Armey advocated the abolition of food stamps and Social Security. He received enormous assistance from Christian activists who had their own reasons for wanting to dismantle Big Government. (Limiting the writ of the federal government, they hoped, would send abortion rights the way of welfare.) Since 1980, 400,000 new Republican voters had appeared in Texas. Many Texas Republicans identified themselves as social conservatives.[61]

The Democrats had little more success in the blue-collar precincts of the North. Reagan carried the ethnic, working-class suburbs of Parma, Ohio, and Macomb, Michigan, 67 percent to 33 percent. In 1960, the Democrats had swept those communities by the same margins. Nationally, the percentage of white workers who identified themselves as Democrats had plummeted by fifteen points since 1980. Younger workers, who were prone to voting Republican, regarded unions as barriers to their employment. Meanwhile, blue-collar social conservatives resented the alliances Kirkland had forged with lifestyle liberals. The majority of Catholics and *working-class women* polled after the election cited an improved economy, social issues, and the presence of Ferraro on the Democratic ticket, as reasons that they voted for Reagan. A retired brewery worker from Texas summed up the good feelings Reagan engendered among blue-collar Democrats: "He really isn't like a Republican. He's more like an American."[62]

During the fall campaign Lane Kirkland had taken heart when western Pennsylvania steelworkers greeted Vice President Bush with jeers. The very fact that Bush had made an appearance in a Democratic stronghold, however, should have alarmed Kirkland. Reagan's campaign staffers knew that socially conservative Catholics were trending toward their man. As for the steelworkers who heckled Bush, they represented no one other than themselves. Kirkland was not alone in misreading the situation. One prominent political historian utterly failed to grasp recent social trends. The Pennsylvania professor happily informed his graduate students that organized labor, allied with a fully mobilized Sierra Club, would sweep Mondale to victory. Surely, the professor continued, voters knew that Reagan was too old and incompetent to be reelected.[63]

In a development that no Democrat anticipated, Mondale relived the McGovern debacle of 1972. The GOP won back seventeen House seats, not enough to exercise informal control of the chamber but still sufficient to keep Tip O'Neill on his guard. Reagan captured nearly two-thirds of the youth vote. Like their grandfatherly president, the twentysomethings of the eighties tended to be optimists on-the-make. Not by accident was Reagan's advertising agency the same one that came up with the "Pepsi Generation" campaign. Feel good, be cool, drink Pepsi, mock the Boomers, and vote for Reagan. The Democrats could not win. Even the angry blue-collar anthems that Bruce Springsteen envisioned as attacks on contemporary conservatism became Reagan theme songs: "Born in the U. S. A., Kick butt on the Commies someday."[64]

Overall, Mondale lost every constituency in the country except for blacks, Reform Jews, union members, and elite journalists. (As in 1980, the media were overwhelmingly against Reagan. On the television networks anti-Reagan coverage outdistanced pro-Reagan coverage by a factor of ten to one.) In sharp contrast to the 1980 election, secular Jews closed ranks behind the Democratic candidate, though Reagan scored well with Orthodox Jews. Mondale secured just 41 percent of the popular vote and carried only the District of Columbia and Minnesota. At that, Mondale barely took his home state, beating Reagan by just under four thousand votes out of two million cast. Mondale, who had spent little time in Minnesota since Carter's defeat, reacted too late to the organizing efforts of religious conservatives. Great numbers of prolifers had moved into both parties. Minnesota's Democratic delegation at the '84 convention contained a large segment of moral traditionalists. They vigorously objected to putting Ferraro on the ticket. When all was said and done,

Mondale's own folks back home were not particularly enthusiastic supporters.[65]

Although Reagan racked up an impressive tally among regular churchgoers, they tended not to be Moral Majoritarians. Most were neither followers nor necessarily admirers of Falwell, Criswell, and LaHaye. The moral traditionalists who voted for Reagan regarded themselves as being in the mainstream of American life. They believed in the separation of church and state and were not inclined to impose their religious beliefs on others. However, such voters, many of whom were once reliable Democrats, concluded that social liberals desired more than the separation of church and state. Mondale's allies wanted to ban God. *New Republic* essayist and Mondale booster Charles Krauthammer understood the situation perfectly. According to Krauthammer there was a "secular tendency" in liberal politics that doomed the Democrats to electoral defeat:

The secularists are the grinches who try to steal Christmas crèches. It is the ACLU that sued Pawtucket, Rhode Island, charging that the city's forty-year tradition of sponsoring a public nativity display at Christmas time violated the First Amendment prohibition against establishment of religion. . . . But the goal of the secularists is not simply to extirpate Christian symbolism from American public life. Their nemesis is religion. Religion is to be kept private. Any public manifestation is to be fought, from school prayer (even a moment of silence, because of its religious connotations) to the national motto (in 1970 the government was sued for "In God We Trust," and won in the Supreme Court).[66]

Republicans could hardly be blamed for exploiting the political opportunities presented to them by the ACLU, NOW, NARAL, and Ferraro. That is not to say, though, that the Reagan campaign could have been a little more circumspect. Reagan was on firm, albeit controversial, ground when he said things like "There is no question that many well-intentioned Great Society–type programs contributed to family breakups, welfare dependency, and a large increase in births out of wedlock." But when Reagan told religious conservatives that if they "sometimes got a busy signal when they were praying, it was just me in there ahead [of them]," some might have thought him to be transparently insincere. Further, while Reagan might have been justified in thinking that God spared him from an assassin in 1981 so that he could do the Lord's work, his efforts to redeem America had been pretty minimal.[67]

Ralph Reed thought that Reagan's support for a constitutional amendment to legalize public school prayer was nothing but a "sop" to religious conservatives. Reagan knew that the amendment would never get out of

Congress, and he did not mind that fact at all. As Reed later recounted, when young Republicans like himself had gone to Washington in 1981, "We viewed ourselves as the mirror image of the leaders of the New Left of the sixties. We saw ourselves as . . . entrepreneurs who were building a new generational consciousness that was pro-Reagan, conservative [and] very aggressive, very creative." Three years later, finding life in the political fast lane too spiritually shallow, Reed had quit drinking and joined an evangelical church. Was genuine moral reform too much to ask of the contemporary American political system? Upset with the "lip service" White House staffers were giving to "family values," Reed headed off to graduate school. God might not be at Emory University, but He certainly was not in Washington.[68]

CHAPTER SIX

"A Thousand Points of Light"

1988

Lt. Colonel Oliver North knew that God wanted him to arm the anti-Communist freedom fighters in Nicaragua and secure the release of American hostages in Lebanon. God, however, works in mysterious ways; He required Iran's help to free the prisoners. If the Iranians demanded sophisticated weapons in exchange for their assistance, so be it. North let the infidels pay top dollar for their arms and then transferred the profits to an account he set up to finance the contras. The White House would not mind. After all, Attorney General Ed Meese championed the contras and often pointed out that "Nicaragua is just as close to Miami, San Antonio, San Diego, and Tucson as those cities are to Washington." Communist Latinos threatened the military security of the Sunbelt, yet Yankee liberals did nothing. Besides, what was so wrong with the Sunbelt's having its own foreign policy? Effete New Englanders had given America World War I and the CIA. It only seemed fair that virile southerners have their chance. North would have to work covertly since he believed congressional Democrats to be "treasonous" allies of Communist Nicaragua. Moreover, if the public found out that the National Security Agency was trading arms for hostages, a terrible political fallout would result.[1]

In 1986, North's dealings with Iran and Nicaragua became public knowledge. God told North to erase his computer disks and shred all his papers pertaining to the Iran-Contra affair. Unfortunately, God forgot to mention that the agency's computer system automatically made backup copies of North's incriminating E-mail. North refused to answer his critics in the media and Congress, prompting Reagan to call him "a national hero." Later, North spun a tale that implicated Reagan and, by extension, Vice President George Bush. Some White House staffers insisted that Reagan was too inattentive to have been involved in North's schemes. The Reagan they knew relied on his cabinet to run the government. North was obviously lying. Other staffers depicted a president who never missed a detail—with *one* notable exception. *Saturday Night Live* offered its own take on the Reagan White House. Phil Hartman's Reagan was a smiling, shallow glad-hander who posed for pictures with children. But when reporters left the Oval Office, Reagan became super president—fluent in Arabic, able to calculate international currency conversions off the top of his head, and handle military logistics for the contras. Many conservatives wanted North to run for the Senate. Others wished North would "fall on his sword and not be heard from again."[2]

The tide appeared to be against Reagan. In the 1986 congressional elections, Republicans lost control of the Senate. Five southern Republicans, including Jeremiah Denton of Alabama, were cast out of office. Although the budding Iran-Contra scandal hurt the GOP, a large black turnout in the South helped the Democrats. Barely 40 percent of Southern whites voted Democratic. On the other hand, the southern Senate races were tight. Denton lost by only 7,000 votes. Moreover, the Dixie Democrats were staunch social conservatives. The only thing they had in common with northern liberals was their sensitivity to the black vote. If there were no clear civil rights issues involved in the matters that came before the Senate, southern Democrats sided with Republicans. (Denton's victorious challenger, Richard Shelby, later joined the Republican Party. When Shelby switched parties after the '94 congressional elections, barely a third of southern whites supported the Democrats. Bushels of black ballots could not make up for the wholesale defection of whites.)[3]

Unhappily for the White House, the first important matter that came before the Democratic Senate concerned civil rights. In 1987, Reagan nominated Robert Bork to the Supreme Court. Norman Lear of the People for the American Way led the charge against Reagan's nominee. In all, Lear's group, the ACLU, the National Abortion Rights Action League, AFSCME, and the NAACP spent $15 million on television and newspaper advertising. Lear sought to persuade the public that Bork was the personification of evil in judge's robes. Never in American history had a well-financed lobby intervened so effectively in a Supreme Court nomination.[4]

Syndicated columnist Garry Wills also slammed Bork, taking exception to the jurist's views on abortion and pornography. According to Wills, banning abortion was unfair since the burden of sacrifice rested entirely upon the mother. The fetus had no career and income to give up and bore no responsibilities to society. Unable to reciprocate, the fetus could not claim more rights than the mother. The fetus, therefore, had no right to life. In the same vein, Wills argued that Bork's criticism of pornography was nothing less than moral totalitarianism. Pornography, Wills insisted, caused no societal damage. Religious beliefs should not shape public policy—unless, of course, the issue was the death penalty, and not abortion or pornography. Then Catholic liberals like Wills and New York governor Mario Cuomo claimed that their religious beliefs did not permit them to endorse capital punishment. Echoing Wills, Teddy Kennedy opined: "Robert Bork's America is a land in which women would be forced into back-alley abortions, blacks would sit at segregated lunch counters, rogue police could break down citizens' doors in midnight raids." (And, perhaps, drunken senators who drove off bridges and allowed their female passengers to drown would go to jail. Perhaps not.)[5]

Bork's nomination was doomed. He had no money to fight Lear and, worse, the Left had caught conservatives flat-footed. Moreover, Bork's views on every single political issue of the past thirty years were well known. Although he might have been within his legal rights to have fired the Watergate special prosecutor, politically it stank. Worse, Bork had gone the extra mile in the Ford administration to combat federally funded abortions. (Most men in his position would have feted the prolifers and then betrayed them.) Likewise, Bork's arguments against the civil rights legislation of the early sixties came back to haunt him. Although he had clearly eschewed racist arguments in making a case for the preservation of state's rights and free association, intellectual subtleties did not play well with the civil rights establishment.[6]

The Senate's southern Democrats could easily dismiss Norman Lear. They could not, however, afford to ignore their angry black constituents. EEOC chair Clarence Thomas and Congressman Jack Kemp pointed out that conservatives had only themselves to blame for Bork's defeat. Intentionally or not, the Right fostered distrust among blacks and fair-minded whites. Thomas, for instance, had long chastised conservative supporters of the segregated Bob Jones University. Kemp agreed, concluding:

Bork stood for the idea that the courts should interpret the law, not legislate. Americans believe this, but also believe it matters whether the law being faithfully interpreted is right or wrong. And, until conservatives gain a more consistent reputation as defenders of equal opportunity (not the liberals' racial quotas), they will be in a poor position to allay fears that they don't want to, or are unable to, correct any legal anomalies that might crop up.[7]

Racial politics and his paper trail aside, Bork simply did not come across well at the televised Senate hearings. He made no effort to disguise his contempt for liberals. Granted, listening to Kennedy talk about legal ethics would have taxed anyone's patience. So too, Senate Judiciary Committee chair Joe Biden of Delaware did not impress Bork. Delaware's "Golden Boy" senator had just been forced to drop out of the Democratic presidential primaries. Not only had he plagiarized his stump speeches, he created make-believe working-class roots. Then it came out that Biden, who liked to portray himself as a scholar, had plagiarized a law school paper. Moreover, if student draft deferments had been strictly based on academic achievement, Biden would have been thrown aboard the first military transport to Saigon. Certainly Biden and Kennedy merited Bork's disdain. Practical politics, though, demanded that Bork not show his true feelings lest he alienate the other senators and look arrogant to the viewers at home. As the president of DePauw University often said, "The world is run by 'C' students." (DePauw's faculty cynics recalled these words when Senator Dan Quayle, an academically undistinguished alumnus, received an honorary degree.)[8]

With Reagan's political magic evaporating, disaster loomed. On October 19, 1987, the stock market took a plunge, wiping out $560 billion in assets. Although the market recovered, the crash unnerved a lot of Americans. In the course of racking up a trillion-dollar debt the Reagan administration borrowed money from foreigners and savvy American investors. Flushed with cash and collecting interest payments from the U.S. Treasury, Germans purchased RCA, Japanese bought Sony, Australians acquired Twentieth Century Fox, and British Petroleum took over Standard Oil of Ohio. Eighty percent of the profits generated by foreign-controlled corporations went back to Japan and Europe. American executives and government bondholders did well, with the number of billionaires and millionaires doubling during the Reagan boom. In 1979, CEOs made twenty-nine times what their assembly-line workers earned. Nine years later, in real dollars, CEOs were making *ninety-three* times what they paid their blue-collar employees. Overall, a quarter of the labor force—mostly those born after 1960—worked part-time. "Temps" received low wages and no health-care benefits. Meanwhile senior citizens received $400 billion annually in entitlements. Their wealth came from the soaring payroll taxes deducted from the earnings of struggling Baby Busters. Many Americans told pollsters that they thought their future prospects were bleak.[9]

CEOs were not shy about disclaiming any responsibility for the support of local communities, their employees, and charities. U.S. Steel's David Roderick remarked, "There is a feeling in this country—wrongly so— that corporations are to step up and fill the void." (U.S. Steel abandoned many of its mill operations, choosing to buy an oil company instead of investing in its basic product and labor force.) Other CEOs complained that they wanted Reagan to deregulate business, not exhort them to increase their charitable giving. Libertarians meanwhile praised the "creative destruction" unleashed by the free market. They contended that government should eliminate its social welfare functions and step out of the way of private enterprise. Indeed, the federal deficit could be abolished if entitlements were eliminated. As for the tens of thousands of unemployed steelworkers, they should stop looking to government and corporate-sponsored charities for succor. Such people needed to move to the booming Sunbelt, abandon the communities of their childhood, and learn to be self-reliant.[10]

Some voices on the Right dissented from this new Social Darwinism. *Christianity Today* decried an economy that forced mothers to work long hours for little return while their children were sent to day care. Free marketers, Christian conservatives warned, threatened the traditional family and fostered a materialistic, Godless culture. The reporters for *Christianity Today* offered an insightful observation on "Supply-Side Morality." To wit, a nation that tolerated unemployment and poverty could never truly prosper, economically or spiritually:

Unemployment is dangerous to all because it undermines self-reliance, weakens individual character, and keeps the individual from fully participating in the maintenance of society as a whole. We have lost sight of this simple truth in our own self-obsessions. The dignity of the individual and the morality of an economic program are intimately related, and thus the critical importance of supplying meaningful jobs for all people.[11]

Peggy Noonan, who had penned Reagan's best speeches on the meaning of self-sacrifice, wished Americans were less acquisitive and more willing to volunteer their time to charity. She also expressed her annoyance with corporations that discarded their hard-working employees in order to enhance the bottom line. Noonan had especially harsh words for her former employer, CBS:

What the accountants and their bosses did not understand is that when you "waste" money by keeping a great man who has passed his prime on the payroll years after his daily contribution has ended, the widest impact is not on the great man but on the people who work around him.

They realize the company cares about them in a careless world, they decide to care about the company. And so they come up with their share of the bargain and . . . decide, as the correspondent Bruce Dunning did, to fight his way onto the last plane out of Da Nang [in 1975], where he huddled on the floor and kept his tape recorder rolling and reported live as the plane barely made it up, as desperate people fell from the wheels. He didn't stop talking, and you could hear the terror of what was happening through the terror of his shaking voice. There has never been a better moment in broadcast journalism. Dunning was later demoted.

CBS saved money, but it spent loyalty as if it was going out of style, which perhaps it is.[12]

Noonan was no happier with the country-club Republicans. She later wrote that GOP liberals and the "paleo-conservatives" had not welcomed blacks and ethnics who had left the New Deal Church. (Paleo-conservatives—so-called because their beliefs were to be found in the bedrock far beneath the New Deal—castigated "impostors" like Noonan, believing that such GOP converts had retained their Democratic sensibilities.) Noonan railed at the Ivy League Republicans whenever they reviled religious conservatives. To the blue bloods, Gary Bauer and other Christian staffers in the White House were "trailer-park" religious nuts. Nancy Reagan, Noonan noted in 1990, was no better. The first lady had begged her Beverly Hills friends to persuade the president "to stop talking about abortion. It's turning everybody off. He already has those people, it does him no good." Noonan readily admitted that she was no saint herself. However, when she had used off-color language around Reagan's blue-blood staffers it was not because she took any pleasure in swearing; rather, she swore because "that's how Protestants who went to Harvard think the working class talks."[13]

Paul Weyrich concurred with Noonan. He argued that the country clubbers—"this elitist group that has controlled the Republican party"—felt threatened by religious idealists. Weyrich fretted that liberal Republicans regarded religious conservatives in the same way Democrats viewed blacks—as a bloc of reliable voters to be "trotted out every four years" and then ignored until the next election. Conservative activist Gary Jarmin concurred, observing that "your three-martini Episcopalians just don't have a lot in common with a tee-totaling Baptist. They don't move and live and work in the same circles." A Christian Voice member from

Virginia put it in more bluntly: "They despise these unwashed low-income Christians coming in singing their hymns and trying to take the party away." Charles Colson sadly concluded that the liberal, or "pragmatic," Republicans in the White House had won the struggle for the soul of the GOP. "Despite unprecedented access to the Oval Office," Colson wrote in 1988, "most items on the evangelical social agenda have been either defeated or shelved." The courts, the universities, and the media remained firmly in the hands of social liberals and their GOP collaborators.[14]

Bob Tyrrell of the *American Spectator* pointed out that if social conservatives failed to advance their agenda, it was not entirely the fault of Reagan's "preppie" advisors. The Moral Majority, Tyrrell maintained, had failed to reach out to libertarians and make sufficient ideological compromises. Tyrrell may have been right. On the other hand, there were libertarians who wanted nothing to do with religious conservatives. As a lark, P. J. O'Rourke had vacationed at Heritage USA, a Pentecostal resort in South Carolina operated by evangelist Jim Bakker. After observing that he and his girlfriend were "wearing the only natural fibers for 2,300 acres in any direction," O'Rourke held forth on the kind of people who attended prolife rallies, spoke in tongues, and made pilgrimages to Heritage USA:

You know what you've got here? This is white trash behaving itself—the only thing in the world worse than white trash *not* behaving itself. These people aren't having any fun. They should join the Klan. They'd be better off. They could hoot and holler and what-not. The Klan doesn't do all that much really bad stuff anymore because there are too many FBI double agents in it. And if these folks joined the Klan, they could smoke and drink again. Plus, they'd get to wear something halfway decent, like an all-cotton bed sheet.[15]

Setting aside the feud that had simmered among libertarians, social conservatives, and preppies since 1981, there was the small matter of finding an heir to Ronald Reagan. Even disillusioned social conservatives believed that sympathetic rhetoric and legislative inaction were preferable to the alternative—the election of an activist social liberal. Of course, among some conservatives there were Republican presidential candidates less popular than Walter Mondale. Weyrich and Newt Gingrich—the libertarian-leaning representative from Georgia—emphatically agreed on one point: Vice President George Bush was an inarticulate preppie nightmare. Free marketers thought Bush was just another tax-and-spend liberal, and a few Christian conservatives saw him as a prolife backslider. The vice president's tongue-tied pronouncements did not enhance his appeal to conservatives, nor did they impress the general public. Bush had once angrily insisted that he was a fervent conservative. "But," he continued, "I'm not a nut about it." (Among friends, Bush had this to say about religious conservatives: "F--- 'em. . . . You can't satisfy those people.") At an official tour of Auschwitz, Bush expressed a thought that no doubt came to the mind of many a reflective Yalie: "Boy, they were big on crematoriums, weren't they?"[16]

Some social conservatives had other reasons to find Bush lacking. After eight years of Republican rule, the moral health of America was no better than it had been when Reagan and Bush arrived in Washington. Indeed, the dominant secular culture corrupted the devout as well as the un-churched. According to a national survey of fundamentalist teenagers, a quarter had engaged in sexual intercourse. More than half of these Christian youths reported that they had gleaned their knowledge of sex from Hollywood. Sex-filled films were not the only reason teens became spiritually tarnished. According to *Christianity Today,* heavy-metal rock bands and their corporate sponsors—notably CBS Records—placed teens under a "Satanic spell." Bands like "Judas Priest" brainwashed young males into killing their families and themselves. Similarly, Billy Idol, Madonna, and MTV videos promoted sexual promiscuity and violence. Social conservatives also aimed barbs at Dr. Ruth Westheimer, a television talk-show host, author, and self-styled "sexpert." *Christianity Today* editorialized that "Dr. Ruth writing a book on the *ethics* of sex is a little like Jack the Ripper writing a book on the ethics of population control."[17]

While rock music and "Dr. Ruth" corrupted the morals of young Americans, gays moved into the sanctuary of the church. Conservatives in the United Methodist Church contested the religious propriety of or-daining gay clergy. As Methodist ministers and bishops began dying from AIDS, the question of gay rights was raised more frequently at church conventions. Year after year the United Methodist Church experienced a widening cultural rift between its morally traditional, small-town members and its cosmopolitan campus and seminary constituencies. The Evangelical Lutheran Church had no such problem. Gays from the church's Berkeley seminary were readily ordained. In Chicago, gay priests and lesbian nuns lobbied on behalf of a homosexual rights ordinance. Cardinal Bernardin gingerly explained his opposition to the proposed law:

Four principles shape the Catholic Church's teaching about homosexuality and gay/lesbian rights:

1. Some people, through no fault of their own, have a homosexual tendency or attraction. The tendency is not immoral or sinful.
2. There is no place for arbitrary discrimination and prejudice against a person because of sexual tendency. All people have a right to decent employment, housing, and public accommodations.
3. However, homosexual activity and its advocacy, as distinguished from homosexual tendency, is objectively morally wrong.
4. Parents have a right to keep their children free during their formative years of any person(s) or influence(s) that would advocate homosexual practice.[18]

At Georgetown University, the federal judiciary ruled, the Jesuits had to provide funds to gay student organizations. Since federal money was involved in some student activities, the courts decided that they had the legal authority to set aside religious doctrine. In a case involving Pennsylvania's Grove City College, however, the Supreme Court concluded that only educational programs directly receiving federal funds fell under Washington's writ. Senator Kennedy quickly put forward the Civil Rights Restoration Act of 1988. Kennedy's law, passed over Reagan's veto, asserted that if students received federal grants and loans, then Washington had jurisdiction over *all* college functions. The only alternative universities had was to follow the example of Michigan's libertarian-minded Hillsdale College and not certify students for federal grants or guaranteed loans. Hillsdale found other sources of funding for its students. However, not every college could go to the Coors family and ask for a check. Grove City's president warned that no employer or college was safe: "Today the federal bureaucracy can reach into virtually any grassroots entity." Since "public policies are increasingly at odds with Biblical values," he concluded, "Christians must segregate themselves from secular society."[19]

Although Reagan had promised fundamentalists and Pentecostals that he would save the American legal system from the forces of social liberalism, many judges continued to jump whenever the ACLU threatened a lawsuit. According to the ACLU, any mention of religion in the public schools was unconstitutional. Conservative Protestants and Catholics complained that the public schools, in their effort to maintain the separation of church and state, were promoting anti-Christian attitudes. Liberals curtly dismissed anyone critical of the ACLU and secular education. If their children were enrolled in a public school—a *big* if—white-collar professionals brooked no carping from the less enlightened. As one upper-middle-class Protestant said in explaining the political and educational controversies taking place in his community, "You have to understand the neighborhood changed when the whites moved out and the Irish Catholics moved in."[20]

Not surprisingly, religious academies continued to flourish. So too did home schooling. In the late seventies thirteen thousand children had been taught at home. By the end of the eighties more than one million children had been taken out of the public school system and educated at home. *Christianity Today* reported that one benefit of home schooling was that the "children appeared to be less peer-oriented than those in [public] schools." Rev. Mike Farris, the president of the Washington state chapter of the Moral Majority, championed home schooling. He called secular education "a Godless monstrosity" and exhorted "every born-again Christian in America to take their children out of public schools." (The Baptist minister and his wife taught their nine children at home.) Farris also explained why the public schools had an obligation to censor immoral materials: "Just as I don't think a black kid should be forced to read Mark Twain because of the word 'nigger,' religious Christians shouldn't be forced to read books offensive to them." Among the books Farris found objectionable were *The Wonderful Wizard of Oz* and *The Diary of Anne Frank*. The former "condoned the practice of witchcraft"; the latter "promoted the belief that all paths lead to God." (By knocking Anne Frank, Farris unintentionally made himself appear anti-Semitic. Conservative Jews, locked in a power struggle with their liberal counterparts, did not need Christian "friends" like Farris.)[21]

In 1988, the federal judiciary dealt a blow to social conservatives. Five years before, Larry Flynt's *Hustler* magazine had published a parody advertisement which suggested a drunken Jerry Falwell having sex with his mother in an outhouse. Falwell filed a defamation suit against Flynt. The clergyman won his suit in the lower courts. Reagan's Supreme Court, however, ruled in favor of Flynt. The justices claimed that Flynt's free-speech rights outweighed Falwell's right to protect his family and reputation. To Falwell, the issue was not the First Amendment; rather, the controversy was about pornography, which was "no longer a thing restricted to back-alley book shops and sordid movie houses. Now pornography has thrust its ugly head into our everyday lives and is multiplying like a filthy plague." The stakes in the lawsuit were enormous. By the eighties pornography was an $8 billion-a-year industry whose influence reached deep into American society. The directors of the *Playboy* Foundation, for example, gave $150,000 to the ACLU, and several of them sat on the board of its Illinois chapter. *Playboy* also shared the wealth with Planned Parenthood and NARAL. Closing down the pornography industry, religious conservatives believed, would go far to "defund" the Left. That consideration made Falwell's legal defeat all the more disappointing.[22]

Only after much pleading had Ed Meese established the Presidential Commission on Pornography. The eleven members of the commission held hearings in 1985 and 1986. Unlike Nixon's 1970 Commission on Pornography, Reagan's group roundly condemned smut. James Dobson, the president of Focus on the Family and a member of the Reagan commission, insisted that *Hustler, Playboy,* and *Penthouse* gave aid and comfort to pedophiles. Commission witnesses, a number of whom were ministers and professors from religious colleges, claimed that pornography stimulated sexual promiscuity and was responsible for two million cases of gonorrhea in 1984. If the connection between pornography and social diseases appeared less than firm, one Calvin College political scientist raised a good point. In response to liberals who claimed that smut did not influence social behavior, the professor said, "If they are to be consistent [they] have to argue that good literature and ennobling art also have no effect"—an admission Garry Wills and other liberal fans of the National Endowment for the Arts seemed unlikely to make.[23]

Dobson, as well as Cal Thomas of the Moral Majority, complained that Meese had given the commission little time and money to expose the pornography industry. They regarded Reagan's pornography commission as little more than sop. Frustrated, religious conservatives took their war against smut to the streets. Church groups in 150 cities picketed Revco, 7-Eleven, and other stores that sold *Playboy* and *Penthouse*. At first, a 7-Eleven spokesman defended the store's policy, arguing, "We are not in the position to make moral judgments for our customers." The picketing, however, took its toll on convenience-store sales. Several thousand Revco and 7-Eleven shops stopped carrying pornographic magazines. In Minneapolis, Indianapolis, and Fort Wayne, Catholics, fundamentalists, and Pentecostals joined forces to picket sex shops and pass anti-smut ordinances. Fort Wayne's homosexuals rallied to the defense of their favorite video store and staged counterpicketing at a Pentecostal church. One homosexual protester wore a nun's costume, seemingly unaware of the difference between Catholics and Pentecostals.[24]

Angered by the anti-smut crusade, the ACLU and Representative Bar-

ney Frank of Brookline, Massachussetts, asserted that religious conservatives wanted to stifle free speech. An openly gay politician, Frank was
particularly irate, having no use for "homophobic" social conservatives.
Frank's lover had operated a male prostitution ring out of Frank's Washington apartment. Brookline's tolerant voters did not object to the behavior of their congressman though the Religious Right had a field day.
Cardinal Bernardin defended the anti-pornography movement: "We are
against censorship, but we are also against obscenity, which is not protected by the Constitution." Further, the cardinal told Frank and the
ACLU, pornography was "morally evil because it undermines human
dignity."[25]

While smut opponents mobilized, a segment of the prolife movement
was becoming more militant. Having lost faith in the political system,
Randall Terry, a blue-collar Christian, founded Operation Rescue in 1987.
Terry's group, modeled after King's Southern Christian Leadership Conference, staged nonviolent protests at abortion clinics. From Atlanta to
Los Angeles, Operation Rescue blockaded abortion facilities and its volunteers went to jail by the thousands. Taking a leaf from the Left, Terry
engaged in visually stunning political theater. He was the first prolife
protester to carry an aborted fetus around with him for the benefit of the
television news cameras. He also made no apologies for stirring up controversy and provoking confrontation:

Every major political change in our society has been preceded by social upheaval.
. . . We've been working on a political solution for fifteen years, and it has failed.
Our ranks are growing because people are realizing we have missed the boat.
Instead of trying to fill the halls of Congress, we should have been filling the
abortion clinics with people who want to stop the killing.[26]

Abortion sympathizers in the media decried Terry's tactics, mocked his
humble origins, and ridiculed his religious fervor. Little did they understand that their disdainful attitude enhanced Terry's credibility among
prolifers who otherwise would have been put off by his tactics. Falwell,
Pat Robertson, and Atlanta Archbishop Eugene Marino endorsed Operation Rescue, although other prolife clergy kept Terry at arm's length.
Typically, liberals missed the most striking feature about Operation Rescue. Here was a situation in which conservatives revolted against the very
government they had brought to power. It was almost as if radical abolitionists had elected Abraham Lincoln president and then turned against
him when they realized he would end slavery only if no other options
remained open. (Not by accident had Falwell compared Operation Rescue

to the Underground Railroad.) For social conservatives, a question hung in the air: Was it time to run one of their own for president, to separate themselves from what they considered to be morally illegitimate authority, or to give the GOP another chance?[27]

Pat Robertson gave his answer to the GOP regulars: he entered the Republican presidential primaries. At first, George Bush and the media laughed off the Robertson challenge. How could anyone take seriously a candidate who, on his own television show, asked God to divert a hurricane from CBN's headquarters? What Republican country clubbers did not appreciate was that a person who could comfortably pray on television while several million people watched was not afraid to act on his convictions. Such a person could attract hundreds of thousands of committed supporters whose moral beliefs weighed more heavily than any loyalty to Reagan's heir-apparent. Even while the Bush campaign ridiculed Robertson, the Virginian had taken control of the GOP in Alaska, Hawaii, Nevada, and Washington. Robertson also organized loyalists in Iowa, Michigan, and Oklahoma. To Bush's amazement, Robertson placed ahead of him in the Iowa caucuses and won Michigan. Only a great deal of backroom dealing with Michigan GOP leaders rescued Bush's fortunes. The county GOP chairs were in Bush's corner and they determined how many delegates each candidate received. Robertson inevitably failed to receive his fair share.[28]

In Michigan, prolife Catholic laity and black Pentecostal clergy energized Robertson's campaign. The GOP legislators who had fallen in behind Bush did not know what was happening—an understandable development since few of Robertson's followers had previously participated in Republican Party functions. They were the kinds of folks who avoided the caucuses and primaries of either party and then voted Republican in the general election. Robertson was leading an insurgency in Michigan, one that implicitly rebuked both major parties:

If principled citizens were in positions of governmental authority, would we have pornography running unchecked in our communities? Would God be banned from our public schools? . . . Would criminals appear to have more rights than their victims? Would homosexuality be applauded as a viable alternative lifestyle and its expression taught to our children and protected by law? Would the traditional Judeo-Christian view of the family be subjected to ridicule and attack?[29]

GOP leaders were irate. George Bush's son Neil likened the factory workers and shopkeepers who supported Robertson to "cockroaches issuing out from underneath the baseboard." Michigan state Senate leader

John Engler castigated religious conservatives for placing their moral agenda ahead of the party's electoral interests. Engler subsequently changed his tune when he needed the help of social conservatives to win the 1990 gubernatorial election. Jack Kemp joined the GOP chorus, grousing that "Robertson has a very negative conservatism. If you heard him speak, it would sound like Reagan lost in 1980." (This was, of course, precisely the point. Reagan had won and had not made much of a difference so far as abortion, drug abuse, and illegitimacy were concerned.) After Bush secured the presidential nomination, Kemp assured reporters that Robertson "is as welcome to our party as Jesse Jackson is to the Democratic Party." Kemp kept a straight face.[30]

In the South one thousand cheering Amway distributors followed Bush from Atlanta to the sea. Amway wanted southern voters and the national media to think that Bush was gaining momentum. Senator Goldwater helped the cause by giving Bush his blessing. Falwell, Ed McAteer of the Religious Roundtable, and W. A. Criswell followed Goldwater's lead. They believed that Bush's nomination was inevitable—and desirable. Few of the fourteen million Southern Baptists supported Robertson. Among the leaders of the National Association of Evangelicals, just 12 percent preferred Robertson to Bush. South Carolina, a bellwether state of Dixie conservatism, went decisively to Bush. Across Dixie, two-thirds of the South's voters informed pollsters that they would never vote for Robertson. His charismatic faith did not sit well with many Southern Baptists. Moreover, Robertson had a streak of patrician paternalism that upset the GOP's anti–Big Government legions. On the campaign trail Robertson had said that he wanted to bring a message of hope to "the steelworkers in Pittsburgh and the autoworkers in Detroit, and the inner-city black people. I cared about them and I wanted to see a government that would make life better for them." This was evidence enough to the conservative Washington *Times* that Robertson was a dangerous populist who did not represent "mainline Republican thought."[31]

On *The 700 Club* Robertson found it easy to mobilize his viewers in the crusade against evil. CBN sowed the seeds for a growing social movement, wisely avoiding sectarian controversies and emphasizing moral issues that united Baptists, Catholics, Orthodox Jews, and Pentecostals. What worked in the CBN studio, however, did not translate well out on the hustings. Wherever Robertson went, trouble followed. Hoping to demonstrate his commitment for justice to all citizens, regardless of race or creed, Robertson announced his presidential candidacy in the New

York slum where he had once preached—Bedford-Stuyvesant. Homosexuals and Norman Lear's People for the American Way disrupted the event. Orthodox Jews who showed up to support Robertson and condemn homosexuality were cursed and called "Nazis." In turn, Robertson referred to his foes as "anti-Christian atheists." He also contended that liberal Jews like Lear and the founders of ACT-UP, a militant homosexual lobby group, were "intent on diminishing Christian influence in the public life of America." Secular Jews branded Robertson an anti-Semite; Orthodox Jews cheered him.[32]

Social conservatives like Robertson blamed gays for the AIDS epidemic and saw them as a driving force behind the spread of pornography. Responding to liberals who wanted to spend more federal funds to combat AIDS, CBN's leader said:

You can't throw money at a disease and think it's going to go away. That isn't the way to solve it. That's not the problem. There's only so much research you can get out of money. After a while, the answer's got to be in somebody's common sense. Why do we have AIDS? Ninety-two percent of the AIDS cases are male homosexuals or intravenous drug users. All these people have to do is stop. If we want to stop AIDS today all we have to do is practice abstinence and stop shooting intravenous drugs into our arms.[33]

Although Robertson correctly pointed out that actions had consequences, politically he did his cause little good. In the abstract most Americans believed people should be held accountable for their behavior. Consequently, violent criminals must be sent to prison, not therapy. On the other hand, most Americans are compassionate folks who do not like to see anyone suffer. A deft politician had to convey compassion *and* hold people responsible for actions that hurt themselves and others. Robertson was not that kind of politician. Moralists make politics exciting and force entrenched elites to address important social problems. They do not, however, ascend to the White House. Lincoln talked the talk but never walked the walk. Even Franklin Roosevelt, who castigated the money changers in the temple of democracy, did not threaten to impoverish the DuPonts. Tax till they screamed, you bet; destroy, not hardly.

Other developments also hurt Robertson. Just as he launched his presidential campaign, Jim Bakker and Jimmy Swaggart brought shame to the Pentecostal faithful. Bakker, who once worked for Robertson, had built his own religious television empire, the PTL ("Praise the Lord") Club. In some months Bakker solicited $10 million in donations from his working-class viewers. Bakker preached "seed faith," or "prosperity gospel." If you sent money to PTL, God would reward you ten times over. Bakker gave himself a $600,000 a year salary, as well as several yachts and mansions. Even his doghouse had air conditioning. Along the way Bakker paid a church secretary $265,000 to keep quiet about their affair. The Assemblies of God "minister"—Bakker was never ordained—also had homosexual encounters. Although homosexuality offended Pentecostal sensibilities, the IRS was more concerned that Bakker had used the PTL Club as a front to avoid paying $56 million in taxes. Bush, who had solicited Bakker's endorsement and had three staffers working for the PTL Ministry, maintained an air of shock. As with the Iran-Contra affair, Bush had been "out of the loop." (Or, as Bush impersonator Dana Carvey said, "I was loopless.")[34]

Another Bush partisan, Jimmy Swaggart, soon found himself in hot water for having had intercourse with prostitutes. A crusader against pornography, Swaggart enjoyed kinky sex. He did not, however, approve of rock 'n' roll. Swaggart often preached that rock music was inspired by Satan. Swaggart's cousin, Jerry Lee Lewis, emphatically concurred, saying that he *hoped* his songs won souls for the Anti-Christ. By the time Swaggart's clandestine sex life came to light, he was a wealthy man with a television audience that numbered in the millions. Although many Pentecostals forgave him, one cousin was less charitable. Commenting on a neighbor who had fallen into disfavor, she said: "This poor little Assemblies of God man was arrested over here. He raped his four children and the animals that he had there—two sons, two daughters, two dogs, and they're lookin' at the parakeet. But the real tragedy is that he sent his last five dollars to Jimmy Swaggart."[35]

Robertson's campaign suffered in the wake of the Swaggart and PTL scandals. Journalists and academics mercilessly ridiculed the Christian Right. Sometimes their witticisms were funny: "What do the letters PTL stand for? Pass the Loot." More commonly, their comments were laced with the kinds of sneers conservatives expected from Ivy League professors. Televangelists were "bizarre" con artists whose number-one charity was themselves. That was unfair. Robertson dedicated millions of dollars to Operation Blessing, a charitable organization that worked with fifteen thousand congregations to provide drug counseling, medical care, and other kinds of assistance to the poor. That fact, however, got lost. Donations to CBN, as well as to Falwell's *Old Time Gospel Hour*, fell precipitously. (Even before the PTL scandal broke, conservative clergy had been experiencing difficulties. Falwell disbanded the Moral Majority in 1986 so that he could devote more time to improving the financial position of the Thomas Road Baptist Church. Meanwhile, Timothy LaHaye's American Coalition for Traditional Values was wracked by scandal in '86 when reporters revealed that the cultist Sun Myung Moon was a major sponsor.) Through 1987 and 1988, CBN lost $16 million. A Gallup poll that asked people whom they would least like to have as neighbors showed born-again Christians topping the list. Episcopalian and Presbyterian clergy, who had spent the eighties watching angrily as their flocks defected to Pentecostal and fundamentalist churches, were overjoyed at their rivals' misfortunes.[36]

Flailing about helplessly, Robertson questioned whether Bush had anything to do with the IRS investigation of the PTL Club and the exposure of Bakker's and Swaggart's sexual adventures. Robertson also had to be gnashing his teeth at just how unfair the whole situation was: *Bakker and Swaggart were Bush supporters yet their peccadilloes redounded to Robertson's discredit.* To country-club Republicans Robertson's gripes were further evidence of his conspiratorial mind-set, galloping paranoia, and unjustified feelings of persecution. After all, would George Bush, a former director of the CIA and political protégé of Richard Nixon, really reach into a bag of dirty tricks to derail Robertson's presidential campaign? Only a ranting lunatic could ever think of such a thing about "Poppy Bush." When you "prep" with a man, and later share the same caddie, you can vouch for his character.[37]

While Bush handily won the Republican presidential nomination, the Democrats put on a remarkable show. Representative Richard Gephardt of Missouri had compiled an impressive legislative record as a fiscal and moral conservative. He voted against extending the ratification deadline of the ERA, opposed raising the minimum wage, decried busing, ridiculed the Consumer Protection Agency, and championed a constitutional ban on abortion. The Missouri Democrat even called Reagan "a disappointment to those in Congress who represent constituencies for whom . . . social issues represent the government's resolve to reverse the misguided social trends of the sixties and seventies." Then, just before the Democratic presidential primaries, and after attending several of Pamela Harriman's parties, Gephardt repudiated every conservative position he had ever taken. It seemed that he had only been funning the rubes back home in Missouri. When his rivals contrasted the 1988 Gephardt to the 1984 Gephardt, voters walked away from him in disgust.[38]

Senator Al Gore, Jr., of Tennessee fared no better. A lackluster preppie who had entered politics only to save his father's Senate seat, Gore billed himself as a true son of the South. (Al Gore, Sr., had thought that filming a campaign commercial with junior in uniform and astride a horse would help his own 1970 reelection prospects. He was wrong, and Al junior thus became one of the few rich kids to go to Vietnam.) Hoping to recreate the magic of Jimmy Carter's '76 primary run, young Gore moved simultaneously to the left and to the right. Prior to the 1988 primaries, Gore's wife, Tipper, had orchestrated a congressional hearing that decried obscene rock lyrics. Once Gore entered the primaries, he went to Los Angeles to inform music industry executives that he would be delighted to take their campaign contributions. Besides, Tipper had been once been a member of an all-girl rock 'n' roll band, and they both really dug The Grateful Dead. While debating Governor Michael Dukakis, Gore accused him of being soft on Communism and derided him for allowing violent criminals out on weekend furloughs so that they could commit rape. The Massachusetts governor, Gore insisted, was a McGovern liberal trying to pass himself off as a moderate Democrat. Although Gore floundered, with Jesse Jackson's black voters depriving him of a southern sweep, the senator had drafted the GOP playbook that Lee Atwater would use against Dukakis.[39]

Colorado senator Gary Hart, who had been leading Dukakis in party polls, self-destructed. A man who bragged about having an "open marriage," with his wife remaining safely tucked away in Colorado while he lived in Washington, Senator Hart had an enormous libido. Daring the tabloids and scandal-hungry journalists to follow him around, Hart was caught with his pants down and in the arms of a young lady. Her name was Donna Rice, a woman who was nearly half his age and whose previous claim to fame had been an appearance on the stylish television series *Miami Vice*.[40]

A photographer aboard the good ship "Monkey Business" captured Rice and Hart in tight embrace as they cruised the Caribbean and discussed foreign affairs. Hart defended his right to commit adultery, contending that just because he lied to the press about his personal life, cheated on his wife, and accepted cruises from campaign supporters, he was not unworthy to be president. Besides, Hart said self-righteously, unlike Reagan he had never been divorced. Repeating their 1980 performance with Teddy Kennedy, liberal columnists wrote that a candidate's character was irrelevant. Hendrick Hertzberg of the *New Republic* cried that Hart was a victim of "Islamic justice"; *Washington Post* columnist

Richard Cohen felt the senator had been victimized by "sexual McCarthyism." Pulitzer Prize–winning historian James MacGregor Burns—a Kennedy family friend—denounced a press that used "old-fashioned, puritanical" standards to judge a candidate's character. Few Democratic primary voters heeded the voices of the liberal elite. One Iowa Democrat put it simply, "If [Hart] can't be true to his family, what reason do we have to think he would use proper judgment about anything else?" Even Hart's Yuppie followers wrote him off.[41]

Once again, Jesse Jackson entered the Democratic primaries. To stave off charges of anti-Semitism, Jackson surrounded himself with Jewish advisors. Gloria Steinem, Robert Borosage of the leftist Institute for Policy Studies, and Barney Frank's sister, Ann Lewis, climbed aboard the Jackson campaign. (As Orthodox Jews and Zionists asserted, one was more likely to find Jackson's Jewish supporters at a PLO fund-raiser than attending temple.) Jackie Jackson urged her husband not to make too many concessions to "the Jews." He heeded her advice. Farrakhan remained an important ally, and the campaign's black staffers did not hesitate to express their hatred of Jews. (In the Jackson campaign "Jew" had always been shorthand for "white.") Jackson's Pennsylvania campaign chair begged him to stop addressing working-class whites and to focus on black Philadelphia. He also warned Jackson to get rid of a "Jewish lesbian" on his staff and blamed "the Jews" for wrecking Jackson's electoral prospects in New York. Even though secular Jewish reporters for the *Village Voice* and the *Nation* endorsed Jackson, New York's religious Jews wanted nothing to do with him. Growing increasingly testy, Jackson verbally and physically abused his white staffers, hurling obscenities at them and roughly shoving them out of his way. The white liberals who worked for Jackson put up with this treatment because they viewed him as a social democrat who would launch another Great Society, this time without a Vietnam War. One just had to separate the message from the messenger.[42]

To head off media attacks, Jackson's supporters launched a preemptive strike. Anyone who criticized Jackson, according to the Congressional Black Caucus, was a racist. Liberal white journalists, not wishing to appear racist, gave Jackson the most favorable coverage of any primary candidate, Democrat or Republican. The media made much of Jackson's landslide win in South Carolina, neglecting to mention that most of the state's whites were voting in the Republican primary. So, too, in Michigan the media marveled at his ability to mobilize blacks, Hispanics, and whites. Jackson mainly owed his Michigan victory, however, to blacks. The whites who voted for him lived in the affluent, liberal precincts of Ann Arbor and East Lansing. (Nationally, a quarter of Jackson's voters had graduate degrees.) He also picked up considerable support from Michigan's Arab-American voters. White ethnics and workers were missing from Jackson's political equation, even though he billed himself as the populist champion of blue-collar America. After the '88 election Jackson admitted that he thought it pointless to reconstruct the New Deal coalition. Southern whites and northern ethnics were forever lost to the GOP—and good riddance. Jackson dreamed of building a new Democratic majority with Arabs, blacks, feminists, gays, and Hispanics—a rainbow coalition.[43]

When all was said and done, Jackson's political crusade never seriously addressed the moral dimensions of poverty. Since 1970 the black under-class had increased by a factor of three. No matter how extensive the economic and educational opportunities for blacks were, there remained an intractable, violent underclass. White leftists, the very people who voted for Jackson and filled his campaign coffers, persisted in their deni-gration of the traditional family. They ignored evidence that showed that the children of intact families had far lower rates of incarceration and welfare dependency. While Jackson criticized illegitimacy on the cam-paign trail, his white benefactors insisted that heterosexual marriage was a superfluous relic from a bygone, patriarchal order. Inner-city teenagers seemingly concurred. Several unwed mothers happily informed a CBS reporter that welfare enabled them to avoid marriage. They also observed that if welfare were abolished they would have to stop making babies.[44]

Liberals painted a world in which racist whites routinely attacked mi-norities. Black assaults on whites seldom received much attention. Indeed, it was a federal crime for a white bigot to attack a black, but racially motivated assaults on whites were not considered civil rights violations. In 1987, a young black woman from New York, Tawana Brawley, attracted widespread sympathy when she claimed to have been assaulted by white police officers. She had lied, but black militants and white radicals insisted that Brawley was a typical victim of "institutionalized racism." The statis-tics on violent crime contradicted their claims. In general, half of the victims of black crime were white; barely 2 percent of blacks were harmed in any way by whites.[45]

In the eighties more crimes than ever were committed by drug addicts. Eighty-four percent of the criminals arrested in New York in 1988, for instance, were stoned. Overall, between 1979 and 1988 New York State saw drug-related crimes increase by 500 percent. Nearly nine of every ten

Washington blacks—most of them junkies—had a police record; 42 percent were either in jail or awaiting trial on any given day. Drug usage, and particularly the smoking of crack, soared in the nation's capital. The drug subculture in Washington was so pervasive that its residents spent more money on crack than on food or drink. Crack was such an addictive drug that female junkies sold their bodies over and over again. Sexually transmitted diseases soared. In Reagan's second term the rate of syphilis infection in Washington rose 90 percent. Nationally, blacks were fifty times more likely than whites to have contracted a social disease.[46]

Conservatives had long characterized the decades of the sixties as an era of escalating crime and galloping moral decay. However, it was in the age of Reagan that American cities became virtually uninhabitable. Violent gangs went about their business unchecked by the judicial system. Meanwhile crack and heroin showered the streets. America had become more violent, more dangerous, and more divided racially and economically. Reagan's promises to combat drugs and crime were not kept. Ed Meese was left with one rejoinder to his critics: at least drug usage among *white suburbanites* declined in the eighties. Most white Americans could agree, though, that inner-city blacks had the right not to be gunned down by drug dealers. Federal and state law enforcement agencies seemed to have abandoned the urban poor to dope-dealing predators.

In 1987, Detroit recorded 686 homicides. The city's black academics and politicians blamed whites, not gangs, for the "genocide." Irresponsibly, Mayor Coleman Young opposed all calls to disarm the city's gangs. His reasons were astounding: "I'll be damned if I'm going to let them [white police officers] collect guns in the city of Detroit while we're surrounded by hostile suburbs and the whole rest of the state who have guns, where you have vigilantes, practicing Ku Klux Klan in the wilderness with automatic weapons." In Young's world, white suburban parents—after they dropped their children off for soccer practice—careered through the city blasting away at blacks. Equally deluded, Arthur Johnson, the leader of the Detroit NAACP and a Wayne State University vice president, claimed that Detroit would never become a better place to live until white racism was eradicated. White racism apparently forced poor blacks to kill one another, bear children out of wedlock, and turn twelve hundred buildings every year into bombed-out crack houses.[47]

The Urban League agreed with Young and Johnson. Black victims of white racism could be saved only by affirmative action. Civil rights leaders never explained how preferential admission to Berkeley would reduce

Detroit's homicide rate. They also refused to engage in a honest discussion of affirmative action. Instead, black activists charged that Reagan had undermined civil rights enforcement and declared that quotas represented a measure of justice for poor minorities. The NAACP, the Urban League, and the Congressional Black Caucus were wrong on both counts. First, the Reagan administration had done nothing to abolish quotas. Second, in the case of Berkeley and other elite universities, the group that experienced the most inconvenience by the creation of admissions quotas were not "privileged" whites but the children of poor Asian immigrants. If not for the quotas, Asian Americans would have constituted half, instead of a quarter, of Berkeley's student body. A fifth of the Asian Americans denied admission to Berkeley had perfect grade point averages and outstanding Scholastic Aptitude Test scores. The majority of middle-class blacks who were admitted in their place had less admirable academic records. Thousands flunked out or sought sanctuary in black studies programs.[48]

Theologian Anthony Evans, a member of the National Black Evangelical Association, summed up the dilemma ordinary, law-abiding minorities faced every election year: "We are sociologically Democratic, but morally Republican. In my opinion, a vote for Jesse Jackson is a vote for a very immoral platform. But to vote Republican is to vote for a sociologically insensitive platform." Even the GOP's sensitive white Christians thought that the preservation of the family, abortion, and the spread of pornography were more important matters than improving race relations. On the other hand, Bishop J. O. Patterson, the president of the four-million-member Church of God in Christ, the second largest black denomination in America, offered a way out of the dilemma Evans posed. Patterson endorsed Pat Robertson. Not knowing what to make of blacks who did not support Jackson and not wishing to deal with national polling data that showed most minorities to be far more socially conservative than the civil rights leadership, the secular media remained silent.[49]

Racial reconciliation and social responsibility, Peggy Noonan believed, had to be at the heart of Bush's '88 campaign. In the Republican convention speech she wrote for Bush, Noonan envisioned a candidate who would reject "the careless effulgence of the Reagan era" and exhort Americans to embrace the ethos of voluntarism. All Americans, black and white, middle class and poor, could join together, becoming "a thousand points of light" that would illuminate the land. The Catholic social thought that infused Noonan's writing, however, did not undergird Bush's general election strategy. "Saint Peggy" never had a chance against

Lee Atwater, "The Republican Prince of Darkness." Atwater, fearful that the Reagan Democrats might return home in 1988, launched a full-scale cultural war against Bush's Democratic opponent. In 1984, liberals had griped that Reagan made them look like flag-burning, criminal-coddling, atheistic radicals. By the time Atwater finished with Michael Dukakis, the Democrats were mourning Reagan's restraint and diplomacy.[50]

Dukakis's victories in the Democratic presidential primaries were hardly a result of his abilities as a campaigner. Affluent Greek-Americans had showered Dukakis with millions of dollars, enabling him to pay for an army of campaign workers and spend a fortune on advertising. His primary rivals never caught up to him in the money race. Then luck played a role. Biden and Hart, whose passion made them far more attractive than the bland, technocratic Dukakis, fell apart. The man Dukakis had thought would be a problem, Al Gore, fared miserably. Gore had counted on winning the nomination by sweeping the southern primaries. Thanks to the black vote, however, Gore could not carry his own region. Only Jackson remained. Dukakis staffers banked on the fact that Democratic primary voters, liberal though they were, would not think a black man, *this* black man, was electable. (Many Jews flatly refused to vote for Jackson.) As the last white guy standing, Dukakis won the nomination by default. Atwater could not believe his good fortune:

The happiest I was during the entire 1988 campaign was the weekend after Dukakis' nomination when the papers and television had all these photographs of him sitting around in a wrought-iron leisure chair with all his Brookline friends on Martha's Vineyard with a brand new pair of deck shoes, his little khakis, and his starched blue shirt. I knew we had this guy's ass. They don't understand that swing voters are antielite and antieffete.[51]

The Bush campaign, having been tipped off by Al Gore, looked into Dukakis's record as an enforcer of law and order. Atwater hit pay dirt. In 1974, Willie Horton had brutally murdered a teenage gas-station attendant. He was sentenced to life in prison without any chance of parole. Twelve years later, under a program administered by Massachusetts and supported by Governor Dukakis, Horton received a weekend furlough from prison. Horton did not return. Instead, he went to Maryland, where he raped a woman and knifed her husband. Horton was black, all of his victims were white. In the aftermath of the Horton incident, Dukakis refused to change the furlough policy and informed the Maryland couple that he would not meet with them—let alone offer them an apology. Only an irate state legislature, over Dukakis's vehement objections, halted the practice of giving weekend passes to convicted murderers. Dukakis later blamed his Republican predecessors for having created the weekend furlough policy in the first place. Dukakis, however, could have changed the policy at any time. The governor did not do so because he believed in prisoner rehabilitation. According to Dukakis, weekend passes were one way to make criminals feel better about themselves, socialize them, and thereby cure their violent natures.[52]

Atwater insisted that he did not know Horton was black. Moreover, Atwater claimed that he studiously avoided turning Dukakis's law-and-order record into a racial issue. Liberal critics and black activists were not mollified. Sidney Blumenthal of the *New Republic* charged that one Bush campaign advertisement deliberately showed black and Hispanic prisoners leaving jail through a revolving door. This was patently false. During the shooting of the commercial at a Utah prison, Bush's staffers were horrified to see that half of the actual felons being filmed were black. They immediately replaced the minority prisoners with white actors—most of whom were young Mormon Republicans. Despite this gesture, Democratic convention chair Ron Brown, an ally of Jesse Jackson's, argued that no *white* politician had the right to bring up the crime problem since it was implicitly racist. Few Democrats bothered to point out that Brown's reasoning itself was racist. Brown also did not appear to be bothered by the fact that half of the victims of violent crime committed by blacks were black. Similarly, Dukakis's campaign manager, Susan Estrich, insisted that any discussion of black rapists was racist. By what intellectual avenue the Harvard Law School professor came to that conclusion she did not reveal. Estrich had, however, been raped by a black man and admitted that she felt uncomfortable around minorities. Hers was a case of classic liberal guilt.[53]

Bush hammered away at Dukakis. Before long it looked as if Willie Horton had become Dukakis's running mate. Atwater also went after the governor for vetoing a state bill to allow students to recite the Pledge of Allegiance. Dukakis asserted that the bill was unconstitutional. He knew, however, that it was up to the courts to make such a ruling. Dukakis made matters worse for himself by vigorously denouncing the death penalty, even though 79 percent of the public favored executing killers. Amazingly, on national television, in response to a question about whether or not he would support the death penalty for someone who raped and killed his own wife—a softball question that was virtually an invitation to Dukakis to shed his passionless, cold-fish image—Dukakis flatly replied that he could see no legal basis for such action. Many Reagan Democrats, who had been abandoning Bush, were shocked. Piling mistake upon mistake, Dukakis also boasted of his membership in the ACLU, but only after weeks of running from the "L" word (liberal) label with which Bush was successfully tagging him. After observing decades of political activism in the courts, many Americans must have thought that the initials ACLU stood for the American *Criminal* Liberties Union. Atwater's private polling persuaded him that while most voters did not want legislation to regulate private morality—much to the chagrin of the Religious Right— they supported increased government action to curb crime and drugs. The Bush campaign would give voters what they wanted.[54]

Dukakis thought he had several factors in his favor. First, he took credit for the "Massachusetts Economic Miracle." As textile mills went out of business, museums and high-tech boutiques took their place. Thousands of new, good-paying state-government and software engineering jobs sprung up around Boston. Dukakis boasted that even McDonald's workers made $10 an hour. There were a few problems with this picture. To begin with, if McDonald's workers made $10 an hour, their pay scale was relative to the high cost of living. One-room apartments in Boston rented for $1,200 a month. Moreover, much of the state's economic boom depended upon federal defense spending. Dukakis condemned the Reagan arms race yet rejoiced in the prosperity that came with "Star Wars" research grants. Sadly for the governor, the bottom fell out of the Massachusetts economy in the summer of '88. The state's finances were in disarray and the deficit rose to $1 billion.[55]

Beyond competency, Dukakis had claimed to be an exemplar of honesty. Conversely, it followed, the Republicans were dishonest. "Fish," Dukakis said in reference to the Reagan White House, "rot from the head down." At the Democratic National Convention and on the campaign trail, Dukakis and his supporters tried to make Iran-Contra and the purported ethical lapses among Reagan's staffers an issue. As in 1984, the Democrats failed to make their case. Part of their difficulty might have been with the party's messengers. On television Teddy Kennedy had mocked Bush for his involvement with the Iran-Contra scandal, repeatedly saying, "Where was George?" The question was entirely fair but Kennedy should not have been the person asking it.[56]

Failing everything else, Dukakis tried to divert attention from himself and force voters to take a close look at Bush's running mate, Senator Dan Quayle. The heir to Eugene Pulliam's billion-dollar publishing empire,

Quayle had been kept away from the day-to-day operations of the business. Like Gore and Kennedy, Quayle's fate was to enter politics and live on an allowance. Although the Pulliams were ardent supporters of the Vietnam War, young Quayle used his family contacts to get him into the Indiana National Guard. Fewer than 2 percent of the 400,000 men lucky enough to get into a Guard unit were sent to Vietnam. Dukakis, believing that turnabout was fair play, wanted to make Quayle's patriotism a matter of public debate. Bush, after all, had been calling his own patriotism into question every time he mentioned Dukakis's veto of the Pledge of Allegiance bill and posed for colorful pictures at American flag factories. (Country-western star Loretta Lynn, who campaigned for the vice president, brought out into the open what Bush had been insinuating. She wanted to know what kind of American had a moniker like Dukakis: "Why, I can't even pronounce his name!")[57]

Quayle was not a popular choice among Republicans. Indeed, party leaders thought Bush was joking whenever he mentioned Quayle's name as a possible vice-presidential candidate. Bob Tyrrell wrote off Quayle as an ingrate when he said he preferred the liberal *New Republic* to the conservative *American Spectator*. Illinois congressman Henry Hyde did not regard Quayle as a reliable ally in the prolife movement. Hyde told reporters that he was "underwhelmed" by Bush's choice. The Indianapolis *Star* and the Arizona *Republic*, both owned by the Pulliam family, chided Quayle's decision to avoid the Vietnam War and questioned his fitness for office. (With Eugene Pulliam's passing, his board of directors allowed for more editorial discretion than had once been the norm.) Quayle's military record, however, did not play much of a role in the election. Quayle, after all, was just the vice-presidential candidate and, as wits pointed out, if an assassin ever got Bush, the Secret Service had orders to shoot him.[58]

There was a more important reason that Quayle did not have to answer for his actions. Sixty percent of his peers had never served in the military. More Boomer voters were sympathetic to draft avoidance than not. Besides, the Democrats could not really take the high ground. Although Democratic vice-presidential candidate Lloyd Bentsen had fought in World War II, his sons sat out the Vietnam conflict in the Texas National Guard. (The same was true for the Bush boys. With so many sons of millionaires in its ranks, the Texas Guard was more exclusive than the Newport Yacht Club.) Even Dukakis, it should be remembered, had held onto a college student deferment until the Korean War had ended; then he did his compulsory military service. Cynical voters did not expect Boomer politicians to have ever placed their lives at risk. Quayle admitted—and Arkansas governor Bill Clinton concurred—that "from a political point of view, it looks better on a resume to have served in Vietnam." Better, but not necessary. There were seventy-six million Boomers in the electorate. Just two million had gone to Indochina. In contrast to Boomers, Baby Busters were more critical of the Quayles and Clintons. Boomer *voters,* however, far outnumbered Baby Buster voters. As for World War II vets, they were either dying off or, if alive and kicking, unlikely to criticize any Boomer politician who advocated increasing their Social Security payments.[59]

Heading into the final days of the fall campaign, there appeared to be no way Dukakis could win. Despite the efforts of Bush's socially liberal followers to move the GOP away from hard-line opposition to gay rights and abortion, conservatives simply could not bring themselves to vote for Dukakis. Prolife bishops from Hartford and New York, ignoring Cardinals Bernardin's and O'Connor's calls to stand a little more apart from politics in this election, charged that Democrats had "abandoned the Catholic Church." Unable to treat with respect those people whose moral values informed their politics, Senator John Glenn of Ohio responded with innuendo: "The last thing we need is the Gospels of Matthew, Mark, Luke, and John rewritten by Meese, Bakker, Swaggart, and Falwell." Given Glenn's attitudes, and the studiously secular air Dukakis maintained, it was not surprising that social conservatives expected the worst from Democrats. One California Pentecostal who resented the way in which Bush had treated Robertson still found Bush to be the lesser of two evils:

Real born-again Christians don't vote Democratic—if they read. They're not going to put a guy in there that's against Christianity.

There's no way I [can] vote for Dukakis and be a Christian. The guy doesn't believe in saluting the flag, he believes in abortion. He believes in taxpayers paying the bill, the government picking up the tab for abortion. I don't go for his releasing these here guys on a lifetime sentence for the weekend. That guy'd never make a president we want.[60]

Jesse Jackson gave the electorate another reason to distrust Dukakis and write him off as a spineless politician. Dukakis had never warmed to Jackson, in part because the governor did not believe there was any room in politics for passionate preachers—liberal or conservative. Additionally, Jackson reminded Dukakis of the backroom-dealing, on-the-make Irish politicians who plagued him back in Massachusetts. Moreover, Dukakis did not like talking about racial issues. During the bitter Boston busing controversy of the seventies Dukakis took no position one way or the other. Dukakis was no bigot. He may have even occasionally waved to the black maids who commuted from Roxbury to Brookline four days a week. That was all well and good, but Jimmy Carter, Mario Cuomo, and Tip O'Neill ganged up on Dukakis and told him he had to make some concessions to Jackson. Dukakis promised more federal money for the Rust-belt cities and pledged his support for affirmative action.[61]

Southern Democrats were outraged. As Virginia senator Chuck Robb, a founder of the centrist Democratic Leadership Council, said, the party should no longer appease its black militants. Indeed, government could not do much to help blacks since they had created many of their own problems. "While racial discrimination has by no means vanished from our society," Robb asserted, "it's time to shift the primary focus from racism—the traditional enemy without—to self-defeating patterns of behavior—the new enemy within." Al Gore and Bill Clinton agreed with Robb. Gore seemingly had little use for liberals who pandered to Jackson, and Clinton dismissed Dukakis as a hopeless Yuppie. Dukakis, southern Democrats complained, did not understand the aspirations of decent, hard-working white people.[62]

Paradoxically, though Dukakis annoyed southern Democrats, he failed to appease Jackson. Throughout the Democratic convention and into the general election campaign, Jackson bad-mouthed Dukakis. He even cast Dukakis in the role of an exploitative Mississippi planter: "It is too much to expect that I will go out in the field and be the champion vote-picker and bale them up and bring them back to the big house and get a reward of thanks." Jackson's words had their intended result. Black voter turnout fell by as much as ten percentage points, costing the Democrats dearly in the South and the northern industrial states. It is interesting that before the Democratic convention Dukakis had led Bush in the public opinion polls by ten points or more. That is, Dukakis decisively led Bush everywhere but the South. In Dixie, Bush retained a considerable lead over Dukakis. When Dixie's ballots were counted, Bush defeated the Democratic nominee by eighteen points—nearly three times his margin of victory in the northern states. Dukakis's advisors had been urging him since the spring to write off the South, but the governor doggedly continued to campaign there. Few southern whites would vote for Dukakis, and many blacks were planning to stay home on election day.[63]

Although the media predictably lined up against the Republicans, this time the flagships of the liberal press declined to endorse the Democratic candidate. Martin Peretz, the publisher of the *New Republic*, pithily observed that "to know Dukakis—to know him even from afar—is to dislike him." The *Washington Post* did not consider Dukakis worthy of its approval, mostly because he had repeatedly denied that he was a liberal. Rather, he was a "progressive," a Reagan Democrat if you will. In truth, Dukakis was a social liberal whose economic policies tended toward the conservative. Dukakis, like Gary Hart, thought that by repudiating the economic tenets of the New Deal, while embracing abortion, he could resurrect the Democratic majority. Working-class voters were not buying what Dukakis had to sell. Once again, the Republican presidential nominee won the blue-collar vote. In Pennsylvania, Dukakis basically told unemployed steelworkers to get a life and then threatened to take their guns. Sixty percent of Pennsylvania's adult males were gun owners—many belonged to the National Rifle Association. Dukakis must have never seen the movie *The Deer Hunter*; if he had, he was so deracinated that he could not understand the almost spiritual allure hunting had for blue-collar ethnics. The governor paid dearly for his alienation of workers, ethnics, and hunters. Bush carried Pennsylvania, as well as Ohio and Michigan.[64]

Dukakis managed to win ten states—though only New York and Massachusetts offered him a nice pot of electoral votes. He improved upon Mondale's showing in 1984—no great achievement. Dukakis ran better than Mondale had with Boomers, middle-class retirees, and single women. He decisively lost Baby Busters and married mothers. Although Bush experienced some slippage in support from fundamentalists and Pentecostals—ten percentage points from Reagan's '84 tally—they did not defect to Dukakis. Such religious conservatives simply followed the example of their black brethren and stayed home. The Democrats retained control of the House and Senate. Their actual share of the raw vote, however, gave them barely a two-percentage-point margin over the Republicans. Overall, 45 percent of the voters split their tickets, the highest proportion since 1948. The Republican lock on the White House remained safe. Congressional Democrats, on the other hand, could not breathe easy. Their control of the House and Senate was weak. A moody electorate might subsequently swing to the right.[65]

George Bush had won because he was not Michael Dukakis. In 1980 and 1984, Reagan had waved the flag and successfully combined economic and cultural issues. Bush tried to perform the same magic in '88, but his was a soulless, cynical campaign. At least Reagan believed that abortion was morally wrong, even if he was not going to go out of his way to push for a constitutional ban on the practice. Bush simply recited whatever catchy phrase Atwater placed in front of him. As political issues, Willie Horton and the Pledge of Allegiance did not last a day beyond the presidential election. Law and order, and patriotism were disposable campaign tactics that had no place in Bush's ideological makeup. And, so far as Bush's ideology went, he believed in being president. Lee Atwater, who would shortly die from a brain tumor, ruefully summed up his own political life, "You can acquire all you want and still feel empty." Little could Atwater know that he had also written the epitaph for the Bush presidency.[66]

CHAPTER SEVEN

"Godspeak"

1992

"The liberation of Kuwait has begun." With those words the Bush administration launched a one-hundred-hour ground war against the Iraqi army that occupied Kuwait. Since the summer of 1990, when Saddam Hussein invaded oil-rich Kuwait, the Left had snapped at Bush's heels. Jesse Jackson and essayist Barbara Ehrenreich condemned the American military buildup in Saudi Arabia. As Ehrenreich argued, "I'm more worried in the long run about the belligerence of George Bush than of Saddam Hussein." When America and its allies commenced bombing Iraq in January 1991, the minuscule campus antiwar movement became excited. In Ames, a few dozen demonstrators from Iowa State University gathered downtown. One student radical summed up what she saw as the connection between Bush's domestic and foreign policies. "The same government that persecutes Saddam Hussein," she argued, "persecutes me." It seemed that white racisthomophobic America would not give legal recognition to her lesbian marriage. No one listening to the young activist pointed out that if given the opportunity, Hussein would execute people like her.[1]

Conservatives have often said that the student militants of the sixties became the tenured radicals of the nineties. There is much truth in that contention. Academic activists openly expressed their hope that protest against the Persian Gulf War would spark a sixties-style revolt. Theirs was an undying faith that some Boomers proclaimed on the T-shirts they wore: "The Nineties Will Make the Sixties Look Like the Fifties." (To which cynics replied, "The Nineties Will Make the Sixties Seem Like Thirty Years Ago.") On a number of campuses, administrators forbade students from selling anti-Hussein T-shirts. Such T-shirts were racist.

Looking about at a reactionary, imperialistic America, Wisconsin chancellor Donna Shalala proclaimed: "The university is institutionally racist. American society is racist and sexist. Covert racism is just as bad today as overt racism was thirty years ago." Fortunately, enlightened academics offered solutions to combat American racism and colonialism: speech codes, multicultural curriculums, and greater hiring and admissions quotas. If leftists could not win at the ballot box, and failed to stymie Bush's foreign policy, at least they had the College of Arts and Letters. With 40 percent of all faculty members working part-time, underemployed Baby Busters wondered why senior professors did not focus their attention on more immediate problems.[2]

In many ways the academic Left and President Bush had a lot in common. Both had no understanding of the American people. Most Americans could laugh at the well-paid white professors who railed against oppression. Bush, on the other hand, was not so funny. Although America triumphed in the Persian Gulf, the celebrations over Hussein's defeat were short-lived. (The fall of the Soviet Empire in 1989 did not even occasion a victory parade.) Bush waxed happily along with a 91 percent public approval rating in the immediate aftermath of Hussein's defeat. However, there was no depth to his support. Bush boasted that America had learned its "lesson" from Vietnam; we were now prepared for a full-scale war. The president, though, failed to grasp the most important lesson Vietnam had to teach. A failed foreign policy can cause no end of political grief. Conversely, a successful foreign policy can do a president little long-term good. Americans expect a winning foreign policy as a matter of course. Further, domestic affairs are almost always more important to voters than diplomatic triumphs. Presidents and professors may care about Saddam Hussein; ordinary Americans worry about making their mortgage payments.[3]

Paul Weyrich warned fellow conservatives that victory in the Persian Gulf would not help Bush with voters. Indeed, three-quarters of the electorate in 1991 believed that the nation was on the wrong track. Voters were on to something. Crime, unemployment, and taxes continued to mount. While the population of decaying industrial centers from New Haven to Milwaukee declined, violent crime and robberies rose. In the case of New Haven, robbery had increased by 10,000 percent since the sixties. Poorly financed and understaffed urban police departments could not cope with crime. Suburban communities and businesses understandably lost patience with municipal, county, and state law enforcement agencies. By the end of Bush's term 1.5 million private security guards were in place to do what government could not: maintain order.[4]

The recession that began in 1990 worsened every successive month. Nationally, the unemployment rate stood at 7 percent. In contrast to the '82 recession, white-collar workers were hit hardest. Those born after 1960 made up two-thirds of the unemployed, even though they accounted for just 17 percent of the work force. Even the Baby Busters who retained their jobs or found new employment did not tend to fare well. While the incomes of senior citizens grew in the eighties and nineties, Baby Busters suffered a 27 percent loss in wages. Additionally, they were two times more likely to be underemployed than Boomers. Employers from Boeing to Greyhound—with union collaboration—established a two-tier wage system, paying Baby Busters 40 percent less than what they gave Boomers for the same work. It did not matter if the Baby Buster was a meat cutter at Kroger's or a recent Ph.D. who may have gotten a rare tenure-track job. The wage scale punished the young. Baby Busters found themselves discriminated against by the unions and by the very academics who were so intent upon promoting social justice in America. Merit had no place in higher education and the union shop.[5]

As had been true in the eighties, unions blamed unfair Japanese competition and the GOP for undermining their clout in the labor market. The UAW alone spent $20 million on advertising to attack its Japanese and Republican tormentors. (In Latrobe, Pennsylvania, a UAW local raised its public profile by imploring young people to demolish a Honda Civic.) Labor bosses sought to persuade younger workers that they should join a union, have mandatory dues deducted from their paychecks, and accept the imposition of a discriminatory wage scale. Rustbelt corporations joined labor's chorus against Bush and the Japanese. Desperate to appease Lee Iacocca, a charismatic Chrysler executive and possible presidential hopeful, Bush brought the Rustbelt CEOs along on a trip to Japan in early 1992. To Bush's dismay, the Japanese businessmen ridiculed their American counterparts. Their attitude was understandable. When a company like United Airlines sees its profits plummet by 71 percent, and then rewards its chief executive officer with an $18 million salary, mockery was appropriate. American prestige suffered a further blow when Bush vomited on the Japanese prime minister.[6]

While the Bush administration revealed its hollow core, Charles Murray, a conservative intellectual, drew attention to one of the social consequences of Reaganomics. Wresting with his libertarian and Catholic sensibilities, Murray confessed that he was "trying to envision what happens when ten or twenty percent of the population has enough income to bypass the social institutions it doesn't like in ways that only the top fraction of one percent used to be able to do." Murray did not like to see America become like Brazil: a place in which a highly educated post-industrial elite lived in gated communities while the public institutions about them collapsed. A "caste system," Murray lamented, had been taking shape since the seventies in which the aging, economically ravished city became "an urban analogue of the Indian reservation."[7]

Historian Christopher Lasch concurred. He believed that America's elites—regardless of whether they were conservative stock analysts or liberal Hollywood directors—lacked any sense of social responsibility and national identity:

To an alarming extent, the privileged classes—by an expansive definition, the top twenty percent—have made themselves independent not only of crumbling industrial cities but of public services in general. They send their children to private schools, insure themselves against medical emergencies by enrolling in company-supported plans, and hire private security guards to protect themselves against the mounting violence. It is not just that they see no point in paying for public services they no longer use; many of them have ceased to think of themselves as Americans in any important sense, implicated in America's destiny for better or worse. Their ties to an international culture of work and leisure—of business, entertainment, information, and "information retrieval"—make many members of the elite deeply indifferent to the prospect of national decline.[8]

Mainstream politicians were not about to take Lasch's and Murray's concerns to heart. Conservatives wished only to read Murray's devastating critiques of welfare and Lasch's sympathetic essays on family values. Their thoughts on the spirit of community were ignored. Similarly, liberals, who considered Lasch to be an apostate and Murray a racist, refused to open their minds. In some ways the media were even less helpful than the politicians. Journalists seemed incapable of addressing the big issues confronting society. Often, they placed political drama before substance. Would House Speaker Jim Wright of Texas and House Whip Tony Coelho be forced to resign once Newt Gingrich exposed their financial dealings to the public? Would Bush renege on his 1988 pledge: "Read ... My ... Lips ... No ... New ... Taxes!" The answers to these questions were yes, yes, and, as Bush said to reporters when he raised taxes in 1990 by $134 billion, "Read My Hips!"[9]

The peccadilloes of Bush, Coelho, and Wright, frothy though they were, did not begin to deal with the issues Lasch and Murray raised. Worse, no one in Washington appeared worried about the prospects of a society in which six of every ten women with pre-school children had to work. Three-quarters of women with children under eighteen were also in the job market. Most were working out of economic necessity—not by choice. Young parents either paid for day care out of their slim earnings or let their children be baby-sat by the television set.[10]

There was a related development that also merited attention. In 1990, just a quarter of all households had children living at home. Senior citizens, older Boomers whose children had moved out, and never-marrieds made up the bulk of the electorate. (In 1991, one-third of American women in their twenties were single, compared to one in ten just twenty years before.) Singles, seniors, and "empty-nest" Boomers were the vocal majority who voted against public school and municipal playground levies. Not surprisingly, politicians who thought about giving tax breaks to families had to think twice. After a decade of conservative governance, Americans had an economic system that hurt families and a political culture that appeared unwilling to prevent the dissolution of the social order.[11]

Some conservatives tried to make light of the economic situation. They insisted that Reaganomics had created little social dislocation. Anyway, leaving aside economic and moral issues, Bush was destined to "go down in history as one of America's great commanders-in-chief." (This observation was a little far-fetched since Hussein, the man whom Bush called "worse than Hitler," remained in power.) Other conservatives, including a few marginal figures who served in the Bush administration, were more agitated. William Bennett, the vocal education secretary in Reagan's second term, and now Bush's "Drug Czar," pulled no punches. He blamed Hollywood for glamorizing anti-social behavior and exhorted Americans to eradicate the criminal element—without any interference from civil libertarians:

Imagine that you own a beach house and discover a school of great white sharks in the water just off your property. They don't leave. As the people continue to swim, the casualties mount. What do you do? You certainly should provide for hospitals, health care, emergency services, rehabilitation, therapy, and artificial limbs. And you should certainly teach people not to go into the water, and take particular care to tell the children that they should not go near the water.

But is there something else you should do, perhaps something else you should do before anything else? Of course there is. *You need to get the damn sharks out of the water.* Drive them out, surround them, net them, spear them, you do whatever it takes, but you get rid of them.[12]

Jack Kemp, whom Bush plucked from Congress to serve as secretary of housing and urban development, offered a number of innovative policies to deal with inner-city crime and joblessness. One of Kemp's ideas was to sell discounted public housing units to their tenants; he believed that ownership promoted individual responsibility. The HUD secretary also championed urban enterprise zones, hoping that targeted tax breaks would encourage businesses to locate in areas of high unemployment. Whether or not Kemp's solutions were workable, he was at least trying to bridge the gap between the political establishment and the mostly black prisoners of urban poverty. As Kemp was fond of saying, conservatives "should have been there on the freedom marches and bus rides" of the sixties. (Newt Gingrich agreed wholeheartedly. In 1986, Gingrich, who had no significant black constituency to answer to, rounded up reluctant Republican votes to make the younger Martin Luther King's birthday a national holiday.) Unfortunately for Kemp, Bush did not appreciate moralists. After all, he had brought Kemp and Bennett on board only to mollify conservatives. The president was not interested in their ideas.[13]

Wall Street Journal editor David Frum dismissed Bush's staffers as "unideological opportunists." Similarly, John Podhoretz, a conservative journalist and son of a prominent intellectual, marveled at the difference between the Reaganites and "the Bushies." Many of the Reaganites had been "true believers" whose family obligations left no time to go out for a drink after work. The Bushies were another story. Podhoretz described the young women who worked for Bush as the "finest flowering of female Republicanism"—debutantes who would not be caught dead in polyester. Male Bushies clothed themselves in $750 suits from the best boutiques. No J. C. Penney bargain basement sales for them. Whatever their differences, whether their wealth came from trust funds or personal allowances, or whether they were graduates of Dartmouth or Yale, the Bushies had one thing in common: they loathed the Reaganites. A number of the older Bush staffers had served in the Ford administration. After a long Reagan-imposed exile from federal employment, they were looking for paybacks.[14]

GOP liberals first went after Doug Wead, an evangelical who had served Reagan as liaison between the White House and the Religious Right. In a White House that was, unofficially, prochoice and tolerant of diverse lifestyles, Wead clearly did not belong. When he questioned the wisdom of inviting militant gays to the White House, Wead was fired. Pat Robertson was not surprised. Given his experience with Bush in the 1988 primaries, as well as the president's opposition to the censorship of textbooks and television—"Closing our children off from the outside world will not protect them," Bush insisted—Robertson was not inclined to be charitable. Confronting the president in 1989, Robertson mused, "Isn't it interesting that you have no difficulty identifying evangelicals and their allies during the campaign, but you cannot find them after the election?" Randall Terry, the organizer of Operation Rescue, was even less politic. Angered that Christie Hefner, the publisher of *Playboy,* could get an audience with Bush while he could not, Terry accosted the President on a New England golf course. Bush fled, letting the Secret Service deal with the prolife activist.[15]

Bush's relationship with ordinary voters was no warmer. His regime saw regressive Social Security payroll taxes rise and 68,000 pages of onerous federal regulations become the law of the land. Bush did not like making public appeals. He preferred cutting private deals with a Democratic Congress that was inclined to raise taxes and increase entitlement spending. Bush had no common touch, let alone a sense of how to play democratic politics. This explained why he tried to persuade the IRS to stop investigating the wealthy for tax evasion. After all, he knew these folks and, besides, they could afford tax attorneys to fight the government. It would be far more financially productive, Bush thought, for the IRS to go after middle- and working-class taxpayers who lacked the financial means to resist. Bush also opposed extending unemployment benefits and nodded when his budget director, Richard Darman, told him that he was so popular that "you could go out there and tell them [the American people] that a depression is upon us and no one would even notice." (Mario Cuomo and the Democratic Party's leading stars agreed with Darman. The first string declined to run against Bush leaving it up to benchwarmers like Arkansas governor Bill Clinton to take on the president.)[16]

To Bush's shock, reality finally intruded upon the White House. Pat Buchanan, who had acquired a personal following through his newspaper columns and cable television appearances, challenged Bush in the '92 primaries. At first, the administration argued that "a vote for Pat Buchanan is a vote for Ted Kennedy." When no one outside the White House could figure out what that meant, Bush's staffers called Buchanan "wacky." Buchanan, one must remember, was the person who fantasized about Jesse Helms's taking over CBS and turning the network into the "Conservative Broadcasting System." More troublesome, Buchanan opposed Bush's efforts to reduce international tariff barriers. Unlike Bush, the pundit, linking trade policy to foreign aid and military intervention abroad, responded to the issues Lasch and Murray had raised. Buchanan's answer was "America First—and Second, and Third." The time had come, Buchanan contended, for a nationalist trade policy that protected American jobs from overseas competitors who paid poverty-level wages. Taunting the president in New Hampshire, where the unemployment rate was twice the national average, Buchanan said, "Mr. Bush, you recall, promised to create thirty million jobs. He didn't tell us he would be creating them in Guandong Province [China], Yokohama, or Mexico."[17]

America's financiers and their libertarian allies in the media cried foul. The *American Spectator, Human Events,* and the *Wall Street Journal* tore into Buchanan. Libertarians argued that cheap imports provided gainfully employed consumers with inexpensive goods. Moreover, the illegal immigrants from Mexico and other Third World countries that Buchanan denounced gave Sunbelt employers an affordable labor pool. Further, if Bush and the Democratic Congress were successful in negotiating a special trade agreement with Mexico, American companies would find it easier to relocate. Mexico gave U.S. corporations an ideal environment in which to work. Low wages, no environmental regulations to contend with, and a government that was more than happy to shoot down malcontents who might want to organize an independent union. While such arguments won kudos in the nation's libertarian think tanks, they did not play well with millions of Republicans. Buchanan carried 37 percent of the New Hampshire primary vote.[18]

Despite decent showings in New Hampshire and other primary states, Buchanan was not an especially popular figure. He proved even better than George Wallace at making enemies. On the cultural front Buchanan went after the National Endowment for the Arts, chastising the federal agency for "subsidizing both filthy and blasphemous art." While Brookline ridiculed his "Puritanism," social conservatives wondered why homosexual artists who submerged crucifixes in their own urine or photographed themselves with bullwhips shoved up their anuses had any claim to the taxpayers' money. As Buchanan had said on an earlier occasion: "A visceral recoil from homosexuality is the natural reaction of a healthy society wishing to preserve itself. A prejudice against males who engage in sodomy with one another represents a normal and natural bias in favor of sound morality." Blindsided, the Bushies denounced the censorship of "gay art." Then, after consulting their polls, they fired the director of the endowment.[19]

For many politicians, earning the hatred of libertarians, country clubbers, and gays would have been enough for one lifetime. Buchanan, how-

ever, never minced words with any group he found bothersome. During
the Persian Gulf War, which he vehemently opposed, Buchanan claimed,
"There are only two groups that are beating the drums for war in the
Middle East—the Israeli Defense Ministry and its amen corner in the
United States." In case Jews detected some ambiguity in his words, Buchanan clarified the situation by noting that the American soldiers who
would likely die in the war would be "kids with names like McAllister,
Murphy, Gonzalez, and Leroy Brown." Buchanan seemed to be saying
that the foxholes would not be filled with Shapiros and Rabinowitzes.
Angered, John Judis of the *New Republic* and A. M. Rosenthal of the *New
York Times* dredged up every allegedly anti-Semitic utterance Buchanan
had ever made. William F. Buckley distanced himself from Buchanan,
though less squeamish members of the Right backed up the pundit. In
one of its most hypocritical moments the Bush administration implied
that Buchanan was a Nazi who had called into question the loyalty of
American Jews. Privately, Secretary of State James Baker, angered by what
he considered to be Israeli intransigence on the Palestinian question, said,
"F--- them [the Jews]. They didn't vote for us."[20]

Far from being chastised, Buchanan stepped up his crusade against
Bush. In Michigan, where GM had announced yet another round of la-
bor-force reductions, Buchanan told his white ethnic audiences that, "Mr.
Bush's campaign is virtually a wholly owned subsidiarity of Japan, Inc."
The president, he continued, "has got too many advisers around him or
close to him who have interests or linkages to foreign interests and are
arguing for these interests, rather than objectively for what is best for the
United States." In the South, Bush called Buchanan's patriotism into
question. Buchanan's director of communications retorted: "I don't think
Pat Buchanan is vulnerable on the Gulf War issue. After all, Saddam
Hussein still has a job while a lot of Americans do not." For all his rebel
fury, Buchanan did not sweep the South. His criticisms of the free market
and calls for trade protection did not go over well in a region that had
weathered the recession better than the Rustbelt. Indeed, South Carolini-
ans had given BMW $130 million to help the German corporation build
a factory in their state. (Southerners like to say that BMW stands for,
"Bubba Makes Wheels.") Far from keeping foreign competitors out, Sunbelt entrepreneurs and politicians wanted the lower-paying—preferably
non-union—jobs that came with overseas investment.[21]

If divided economically, southern whites and northern ethnics found
common ground in their opposition to racial quotas. Buchanan did not

question whether blacks deserved equal treatment. He believed all law-abiding, hard-working Americans should be treated the same. For Buchanan, quotas were a class, not a civil rights, issue. He argued that the affirmative action policies championed by upper-class whites discriminated against humble citizens. Pointing to Bush's support for the 1991 Civil Rights Act, Buchanan rekindled the fires of blue-collar populism:

Mr. Bush promised he would veto a quota bill, and then . . . he caved in. . . . Now if you belong to the Exeter-Yale GOP club, that's not going to bother you greatly because, as we know, it is not their children who get bused out of South Boston into Roxbury, it is not their brothers who lose contracts because of minority set-asides, it is not the scions of Yale and Harvard who apply to become FBI agents and construction workers and civil servants and cops, who bear the onus of this reverse discrimination. It is the sons of middle America who pay the price of reverse discrimination advanced by the Walker's Point [Bush's Kennebunkport home] GOP to salve their social consciences at other people's expense. If I am elected, my friends, I will go through this administration, department by department, agency by agency, and root out the whole rotten infrastructure of reverse discrimination, root and branch.[22]

After twenty years of quotas the vast majority of whites, as well as a growing number of blacks, were questioning the wisdom of affirmative action. Paradoxically, while black education, income, and social status had greatly improved since the sixties, many activists insisted that discrimination was worse than ever. Liberals argued that only quotas could combat "toxic racism." Coretta Scott King, the widow of the slain civil rights leader, and liberal activist Joseph Califano contended that more civil rights legislation and anti-poverty spending were necessary. (*Combined* federal, state, and local welfare spending in 1992 amounted to $305 billion.) In contrast, whites, who had become more racially tolerant in the past three decades, were losing patience with blacks. According to a 1991 University of Chicago poll, three of four whites thought blacks preferred to subsist on welfare, and 56 percent believed minorities were prone to violence. Interestingly, an equal proportion of both races—two-thirds—thought that Asian immigrants were harder workers than blacks.[23]

Whites were becoming frustrated with black activists and their white apologists. Jim Sleeper, a *Village Voice* columnist, was a rare person on the Left who criticized black militants. According to Sleeper, there were "professional blacks (not to be confused with black professionals) who've developed a predictable stake in expanding the boundaries of racism in pursuit of moral and practical exemptions from social obligation." Sleeper hit it on the head. Professional blacks responded to any criticism of crime, illegitimacy, and quotas by race-baiting their white critics. On the nation's campuses race-baiting was in fashion. From Smith College to SUNY-Binghamton, black students, and a few secular Jews, filed false assault and vandalism reports. They then used such "racial incidents" to rally the community against discrimination. Far too often white journalists reported on the demonstrations without bothering to learn the facts.[24]

Professional blacks counted on minorities to stand blindly by their political leaders. In 1991, a gang of black teens brutally assaulted three suburban whites who had come downtown to view Detroit's Fourth of July fireworks display. The black jury acquitted the gang leader. In a strange twist to the case, Mayor Coleman Young interviewed the eyewitnesses and allegedly questioned the accuracy of their accounts. Angered, the white victims lashed out at Young, claiming that he had personally footed the legal bills for the black defendants. For all of that, however, Young's behavior was a model of restraint compared to the deeds of his Washington counterpart. When Mayor Marion Barry stood trial for smoking crack, black jurors and the minority electorate at large championed his cause. Ignoring the evidence, the NAACP and Jesse Jackson declared that Barry was the victim of a "racist prosecution." Just as disturbing, even though Washington had become America's "murder capital," few blacks held Barry accountable. White liberals uttered patronizing comments on the need for racial sensitivity and then retreated to their gated settlements in suburban Chevy Chase.[25]

In their flight from urban decay, whites (and middle-class blacks) had made America a suburban nation. (Conservative wits noted that in Camden, New Jersey, even the Mafia relocated to the 'burbs.) The cities that had once given the party of the New Deal its shock troops no longer decided presidential elections. Suburban and small-town living, however, did not always offer a sanctuary from violence. The threatening underclass could no longer be confined to the inner cities. Traveling west on I-80 from Chicago, the Crips and Bloods turned Davenport and Des Moines, Iowa, into crack distribution centers. In Davenport, a decaying industrial town on the Mississippi, twenty-five hundred gang members stalked the streets. To the astonishment of Iowans, 40 percent of the gang recruits were local white youths. "These little white s---heads," a Davenport police officer said, "act black, they talk black, they think they're tough, but they are mutts without their gangs, just idiots. They get recruited by the older black gang members who run them like tops." Paradoxically, gangs had become the most racially integrated institutions in America.[26]

William Bennett argued that the recording industry had to take some responsibility for luring white and black youths into a life of crime. Time-Warner, for instance, eagerly marketed the violent, sexist, rap music of the inner city to its most enthusiastic customers—the white teenage boys of the suburbs and small towns. Rapper Ice-T, who easily moved between recording studio and Hollywood movie lot, exhorted teens to gun down white police officers and Korean merchants. Far from condemning such racist attitudes, the Left praised rappers as the authentic voices of black America. From Pittsburgh to Brookline, white liberals drooled over rap groups like 2 Live Crew and the Geto Boys. Such rappers, liberal academics and journalists argued, should not be dismissed as a misogynist or profane. In reality, rappers were liberating black sexuality from the racist confines of white middle-class norms, while, in the process, becoming the Shakespeares of the contemporary scene. "Suck my d—k, b—ch, and make it puke," 2 Live Crew rapped, "Lick my ass up and down. Lick it till your tongue turn doo-doo brown."[27]

Against this backdrop of gang violence and moral decay, two developments forced Americans to examine the state of race relations. In 1991, Bush nominated Clarence Thomas to the "black seat" on Supreme Court. Patricia Ireland, the president of NOW, boasted to the media that "we're going to Bork him." Oregon senator Bob Packwood, a liberal Republican and ally of NOW, also went on the attack against the prolife jurist. Norman Lear and Teddy Kennedy reassembled the anti-Bork coalition. Meanwhile, Virginia's first black governor, Doug Wilder, a prochoice Democrat, asserted that Thomas, having been raised a Catholic, was not fit to be on the nation's highest court. "How much allegiance is there to the Pope?" Senator Howard Metzenbaum of Ohio weighed in, claiming that Thomas's conservative ideology made him an unfit judge. Eleven years before, when supporting Ruth Bader Ginsburg's nomination to the U.S. Court of Appeals Washington Circuit, Metzenbaum had asserted that ideology should not be a basis upon which to reject judicial nominees. Ginsburg was, like Metzenbaum, an advocate of abortion on demand and racial quotas.[28]

At first, the hearings went well for Thomas. But then Senate liberals sprang a surprise on the jurist. Anita Hill, a former EEOC staffer who had worked with Thomas, claimed that he had sexually harassed her. Although Hill captured much sympathetic media attention, she had no evidence to support her charges. Worse, no credible witnesses came forward to corroborate Hill's story. This was remarkable. In cases of sexual

harassment, especially when, as in the Thomas matter, the incidents sup-
posedly took place over a number of years, there is usually more than one
victim. Senator Packwood, for instance, had long made it a habit to stick
his tongue into women's mouths. With Packwood, there was a pattern of
abuse, as well as a number of potential witnesses. Unfortunately, Packwood's victims tended to be ardent feminists who so valued his prochoice
stance that they were unwilling to expose him. Instead, they redirected
their anger against Thomas. (Feminists also did not say much about the
antics of another congressional champion of Anita Hill. Over the Easter
weekend in 1991 Teddy Kennedy had gone out on a drinking binge with
his nephew, William Smith. Kennedy apparently passed out before Smith
allegedly raped a young woman. As Buchanan said about Kennedy's
Easter escapade, "What other fifty-nine-year-old do you know who stills
goes to Florida for Spring break?")[29]

Resenting the attacks on his character, Thomas denounced the Senate
Judiciary Committee hearings as a "high-tech lynching of an uppity
black." Despite the hostility of the NAACP, most blacks believed Thomas
had been done wrong. Tony Brown, a television journalist, embraced
Thomas and ridiculed the Congressional Black Caucus, which had come
out against the conservative. "Where do you get the power to organize
thirty million black folks," Brown asked the Congressional Black Caucus,
"when only 27 percent of them agree with you?" Brown further endeared
himself to civil rights activists by accusing them of practicing a "crude
intellectual fascism when a black strays from the liberal plantation."
Southern Democrats, fearing a backlash from their black constituents, had
little choice but to confirm Thomas. Hill, once an undistinguished law
professor in Oklahoma, hit the lecture circuit, pulling down $10,000 for
each appearance and hobnobbing with the likes of Donna Shalala and
Arkansas first lady Hillary Rodham Clinton.[30]

Intense coverage notwithstanding, the media failed to explore an important aspect of the Thomas story. His nomination revealed troubling
rifts within the conservative movement. Social conservatives like Kemp
and Bennett backed Thomas to the hilt. To Bennett, Thomas showed
minorities that they could escape from the clutches of an irrelevant civil
rights establishment. Thomas had impressed Bennett and Kemp with his
eloquent testimony on the importance of moral values and his belief that
blacks should not permit racism to drive them into self-destructive hatred
of whites. Born into a dirt-poor Georgia family, Thomas noted that "I

grew up under state enforced segregation, which is as close to totalitarianism as I would like to get." Convinced that government should play a role in combating discrimination, the EEOC under Thomas nearly doubled the number of cases litigated in the courts and (in what might seem like an ironic development to some), initiated the first case against sexual harassment in the workplace.[31]

Where Kemp and Bennett cheered Thomas, other conservatives expressed disgust. Llewellyn Rockwell of the Alabama-based Ludwig von Mises Institute—a libertarian think tank—thundered: "Thomas calls the segregation of the Old South, where he grew up, 'totalitarian.' But that's liberal nonsense. Whatever its faults, and it certainly had them, that system was far more localized, decent, and humane than the really totalitarian social engineering now wrecking the country." Senator Jesse Helms, though not opposing Thomas, remained an unreconstructed rebel. In his 1990 campaign against Harvey Gantt, a black liberal and ardent supporter of abortion and affirmative action, Helms aired commercials showing a deserving white man losing a job to an unqualified minority. While provocative, the commercial did show a probable consequence of a Gantt victory. There was no excuse, however, for Helms to mail notices to 125,000 blacks warning them that they might be guilty of voting fraud if they showed up at the polls.[32]

Though having no use for Anita Hill, the *American Spectator* warned libertarians that Thomas would not eliminate hiring quotas. His record at the EEOC and the agency's subsequent actions against employers after his departure marked Thomas as a man who was overly fond of Big Government. The *American Spectator* had a point. One was hard pressed to understand why the EEOC in 1989 prosecuted a freight-hauling company for refusing to hire drivers who had been convicted of larceny. The EEOC said that since minorities disproportionately committed felonies, the firm's hiring practices resulted in racial discrimination. A federal judge in Florida, who happened to be Hispanic, heard the EEOC case. He was not impressed by the "condescending attitude" of the EEOC:

[The] EEOC's position that minorities should be held to lower standards is an insult to millions of honest Hispanics. Obviously a rule refusing honest employment to convicted applicants is going to have a disparate impact upon thieves. That apparently a higher percentage of Hispanics are convicted of crimes than of the "white" population may prove a number of things such as: 1) Hispanics are not very good at stealing; 2) whites are better thieves than Hispanics; 3) none of

the above; 4) all of the above. . . . Regardless, the honesty of a prospective employee is certainly a vital consideration in the hiring decision. If Hispanics do not
wish to be discriminated against because they have been convicted of theft then
they should stop stealing.[33]

Clarence Thomas and Anita Hill became forever linked in the public
mind just after Rodney King became famous. In March of 1991, Rodney
King, who had been racing through Los Angeles while drunk and stoned,
was arrested. He was out on parole for robbery. The LAPD, captured on
videotape, beat King. A public outcry forced L.A. officials to put the police
officers involved in the King beating on trial. One year later an all-white
jury acquitted the defendants. Soon, thirty-five thousand Crips, Bloods,
and members of other gangs led a riot that left fifty-eight people dead
and caused a billion dollars in property damage. The riot served notice
that the melting pot was cracked. Illegal Mexican immigrants accounted
for one-third of those arrested, while 80 percent of the looted and
burned-out businesses were owned by Korean immigrants. Only one hundred of the twenty-five hundred Korean shops subsequently reopened in
their old neighborhoods. Thousands of Koreans moved to Seattle or returned to their homeland.[34]

Assistant LAPD chief Robert Vernon, a born-again Christian who had
found the King beating reprehensible, blamed Mayor Tom Bradley for
crippling the department. Bradley, Vernon charged, had reduced the size
of the police force and, at the urging of civil libertarians, made it more
difficult to disrupt gang activities. (Bradley had been one of the first black
members of the LAPD.) Jesse Jackson and Watts congressman Maxine
Waters led rallies against the "racist" LAPD. Conservatives countered that
if the LAPD was so racist, why did the officers who captured King not
beat up his black passengers? Worried about further rioting, the U.S.
Justice Department charged the officers with violating King's civil rights.
In the federal trial, with several black jurors on board, the policemen were
convicted. (White jurors feared a second riot and thus voted to convict.)
King went on to collect nearly $4 million in civil damages from Los
Angeles. Later, police officers in California and Pennsylvania picked him
up on a variety of offenses—including spousal abuse. Fearing adverse
publicity, lawsuits, and federal prosecution, the cops usually let King go.[35]

On the left, Waters called the L.A. riots a "rebellion" against white
racism and Republican fiscal policies. She and Jesse Jackson even arranged
for a "summit meeting" with gang leaders. At the other end of the ideological spectrum, Buchanan proffered a quick remedy to urban disorder:

"Rioters do not need to hear a lot of bull hockey about 'connecting' and 'dialogue,'" Buchanan contended. "They need to hear through a police bullhorn the three little words that say it all, 'Lock and load!'" As conservatives were wont to say, poverty could not be eradicated until poor blacks stopped preying upon one another and bearing children out of wedlock. To the surprise of some conservatives and liberals, Representative John Lewis of Georgia, a black veteran of the sixties civil rights movement and onetime seminarian, concurred:

Increasingly over the past thirty years, crime and violence have been allowed to run virtually unchecked through poor black communities. This widening gyre of destruction first stripped communities of businesses and jobs. It broke down housing. It made schools places of fear, where a quarter of the students might carry weapons for self-defense, and learning was always a casualty. For as life became more dangerous, more subject to hazardous fate, so it became progressively difficult to raise children in the settled peace they require. And more and more the most conspicuous models of success were the racketeers, the pimp, and the insidious drug dealer. So more and more children, deprived of reasonable nurture, were sucked into the vortex, to become in their turn the abusers and the destroyers of the children who came after them.

It is not only poverty that has caused crime. In a very real sense it is crime that has caused poverty, and is the most powerful cause of poverty today.[36]

Religious conservatives endorsed the congressman's heartfelt words. Indeed, Southern Baptist clergy wanted blacks like Lewis to become part of their spiritual community. Since 1989, the Southern Baptist Convention had established 150 churches in predominately black neighborhoods. Southern Baptists pledged that blacks, as well as Hispanics and Asians, would never again be turned away by white deacons. The Southern Baptist Convention, like fundamentalist churches in general, grew larger. Such churches attracted young white and minority couples who had grown disgusted with what they regarded as the moral relativism of the mainline Protestant denominations. They listened to one of the thousand Christian radio stations operating in the nation and purchased child-rearing books at the Christian shops that infiltrated suburban shopping malls. A 1990 Gallup poll revealed that 38 percent of voters could be described as moral traditionalists. These were people who sought sanctuary from a violent, corrupt society. At the same time the faithful wanted to make their communities better places in which to live.[37]

After the '88 election Pat Robertson had sensed that the time was ripe for a second wave of religious activism. Robertson, however, vowed not to make the same mistakes that limited the political effectiveness of the

Moral Majority. GOP strategist Ralph Reed, with a freshly minted history Ph.D. from Emory, came on board to run day-to-day operations of the Christian Coalition. Reed announced that the Christian Coalition would focus on political contests at the local—as well as the federal—level and be more aggressive in reaching out beyond its Pentecostal base. "We believe that the Christian community in many ways missed the boat in the nineteen eighties by focusing almost entirely on the White House and Congress," Reed stated, "when most of the issues that concern conservative Catholics and evangelicals are primarily determined in the city councils, school boards, and state legislatures." Casting a wary eye at the Bush administration, Reed quietly mobilized the party's grassroots. "We think the Lord is going to give us this nation back one precinct at a time, one neighborhood at a time, and one state at a time. We're not going to win it all at once with some kind of millennial rush at the White House."[38]

While Bush purged the White House staff of social conservatives, the Christian Coalition ran candidates in a thousand local elections. Reed's troops won 40 percent of the contests they entered in 1990 and 1991. Working almost exclusively through the churches, the Christian Coalition initially escaped the attention of the GOP country clubbers and hostile reporters. (Eluding notice did not require much effort. In 1990, a year after the founding of the Christian Coalition, liberal academics and journalists were still writing the obituaries of the Religious Right.) Reed urged Christian activists not to "stick your head up, you can be shot." Rather, a Christian should "paint [one's] face and travel at night." Reed then described the church as a nineties equivalent of the Ho Chi Minh Trail— a sheltered route by which to resupply guerilla forces. "The advantage we enjoy," Reed noted, "is that liberals and feminists don't generally go to church; they don't gather in one place three days before the election. We can print twenty-five million voter guides and insert them in the bulletins of ten thousand churches across the country."[39]

One Oregon member of the Christian Coalition succinctly explained why he had become politically active. "The things that I believe in and that are important to me, I felt were being targeted [by liberals]. It's like when I was in Vietnam. When someone was targeting you, you knew." This vet, like others who enlisted in Robertson's crusade, felt as if secular society had declared war on Christians. Cal Thomas, a syndicated Christian columnist, had an appearance on ABC's *Good Morning America* canceled in 1990 because "producers feared he would quote Bible verses on the air." Michael Medved, a film critic and conservative Jew, observed that "for many of the most powerful people in the entertainment business, hostility to traditional religion goes so deep and burns so intensely that they insist on expressing that hostility, even at the risk of commercial disaster." Hollywood's secularized scriptwriters, directors, and producers loathed Judeo-Christian morality and wallowed in sex and violence. Since the sixties the proportion of G-rated films suitable for family viewing had fallen from 41 percent to 13 percent. Film and television producers invariably depicted prolifers as bomb-wielding religious nuts. They also brought graphic "splatter shots" and soft-core sex to the heartland.[40]

The Christian Coalition sent nearly two million postcards to television executives imploring them not to advertise condoms. In Colorado, the Christian Coalition successfully amended the state constitution to prohibit gay affirmative action. Meanwhile in Bovard County, Florida, Baptists, Catholics, and Pentecostals joined forces to defeat a gay-rights ordinance. (As if hurtling through an alternative universe, the United Methodist Church in 1992 narrowly decided that homosexuality remained somewhat sinful. However, the governing body of the church did, at the prompting of lesbian delegates, say that prayers could begin with "Our Mother who art in Heaven.") Irate at efforts to curb gay power, Teddy Kennedy and Brookline's Barney Frank authored legislation in 1992 that would grant legal recognition to gay marriages and nullify local sodomy statutes. Social conservatives lambasted the proposed legislation, calling it a mortal threat to "family values."[41]

Paying little heed to the Christian Coalition, Bush awoke too late to prevent social conservatives from acquiring a presence at the '92 Republican National Convention. Forty percent of the GOP delegates, including many pledged to Bush, were evangelicals. Twenty percent of the two thousand delegates openly affiliated themselves with the Christian Coalition. Across the nation, religious activists, having learned their lesson in 1988, took over the GOP's county-chair positions. Bush partisans could not manipulate the delegate selection process as effectively as before. GOP liberals, *Christianity Today* reported, had no choice but to learn "Godspeak."[42]

Vice President Dan Quayle, whom the Bushies had virtually exiled from the White House, was now called upon to shore up their "family values" image. Appearing before various Protestant groups, Quayle read from a well-crafted speech that linked family dissolution to the L.A. riots. He mentioned in passing that Hollywood glorified illegitimacy, citing as an example the television series *Murphy Brown*. Media critics recast the story to make it appear as if Quayle had spent all his time chastising a *fictional* unwed mother. Quayle's advisors paid little mind to liberal pundits. They needed to score points with the GOP's social conservatives. In that, Quayle's staff achieved a partial victory. Conservative columnist Mona Charen heaped praise upon Quayle and accused "liberal elitists" of corrupting America's morals. Quayle, though, did little to improve Bush's reputation with the Right. At the Republican convention in Houston, Quayle led a pep rally. "Do we trust Bill Clinton [the Democratic presidential nominee]?", Quayle asked. The crowd cried, "No!" Then Quayle said, "Do we trust the liberal media?" Again, the delegates shouted, "No!" Thinking that he had whipped up enthusiasm for Bush, Quayle made his pitch: "Who do we trust?" The religious conservatives cried, "Jesus!"[43]

Bush plunged ahead, determined to be the "family values" president. A year before the '92 election Bush told several religious publications that he believed in voluntary school prayer. As for the distribution of condoms to teenagers in the public schools, the president noted that he was against the practice. However, neither prayer nor condoms was a federal issue. In truth, Republican liberals did not think anything on the social agenda fell under the purview of the White House—from abortion to crime, such matters were best left to the states. (The Bushies had the similar thoughts about the economy: corporate executives, not government, would do what was best for America.) In 1992, religious conservatives noted, Bush became a country-club messiah. To the disgust of liberal Republicans like California governor Pete Wilson and Massachusetts governor William Weld, the Bush platform grudgingly remained true to its Reaganite principles. The Republicans opposed abortion, criticized same-sex marriages, and asserted that "elements within the media, the entertainment industry, academics, and the Democratic Party are waging a guerrilla war against American values."[44]

Hoping to reassure the party's economic populists and social conservatives that they truly were born-again Republicans, Bush permitted Buchanan and Robertson to address the convention. Quayle's wife, Marilyn, joined the lineup, as did Ronald Reagan in what turned out to be his last appearance at a national political convention. (White House staffers were worried that Reagan would not endorse Bush. They had cause for concern. Reagan confided to friends that he had "really effed it up" by choosing Bush as his running mate in 1980.) Attempting to make up in stridency what she lacked in common sense, Marilyn Quayle observed that many of her fellow Boomers never "took drugs, joined in the sexual revolution or dodged the draft." She was absolutely right. However, raising the issue of military service—and by extension implying that Democrats like Bill Clinton were unpatriotic—was unwise. The Bush administration contained a number of people who avoided Vietnam. In addition to Dan Quayle, Defense Secretary Dick Cheney and economic advisor Michael Boskin had ducked the draft. Ironically, Marilyn Quayle did not realize that when she condemned Clinton for participating in an overseas antiwar protest she also implicated Boskin. The economist had organized the 1969 British demonstration in which Clinton took part.[45]

Buchanan proved to be the most riveting—and controversial— speaker at the GOP convention. "My friends," Buchanan roared,

this election is about more than who gets what. It is about who we are. It is about what we believe and what we stand for as Americans. There is a religious war going on in this country for the soul of America. It is a cultural war as critical to the kind of nation we shall be as the Cold War itself. And in that struggle for the soul of America, Clinton and [Hillary Rodham] Clinton are on the other side and George Bush is on our side.

Of course, Buchanan knew that Bush had little choice but to be "on our side." The media, though, did not appreciate talk about a "culture war"— especially since they were "on the other side." *Newsweek* called the Republican convention "wall-to-wall ugly"; *Time* accused Buchanan of fomenting civil unrest; and the Boston *Globe* argued that anyone who wanted to ban pornography and abortion was a "puritanical" tyrant. Not used to the hostility of the media elite, White House staffers—most of whom favored unrestricted abortion and gay rights in any event—wilted. After the convention, liberal Republicans commenced the long march back to Newport. "Poppy Bush" would have to win reelection without their assistance.[46]

Unlike the Bushies, the Reaganites had never given much heed to the liberal media. Reagan's staffers believed that the public paid more attention to happy pictures than to the negative commentary that accompanied his "photo opportunities." Then again, if reporters were hostile to Republicans in '80, '84, and '88, it was also true that they had not been enamored of the Democratic candidates. The '92 election was different. This time newspaper reporters and television correspondents loved the Democratic nominee. The *Washington Post* gushed that Bill Clinton and vice-presidential-candidate Al Gore were the "New Heartthrobs of the Heartland." Predictably, 70 percent of Bush's network news coverage was negative. In contrast, the majority of television stories on Clinton were highly favorable. When the tabloids reported on Clinton's affair with Gennifer Flowers, the *New York Times* and the *Washington Post* buried the story. At PBS, the MacNeill/Lehrer NewsHour tried to ignore stories about Clinton's sex life. Meanwhile a producer at ABC's *Primetime Live* offered to help Clinton engage in "damage control." Hillary Rodham Clinton weighed in, persuading her media favorites to report that Bush slept around on his matronly wife.[47]

Bill Clinton often told major political journalists such as Sidney Blumenthal, Ronald Brownstein, E. J. Dionne, Thomas Edsall, and Joe Klein that he had embraced their ideas. Only his election, Clinton informed fellow Boomers, would transform their vision of America into reality. In turns flattered and suspicious, the high-profile journalists could not help but feel that they did have a stake in seeing Clinton triumph over Bush. (Blumenthal eventually became a Clinton staffer.) Initially, Joe Klein was infatuated with Clinton. By the end of the campaign, however, *Newsweek*'s ace correspondent believed that Clinton more appropriately belonged in a seamy political novel, not the White House. Klein was wise to see the shadow of Richard Nixon behind the Arkansas governor. When journalists went to Little Rock to ask the locals about their hometown hero, the Clinton campaign had them tailed and ordered state employees not to talk to outsiders. Boomer journalists came away from their Arkansas sojourn deeply disturbed. The more paranoid members of the press corps even began using public pay phones because they feared that the good people of Dogpatch had bugged their hotel rooms. *And these were liberal journalists who had harbored only goodwill toward Clinton.*[48]

In addition to the media, the Clintons relied on their Hollywood connections for advice and technical expertise. (Four years before, Dukakis had contemptuously dismissed the activists on the Left Coast as flakes.) Producer Linda Bloodworth-Thomason steered the media away from "bimbo eruptions." The focus, she insisted, must be on Clinton's youthful dynamism and the dismal state of the Bush economy. Another Hollywood producer, Mort Engelberg, who had enriched American culture with the "Smokey and the Bandit" films, helped put together a midwestern bus tour for Clinton and Gore. Engelberg thought that the touring "Bubba Mobile" would underscore Clinton's attachment to the wonderful white folks who lived in small-town America. Leaving nothing to chance, Clinton's Hollywood friends directed him toward media outlets where he would not have to worry about answering intelligent questions. Whether playing the saxophone on *Arsenio*, feeling someone's pain on *Donahue*, or hanging out with the pierced-navel crowd on MTV, Clinton generated feel-good media coverage.[49]

In one of his most calculated ploys, Clinton repeatedly snubbed Jesse Jackson and the civil rights establishment. At the 1991 Democratic Leadership Council meeting in Cleveland, Clinton successfully kept Jackson off the speaker's podium. Ignoring Jackson's cries of pain, Clinton then denounced the '91 "quota bill." A year later, seeking to attract support from Reagan Democrats and white southerners, Clinton staged an appearance at a Georgia prison, where he stood with his back to dozens of docile black prisoners. The photograph evoked disturbing memories of a bygone age when planters herded their slaves to the cotton fields. Clinton counted on southern blacks to look at the picture for what it really was: a shuck-and-jive show for the redneck seniors who still clung to the Democratic Party. Race-baiting, apparently, was a permissible tactic so long as a liberal did it. Besides, the only people really harmed by Clinton's actions were the largely black, sometimes mentally incapacitated, prisoners he put to death in Arkansas. There were good arguments to be made for executing violent criminals, black or white. However, with Clinton, one never knew if he actually believed in retributive justice or—recognizing that the vast majority of Americans embraced capital punishment—merely wanted to stack up corpses on his way to the White House.[50]

At Jackson's 1992 Rainbow Coalition conference Clinton hit pay dirt. Sister Souljah (a.k.a. Lisa Williamson), a young college graduate who posed as a ghetto gangsta rapper, praised the L.A. rioters. She informed the *Washington Post,* "If black people kill black people every day, why not have a week and kill white people?" Clinton, knowing that Jackson would leap to Sister Souljah's defense, sharply criticized her remarks. Jackson, whose decision not to run in the Democratic primaries had enabled Clinton to capture the black vote, sourly informed reporters that the governor had ambushed him. Sister Souljah charged that Clinton was making her the "Willie Horton" of the '92 campaign. Editors and reporters for the *New York Times* and the Boston *Globe,* as well as members of the Congressional Black Caucus, concurred with Souljah. One side effect of Clinton's remarks was a little additional support from bitter working-class whites. A Philadelphia electrician told the political journalists who interviewed him, "The day [Clinton] told off that f---ing Jackson is the day he got my vote."[51]

Whatever his own faults, Jackson did have Clinton's number. Although liberals accused Buchanan of being a racist, at least his condemnation of crime and quotas was sincere. Clinton, on the other hand, effortlessly bent to the prevailing political winds and deceived voters whenever it suited him. For instance, Clinton made it a centerpiece of his campaign that he came from humble "Bubba" origins, having grown up the son of a poor widow in the aptly named town of Hope, Arkansas. Actually, Clinton was raised by a prosperous uncle in the state's most infamous city, Hot Springs—a place where gamblers, prostitutes, and back-alley abortionists flourished. The *American Spectator*'s humorists liked to point out that "when Clinton says he grew up with outdoor plumbing he means he used to pee in the family swimming pool." While posing as a populist, Clinton spent most of his time eagerly stroking industrialists, Georgetown socialites, and Hollywood movers and shakers. When the time came to run for president, Clinton was, as even the *New York Times* admitted, "a money-raising dynamo." Wal-Mart, Tyson Foods, Washington lobbyists, Wall Street brokerage firms, and Pamela Harriman poured millions of dollars into Clinton's coffers. He had no trouble outspending his weak rivals in the Democratic primaries and subsequently burying Bush under a mountain of cash.[52]

Desperate, White House staffers tried to paint Clinton as a McGovern liberal. Their efforts were not wildly successful because Clinton was able to blend McGovernite beliefs with Nixonian impulses. Of course, "Mc-Nixon" was hard for *anyone* to pin down. David Mixner, who was last seen driving Richard Daley from the 1972 Democratic convention, answered Clinton's call to work for his campaign. Clinton met with gay and lesbian activists like San Francisco supervisor Roberta Achtenberg and industrialist James Hormel, as well as Patricia Ireland, NOW's bisexual leader. (By 1992 40 percent of NOW's membership was lesbian or bisexual.) In return for their contributions—which amounted to $3.5 million—Clinton privately endorsed gay rights. Once elected, Mixner believed Clinton would keep his word and become the gays-rights president. After all, they had been friends since their days in the antiwar movement.[53]

An ecstatic Mixner recounted that meeting with Clinton and his staff was "like a reunion from the sixties." By that, Mixner meant Clinton's advisors came from the ranks of the protest generation. Mixner, however, should have looked more closely at the seriousness of Clinton's commitment to the gay agenda. After all, Clinton met his gay friends on the quiet and, when Bush charged that the governor's staffers were McGovernites, he hotly denied it. Clinton declared that he was no stinking liberal, even as AFSCME, the NEA, NOW, and NARAL filled his coffers and mobilized their troops behind his banner.[54]

In public, Clinton insisted that he was quite conservative. He noted with pride how he had, against the vehement opposition of the National Education Association, required Arkansas school teachers to take competency exams. What Clinton did not say was that *college-educated teachers took English and mathematics exams intended for eighth-grade students*. It appeared as if the NEA criticized Clinton's initiative simply to make him look good to the millions of voters who thought that the teacher's union was the greatest obstacle to education reform. When questioned about his position on providing vouchers to parents that would allow them to place their children in the private schools of their own choosing, Clinton said, yes, he was in favor of choice—but only for choice within the public educational system. In other words, Clinton believed in no choice at all. Critics pointed out that New York City's parochial schools annually spent $1,700 on each student and had a 99 percent graduation rate. In contrast, the public schools spent $7,100 per child and graduated only 38 percent of their students. Clinton changed the subject. Interestingly, he was himself educated at private schools. Further, Clinton had no intention of enrolling his daughter, Chelsea, in Washington's public schools. Luckily for the Clintons, they did not need vouchers to cover Chelsea's educational expenses. Hillary made enough money to send their child to a fine private school.[55]

"McNixon" played other games. He claimed to have cut welfare rolls in Arkansas by 17,000. In reality, the welfare caseload increased by 12 percent over the course of the eighties. Recognizing that the majority of Americans feared Big Government *and* worried about rising health care costs, Clinton offered to defy logic. He vowed to eliminate one hundred thousand federal jobs, cut taxes, and create a mammoth, not to mention lavish, national health insurance program. On the abortion front, Clinton claimed that he was morally opposed to the procedure. Then, revealing another aspect of his personality, Clinton prevented the Catholic governor of Pennsylvania, Bob Casey, from addressing the Democratic convention. Clinton did not want prolife speakers at the podium—especially one who had fought Planned Parenthood all the way to the Supreme Court over a legislative effort to impose limits on abortion. Having snubbed Casey, Clinton then snagged an invitation to the University of Notre Dame, where he touted the joys of family life. Sounding defensive, Notre Dame's liberals told campus prolifers that Clinton was a graduate of a Catholic college—as if that fact mattered more to him than his relationship with NOW and NARAL.[56]

Despite image-enhancing assistance from Hollywood and the media, most voters did not trust Clinton. Among New York's and Connecticut's *Democrats,* more than half informed pollsters that Clinton was dishonest and lacked integrity. However, they would still vote for him because they blamed Bush for the recession. Hammering away at the Bush economy, though, did not guarantee Clinton victory. He needed Ross Perot to run as a third-party candidate. As America's "first welfare state billionaire," Perot had grown rich in the sixties by creating sophisticated computer records for the Social Security Administration. The Texas businessman appealed to the Sunbelt's disaffected libertarians. They did not like the government's telling them what to do. Whether it involved higher taxation or the curbing of abortion rights, Perot's followers despised religious conservatives and liberal do-gooders in equal measure. Fortunately for Clinton, Perot could take millions of votes away from Bush without there being any danger of the Texan's winning. Perot had revealed a pattern of arrogance, paranoia, and a penchant for spying on his employees that made Nixon look harmless in comparison. (David Frum of the *Wall Street Journal* called Perot a "sinister demagogue.")[57]

As Clinton expected, Perot won 19 percent of the popular vote. Nearly every vote Perot received came from angry Republicans. Clinton's victory, however, was nothing to crow about. By winning just 43 percent of the popular vote, Clinton exposed the rotten core of the Democratic Party. Even though the Democrats ran an all-southern, and purportedly centrist, ticket, Clinton and Gore lost their native region to Bush. In Georgia and in Gore's home state of Tennessee, only Perot's presence turned what would have been a Bush blowout into a slim win for Clinton. More embarrassing, more than two hundred Democratic officeholders, most of them southerners, switched to the GOP. Southern blacks continued to vote Democratic while whites confirmed their Republican loyalties. In Alabama, barely 14 percent of white men considered themselves Democrats. Among all white voters in South Carolina, just 20 percent continued to back Democratic candidates. Almost without exception, every southern white who clung to the Democratic Party was a senior citizen who believed Clinton when he warned that the Republicans would abolish Social Security.[58]

Clinton's appeal to seniors, southern and northern, was enormous.

World War II veterans, who might have been expected to look askance upon an antiwar activist, supported Clinton. (With an eye to the future, Clinton in 1969 had fretted that his evasion of the draft might affect his "political viability." He need not have been worried.) Bush, himself a World War II combat veteran, could not carry his own generational cohort. Then again, Clinton, despite efforts to tap into the "Pepsi Generation" by appearing on MTV, did not win over the majority of Baby Busters. To them, Clinton was like the smarmy Boomer uncle who encouraged the old folks to spend as if there were no tomorrow, took his percentage off the top as executor of the estate, and then left the young heirs with backbreaking debt. So long as seniors could be bought off by Social Security and Medicare, there would be Boomer liberals clinging desperately to power and writing checks on accounts with insufficient funds. Time, however, was running out for the Democrats. By 1992, 60 percent of the electorate had been born after FDR's death. Few Boomers had any *real* commitment to the New Deal. For those who came of voting age in the eighties, just a minority identified with the Democratic Party. Moreover, Baby-Buster Democrats were lifestyle liberals who, like their conservative counterparts, tended to regard Social Security as a generational scam. The New Deal Democrats were truly the last of their tribe.[59]

Of the nation's 435 congressional districts, Clinton took a majority of the vote in only 98. Clinton had no electoral coattails, running behind *every* single House Democrat. He captured less than half of the Catholic, union, and working-class white vote. AFSCME and the NEA may have pulled out all stops to elect Clinton, but blue-collar workers were well aware of how cozy the Arkansas governor was with low-wage employers. In Pennsylvania, union members recoiled from Clinton's prolife position and fretted that the Democrats would bankrupt the country rather than cut entitlement spending. Blacks, Jews, and seniors were the only voters to back Clinton in great numbers. Indeed, Bush's Jewish support had fallen twenty percentage points since 1988 because of his efforts to pressure Israel to negotiate with the Palestinians. Jews also mistakenly believed that Buchanan had taken over the GOP. As for blacks, they did not give Bush any credit for ultimately supporting the 1991 "quota bill." Bush lost what little black support he ever had because minorities were willing to accept criticism from Clinton but not Buchanan. The GOP scored best among two-parent families that were more socially conservative than singles, childless couples, and empty nesters. White families did not care for abortion, gay activism, and Bill Clinton.[60]

In the postmortems on the election, liberals and conservatives agreed that the recession had wounded Bush. Indeed, two-thirds of the voters considered the economy to be the most important issue in the '92 campaign. GOP liberals, as well as media pundits, though, came up with an additional explanation for Bush's defeat. Buchanan, the Christian Coalition, and social conservatives in general had alienated the electorate. Although this interpretation became part of the perceived wisdom on the '92 election and encouraged liberal Republicans to try to "take back" their party before the next presidential campaign, it was wrong. Despite what liberal Republicans said, the GOP platform of 1992 was no more "extremist" than the ones that Reagan and Bush successfully ran on in '80, '84, and '88. Moreover, various academic studies of the '92 election revealed a fact that the country clubbers and network broadcasters found too inconvenient to accept. If not for the mobilization of social conservatives, Bush would have lost in a landslide, not a squeaker. Social conservatives could also point out that although they may not have loved Bush, they did not, like liberal Republicans, desert the flawed incumbent for the smooth-talking Clinton.[61]

At the state level religious conservatives scored impressive victories. In South Carolina alone the Christian Coalition distributed 840,000 voter guides just before the election. The guides had an effect, sealing the fate of one Democratic representative. Although liberal Republicans in California battled the Christian Coalition and helped elect Democratic candidates, theirs was a losing cause in rest of the country. Christian conservatives in 1992 won hundreds of school board, city council, and state legislative races in Florida, Iowa, Kansas, Oregon, and Texas. Ralph Reed admonished the petulant Bushies that they would have to work with social conservatives if they expected to rebuild the Republican Party. Gary Bauer, a former Reagan administration staffer and now president of the Family Research Council, informed GOP liberals and libertarians that "radical individualism" must be balanced "with a sense of community, a sense of having obligations to one another." Abortion, crime, and gay power were issues, Bauer believed, that went to the heart of what ailed America. People were going to have to give up some of their rights "to do their own thing" if America was to endure. The Republicans who defected to Perot and Clinton would never accept such restraints on their freedom.[62]

The GOP coalition had started to come apart at the seams. Still, social liberals had cause for circumspection. With 43 percent of the vote, Clinton could hardly be hailed as the harbinger of an electoral realignment. If anything, the '92 election demonstrated that the class, racial, and religious divisions that tore America apart in the sixties had only mutated—not disappeared. Prolifers might win a governorship in Michigan while pro-choice liberals and libertarians would triumph in Florida. Taken together, such electoral results underscored the fact that there was no common vision, no universally accepted beliefs to unite the country. Conservatives complained that Social Security was destroying America's future. Nothing was done. More and more prolifers, frustrated after twenty years of political stalemate, increasingly believed that they lived in an genocidal, Nazi-like state. One might have reasonably asked after the election: If the enormously popular Reagan had ultimately failed to restore faith in America's civil institutions, curb federal spending, and bring order back to the cities, how could someone so politically weak and flawed as Clinton possibly succeed?[63]

CHAPTER EIGHT

"Don't Ask, Don't Tell"

1996

Having run as a conservative, Bill Clinton governed as a liberal. The results were disastrous. Honoring his pledge to David Mixner, Clinton tried to end the military's prohibition against homosexual conduct. Roger Wilkins lauded the presidential initiative. According to the civil rights activist, Clinton was following in the footsteps of Harry Truman, who had ended racial segregation in the military decades before. However, most Americans—white and black—were not as enthusiastic. Senator Sam Nunn of Georgia rallied conservative Democrats against Clinton, prompting Mixner to accuse the southerner of being a sexual bigot. Lesbian activist Roberta Achtenberg, whom Clinton had installed as an assistant secretary in the Department of Housing and Urban Development, joined the battle, dubbing Nunn and his ilk "hate mongers."[1]

To Mixner's astonishment, General Colin Powell, America's highest-ranking black officer, voiced the opinion that homosexuals should not be in the military. Given Clinton's own efforts to avoid military service in the sixties, the last thing he needed was a well-publicized battle between a black Vietnam veteran and a gay antiwar organizer. Looking for a way out of a mess of his own making, Clinton suggested a "don't ask, don't tell" policy. Soldiers should neither be asked about their sexual orientation nor tell anyone whether they were gay. In practice, Clinton's policy meant that gays would continue to be discharged for sexual misconduct. Mixner soon found that he no longer had access to Clinton. Tellingly, when AIDS activists later showed up at the White House for a meeting, Clinton's security personnel wore rubber gloves.[2]

Burned by the gay rights controversy, Clinton nonetheless forged ahead. To appease NOW and NARAL, Clinton lifted a gag rule that forbade federally funded clinics from providing information on abortion. He also appointed two prochoice judges to the Supreme Court: Ruth Bader Ginsburg and Stephen Breyer, an acolyte of Teddy Kennedy's. Since Anthony Kennedy, Sandra Day O'Connor, and David Souter were disinclined to outlaw abortion, Clinton's actions helped maintain a prochoice majority. The Catholic bishops were displeased. After all, some of the judges who upheld the constitutionality of *Roe v. Wade* had been brought up in the Catholic faith. Only Antonin Scalia, Clarence Thomas, and Chief Justice William Rehnquist were reliable moral traditionalists. (In 1996, they were the only dissenters when the Supreme Court killed a Colorado law that barred gay affirmative action. Scalia fumed, "While the present court sits, a major undemocratic restructuring of our national institutions and mores is constantly in progress. Day by day, case by case, it is busy designing a constitution for a country I do not recognize.")[3]

During the '92 election Clinton had promised to give the middle class a tax cut. Instead, he raised taxes on "the rich," defining anyone who made more than $30,000 a year as wealthy. Among Clinton's other campaign pledges, he had vowed to "review" federal affirmative action policies, "end welfare as we know it," and to reform America's health care system. Clinton quickly "reviewed" affirmative action. Not only did he endorse quotas, Clinton announced that his administration would "look like America." Although Clinton appointed plenty of blacks and women, none of his advisors looked like struggling working stiffs. (Even Clinton's black cabinet appointees were millionaires.) So far as "ending welfare as we know it," Clinton let the matter drop. When it came to reforming health care, most Boomers and Baby Busters thought Clinton had been talking about containing Medicare and Medicaid costs. Instead, the first lady, who headed up a federal task force, wanted to create an elaborate national health insurance program that would be more costly than Medicare and Medicaid. Seniors were thrilled, but their grandchildren had wanted Big Government curbed, not expanded.

The Clintons found themselves embroiled in controversy at the very beginning of their White House tenure. First, Clinton had paid a private detective $100,000 to visit his girlfriends and threaten to "shred their reputations" if they told their stories to the media. Then the first lady fired the members of the White House travel office and placed its director on trial for financial misconduct. There was no truth to the charges. It seemed that some of Hillary's Hollywood friends wanted to run the travel office. Wishing to reward her allies, the first lady sent the FBI after the federal employers she wanted ousted. Years before, Hillary had denounced President Nixon for abusing his power. However, once in the White House, she had a change of heart. In addition to deploying federal agents against government employees, Hillary obtained classified FBI files on several hundred Republicans. Conservatives suspected that Hillary was looking for dirt on her political opponents. A disaffected FBI agent complained that the Clintons were the kind of "people we used to arrest." (Nixon, whom Clinton had graciously invited to the White House for an overnight stay, found himself liking the eager-to-please president. Hillary was another matter. Nixon must have seen a dark, vindictive personality that hit a little too close to home.)[4]

In 1992, Clinton had complained about the deteriorating quality of American life. He implied that once the "Reagan-Bush" team was replaced, a renewed sense of social responsibility would flourish among all sectors of the nation. To his apparent astonishment, Clinton's own supporters had no intention of being cooperative. When Clinton asked his friends at the television networks to restore "the family hour," they adamantly refused. Shows featuring profanity, simulated sex, and violence were broadcast in the early evening slots that had once been reserved for *The Wonderful World of Disney*. To the horror of social conservatives, the networks were televising eight scenes of premarital sex for every act of affection between a husband and wife. Clinton's Hollywood allies insisted that shows about dysfunctional families and horny teens were more realistic and generated greater advertising revenue than programs featuring well-behaved children and loving parents.[5]

Were the networks holding a mirror up to society or contributing to America's moral debasement? In 1994, forty-four million young people were single, compared to twenty-one million just twenty years before. The longer someone remained unwed, the more sexual partners he or she may have accumulated. Television executives claimed that shows like *Melrose Place* accurately reflected America's single-sex scene. Perhaps. But many people take their cues from the Hollywood culture machine. In Philadelphia, for instance, investors built an apartment complex for single professionals. A publicist for the complex cheerfully told reporters, "We're selling sex," while residents boasted that their lifestyles were reminiscent of *Melrose Place* and *The Love Connection*. One software consultant, who had been with six women in six months, insisted that he was just trying out the merchandise before settling down.[6]

While the controversy over television sex raged, the number of father-less children continued to rise. By 1993, three million youngsters lived with their grandparents—usually because their mothers could not or would not parent. At the same time, rates of teenage drug addiction and suicide rose to a twenty-five-year high. One of Clinton's first acts as president had been to slash funding for the White House Office of Drug Strategy, which coordinated all federal anti-drug programs. Teenage narcotics abuse soon shot up by 78 percent. Marijuana also enjoyed a new surge in popularity among junior high school students who could point to the fact that President Clinton had smoked "doobies" in the sixties. (In 1992, Clinton asserted that he had never inhaled. After he became president, Clinton informed a MTV audience that if he could it to do all over again, he would inhale.)[7]

Civil libertarians continued to resist efforts to crack down on anti-social behavior. New York City's ACLU chapter in 1996, for instance, challenged a municipal ordinance regulating the distribution of pornography in residential neighborhoods. Smut-shop owners were grateful. Nationally, ACLU attorneys fought state and federal efforts to prosecute hardened juvenile offenders as adults. Social liberals argued that punishment was no way to deter young felons. Instead, social workers and schoolteachers needed to work on improving the self-esteem of criminally inclined youngsters. Liberals refused to read university studies that showed violent juveniles had self-esteem to spare. Between 1992 and 1996 the number of murders committed by teens rose 22 percent. In 1994 alone, 2,800 juveniles were wanted for murder. Very rarely did violent offenders, juvenile or adult, go to prison. Of the 641,000 people arrested in the early nineties, fewer than 20 percent ever went to prison. Among those convicted of murder, most served no more than six years of jail time.[8]

When social workers exhorted teens not to drop out and pursue a life of crime, they did not realize that public schools were just the place in indulge in anti-social activities. From 1992 to 1994, eighty-five homicides were committed in public schools. In 1996, the American Medical Association issued a "report card" on teenage violence. The AMA's members, tired of patching together bullet-ridden teens, gave America a grade of D when it came to deterring violence. Federal law enforcement officials predicted that within the next decade the number of juveniles arrested for murder would increase by 145 percent.[9]

Violence and callousness loomed ever larger. In Philadelphia, a young man robbed a neighbor's house while his own home burned to the ground. His neighbors had gone outside to fight the fire and save the thief's sister and nine-year-old cousin. (The thief's relatives died in the blaze, but he did net $100, which he spent on beer.) For three months in 1995, fifty soldiers from the Indiana National Guard helped the city of Gary maintain order. Murders fell by 40 percent but immediately shot up again after the Guard left. A year later, gang shootings at Gary high schools and public housing projects prompted Mayor Scott King to declare a state of emergency.[10]

In Chicago, some politicians, white and black, pleaded for the United States Army to occupy the city's housing projects. Bridgeport, Connecticut, officials and the state police took direct action. They established checkpoints on all roads into the city. In 1996, Bridgeport arrested 150 automobile drivers every week—most for possession of drugs and illegal firearms. Although a few blacks complained about being searched, others expressed their gratitude. One Bridgeport resident observed that he had been stopped twice, but "I didn't mind it one bit. Maybe it will make some of the knuckle heads around here realize life isn't a joke." Meanwhile in Atlanta, white liberals complained about Beverly Harvard, a black police chief who was determined to keep '96 Olympic tourists safe from gang assault. They contended that Harvard's crackdown on gangs had only pushed criminal activity back to the poorest neighborhoods. White suburban liberals thus found themselves in the decidedly awkward position of insinuating that a black woman was racist.[11]

As public institutions like law enforcement struggled (and often failed) to deal with social disorder, the citizenry came up with its own responses to the collapse of America's public institutions. Ever larger numbers of Americans carried legally concealed guns. In 1986, only six states allowed the practice. Ten years later, thirty-one states made it easier to carry hidden weapons. A University of Chicago study, which caused liberals no end of grief, revealed a substantial drop in violent urban crime when law-abiding citizens were able to fight back. Since 1992, concealed weapons had deterred three thousand rapes and eighteen hundred homicides. Meanwhile, in San Diego two hundred unarmed citizens patrolled the local airport looking for drug smugglers and illegal Mexican immigrants. "This is a domestic Vietnam War," said one member of the U.S. Citizen Patrol. Latino activists and liberal white lawyers demanded that the Clinton administration prosecute patrol members for "impersonating" federal officers.[12]

If some Americans became vigilantes, others withdrew from the "public square." One Ohio business executive contended that taxpayers should sharply reduce funding for higher education since too many people already had college degrees. (In terms of state support for higher education, as well as in the proportion of residents who obtained university diplomas, Ohio ranked at the bottom along with Mississippi.) This businessman also observed that he located his plants in rural areas that had not been contaminated by urban people and college graduates. Japanese-owned companies in the United States had adopted the same strategy years before.[13]

Elsewhere in the nation education reformers touted vouchers and school choice. They pointed to a pilot program in Milwaukee where the Catholic diocese educated minorities for half of what the public schools charged. In New York City, poor children who attended parochial schools were more likely to go to college than publicly educated youths. Private education, conservatives argued in the nineties, was superior because the unions and the "educrats" had no role to play. Although the NEA declared that the proponents of vouchers really wanted to close down the entire public school system, conservatives hardly needed to undertake such an effort. Given the rising levels of teenage crime and illiteracy, coupled with the fact that great numbers of senior citizens voted against school levies, public education was already in serious trouble.[14]

While public schools steadily lost support, millions of Americans continued to abandon their liberal Protestant churches. In 1996, four hundred theologically conservative "megachurches," with congregations of more than ten thousand, offered courses in Christian music, drama, and dance. For Baby Busters and Boomers, the vast evangelical church network provided sheltered environments in which they could establish a community separate from the secular culture. Such Christians could vacation in Branson, Missouri, where the hotels' cable system did not carry MTV and the country-western performers were well scrubbed. (Branson, enthused Cal Thomas, was "a town that slime forgot.") If there was no time or money to go to Branson, religious traditionalists could play board games such as "Bibleopoly" and "The Way of Peace." In the latter game players learned what Jesus would say to Congress on issues like school busing and welfare payments to unwed mothers. By 1995, one million Christian games were being sold annually.[15]

Christians could join Promise Keepers, an organization of several hundred thousand men led by Bill McCartney, at one time the University of

Colorado's football coach. Founded in 1990, Promise Keepers was an "apolitical" group that held all-male prayer rallies. Its members vowed to be good fathers and husbands, promote racial and religious toleration, and obey God's laws. Shocked that male Christians would come together to pray for the salvation of the American family, NOW often staged protests at Promise Keepers rallies. Liberals also questioned whether an organization that condemned gay activism and abortion could accurately claim to be apolitical. As McCartney, a Pentecostal convert, responded, "If a guy is inspired [by Promise Keepers] to run for the local school board, it'll be between him and the Lord."[16]

Most Americans neither joined Promise Keepers nor vacationed in Branson. Instead, they dropped out of both the religious and secular cultures. Since 1975, membership in fraternal organizations and women's clubs had fallen by half. The number of people volunteering to assist the Red Cross and the Boy Scouts declined by a third. (Many Americans, especially teens, spent more time watching television than in any other kind of activity.) Wearying of suburban traffic jams and juvenile crime, and not inclined to move to the city, greater numbers of people headed to the "exurbs." From 1990 to 1994, three-quarters of America's rural areas saw their populations increase. Ideally, white-collar workers could work from their home computer stations and ignore the larger, unsettling world. Some, depending upon their financial situation, might find time to become involved in community affairs and local governance.[17]

Given mounting disaffection with the nation's public institutions, it was hardly surprising that by 1995 three of every four Americans did not "trust government to do what is right." Baby Busters expressed the greatest contempt for politicians, eyeing both Democrats and Republicans with suspicion. They also had little patience for Boomer activists like the Clintons. As one Houston thirtysomething said in 1996, he was "sick of hearing about how Boomers changed things. They didn't change anything. All they did was tear down. They think nobody remembers. But growing your hair long, sleeping around, smoking a bunch of dope— what the hell good does that do for the country?" This fellow may have been upset by the fact that some Boomer professionals had been able to walk into good-paying jobs with little effort and seldom passed up an opportunity to brandish their credentials as friends of oppressed minorities. Perhaps when Baby Busters cheered as "Forrest Gump" punched out the abusive president of the Berkeley SDS, they saw their own smug Boomer bosses going down for the count.[18]

Clinton did have one bit of luck in the first two years of his administration. The "Bush recession" was over by the time he assumed office. Still, the economy had problems that would not go away. Ignoring the objections of the Rustbelt union chiefs, and with the enthusiastic support of Sunbelt Republicans, Clinton pushed the North American Free Trade Agreement (NAFTA) through Congress in 1994. (On the Right, only Pat Buchanan and Paul Weyrich opposed NAFTA.) Clinton predicted that NAFTA would create 200,000 new jobs by 1995. Instead, 225,000 jobs were lost as American industrialists relocated to low-wage Mexico. (Even before Mexico became a corporate "El Dorado," a number of U.S. businesses had sought out cheap labor in Indonesia.) Desperate for any kind of business, Rustbelt communities sought casino franchises. While some people might obtain jobs as card dealers and bartenders, the economic and social costs far outweighed whatever employment opportunities that came along. The Chicago *Tribune* reported that Gary's casinos drained $240 million annually from the local economy. Legalized gambling devoured financial resources that might have been used to build new plants and urban infrastructure. A nasty side effect was that casinos attracted drug peddlers, prostitutes, and muggers.[19]

For auto- and steelworkers who still had jobs, life was pretty good. As had been true since the early eighties, many unionized plants allowed their labor force to age in place. (The average age of a Big Three autoworker in 1995 was forty-five. Autoworkers at Japanese-owned, non-union firms in the United States were much younger.) College graduates looked longingly at assembly-line jobs that paid more than they could make as temps, video-store clerks, and teachers. Even if college-educated Baby Busters obtained a hard-to-get factory job, they would have to accept a two-tier wage system. Still, receiving ten dollars an hour—instead of nineteen as did their Boomer counterparts—was better than working for minimum wage at Blockbuster. To reduce generational tensions, the UAW had the American automakers segregate their Boomer and Baby Buster employees. Consequently, when generational strife did develop, it usually involved Boomers and seniors. For instance, retirees from the Wheeling-Pittsburgh Steel mill in West Virginia precipitated a strike and plant shutdown. Seniors argued that they could not manage on their (largely tax-exempt) Social Security, $600-a-month company pensions, and Medicare. They wanted heftier pensions, even if it meant driving Wheeling-Pitt into bankruptcy.[20]

By the nineties it was evident that, as MIT economist Lester Thurow observed, one-earner families were on the verge of extinction. Millions of men under the age of thirty-five could not support a family with just their income. When wives had to work, a price had to be paid. A 1994 study revealed that children whose mothers worked full-time were 45 percent more likely to be sexually active than youngsters who had either parent at home. If that was not worrisome enough, fewer families could afford to become homeowners.[21]

Corporate executives, far from reassuring their employees, justified "downsizing" the labor force while giving themselves huge bonuses. The fact that American goods were better made than had been the case in previous years mattered little when executives calculated the bottom line. A growing number of businessmen, including the heirs of the Campbell Soup fortune, went so far as to renounce their American citizenship and move their residences overseas out of the tax man's reach. Significantly, one of every three downsized white-collar workers who found a new job made less money. (In New Hampshire, where service and retail employ- ment had replaced construction and manufacturing jobs, blue-collar wages fell from $600 to $380 weekly.) Payroll deductions for Social Secu- rity, Medicare, and Medicaid placed added burdens on families. In 1970, Medicaid had been a $5 billion program. By 1995, Medicaid costs had soared to $156 billion.[22]

Ironically, the wealth of those in the highest income bracket grew more rapidly in the first two years of the Clinton administration than during the entire eighties—the so-called "Reagan decade of greed." (Overall, the nation's top 20 percent of taxpayers made more money than the middle 60 percent.) In 1979, the average wage gap between male high school and college graduates was $18,000. Fifteen years later, college-educated males made, on average, $30,000 more than high school graduates. To get the most "bang for your buck," though, you really needed to major in soft- ware engineering, not history, and graduate from Carnegie-Mellon Uni- versity, not Michigan State.[23]

By 1994, the electorate was, as it had been in '92, anxious and angry. Liberals, however, misread the political mood of the country. Six months into Clinton's presidency, historian James MacGregor Burns proclaimed that a new age of progressive reform and government activism had dawned. Burns favorably compared Bill Clinton to Franklin Roosevelt. His judgment failed him. Voters may have tossed a Republican out of the White House in 1992, but two years later they were gunning for Demo- cratic governors and congressmen.[24]

Among the most prominent liberals to be defeated was Governor Mario Cuomo. Over the years New York voters had been remarkably tolerant of Cuomo. They could, at least in part, buy Cuomo's argument that while he thought abortion violated God's commandments, he did not think religious beliefs should influence civil law. Voters even brushed off Cuomo's bizarre assertions that there was no such thing as the Mafia. By 1994, however, New Yorkers had wearied of their governor. He had racked up an enormous state debt, expanded the government payroll beyond all reason, repeatedly raised taxes, and resisted efforts to restore the death penalty. Perhaps most damaging to Cuomo, however, was his unwillingness to condemn black-on-white crime. Far too often Cuomo excused the behavior of violent minority teens. In New York City, where relations between blacks and Jews had steadily deteriorated since Jesse Jackson's "Hymietown" remarks in the eighties, Cuomo lost sufficient support to deny him reelection. Orthodox Jews complained that "the blacks can kill and do anything" without fear of prosecution, while blacks charged Jews with racism. Cuomo could win only with black *and* Jewish votes.[25]

New Jersey and Ohio voters also sent their regards to the Democratic gubernatorial candidates. Governor Jim Florio of New Jersey, whom Cuomo had touted as a presidential prospect, was defeated in 1993. Rising taxes and crime proved lethal to the Democratic incumbent. In 1994, Ohio's Democratic candidate for governor managed to garner just 25 percent of the vote. If his tally had fallen to 20 percent, the Democratic Party, as required by state law, would have lost its status as a major political organization. Subsequent Democratic candidates for state office would have had to petition to be put on the ballot—just like Socialist Workers Party candidates. During the gubernatorial election, Ohio Democrats dismissed the Republican candidate for lieutenant governor as nothing but a housewife and college dropout. Their superior candidate for lieutenant governor, in contrast, was a black, Harvard-educated lawyer. Apparently, Ohio Democrats did not want the votes of working-class whites, high school graduates, and mothers.[26]

The '94 congressional elections—which *Newsweek*'s Eleanor Clift had predicted would leave the Democrats securely in power—radically altered the political landscape. Not only did Republicans regain control of the Senate, for the first time in forty years they captured the House. The white working class, the most alienated constituency in America next to religious conservatives, tossed out their Democratic senators and representatives. In Kentucky, a minister and owner of a Christian bookstore whipped his more politically experienced opponent. Newt Gingrich celebrated the clergyman's victory by throwing what one observer called "a fraternity keg party" for the teetotaler. Meanwhile in the state of Washington, a Pentecostal woman fond of quoting from the Book of Daniel not only won her congressional race but beat up on the GOP establishment. To the horror of country-club Republicans, Linda Smith conducted a write-in campaign that she ran outside regular party circles. Overall, the 230-member Republican Congressional Class of '94 was just as ideologically driven as its liberal counterpart of twenty years before.[27]

In addition to winning the support of white workers, the GOP's congressional candidates received more Catholic votes than the Democrats. That had not happened before in a midterm election. Thanks in part to Ralph Reed, the Christian Coalition had developed strong ties to Catholic clergy and laity. In the spring of '94, Cardinal John O'Connor and Pat Robertson, among other prominent Catholics and conservative Protestants, formed a "spiritual" alliance. They pledged to oppose abortion and support "school choice." The Christian Coalition placed its resources squarely behind the ecumenical initiative. Liberal Republicans were jittery. By 1994, the Christian Coalition dominated GOP organizations in nineteen states, twelve in the Sunbelt. (Liberal Republicans clung to power in Connecticut, Massachusetts, and New York.) Overall, the Christian Coalition claimed nearly two million members, accounted for 40 percent of the Republican primary vote, and had a budget of $25 million. Despite enormous doctrinal differences, Robertson's group recruited Catholics to leadership positions and baptized them as Republicans.[28]

Not only was 1994 a victory for the Christian Coalition—and conservatives in general—it was a big win for southern Republicans. Newt Gingrich, Dick Armey, and Phil Gramm took up leadership positions in Congress while their state-level counterparts swept Dixie. Sixty-three percent of southern whites, regardless of gender and income, voted Republican. In Georgia, all eight white representatives were Republican; the three Democrats were black. Dixie conservatives owed an immense debt to Yankee liberals. First, liberals insisted that congressional districts be apportioned by race in order to facilitate the election of blacks. Thanks to racial redistricting, where there had been five black Democrats in Congress in 1990 there were seventeen after the '94 election. Of course, a number of southern white Democrats, deprived of black votes, lost their seats. Second, liberal House leaders, including House Speaker Tom Foley of Washington, had told Clinton that they would not address welfare reform. Further, Foley added, they would regard any criticism of crime as racist. In this, Foley seemed to be taking a leaf from Tip O'Neill. Given what had happened to Carter's presidency as a result of his failure to put O'Neill in his place, one must wonder if Clinton felt relieved when voters tossed Foley out in '94.[29]

Newt Gingrich was the strategic mastermind behind the GOP's congressional victory. As media pundits observed, Gingrich and Clinton were a lot alike. Both could get carried away by their enthusiasms and lose sight of more important matters. The southern Boomers could, by turns, be charming, dogmatic, petulant, stubborn, and vain. There was, though, one major difference. By nature, Clinton said whatever his particular audience wanted to hear. If Hillary was not around to keep him on the liberal path, Clinton would stray. No one exercised comparable influence over Gingrich. Moreover, the new House Speaker enjoyed playing "chicken" with the Democrats. The problem was Gingrich never knew when to bail out of the car before it went plunging off the cliff.

At the center of the Gingrich Revolution stood the "Contract with America." With great fanfare, Republicans promised to end federal welfare, cut taxes, and balance the budget. Following the counsel of the Heritage Foundation, the "Contract with America" avoided issues dear to the hearts of social conservatives. As a Heritage analyst argued, "Tax cuts cannot only unite the factions of the [GOP] that would otherwise be divided on social issues," they convey "an optimistic message about the future and address the underlying anxiety." Representative Dick Armey of Texas minimized differences between social conservatives and libertarians. The Republican majority leader contended that by trimming the power of the federal government, libertarians could deprive gays of their major ally and "de-fund" federal agencies that social conservatives loathed, chiefly the National Endowment for the Arts. Libertarians and moralists, Armey predicted, would be "singing the same song" in "Freedom's Choir."[30]

Unfortunately for Armey, many of his fellow choir members were tone deaf. Texas senator Phil Gramm, who wanted the '96 GOP presidential nomination, had little use for religious traditionalists. In public, Gramm played avenging Christian and patriot. He was at his God-fearing best in a 1995 commencement address at Jerry Falwell's Liberty Baptist University:

Let's hold violent criminals accountable for their actions and have minimum mandatory sentencing for thugs who sell drugs to our children. Let's stop building prisons like Holiday Inns, make prisoners work six days a week and go to school at night. And when violent criminals brutally murder our neighbors, let's put them to death.[31]

In private, Gramm was neither a superpatriot nor an Old Testament prophet. During the Vietnam War, Gramm had found that he had better things to do than fight for his country—like getting a doctorate in economics. At a meeting with Jim Dobson, the leader of Focus on the Family, Gramm bluntly stated, "I'm not running for preacher. I'm running for president. I just don't feel comfortable going around telling other people how to live their lives." The Texan wished to champion the free market, not waste his time on moral issues. Having once financed a pornographic movie production, Gramm was understandably reluctant to be a *real* crusader against immorality. Then again, Gramm was not even much of a libertarian. While he voted to curb welfare, Gramm protected a special mohair wool subsidy program for Texas sheepherders.[32]

Dismayed with GOP efforts to downplay social issues in favor of tax cuts, religious conservatives raised a ruckus. In 1993, Martin Mawyer, the president of the Christian Action Network, informed the *Washington Post*:

Our goal is not to increase our political power by deceiving the American public through talk of taxes, crime, health care, or NAFTA. Our real concerns are abortion, school prayer, and gay rights, and our mission is to present our case honestly to the American people and give them a chance to decide.[33]

After the GOP captured Congress, Dobson chastised Gingrich and the free marketers, informing them that he would walk away from the Republicans if they did not address abortion. Dobson had grown weary of political compromise, feeling that society was at the point of moral bankruptcy. By way of example, he pointed to 1994 ballot initiatives in Oregon that legalized "doctor-assisted suicide" and essentially decriminalized child pornography. As Dobson and former Reagan administration staffer Gary Bauer contended, "Nothing short of a great Civil War of Values rages today throughout North America. Two sides with vastly differing and incompatible world-views are locked in a bitter conflict that permeates every level of society." Just how bitter that conflict was became evident in 1996. Colorado liberals, looking to cripple Focus on the Family—which was based in that state—put an initiative on the ballot to tax churches and non-profit organizations. The Denver *Post* warned voters that the initiative would result in the closure of YMCAs, among other non-profit institutions. Liberal activists did not care—they belonged to private gyms where they could go to tone their abs. The initiative failed.[34]

Moderate Republicans castigated Dobson and Bauer. Rich Bond, an ally of George Bush's and a former chair of the Republican National Committee, asserted, "Our job is to win elections, not to cling to intolerances that zealots call principles, not to be led or dominated by a vocal few who like to look good losing. That is a sure path to disaster." Pennsylvania senator Arlen Specter, a prochoice Republican and a Jew, went further than Bond, accusing social conservatives of being anti-Semites. In Virginia, Senator John Warner, another liberal Republican, refused to endorse Michael Farris, the 1993 GOP candidate for lieutenant governor. Farris had earlier earned fame among Christian conservatives for advocating the censorship of public school texts. (When Senator Specter accused Christian conservatives of being anti-Semitic, he had activists like Farris in mind. Farris would not have regarded himself as anti-Semitic, even if he did seemingly imply in his criticism of Anne Frank that Judaism was not the true path to God.)[35]

Religious conservatives lost all patience with Warner when he openly expressed his contempt for Oliver North, their pick to run against Senator Chuck Robb in 1994. North may have eluded prison for his role in the Iran-Contra affair and won a following among some conservatives. However, he did not inspire much love among other Republicans. Though the *American Spectator* accused Warner of committing "treason," it was worth bearing in mind that James Webb, a onetime Reagan administration official and Vietnam combat veteran, also campaigned against North. Webb was no liberal. When Nancy Reagan denounced North during the '94 senatorial race, a few conservatives countered that she had helped derail the Reagan Revolution.[36]

Liberal Democrats also attacked the Right. Writing in 1995 for the *New York Review of Books,* Garry Wills and Michael Lind depicted conservatives as paranoid conspiracy mongers, bigots, and dolts. While *Time* and other mainstream publications picked up on their accusations, few journalists pointed out that Wills and Lind had began their careers within the bowels of the New Right. Both found success and celebrity once they turned on their benefactors. Lind, who was a former Heritage Foundation staffer, charged that many conservatives hailed from "the least 'American' section of the country"—the South. With no less disdain, Wills sniffed that "Gingrich looks like a car salesman affecting professorial airs." Although Wills and Lind claimed they were awakening the nation to the threat posed by an anti-Semitic Christian Right, the writers made clear what really bothered them about Pat Robertson and the South: Robertson, like his white Dixie brethren, opposed abortion and gay liberation. (Actually, southern blacks did not approve of abortion and gay rights either, but Lind and Wills could not acknowledge such inconvenient facts without undercutting their argument that social conservatives were white racists.)[37]

Abraham Foxman, the director of the Anti-Defamation League (ADL), weighed in, hurling more politically motivated charges against conservatives. When Gingrich appointed Christina Jeffrey of Kennesaw State College to the position of House historian, Foxman took a fragment of her scholarly work out of context to make it appear as if she were a Nazi sympathizer. Jeffrey's Jewish colleagues were outraged, but Foxman's smears had their intended result. Wilting under the attack of the ADL and the *New York Times,* Gingrich fired his fellow Georgian. Understandably hurt, Jeffrey lamented: "I know the people in Washington just shrug their shoulders and say, 'Welcome to Washington. That's just the way it is.' But, you know, there's a little part of me that says it ought not to be that way. We ought to be able to come in from the hinterlands, every now and then, we peasants with our country ways."[38]

Conservative Jews rushed to the defense of the GOP Congress and the Christian Right. Bill Kristol—a former member of Dan Quayle's staff— stated, "I prefer the Christian Right to the pagan Left." Kristol also declared that Jewish liberals hated Pentecostals and Southern Baptists because such Christians belonged to a lower social class. (Some Jewish liberals, notably Rabbi Simeon Maslin, the head of the Central Conference of American [Reform] Rabbis, had no use for Orthodox Jews either. Any Jew who opposed the causes of social liberalism, Rabbi Maslin believed, was not a true Jew. In 1996, the Central Conference of American Rabbis endorsed same-sex marriages.) Norman Podhoretz denied that conservatives despised Jews. "They hate liberals," Podhoretz observed. "As it happens, most Jews are liberals."[39]

In 1994, seventy-five Jewish conservatives had taken out an advertisement in the *New York Times.* They were upset with Foxman's crusade against the Religious Right. As film critic Michael Medved and Heritage Foundation vice president Adam Meyerson pointed out in criticism of the ADL, "It ill behooves an organization dedicated to fighting against defamation to engage in defamation of its own." Marshall Wittmann, a Jewish analyst at the Heritage Foundation, denied that there was any conflict between Judaism and conservative Christianity. Taking issue with Foxman, Wittmann insisted that, far from trying "to impose their values upon others," Christians just wanted "to prevent the values of others [namely, secular liberals] from being imposed upon them." Foxman, who had not been prepared to substantiate his charges against the Christian Coalition, backpedaled, conceding, "I don't consider Pat Robertson an anti-Semite."[40]

While the battle over Christian anti-Semitism raged, Ralph Reed had to deal with his right flank. Writing in *Policy Review* a year before the midterm elections, Reed pleaded with social conservatives to broaden their appeal. "The pro-family movement has limited its effectiveness by concentrating disproportionately on issues such as abortion and homosexuality," Reed wrote. "These are vital moral issues, and must remain an important part of the message. To win at the ballot box and in the court of public opinion, however, the pro-family movement must speak to the concerns of average voters in the areas of taxes, crime, government waste, health care, and financial security." Reed then reassured the free marketers who read the *Wall Street Journal* that the Christian Coalition thought NAFTA, and reducing federal entitlement spending, were priority issues. Following Reed's lead, candidates who were "approved" by the Christian Coalition in '93 and '94 stressed their opposition to higher taxes, not abortion.[41]

Stunned by the intense criticism he received from social conservatives after the '94 election, Reed clarified his message. He insisted that "traditionalist ends can be advanced through libertarian means." Moreover, religious conservatives must be careful not to "replace the social engineering of the Left with their own government-run Promised Land." What America needed, Reed argued, was a "return to non-governmental solutions" to issues like poverty and welfare. "We've got to challenge the churches, the synagogues, and the families to dig deeper and do more," he contended. Still, Reed recognized that some federal legislation would be necessary to pacify moral traditionalists. With much fanfare the Christian Coalition announced a "Contract With the American Family," as well as its support for a "Religious Freedom Act" that would allow prayer in the public schools and eliminate federal funding of the National Endowment for the Arts. Never at a loss for words, Reed eloquently called for an America in which "more marriages succeed than fail, where more children are born in wedlock than outside of it, and where children are counted both by families and by government as a blessing rather than a burden." For all of that, Reed continued sotto voce, the best thing the federal government could do for American families was to leave them alone.[42]

Jim Dobson would never embrace Reed's pragmatic approach to politics. In 1995, he praised Pat Buchanan and hinted that his two-million-member organization might support a third-party candidate in the forthcoming presidential election. The prospect of another Buchanan run in the GOP primaries did not please Reed—not least because it would tear apart the conservative movement and perhaps the Christian Coalition itself. In 1993, Buchanan had given a rousing address to a Christian Coalition convention. While Reed downplayed cultural issues, Buchanan excited the three thousand delegates with his defense of Christian morality. Even more embarrassing, Buchanan criticized Reed and Robertson for endorsing NAFTA. Aghast, Reed made it clear that, regardless of what the liberal media said, the Christian Coalition did not support Buchanan.[43]

In the Iowa caucuses several prominent state figures in the Christian Coalition broke ranks to campaign for Buchanan. He placed second, picking up enormous support from Catholic precincts in Davenport and Dubuque. Buchanan subsequently won the New Hampshire primary, besting the befuddled Bob Dole. (Senator Dole, despite his Kansas farm ties, had not done well in the Iowa caucuses either.) The New England coordinator of the Christian Coalition, a Buchanan campaign aide in the '92 primaries, praised his former boss for being "right on the money" when it came to the important social and economic issues. In the Louisiana caucuses, Reed turned up at Senator Phil Gramm's side. (Dole stayed out of the state, conceding it to Gramm.) The Texan lost to Buchanan. Louisiana's economic populists and social conservatives—particularly Catholics—rallied behind the onetime *Crossfire* commentator. Fortunately for Reed, the rest of the South, as had been true in '92, turned its back on Buchanan. Twice as many Christian Coalition members voted for Dole than the combative Buchanan. He did not pick up a great deal of support from Southern Baptists and—once again—won few kudos for his complaints about NAFTA and the loss of American industrial jobs. As one South Carolinian free marketer said in response to Buchanan's economic populism, "We can mourn the loss of the textile jobs. But there's no time for nostalgia."[44]

Paradoxically, where economic populism served Buchanan well in the North, it limited his effectiveness in most of the South. Protestant individualism reigned in Dixie. This religious factor, although it should not be overstated, cannot be ignored. As Buchanan liked to say, he gleaned his economic views from Pope Leo XIII and embraced "the old Catholic principle of subsidiarity." In 1891, Leo XIII had stated that workers should expect a living wage. Further, Leo and his successors rejected centralized, bureaucratic dictation from above just as they argued that free-market capitalism had to operate within moral limits. Keeping these Catholic tenets in mind, Buchanan ripped into Gramm. According to Buchanan, Gramm had "bought into the myth of economic man, that everything can be solved with tax cuts, balance the budget, get the numbers right, [and then] the problem is solved." Worse, Gramm looked upon workers as raw materials to be used up and then thrown aside. Workers, and the communities in which they lived and raised families, were central to what made America a great and godly nation. Wall Street brokers and economic conservatives, Buchanan claimed, had "lost their connection to American working men and women."[45]

The attacks Buchanan sustained from GOP businessmen and libertarians were even more shrill than had been the case in '92. That was to be expected. By winning three million primary votes and finishing in second place for the GOP presidential nomination, Buchanan had made himself a bigger target. Heritage Foundation analyst Stuart Butler cried that Buchanan "sounds like somebody from the AFL-CIO. His notion that you've got to protect the market from the threat of competition abroad, and the threat of people raking off excess profits at the expense of the working person, is far to the left of most of the people in the Democratic Party." A few political journalists on the Left had noted the same phenomenon. As a liberal reporter for the *Village Voice* lamented when interviewing Buchanan, "I've been waiting my whole life for someone running for president to talk about the Fortune 500 as the enemy, and when I finally get my wish, it turns out to be you." John Judis of the *New Republic,* who never cut Buchanan any slack when it came to his attitudes toward blacks, gays, and Jews, noted that the feisty conservative was raising points that no one in the Democratic White House or the Republican Congress seemed comfortable discussing.[46]

Bill Kristol, who resented Buchanan's attacks on Wall Street and Israel, derided the pundit as "America's last leftist." The *Wall Street Journal* editorialized that radicals like Buchanan were "McGovern Republicans" bent on destroying the party. William Bennett, now based at the Heritage Foundation, slammed Buchanan. It was one thing to condemn Universal Studios for distributing obscene rap music; it was quite another to criticize corporations that went abroad in search of cheap labor. Gingrich let it be known that there would be no place for Buchanan at the '96 Republican National Convention. (The House Speaker prized loyalty and obedience, two virtues that he thought Buchanan lacked. When Representative Linda Smith, in good Christian fashion, insisted that congressional ethics rules apply to Republicans as well as Democrats, Gingrich made her a "non person.") Corporate executives called Buchanan "dangerous" and threatened to back Clinton unless the GOP silenced him. Only two major businessmen, both dedicated Catholics, contributed to Buchanan's campaign: Thomas Monaghan of Domino's Pizza and John Breen of Sherwin Williams.[47]

At the urging of friends from the Heritage Foundation and the *Wall Street Journal*, billionaire publisher Steve Forbes entered the GOP primaries. Though Forbes spent millions to stop Buchanan, he went nowhere. His problems were many. First, Forbes alienated social conservatives by opposing constitutional amendments to ban abortion and legalize school prayer. Second, Forbes had to rebut Buchanan's "gloom and doom" economic message, while persuading voters that the Clinton economy was veering toward recession. If logic failed Forbes, his political senses were not far behind. With assistance from conservative think tanks, Forbes proposed a single flat income tax. Buchanan had a field day: "Under Mr. Forbes' plan, the middle class loses all deductions for home mortgage interest and church contributions; the federal budget would be thrown scores of billions deeper into deficit, and lounge lizards in Palm Beach pay a lower tax rate than steelworkers in Youngstown." He might have also observed that Forbes's plan, by abolishing the inheritance tax, would net the publisher's heirs an additional $1 billion. GOP primary voters, half of whom made less than $50,000 a year, were not impressed with Forbes. He had hoped voters would look at him as a kinder and gentler Ross Perot. There was, however, an important difference between the two that could not be ignored: Perot had *earned* his billions, Forbes had inherited his wealth.[48]

As the Republican primary season unfolded, party leaders came to an inescapable conclusion—only by uniting behind Bob Dole could Buchanan be defeated. The Republican governors, country clubbers, and the southern wing of the Christian Coalition dragged a sluggish Dole across the finish line. Despite their success in beating Buchanan, few Republicans were happy with their nominee. Free marketers regarded Dole as a tax-and-spend liberal. But that did not matter so much, as David Frum of the *Wall Street Journal* wrote, because "conservatives have long since adjusted themselves to defalcations from duty by Bob Dole." Speaking for many religious conservatives, Cal Thomas observed that Dole was a weak candidate with no principles. Dole also received harsh words from the Republican governors of Illinois, New York, Ohio, and Wisconsin. Indeed, on several occasions Governor George Voinovich made sure he was detained elsewhere when Dole campaigned in Ohio. With allies like these, Dole did not need Democratic enemies.[49]

The Republican capture of Congress had initially disoriented President Clinton. His first reaction was to summon Boomer intellectuals such as Columbia historian Alan Brinkley to his side. An author of an incisive book on New Deal protest politics, as well as the son of an influential NBC commentator, Brinkley urged Clinton "to defend the idea of government without necessarily defending everything the current government does." Clinton, Brinkley observed, also needed to appear presidential. Since Gingrich wanted to claim the Roosevelt mantle, Clinton decided two could play at that game. On the fiftieth anniversary of FDR's death, Clinton went to the late president's "Southern Home" in Warm Springs, Georgia. All Clinton succeeded in doing was to recast himself as a dynamic, heroic leader for the *thirties*. Having failed to project himself as a new FDR, Clinton summoned "personal growth gurus" to the White House for their advice. Conservatives speculated that the gurus told him to get in touch with his inner Republican.[50]

Luckily for Clinton, unexpected opportunities arose in 1995 that salvaged his presidency. In Oklahoma City, an American boy-next-door terrorist bombed a federal office building, killing 168 people. Clinton and the media indicted Gingrich, Jerry Falwell, the National Rifle Association (NRA), and conservative talk-radio personality Rush Limbaugh for creating "a climate in which violence blossoms." Such conservatives, Clinton insisted, "spread hate" and "leave the impression that . . . violence is acceptable." Juan Williams, a black columnist for the *Washington Post*, savaged "angry white men" who planted bombs and had taken "over the agenda here in Washington." While conservatives had grown used to being branded racists and anti-Semites, this was the first time they had been called mass murderers. As he met with the families of the Oklahoma victims, Clinton shed a few tears for the television cameras. His public approval ratings subsequently rose.[51]

Having bettered his political prospects, Clinton baited a trap for Gingrich. Flushed with their newfound power, Gingrich, Armey, and Gramm decided in 1995 that they would rather shut down the federal government than live with Clinton's budget plans. Clinton dared Gingrich to play chicken and the House Speaker took him up on his offer. Twice. Though the libertarians believed that Americans could (and should) live without government services and checks, theirs was a minority position. To Gingrich's chagrin, the media and many voters blamed Republican "extremists" for the inconveniences they experienced. Congressional conservatives further damaged themselves by embracing the legislative agenda of the NRA. A major contributor to Republican candidates in the '94 elections, the NRA expected Gingrich to turn aside federal bans on assault weapons and "cop-killer" ammo. While most Americans believed in the right to bear arms, they thought the NRA had gone off the libertarian deep end. Gingrich and the NRA were making it possible for Clinton to run for reelection as the law-and-order president. It was Gingrich's turn to flounder.

Clinton, however, needed more than funerals and Newt Gingrich to win reelection. After four years in office, Clinton (like Bush) had accomplished little and failed to articulate a vision for the nation. Once again, however, good fortune smiled on Clinton. Political consultant Dick Morris joined the Clinton team. A married man who paid prostitutes to suck his toes, Morris successfully remade Clinton into a Moral Majority–free enterprise Republican. Public opinion polls in 1996 showed that Americans remained responsive to promises to crack down on crime and welfare. Those same polls also revealed that the overwhelming majority of the electorate condemned same-sex marriages. (So poll-obsessed had Clinton become that he even commissioned voter surveys to determine where he should vacation.) Obviously, Morris concluded, Clinton must take credit for the economic "recovery" and run to the right of Dole on social issues. Hillary, in the meantime, had to be put on ice. In short order, Hillary's *policy-making* role in the White House shrank and, one by one, her allies in the administration found other employment. (Morris allowed Hillary to talk about child rearing since it seemed politically innocuous yet quite motherly.) Appearing on *Larry King Live,* Hillary gritted her teeth and assured voters that "there is no left wing of the Clinton White House."[52]

As a conservative, the president had few peers in his own party. Indeed, Clinton said that he would sign a bill barring legal recognition of gay marriages. From the sidelines David Mixner accused Clinton of supporting "a hate-filled and divisive bill for short-term political comfort." Senator Teddy Kennedy charged Clinton with "gay-bashing." (One wit pointed out that the real issue for Clinton and Kennedy was not "same-sex marriage, but same-marriage sex.") After assuring Health and Human Services Secretary Donna Shalala that he opposed draconian welfare reform, Clinton signed off on a Republican bill that limited total lifetime benefits to five years and permitted states to determine how they would deal with poor unwed mothers. Democratic representative John Lewis of Georgia moaned that the "downright lowdown" legislation "penalizes children for the action of their parents." Peter Edelman, a staffer in the Health and Human Services Department resigned in protest. (Hillary and Edelman's wife, Marian, were leaders of the Children's Defense Fund—a welfare lobby organization. Marian Edelman fumed that the president had made "a mockery of his pledge not to hurt children.") Undeterred by criticism from fellow Democrats, Clinton took credit for the popular Republican initiative.[53]

When it came to championing law and order Clinton made Pat Buchanan look like a bleeding-heart liberal. The President praised the efforts of San Diego residents to ferret out drug-dealing illegal immigrants: "We have begun to turn border communities under siege into communities where law and order and safety and security are once again the order of the day." Appearing before a black Pentecostal convention in New Orleans, Clinton called for America's cities to adopt 10:00 P.M. curfews for teenagers. (In 1993, Clinton had allocated federal funds to support "midnight basketball" leagues for urban teens. But that, as they say in politics, was history.) Clinton also addressed the '96 NEA convention, pledging $10 million to help public schools deal with truants. Noticing that many juvenile delinquents smoked cigarettes, Clinton vowed to punish tobacco companies for targeting teens in their advertising. Even though Democrats also received campaign money from the tobacco lobby, Clinton made sure voters identified Gingrich and Dole with "Joe Camel."[54]

Clinton next proposed mandatory drug testing for teens seeking driver's licenses and called for a five-year prison sentence for anyone caught with five grams or more of methamphetamine—a variety of "speed" derived partially from nasal decongestants. "We have to stop it before it becomes the crack of the 1990s," Clinton warned. (Twenty-one of Clinton's staffers failed their drug tests in 1994. They kept their jobs—and their driver's licenses.) Then the president announced a business-government partnership that would, at no cost to the taxpayer, distribute cellular phones to twenty thousand neighborhood crime-watch programs so that volunteers could quickly contact the police. Clinton further promised to establish a federal registry on convicted pedophiles that would assist local law-enforcement agencies in tracking "those who prey on America's children." The president also urged the states to place the names of "deadbeat dads" on the Internet and in post offices. Failure to pay child support, Clinton said, would result in felony charges. (In 1994, the *Democratic* Senate had, without dissent, criticized Clinton for "failing to use existing federal law to prosecute deadbeat parents.")[55]

Maureen Dowd of the *New York Times* could not believe how trivial the Democratic campaign had become. "What bold new visions will the president come up with next?" Dowd wondered. "Will he ask Health and Human Services to make doctors stop putting really old magazines in their waiting rooms?" Dowd had it exactly right. At one point of the campaign, Clinton turned to a handful of hecklers and said, in reference to the efforts of Congress to eliminate federal subsidies for PBS, "I would be screaming too if I wanted a country that took . . . Big Bird away from ten year-olds." Not everyone, however, panned Clinton's act. A number of chief executive officers deserted the GOP for Clinton. Xerox CEO Paul Allaire said, "We share a common view that the president is good for America and good for American business." William Estrey, the Republican CEO of Sprint, the largest private employer in Dole's home state, similarly lauded Clinton. The president, after all, had pushed through NAFTA. As for Clinton's '93 tax hike, it had little impact on executives who employed an army of accountants to shelter their incomes. Buchanan's downwardly mobile middle class bore the brunt of the tax increase, not people like Estrey and Allaire.[56]

Dick Morris made sure that Clinton's campaign was flawless—if vapid and hypocritical as well. Strategists studied Reagan's '84 "Morning in America" campaign intently, determined to make Bob Dole the Walter Mondale of 1996. Clinton ran radio advertisements aimed at religious traditionalists, emphasizing that he too opposed gay rights. The president and Hillary also staged a "photo opportunity" on the steps of a church with Bill holding a Bible in his hands. (Their pose, including the way Clinton grasped his Bible, perfectly replicated a shot of Jimmy and Rosalynn Carter as they left church services during the '76 campaign. No one in the media appeared to notice this remarkable coincidence.)[57]

Despite protests from the Left, the Democratic Party platform that Clinton had engineered exhorted Washington to devolve political power back to the (mostly Republican-led) states. The platform also asserted that "the private sector is the engine of economic growth"—not the federal government. Unlike the 1980 platform that Teddy Kennedy had written, the Clinton model celebrated the traditional family and called for greater police powers to curb crime. Although the blue-collar unions continued to denounce NAFTA, and AFL-CIO president John Sweeney decried Clinton's welfare reform as "anti-poor, anti-immigrant, anti-women, and anti-children," the president had little reason to worry. By 1996, the public-sector unions politically dominated the AFL-CIO; NAFTA did not adversely affect white-collar government employees. Besides, lifestyle liberals persuaded themselves that Clinton was just throwing "boob bait to the Bubbas." It would be business as usual after the election.[58]

While beating up on liberals—who would vote for him anyway—Clinton aroused senior citizens. Visiting the nation's affluent retirement communities, as had every Democratic presidential candidate for the past twenty years, Clinton vowed to "protect and preserve" Medicare from Republican dismemberment. Although Clinton knew full well that Medicare, like Social Security, was bankrupting the country and impoverishing struggling families, the president told Florida seniors, "I don't understand why everybody is going around like Chicken Little." Clinton credited Medicare and Social Security for giving seniors "a lower poverty rate than people under sixty-five" and asserted that "we can clearly balance the budget and dramatically extend the life of the Medicare trust fund without the level of cuts in Medicare and Medicaid" that the Republican Congress advocated. (Clinton admitted that benefits would have to be reduced, payroll taxes further increased, and the retirement age raised *for Baby Busters*. That prospect naturally did not upset seniors.) The AMA, its members having grown fat on Medicare and Medicaid checks, praised Clinton's determination to keep funding federal health insurance programs. Republican doctors, fearing that congressional conservatives might reduce medical benefits, joined the Clinton camp.[59]

The president also played racial politics, though this time around he left Sister Souljah alone. Over the past six years a rash of church fires had occurred, mostly in the South. The network news shows, *USA Today*, the *New York Times*, and civil rights activists seized on the incidents, declaring that black churches had been selected for destruction by white racists. Predictably, Jesse Jackson deplored the "climate of retreat, hate, and ethnic cleansing" that Republicans had engendered in the South. Another liberal black minister echoed Jackson: "There's only a slippery slope between conservative religious persons and those that are actually doing the burning." Clinton and Vice President Gore quickly staged a photo opportunity at a torched black church. The president also set aside $6 million to assist local law enforcement officers in protecting southern black churches.[60]

Despite what Clinton and black activists claimed, the church fires said more about some peoples' attitudes toward Christianity than what they thought about race. Of the 216 church buildings burnt since 1990, the majority had *white* congregations. Moreover, a number of the arsonists were black. There was no organized conspiracy to torch black places of worship. To their credit, religious conservatives ignored the abuse heaped upon them by Jesse Jackson and secular white liberals. Promise Keepers and the Christian Coalition each pledged $1 million to assist in the rebuilding of black churches. Joseph Lowery, the leader of the Southern Christian Leadership Conference rebuffed such overtures, telling white conservatives, "The root of the problem is racism, not the burning of churches." Meanwhile the Southeast director of the NAACP exhorted blacks to spurn aid from Promise Keepers and the Christian Coalition. White Christian conservatives, he argued, were "Trojan Horses" seeking to undermine black solidarity.[61]

Though Clinton was quick to attack white racism—real and imagined—he faltered on the issue of black anti-Semitism. When Nation of Islam leader Louis Farrakhan led his "Million Man March" in Washington in 1995, Clinton praised the organizers' stand against black-on-black violence. The president emphasized that while he did not approve of Farrakhan's criticism of Jews, he thought that the message of the march was laudable. In effect, whites should "separate the message from the messenger." That was impossible. One of the purposes of the rally was to give Farrakhan and his minions a national stage on which they could savage "bloodsucker" Jews. Pat Robertson could only express amazement at the way in which Clinton, the network news shows, and the prestige press gingerly treated Farrakhan—as opposed to their treatment of him—playing down the Black Muslim's hatred of Jews, Christians, and white people in general. A year later, Representative Cynthia McKinney, a black Georgian Democrat, ran an anti-Semitic campaign against her Jewish opponent. Not a word of condemnation came from the White House. McKinney's father, who served as her political advisor, called challenger John Mitnick "a racist Jew" for having criticized Farrakhan. Her father, a member of the Georgia legislature, also distributed to black voters leaflets charging that Mitnick belonged to Jewish groups like the Anti-Defamation

League. (McKinney disavowed her father's comments but retained him as her campaign strategist.)[62]

Black anti-Semitism represented one strand in the conflicted impulses of the black middle class. It is worth bearing in mind that two-thirds of Farrakhan's marchers had annual incomes above $30,000, and one in five earned $75,000. It was not the exploited ghetto poor who cheered Farrakhan but members of a black middle class whose median income outstripped whites'. There was no shortage of bigots among such people. The chair of the Rutgers theater department, for instance, who reportedly denied tenure to a professor because she was "a white Jew b—ch." This black middle class included lawyers and politicians such as those in Dallas who formed a para-military group, the New Black Panthers, to intimidate white and Hispanic school board members. Dallas's black militants also threatened that unless an African-American was hired as police chief, "we're going to be in the streets, physically, literally, shooting [white] folks." Yet it was black middle-class residents in Perrywood, Maryland, who ordered security guards in 1996 to roust Washington youths from the suburb's basketball courts. Meanwhile in suburban Chicago, middle-class blacks protested the placement of low-income public housing units in their neighborhoods. Affluent blacks did not want to associate with poor blacks, even though they often accused whites of being racists for having the same desire.[63]

Kansas City, Missouri, mayor Emmanuel Cleaver, the president of the National Conference of Black Mayors, warned Republicans in 1996 that he would regard any criticism of affirmative action as racist. Knowing that better than three-quarters of the public opposed quotas, Clinton said he was "against reverse discrimination" and then retreated into silence. Though most citizens opposed quotas, American corporations did not. Only 14 percent of Fortune 500 companies used merit alone in making hiring decisions; the rest employed quotas. (Corporations commonly tucked minority employees away in their human resource departments, where they were far removed from the decision-making process. On the other hand, companies could not "downsize" minorities without risking an EEOC lawsuit for discrimination.) In California, conservatives placed an initiative on the ballot to end racial preferences. The initiative was more popular than the Republican presidential nominee and drew support from whites, Hispanics, Asians, *and blacks*. Proposition 209 would be approved by 54 percent of California's voters even as Bob Dole went down in flames.[64]

Across the land, liberals had to go to embarrassing lengths to defend racial hiring and admissions quotas. At Ohio University in 1996, President Robert Glidden overrode a decision by a department faculty committee and college dean to deny tenure to a black man. Glidden claimed that race had nothing to do with his decree while noting that the university needed "role models for minority students"—even if the role models could not survive peer review. A year before, Rutgers University president Francis Lawrence had inadvertently let slip his real reason for supporting admissions and hiring quotas: "Do we set standards in the future so that we don't admit anybody with the [Scholastic Aptitude Test]? Or do we deal with a disadvantaged population that doesn't have the genetic hereditary background to have a higher average [on the SAT]?"[65]

What with the public backlash against crime, quotas, and welfare—a reaction of twenty-five years' standing by the time of the '96 election—Dole should have had little problem defeating Clinton. Polls showed that two of every three voters thought that the country was "on the wrong track." Voters also rated Dole as far more honest than Clinton. The majority thought that the Clintons had tried to cover up several political scandals—including an Arkansas real estate deal that led to the imprisonment of Governor Jim Guy Tucker. But for all of that, as a Gallup poll concluded, "Dole's views [are] more popular than he is." Dole never persuaded the electorate that he should be president, nor did he ever connect with voters. The senator's constant references to his World War II service won him little respect from his own generation, which, as in the '92 election, valued Democratic entitlements over Republican calls for duty. At one point in the fall election, Dole became so irate at Clinton's "Mediscare" tactics, that the seventy-three-year-old politician blurted out, "If I were a senior citizen, I'd be a little fed up with all these ads scaring seniors."[66]

In part, Dole's problems stemmed from the fact that Clinton had tied him to Gingrich. (Gingrich and Dole strongly disliked each other. The House Speaker once called Dole "the tax collector for the welfare state.") As one Michigan Republican said of Gingrich, "If someone could ever turn me off the Republican Party, he could do it." Clinton would get his vote. Another Michigan voter, a political independent, said that she too would vote for Clinton because "I'm afraid the Republicans are going to cut funds for education and day care." In interviews with Ohio voters, the Columbus *Dispatch* found Republicans and independents who mirrored their Michigan counterparts. "Dole seems like he is out to save money for the rich," griped one woman. "I think Dole is too old. He teams up with Gingrich, and I don't care for that man at all." Yet another Ohio voter, who condemned Clinton for laughing off his experiments with marijuana, said that she still could not bring herself to vote for Dole. Once again, the "Gingrich factor" had cost Dole needed votes. (The Heritage Foundation insisted that Gingrich was a great leader who had "won the budget war" against Clinton. If that had been true, "Big Bird" would no longer be feeding at the federal trough.)[67]

As a campaigner, Dole could be extremely lame or just plain nasty. On most days he was simply inept—as when he declined to address a NAACP convention because its leaders were "trying to set me up." Dole added that he preferred a group that "I can relate to." (Denying that his campaign was in trouble, Dole said that he just needed to find the right "wedge issue" against Clinton. While deploying wedge issues against liberals had a venerable history, no previous Republican had ever been so daft as to admit that he wanted to divide Democrats along racial and religious lines.) Hoping to pull himself out of his electoral free fall, Dole tried to connect with his audience through the imagery of popular culture, observing that when it came to dealing with crime, Clinton "talks like Dirty Harry but acts like Barney Fife." That was the best Dole got.[68]

Mostly, Dole hit Clinton for raising taxes and his recent conversion to fiscal and moral conservatism. A California bookkeeper was not impressed. "All he does is complain about the president," she said. "I haven't heard him give me one reason to vote for him." Maybe, as columnist Maureen Dowd concluded, it was not that Dole was excessively negative. Dole's difficulties might stem from the fact that many voters, especially Boomers, did not want to change their own behavior, let alone listen to sermons about duty:

The scary thing about Bob Dole is that, just below the surface, we fear we can't live up to his standards, that he's an old-fashioned curmudgeon who's never going to think we have enough starch. On the other hand, we know we can live up to Bill Clinton's standards.

So it is futile for Republicans to argue that Clinton is flawed because all he does is respond and change. That's exactly why people like him. We are in a consumer culture. Baby Boomers are the most spoiled, over-marketed cohort in history, accustomed to having products tailored to them. Why should the presidency be any different?[69]

Perhaps Dole's worst problem was his inability to inspire trust among social and fiscal conservatives. Tellingly, when Dole discussed his accomplishments as a senator he emphasized the *liberal* legislation that he had helped pass. From saving the food stamp program to making Social Security "solvent" by raising payroll taxes, Dole could have been mistaken for George McGovern. After championing affirmative action for most of his career and then changing his mind only in 1995, in addition to having pushed several hefty tax increases through the Senate, Dole clearly had no bedrock conservative principles. As he told GOP leaders in '95, "I'm willing to be another Ronald Reagan, if that's what you want."[70]

Conservatives did not believe Dole had it in him to be Ronald Reagan, especially after he muddied the GOP's prolife message. For years Dole had been firmly against abortion. Indeed, in his 1974 Senate race he had accused his Democratic opponent, a medical doctor, of having performed abortions. In Kansas that charge was enough to save Dole from voter disenchantment with Watergate and Nixon. By 1996, however, the senator had a change of heart. Dole decided he had to heal the growing breach between liberal Republicans and religious traditionalists. To the outrage of the latter group, Dole's idea of compromise was to cave in to the demands of the GOP's abortion-rights stalwarts. Massachusetts governor William Weld and California governor Pete Wilson insisted that the party platform remove a plank that called for a constitutional ban on abortion. (When religious conservatives won half of the Massachusetts delegate seats to the GOP national convention, Weld tried to remove them. Failing at that, he made sure that the delegates-at-large, who were picked by his country-club and libertarian allies, were prochoice partisans.)[71]

Weld and Wilson picked up important support in New Jersey, Ohio, and Texas. Governor Christie Whitman of New Jersey, the heiress who had derailed Jim Florio's national political ambitions in 1993, urged the GOP to concentrate on tax cutting. Abortion rights, like affirmative action, Whitman said, made good public policy. Ohio's GOP leaders concurred. Of the sixty-seven GOP convention delegates from Ohio, just three wanted to retain the abortion plank. Ohio's businessmen, who ran the state GOP, did not care all that much about abortion. Like their New Jersey counterparts, they wanted corporate tax cuts. In Texas, Phil Gramm and Governor George W. Bush, a son of the former president, rebuked religious conservatives. They did not appreciate efforts to deny Senator Kay Bailey Hutchinson a seat at the Republican National Convention simply because she supported abortion. Senator Hutchinson bitterly complained that she had been victim of a "kamikaze mission [by a] small group that is not in the mainstream of the party." Sunbelt libertarians and Southern Baptists were on the verge of parting ways.[72]

Dole quickly backed away from his liberal Republican allies, claiming that he had been misunderstood. He still opposed abortion but thought that the GOP should welcome people with diverse views on the matter since it was *only* a moral issue. Dole had opened up the proverbial Pandora's box. Gingrich imprudently endorsed Hutchinson and intervened in a New York congressional race where prolifers were trying to unseat a prochoice Republican. In Colorado, moralists and GOP businessmen sniped at one another. The latter group championed abortion and fretted that Pat Buchanan had corrupted the party.[73]

Ralph Reed, who previously had encouraged overtures to prochoice Republicans, now found himself the subject of attack from within the ranks of the Christian Coalition. The political operative rapidly distanced himself from Dole, warning that social conservatives would reassess their support of the GOP presidential nominee. By the fall, Reed emphasized the importance of saving the Republican Congress. As for Dole, Reed predicted that Christian Coalition voters "will act as a firewall that will prevent what is clearly a poor Republican presidential performance from turning into a meltdown." Dole's problem, Reed concluded, had been his unwillingness to make "moral decline and a loss of family values more of a central theme." (Reed possessed a highly selective memory. Dole's stances on moral issues had *not* been the reason behind Reed's decision to back him. Reed, some conservatives fumed, would have endorsed the devil if it meant derailing Buchanan.)[74]

By alienating both prolife and prochoice Republicans, Dole could not take advantage of the fact that Clinton had left himself vulnerable to attack on the abortion issue. In the spring of '96, Clinton vetoed legislation that banned partial-birth abortion. This procedure, usually performed in the final weeks of pregnancy, was particularly grisly. The abortionist reached into the womb and cut open the head of the unborn child, using a catheter to suck out the brains. The dead fetus could then easily be pulled through the cervix. Ron Fitzsimmons, the head of the National Coalition of Abortion Providers, assured the public that partial-birth abortion was a rare procedure performed only to save the life (and fertility) of the mother. He later admitted, "I lied through my teeth." Half of the abortions performed in Cleveland's clinics, for instance, used this procedure. These had generally been elective abortions; neither the health of the mother nor her fertility was at stake. Partial-birth abortions were frequently performed as a matter of convenience or, in a number of cases, to prevent the birth of a handicapped child. (A few parish priests were unkind enough to point out that a woman who underwent a partial-birth abortion would be able to resume sexual activity much more quickly than was the case with a standard abortion.)[75]

Prochoice partisans went all out to fight the partial-birth abortion ban. During the House debate, Representative Patricia Schroeder of Colorado brought in a large color photograph of a happy family that, she claimed, would not have been so happy had the mother been forced to carry a "defective" fetus to term. (Schroeder apparently never saw the Nazi "hygiene" films of the thirties that rationalized state-sponsored euthanasia for the mentally and physically handicapped.) Schroeder then shouted that prolifers had almost killed her years before. It seemed that she had nearly died after the difficult birth of her second child. If partial-birth abortion had been an option she could have been spared her ordeal. (No one in the media sought out the Schroeder children for a reaction to that proposition.) Although most House and Senate Republicans, as well as a few Democrats, ignored Schroeder, Clinton did not. He turned aside the legislation and Senate Democrats subsequently sustained his veto.[76]

America's Catholic hierarchy was outraged. As the bishops informed Clinton:

Your action . . . takes our nation to a critical turning point in its treatment of helpless human beings inside and outside the womb. It moves our nation one step further toward acceptance of infanticide.

We will . . . urge Catholics and other people of good will . . . to do all that they can to urge Congress to override this shameful veto. In the coming weeks and months . . . each of us . . . will do all we can to educate people.[77]

The bishops made good their promise, distributing twenty-seven million prolife postcards at churches. Priests asked parishioners to mail the cards to their senators and representatives. (Southern Baptists joined in the effort, and Norma McCorvey, the plaintiff in *Roe v. Wade,* announced her conversion to the prolife side.) Despite their efforts, however, Catholic clergy failed to sway Senate Democrats. Liberals knew that most Catholics would not vote against them just on the issue of partial-birth abortion. As one Ohio Catholic woman observed, although she thought Clinton's support for partial-birth abortions was horrendous, she appreciated his effort to abolish welfare. The fact that she credited Clinton for "ending welfare as we know it," instead of crediting Congress, spoke volumes about Republican ineptitude. Certainly, Dole had done his cause little good among social conservatives. Rev. Flip Benham of Waco, Texas, who had converted Norma McCorvey to the prolife side, contended that Dole was no better than Clinton:

Choosing the lesser of two evils is still choosing evil. Bill Clinton is driving us off the cliff at 100 mph. Bob Dole is driving us off the cliff at 55 mph., but we're still going off the cliff.

The [GOP] platform means nothing; Bob Dole has said that over and over again. That is a bone the Republican Party throws out every four years to Christians and says, "Eat this."

Bob Dole wants to do everything he can do to dodge the issue (of abortion). He would sell anything for the presidency.[78]

Dole had made just one smart move as he headed into the fall campaign. He named Jack Kemp as his vice-presidential running mate. (It was a shotgun wedding performed at the insistence of economic conservatives. In the eighties Dole had publicly derided Kemp, claiming that the well-coifed Buffalo congressman would love to have a tax deduction for hair spray.) After leaving the Bush administration, Kemp had set up shop at the Heritage Foundation. As a free-lance politician, Kemp devised several proposals to deal with America's problems. While his economic ideas were standard libertarian fare—end welfare, cut taxes, and enact more free trade agreements like NAFTA—he did have something radical to offer social conservatives. According to Kemp, Congress must "support community and individual self-determination through the initiative and referendum process." Kemp thought communities should arrange their affairs as they saw fit without (one must suppose) the interference of the ACLU, the NEA, and the federal courts:

The debate over "community standards" is increasingly a debate over whether communities will be allowed to have any standards at all. Many parents are rendered virtually powerless in the moral and cultural upbringing of their children. It is a frustration that has led to a parental rights movement and a thousand school board fights.

To empower parents and communities in this struggle, Republicans should support the initiative and referenda movement that represents the cutting edge of the effort to enact conservative reforms such as school choice and tax limitation. We should welcome this as an authentic populist innovation.[79]

An infectiously enthusiastic campaigner, Kemp worked Catholic mill towns and black neighborhoods like a reincarnated FDR. In Johnstown, Pennsylvania, Kemp emphasized his support for school vouchers. Subsequently, a number of the city's younger union officers and Catholic laity announced that they would vote for the GOP ticket, largely because of Kemp—and in spite of Dole. Earlier, Kemp had dragged a dour Dole to Mass at St. Joseph's Cathedral in Buffalo. Then the two headed for Pittsburgh, where Kemp acted as the party's voice of prolife morality: "I can't imagine our nation being that city on a hill if we continue to allow the partial-birth abortion tragedy to continue in America." Cutting loose from Dole, Kemp addressed black crowds in Harlem and Chicago. Kemp bewailed the existence of an "an urban inner-city economy that tears your guts out." Seeking to save the black underclass, he recommended the creation of tax-free enterprise zones that would encourage employers to relocate to the ghetto. Underscoring his message that the difficulties of the black underclass were more economic than racial in nature, Kemp held up a dollar bill and boomed, "This is the color of the new civil rights revolution." No national Republican candidate in the past three decades (or even before) had gone to such lengths to extend his hand of friendship to blacks. Kemp, however, did not get many blacks to vote Republican. As Harlem congressman Charles Rangel asserted, "Jack is a very nice guy in a mean-spirited party."[80]

Ultimately, Kemp could not overcome the drag Dole exerted on the ticket. Then again, given what Clinton had in his electoral arsenal, it would have been difficult for any Republican to have won the presidency. Prior to the election Clinton granted citizenship to 1.3 million immigrants. The Justice Department did not have time to check the backgrounds of America's new *Democratic* voters but later found that at least 71,000 had criminal records. Many were not even eligible to become U.S. citizens. More important to Clinton's reelection than fraudulent votes, he had money—lots of it. The AFL-CIO spent $35 million on television ads attacking the "Dole-Gingrich" ticket and the Republican Congress. The president also called upon a wide variety of contributors to fatten his war chest. In addition to Steven Spielberg and Pamela Harriman—his ambassador to France—Clinton drew funds from the Chinese and Indonesian governments. China alone gave Clinton over $3 million, in the apparent expectation that the president would overlook its human rights violations and use of prison labor to undercut American manufacturers. (Labor leaders just closed their eyes.) Vice President Gore did his part, accepting $140,000 from a handful of Buddhist monks who, as cynics pointed out, "had taken a vow of poverty."[81]

Most voters were indifferent to Clinton's fund-raising schemes, although a few thought it was tacky to sell overnight stays in the White House for $50,000 and up. The media generally downplayed Clinton's ethical lapses. When Paula Jones, a former Arkansas government employee, sued Clinton for sexual harassment, journalists ridiculed her working-class origins and hairstyle, while gleefully reporting White House operatives' description of her as "trailer trash." (Anita Hill's feminist supporters also attacked Jones.) *Newsweek*'s Washington Bureau chief, Evan Thomas, who had participated in the pillorying of Paula Jones, subsequently apologized and blamed the media for covering up Clinton's sins:

About 85 percent of the reporters who cover the White House vote Democratic, they have for a long time. There is a liberal bias, particularly at the networks, at the lower levels, among the editors and the so-called infrastructure. There is a liberal bias at *Newsweek,* the magazine I work for—most of the people who work at *Newsweek* live on the Upper West Side of New York and they have a liberal bias.[82]

Although there was little good anyone could say about Bob Dole, the media made no effort to hide their contempt for conservatives. Major newspaper and television reporters were, as academic studies underscored, "two to three times more liberal than the general public." (Eighty-nine percent of Washington's news correspondents voted for Clinton in 1992.) On CNN, Judy Woodruff accused Gingrich of "yanking money away from welfare mothers with small children." Apparently, Clinton had played no role in enacting welfare reform, even thought he took credit for it on the campaign trail. *New York Times* columnist Frank Rich, who had gone to Harvard with Al Gore, intoned that Dole was a tool of anti-Semites like Pat Robertson. On National Public Radio, commentator Andrei Codrescu ridiculed Christian traditionalists, concluding that "the evaporation of four million (people) who believe in this crap would leave the world a better place." (One can imagine the media outcry if Pat Buchanan had called for the "evaporation" of four million Jews or blacks.)[83]

During the Republican convention, the networks televised a speech by Colin Powell that received a lukewarm reception. Liberals claimed that conservatives did not like Powell because he was black, failing to mention that he was also prochoice. Tellingly, only C-Span and "The Family Channel" broadcast a more popular convention address by Oklahoma representative J. C. Watts, a black social conservative and Baby Buster. ABC, CBS, and NBC did not show Watts bringing *white* delegates to their feet, nor did they mention that the Democrats had deployed racist tactics to unseat him. The party of racial reconciliation ran television advertisements showing the high school photographs of Watts and his white opponent. Watts had an "Afro"; the farm-boy Democrat cradled livestock in his arms. The narrator of the advertisement asked which of the two most accurately represented the values of the white, rural district. Oklahoma voters answered that question by reelecting Watts. (Ohio Democrats sank lower than their Sooner counterparts. In their efforts to defeat Representative John Kasich, Democratic operatives informed various media outlets that the chair of the House Budget Committee might be gay. Kasich was a free marketer and Grateful Dead fan, not a homosexual.)[84]

Just before election day, the New York Times and CBS predicted Clinton would beat Dole by eighteen percentage points. Moreover, many media figures concluded, Republicans might lose control of the House. Republicans did surrender a few House seats, but Gingrich kept his majority. The Democrats ran thousands of television ads denouncing "Gingrich & Dole," deployed "Mediscare" tactics among seniors, and persuaded several millionaires to use their own money to run for office. NARAL and NOW recited their shopworn litany about Republican racism, sexism, and fascism, and a miffed Mario Cuomo called House Republicans "rabid revolutionaries." It was all for naught. Of course, even if the Democrats had recaptured Congress, it was questionable what good it would have done the liberal cause. Walter Minnick, the Boomer millionaire who sought an Idaho Senate seat, insisted that although he ran on the Democratic ticket, "I'm not a Democrat." Having worked for the Nixon White House, Minnick was not kidding.[85]

Although Clinton won a second term, he once again proved incapable of securing a majority. Despite the predictions of the media, the president defeated Dole by eight points—not eighteen. As in the '92 election, Clinton's entire margin of victory came from free marketers who deserted the GOP for Ross Perot. (Country-club Republicans also quietly embraced Clinton.) Although Clinton captured a somewhat larger share of the vote in 1996 than had been the case four years before, overall voter turnout had fallen by 6 percent—meaning that just 49 percent of the electorate participated. Clinton's improved performance was chiefly the result of lower turnout, not because he had won many converts to his cause. Indeed, the Clinton electoral coalition remained essentially unchanged: blacks, Reform Jews, singles, and senior citizens. Once again, white southerners, nonunion workers, families, religious traditionalists, and Baby

Busters scorned Clinton. Fortunately for the president, though Baby Busters now outnumbered seniors, they were less likely to vote.[86]

At the state and congressional district level, large numbers of citizens split their ballots, voting for Clinton and their local Republican office-holders. In California, analysts concluded that a quarter of the electorate could be described as socially liberal and economically conservative. Such voters—most of whom were college-educated and tied into the post-industrial economy—liked Clinton because of his support for abortion rights and admired Gingrich for trying to abolish welfare and affirmative action. In Ohio, the Republicans retained control of the legislature and the state's congressional delegation. Only black Cleveland and its Jewish (non-Orthodox) suburbs remained solidly Democratic. Catholic voters tended to divide their loyalties between Clinton and their Republican representatives. (Catholic seniors often discounted what the Cleveland bishop said about Clinton's veto of the partial-birth abortion ban. They were worried about retaining their federal entitlements, not abortion.) Republicans claimed both of Alabama's Senate seats and the governorship. The GOP also picked up its first Senate seat ever in Clinton's Arkansas and took control of the Florida statehouse. In Kansas, Sam Brownback, a stanch conservative and foe of the welfare state, assumed Dole's former Senate seat. (Brownback was *not* Dole's designated successor.) Across the nation, just seventeen Democratic governors clung to office.[87]

In the larger scheme of things, neither Clinton nor Republicans could afford to be cheerful about the election results. Twenty-one percent of the people who voted Democratic expressed the fear that Clinton and his congressional counterparts might return to their liberal ways. If so, such voters would exact their revenge at a later date. Clinton, who ran as a conservative in '96, would have little choice but to govern as one in his second term. (Or, more likely, not govern at all, hoping that voters, and the congressional investigating committees looking into the sources of his campaign financing, forgot that he was president.) Republicans, meanwhile, had their own crosses to bear. Buchananites and Christian Coalition members did not enjoy being taken for granted. Martin Mawyer, who had criticized Ralph Reed's "pragmatic" support for Dole in the GOP primaries, talked loudly about forming a third party devoted to moral issues. ("I don't think people who come from conviction," Mawyer asserted after the election, "can any longer support people of compromise, and I think that's what the Republican Party has become.") Other religious conservatives recommended abandoning the secular political realm altogether, leaving the GOP to its libertarian and country-club constituencies.[88]

Libertarians such as David Frum were no happier with the GOP. He decried a Republican primary process that guaranteed the nomination of "bland candidates who care much more about building a political machine than they do about ideas and principles." (Actually, Dole's backers did have at least one principle: they did not want Buchanan winning the nomination.) Instead of choosing a leader who would attack entitlement spending, Frum argued, Republicans were stuck with "Mr. Dole's mimicry of checkbook liberalism." The libertarians made a valid point but ignored political realities. So long as millions of voters held out their hands for farm subsidies and Social Security, the federal government would continue to mortgage the nation's future. At the same time, Republican pledges to cut taxes, without seriously trimming federal spending, assured the continuation of crippling deficits.[89]

The '96 presidential election proved at least three things. First, Americans were not prepared to make hard choices. Voters wanted Democratic entitlements and Republican tax cuts. Second, as social critic Amitai Etzioni wrote, two distinct blocs of voters had created a political stalemate in national politics. One bloc consisted of libertarians and social liberals who wanted the freedom "to do their own thing" regardless of the cost to society. The other bloc hoped to impose moral order even if meant limiting individual freedom. These two groups contained both Democrats and Republicans. Third, Democratic and Republican politicians had little to offer the general electorate but insincere calls for moral renewal and free-trade nostrums like NAFTA, in addition to a little opportunistic race-gaming. Given this reality, Americans inevitably elected an ineffectual president and a hamstrung Congress. The Roosevelt and Reagan "revolutions" were over. What would come next was anyone's guess.[90]

Epilogue

There Is No Money in Social Conservatism

In 1995, William Bennett criticized the executives of Time-Warner for producing morally offensive rap music. For his part, conservative commentator John Leo called Time-Warner "our leading cultural polluter." An irate Gerald Levin, the chair of the mass-media conglomerate, countered that rap music had socially redeeming qualities. Indeed, Levin said, his son, a New York public-school teacher, used gangsta rap music in his classes as a way "to connect with his students." Two years later, one of Jonathan Levin's students allegedly robbed and murdered him.[1]

If Jonathan Levin had followed the example of his upper-class peers, he would have become a museum curator, corporate lawyer, or Wall Street broker. Few rich, well-educated people choose a career teaching in New York's public schools. Every day, Levin passed through a metal detector on his way to class. Many of his students had never known their fathers; some had close friends or family members who had been killed in drug-related shootings. His was a far cry from the world that the executives of Time-Warner inhabited. Businessmen could usually inoculate their families from the pathologies of modern urban life. Jonathan Levin was the exception that proved the rule. By becoming a public-school teacher he had placed himself at risk.[2]

Record industry executives were not the only people who tried to protect their families from the volatile products they sold. Rapper Notorious B. I. G., after passing a day singing about drug dealing and murder, returned to his gated mansion. "I'm not hip-hop twenty-four hours a day, and I don't play my music in the house," Notorious B. I. G. informed a *New York Times* reporter in 1995. "When I am home, I lay around,

247

snuggle up and play games with my (two-year-old) daughter." In 1997, in rumored retaliation for the murder of rapper Tupac Shakur, Notorious B. I. G. was gunned down. Prior to his own death in 1996, Shakur had gone to jail for sexually abusing a woman.[3]

Notorious B.I.G.'s murder notwithstanding, Bill Clinton insisted that as the law-and-order president he had helped reduce the violent crime rate. Most people, however, did not feel any safer. Indeed, local law-enforcement agencies encouraged citizens to protect themselves. In Toledo, the local chapter of the Fraternal Order of Police opposed municipal gun-control legislation. As the president of the police union said in 1997, "It's our opinion that passage of this legislation will only serve to provide the criminal element with a stronger position for the intimidation and victimization of the honest citizens." The undermanned Toledo Police Department counted on a well-armed citizenry to maintain public order.[4]

Arming oneself did seem to be the most effective way to safeguard home and family. Although some legal initiatives to combat crime were passed in the nineties—notably federal legislation that sent "three-time losers" to jail for life—others met with resistance from the federal courts and the ACLU. In Florida, the Supreme Court ruled in 1997 that the state could not punish prisoners by denying them the right to early release, particularly if the prisons were overcrowded. Three hundred rapists, muggers, and killers immediately went free. Within hours of their release, the convicts murdered two people and committed numerous other crimes. Meanwhile in California, civil libertarians castigated the LAPD for disrupting gang meetings; the ACLU contended that the Crips and Bloods had a constitutional right to assemble. Writing from the American Enterprise Institute, a conservative think tank in Washington, Robert Bork concluded that liberal judges and the ACLU had made a mockery of the Constitution. America was at the point where its citizens would have to start disobeying the law if they expected to obtain justice. The liberal judiciary, Bork believed, had forfeited its moral authority. (When Martin Luther King, Jr., had made a similar argument in the early sixties, Bork skewered him. Thirty years later Bork seemed to be calling for a new era of civil disobedience against established legal authority.)[5]

A number of working-class blacks and Hispanics defended the LAPD. Gang members had to spend so much time eluding the police that they found it difficult to avail themselves of the opportunity to deal drugs and commit murder. Social liberals did not put such a positive spin on the situation. To Jesse Jackson, speaking shortly after Clinton's second inauguration, efforts to deal with crime, quotas, and welfare smacked of racism. Joseph Lowery of the Southern Christian Leadership Conference was even more extreme in his views than Jackson. When confronted with polling data in 1997 showing that the overwhelming majority of white Americans bore blacks no ill will and that a solid majority had no problem with interracial marriage, Lowery vented his spleen. "We're creating a fifty-first state called the state of denial," he fumed. "We just want racism to go away." By Lowery's logic, whites who believed in equal opportunity and law and order were, in reality, irredeemable racists. White America would always be racist, oppressive, and genocidal. (Some members of the judiciary agreed with that assessment. No sooner had California voted to end state-level racial quotas in 1996 than a federal judge sought to set aside the ballot initiative. If you believed that racism was intractable, it seemed, then quotas could never be abolished.)[6]

Lowery and Jackson were perfectly in tune with America's civil rights leadership. In 1997, Rev. Henry Lyons, the president of the National Baptist Convention, found himself embroiled in controversy. His wife, who earlier had been convicted of embezzling federal grants from an alternative school she directed in Milwaukee, discovered that her husband had bought a house for his purported mistress. Angered, Lyons's wife torched the house, confessed to the deed, and then recanted. Lyons, who had recently served a year on probation for federal bank fraud, defended his wife and his female colleague, while justifying ownership of a $700,000 mansion and a Rolls-Royce. Although the news media approached the scandal with great trepidation, Lyons felt he was the victim of white racism. "I'm proud I've enjoyed some financial success," Lyons told his flock. Then, turning to white reporters, the Baptist minister said, "What are you trying to imply? That blacks in this country cannot be successful?" By cynically and transparently stressing race in an effort to divert attention from his brazen transgression, Lyons discredited the civil rights cause and—like Jim Bakker before him—tarnished the reputation of the Christian church. (Though Lyons and Bakker allegedly had much in common, white reporters treated the two quite differently.)[7]

While black activists cried racism, the post-industrial economy continued to bedevil Americans, even the wealthiest. In the summer of 1997, *USA Today* ran a story on millionaires who never quite felt financially secure. (With hundreds of new billionaires appearing in the nineties, some just plain millionaires also experienced feelings of inadequacy.) As one affluent lawyer explained, he would be "more prone to gift-giving" to charities and friends if he only made more money. Even then, when the wealthy donated money to charity, they invariably funded private universities and museums, not churches and public schools. In upper-crust Cape Cod, wealthy retirees refused to vote for school levies. Consequently, one elementary school had its students manufacturing board games for sale to the public. School officials stated that there was no other way to purchase paper, pencils, and other basic supplies. Since this was an "educational project," federal child-labor laws did not apply to the school district.[8]

If the notion of ten-year-olds working for pencil money seems to have been lifted from a Dickens novel, there were still other dismaying developments to ponder. The Department of Labor predicted that through the year 2005 just one in every three college graduates would be able to obtain a job requiring a university education. Two-thirds of the college-educated Baby Busters would be forced to take jobs once reserved for high school graduates. That in turn meant many high school graduates would be displaced. What would happen to them? The employment horizon was not encouraging. With the passage of welfare reform in 1996, Clinton had exhorted businesses to hire poor people. Unfortunately, many long-term welfare dependents were unemployable, lacking basic discipline and skills. State and federal job-training programs often failed to imbue their students with a sustained work ethic. Not surprisingly, some companies, regarding the glut of college-trained youths entering the job market, saw little need to employ the troublesome underclass. Other corporations announced that they were planning more "downsizing" and, therefore, did not want welfare mothers or educated Baby Busters.[9]

Looking for work in the Sunbelt was not much of an option. Thousands of Yankees were moving back North in the nineties, complaining of low wages, high living costs, and soaring crime. They also resented being undercut in the job market by cheap immigrant labor. For every three Ohioans who moved to Florida looking for work in the eighties, two had returned to the Rustbelt by the nineties. Most observed that if they could find a job in Toledo as a tool and die maker—*even in a nonunion shop*—their wages would be twice what they could earn in Florida. After two decades of economic growth, the Sunbelt could no longer absorb Rustbelt refugees, especially since Latin American and Haitian immigrants (legal and otherwise) worked for so little money.[10]

Economics aside, the culture wars showed little sign of abating. Prolifers in 1997 continued to denounce partial-birth abortion and Planned

Parenthood. Supporters of Planned Parenthood claimed that abortion was just one minor option presented to women. Most of its resources, Planned Parenthood insisted, went to helping pregnant women carry healthy babies to term. Abortion foes countered that barely a quarter of Planned Parenthood's clinics provided prenatal care. Other prolifers, weary of debate, had long ago joined Operation Rescue or a predominantly Catholic group, the Lambs of Christ. Father Norman Weslin, who roamed the nation with the nomadic Lambs of Christ, explained to reporters, "It became clear that we had to develop a seriousness on the level of Martin Luther King or Mahatma Gandhi. We had to go inside the [abortion] clinic, put our back against the killing door, and tell the mother that 'we have a place where you can stay, we can take care of anything you need. Just don't kill your baby.'" Since the legal system sanctioned abortion, growing numbers of prolifers felt morally compelled to work outside the law, to the point of disrupting the operation of Planned Parenthood clinics.[11]

In the meantime, Clinton's "gay-bashing" during the '96 election rapidly receded from memory. Indeed, the president pushed for legislation to protect gays from discrimination in the federal work force. Clinton received little help from fellow Democrats. For all of their professed fondness for gays, congressional liberals were not about to risk precious political capital on lifestyle issues. Gays would have to wait for the Democrats to recapture Congress.[12]

Casting about for a politically safe issue, House minority leader Richard Gephardt warned seniors that Republicans wanted to slash Social Security and Medicare spending. With his own eye on the presidential primaries in 2000, Gephardt condemned Clinton and Vice President Gore for conspiring with Newt Gingrich to assault the elderly. (The Missouri Democrat had to be hoping that voters forgot how—in the search for liberal campaign contributions—he had radically modified his conservative views on abortion, tax hikes, and gay rights during the '88 primaries.) Other House liberals stood behind Gephardt, fearful that the Clinton-Gore compromises on entitlement funding would undermine their efforts to take back Congress. In truth, Clinton and Gingrich recommended only a small slowdown in federal spending. Gephardt knew that whatever budget cuts were ultimately put in place would amount to very little. However, the Democrats, having previously endorsed NAFTA and raised taxes on the working and middle classes, had no other economic issue to deploy against the GOP. "Mediscare" would remain a Democratic campaign staple until the last of the World War II generation passed from the scene and the first wave of Boomers made Social Security financially insolvent and politically untenable.[13]

Dissension within Democratic ranks was fully matched on the other side of the House and Senate aisles. Both Gingrich and Senate majority leader Trent Lott of Mississippi came under attack in 1997 by economic and social conservatives. Free marketers thought the GOP's congressional leaders had made themselves junior partners of the Clinton administration. Libertarians like Phil Gramm expected the GOP to slash federal entitlements and give tax breaks to deserving corporations. Talk-radio host Michael Reagan, "the Gipper's" Boomer son, announced that he was leaving the Republican Party. Dismayed by the apparent unwillingness of Gingrich to abolish the Education Department and "business-welfare" programs like the Overseas Private Investment Corporation that gave federal subsidies to American exporters, Reagan contended that "today's Republicans seem content simply to slow creeping socialism rather than reverse it."[14]

In 1997, Republican senator Sam Brownback of Kansas and Democratic senator Joseph Lieberman of Connecticut—an Orthodox Jew who was not at home in his own party—proposed legislation to restore "the family hour" on network television. Lott cut a deal with media executives. In exchange for a pledge from the networks that they would tell viewers which shows contained profanity, sex, and violence, Lott promised executives that Congress would not regulate the content and timing of their broadcasts. The free market, with the help of the Republican leadership, triumphed yet again. Moral traditionalists were aghast.[15]

Social conservatives, including Gary Bauer of the Family Research Council, found other reasons to fault the GOP's power brokers. They were appalled when Gingrich and Lott secured special trading privileges with China. Bauer insisted that "human rights" must be "at the center of our relationship" with China and other nations. Sounding like Jimmy Carter on his better days, Bauer believed that morality and foreign policy had to go hand in hand. A country that used slave labor from its burgeoning population of political prisoners had no business trading with the United States. The Christian Broadcasting Network agreed, developing searing stories on how Chinese corporations flooded America with slave-made goods—destroying U.S. jobs in the process.[16]

The Presidents' Summit for America's Future, held in Philadelphia and endorsed by Gerald Ford, Jimmy Carter, and Colin Powell, among other notables, sparked a rhetorical civil war within conservative ranks. Talk-radio personality Rush Limbaugh called this effort to promote voluntarism "anti-American." Limbaugh is a firm believer in libertarian individualism. The free market took care of all community needs. Disgusted, conservative activist Arianna Huffington, a wealthy Greek immigrant and an organizer of the summit, countered that Limbaugh was "a morally impoverished ignoramus who is increasingly becoming a living warning to young kids of the perils of dropping out of college."[17]

As the Presidents' Summit riveted the attention of the media—and then was quickly forgotten—libertarians and social conservatives drifted further apart. No longer running the day-to-day operations of *National Review,* William F. Buckley had time to reassess his own libertarian and religious ideals. Ultimately, Buckley admitted, he may have been too strong a champion of the free market. Unbridled capitalism often undermined communities and families. There was, in the final analysis, more to life "than merely paying taxes, buying and selling in the marketplace, and voting (occasionally, if at all)." Drawing upon Catholic social thought, Buckley endorsed at least one New Deal–era program: the GI Bill of Rights, which had "enriched America more than it cost the government." He hoped Congress would reward citizens who volunteered service to charities, hospitals, and churches. Those who served their country merited funds to pay for college tuition or for the down payment on a home.[18]

Expressing dismay with radical libertarians and do-your-own-thing liberals, Buckley lamented the "growing national tendency to corruption, or hedonism; an insensitivity to suffering; a callousness that breeds ugliness of behavior." The federal government could, and should, Buckley concluded, promote "the cultivation of virtue" through voluntary, not mandatory, community service. Far from rallying the GOP, however, Buckley became an oddity to be trotted out at conservative functions—no longer a political thinker to be taken seriously. In truth, Buckley's thoughts on duty, service, and virtue seemed irrelevant to the Boomer elites of both parties. A social conservatism that contained within it a critique of the free market might play well with populists but did not warm the hearts of businessmen and think-tank intellectuals.[19]

Libertarian writer David Frum allowed that "social conservatism is potentially more popular than economic conservatism"; however, if "severed from economic conservatism, social conservatism too easily degenerates into mere posturing." As libertarians had been arguing for the past twenty years, cutting taxes and reducing the size of Big Government would cure America's ills. (The causes of social liberalism fed off Washington. Starve the latter you kill the former.) Robert Bork, himself no friend of Big Government, concluded that the libertarians lacked sufficient moral sense. Liberating the free market from federal regulation would not bring about a moral restoration in America. Far from it. Bork argued:

> Free market economists are particularly vulnerable to the libertarian virus. They know that free economic exchanges usually benefit both parties to them. But they mistake that general rule for a universal rule. Benefits do not invariably result from free market exchanges. When it comes to pornography or addictive drugs, libertarians all too often confuse the idea that markets should be free with the idea that everything should be available on the market. The first of those ideas rests on the efficiency of the free market in satisfying wants. The second ignores the question of which wants it is moral to satisfy. That is a question of an entirely different nature. I have heard economist say that, as economists, they do not deal with questions of morality. Quite right. But nobody is just an economist. Economists are also fathers or mothers, husbands or wives, voters, citizens, members of communities. In these latter roles, they cannot avoid questions of morality.[20]

• • •

Bork's distaste for the more extreme manifestations of libertarianism underscored just how fractured the once formidable Reagan coalition had become by the nineties. There was no end of explanations for why this occurred. Arguably, the Cold War provided some of the essential ideological glue that brought together anti-Communist fundamentalists, working-class ethnics, businessmen, and free marketers. Ronald Reagan won two terms in office by playing patriotic tunes and restoring national morale in the wake of the Vietnam War and the Iranian hostage crisis. Reagan, however, was so successful in vanquishing the Soviet Empire and making Americans stand (sort of) tall again in the world, that he eliminated foreign policy concerns from the domestic political mix. Consequently, George Bush did not gain any mileage from the collapse of the Soviet Union and America's victory in the Persian Gulf War.

As America enters the twenty-first century, it is obvious that the bulk of the electorate, in contrast to the dedicated members of the Left and Right, has largely lost interest in what happens overseas. So long as America does not become involved in a losing war, foreign policy matters do not influence internal politics. Foreign policy issues might shape domestic politics, of course, if they were framed in terms of job-destroying imports, overseas relocation of American companies, and Third World immigrants who drive U.S. wages down. Democratic and Republican elites are not about to address any of those concerns lest they arouse their respective free-market and "multicultural, rainbow coalition" constituencies.

The World War II generation, which condemned the antiwar activism of Boomer students in the sixties, grew less and less concerned about the whole matter of military service and patriotism. By the '92 election, Social Security and Medicare counted for more than whether or not Bill Clinton had dodged the Vietnam draft. This situation was not too surprising. David Stockman and the free marketers had so ineptly attempted to dismantle Social Security in the early eighties that they left the GOP vulnerable to Democratic "Mediscare" tactics. In any event, how could seniors condemn social liberals for ducking the Vietnam War when so many libertarians and upper-crust Republicans had done exactly the same thing? Reagan's Boomer heirs were not credible patriots—let alone trustworthy friends of senior entitlements.

Conservatives had more than anti-Communism upon which to build an electoral majority. They identified another enemy that in many ways was just as menacing as the Soviet Empire: Big Government. Yet once they were in the White House, neither Nixon nor Reagan seemed to know what to do about the bureaucratic beast. Nixon may have railed against the rising federal tax burden, liberal civil servants, intrusive government programs, and welfare cheats, but he quickly ran up the white flag. Entitlement spending in the early seventies rose and the federal government built an affirmative action bureaucracy. The situation was little different in the Reagan years.

GOP strategists had hoped that an anti-tax crusade could unite social conservatives and free marketers. That was the expectation of the Heritage Foundation in the seventies and remained central to the conservative credo through Newt Gingrich's "Contract with America." But even before Reagan completed his first term, moral traditionalists groused that their issues never took front seat. As Cal Thomas of the Moral Majority had observed, cutting taxes did not stop abortion. Yes, the same Big Government that strangled businesses with hiring quotas and payroll taxes also attacked private religious academies in the name of civil rights enforcement. In the larger scheme of things, however, free marketers would never really embrace religious conservatives. After all, if one believed in the right to do what you please with your own business, then why should there be governmental restrictions on what took place in your own home? Social conservatives answered that moral limits should be imposed in the marketplace and the bedroom. Meanwhile, Ralph Reed insisted that moral ends could be advanced through libertarian means. As the decade of the nineties came to a close, few religious conservatives believed that to be true.

When social liberals framed abortion in terms of free choice, many Republicans parted ways with fundamentalists, Pentecostals, and Catholics. Even among white ethnics, though, the prolife movement—which had been an unmistakably Catholic cause in the seventies—encountered difficulties. Economic issues frequently drove Catholic voting patterns more than moral matters like abortion. Catholics, as GOP operative Lee Atwater lamented, were incurable New Deal Democrats who distrusted corporate executives and Ivy League lounge lizards. Moreover, the GOP itself did not have a clear prolife policy. For the past two decades social conservatives had written the party's platform but never received more than rhetorical support from Reagan and Bush. By 1996, Dole was not even prepared to concede that much to prolifers. Frustration with a judicial system that seemingly condemned innocent "unborn children" to death but protected the civil liberties of criminals has led many conservative activists to advocate taking the law into their owns hands.

Religious conservatives have found themselves in a quandary. Liberal legislative and judicial activism has made them leery of government power. Traditionalists have also seen how secular politics seemingly triumphed over the spiritual mission of liberal Protestant denominations and Reform Judaism. Reagan played to social conservatives' fear of Big Government coercion and argued that religious traditionalists had to mobilize politically to defend their values. Mobilization is one thing, executing policy quite another. Libertarians and country-club Republicans wanted Southern Baptist and Pentecostal votes but not their issues. Symbolism was preferable to action. By the logic of their circumstance, members of the Moral Majority and the Christian Coalition had to condemn liberal activism and the politicization of Christianity, while lining up at the ballot box to demand federal and local regulation of morals. To their credit, moralists like Cal Thomas were not entirely comfortable with their political roles and never abandoned their embrace of a Christian counterculture separated from secular society.

Reagan Democrats and conservative populists like Paul Weyrich and Pat Buchanan believed that government could do a few good things. While welfare and quotas were to be dispensed with, the new post-

industrial order seemed to demand some federal action to help beleaguered working and middle-class Americans. Since McGovern's capture
of the Democratic presidential nomination in 1972, liberals have elevated
the cultural agenda above the class issues that made the New Deal majority possible. (Liberals also dispensed with the distinction between the
deserving and undeserving poor when it came to social welfare policies.)
Carter tried to reverse course in 1976, but failed to bring social liberals,
the Democratic Party's most important voting bloc, into line. Clinton's
corporate backing and championship of NAFTA served final notice that
working people could expect little from free-market Democrats—or Republicans for that matter. Who speaks for the struggling American family
threatened by cheap overseas labor, declining incomes, and burdensome
payroll taxes? Not Clinton, not Gingrich, and not the public-sector unions. Pat Buchanan could hardly resist stepping into this political vacuum.

American economic angst is understandable. Despite great gains in the
quality of American-made goods since the seventies, many highly profit-
able corporations are not about to permit their employees to share in
their success. No matter how many blue- and white-collar workers have
been "downsized," replaced by machines, or turned into temporary, low-
paid employees in the past twenty years, stock investors continue to demand greater profit margins. In 1997, a market analyst observed that in
the eighties corporations worried about the bad publicity that came with
every layoff. By the late nineties, however, the consultant concluded, companies no longer cared what the general public thought since they "have
gotten used to" generating bad feelings. At the same time, employees had
come to regard themselves as expendable. That did not mean, though,
that workers were happy about their situation.[21]

In an economy of temps and depressed wages, young mothers had
little choice but to enter the labor market. The absence of both parents
from the home helped raise rates of juvenile delinquency and illegitimacy.
Families also suffered as payroll taxes rose to ensure high living standards
for seniors. The resulting "family gap" in voting patterns between parents
and those without children was a reflection of both morality and economics. Young families and seniors increasingly squared off over entitlements
and public school levies, while parents deplored what they saw as a profit-
driven effort to sell products with riveting images of sex and violence.
However, the "family gap" did not prove decisive in the outcome of
national elections in the eighties and nineties for at least two reasons.
First, families represented a minority of the electorate. Most Americans

were either single or "empty-nest" Boomers and seniors. Second, the economy, while hurting many families, helped others. The "class gap" between economically insecure couples with low-wage jobs and those who had well-paid careers limited the electoral impact of the "family gap."

The "class gap" also partly explained why the economy of 1992 sunk Bush's presidency while the economy of 1996 helped Clinton's reelection campaign. In 1992 working- and upper-middle-class voters felt threatened by unemployment and corporate restructuring. Four years later, as the wealth of the top 20 percent of the population rose faster than it had in the Reagan eighties, white-collar voters believed that the worst was over and that they were immune from future economic dislocation. (Similar conditions, perceptions, and sentiments were at work in the '84 presidential election.) Besides, as historian Christopher Lasch had observed, in a new age of mobile capital and the Internet, "knowledge workers" could find income elsewhere. They were not tied to a particular locale or even a nation, unlike manufacturing and service workers.

Paradoxically, while conservative congregations grew and moral traditionalists loomed ever larger at the polls, their relative political power in the inner circles of the GOP remained limited throughout the eighties and nineties. At the same time, social liberalism lost at the polls, and those religious denominations most attuned to the new liberationist ethos—the Episcopal Church and Reform Judaism, for instance—saw their ranks decline. Yet the Democratic Party continued to be largely responsive to the political agenda of the National Organization for Women and the National Abortion Rights Action League. Social conservatives are a constituency to which GOP regulars pay lip service but do not allow to shape actual policy. In contrast, social liberals do not have to pound at the door to be let in. Rather, they are in a position to keep conservative dissenters in the Democratic Party out. This fact of life helps explain why Clinton is prone to attacking his allies publicly and then, when the media have lost interest, returns to the liberal fold.

The secular media have proven to be implacably hostile toward social conservatives and even the GOP candidates who have given only *rhetorical* support to the Moral Majority and the Christian Coalition. This is not surprising, given that nine of ten elite journalists voted for Clinton. Since at least the 1980 election there have been numerous instances in which media personalities distorted events, mercilessly ridiculed religious conservatives, and displayed a class snobbery worthy of a Boston Brahmin. In response, conservatives have cultivated their own media, from religious broadcasting networks such as Robertson's CBN, to the libertarian-minded *American Spectator*. With the proliferation of cable channels and narrowly targeted magazines in the eighties, Americans have segregated themselves into small, mutually suspicious tribes. Liberals are fond of complaining about Rush Limbaugh, but where is the objective alternative to be found in the national media? What Americans get are characterizations of religious traditionalists as small-minded anti-Semitic bigots who wear "Charlie's Angels' " hairdos and would like nothing better than to burn down black churches. When black Pentecostals and Orthodox Jews campaigned for Robertson in the 1988 GOP primaries, they were usually ignored by the media.

Reporters, as is true with liberal activists and members of the Religious Left, have their own definition of what constitutes correct moral behavior. In 1972, religious liberals tried to direct the moral debate away from abortion, crime, and pornography and toward issues like the Vietnam War, poverty, and discrimination. By their standards, McGovern was more moral than Nixon. When Geraldine Ferraro denounced Reagan as a proponent of immoral policies in 1984, she was simply replaying the McGovern gambit while, of course, hoping to direct attention away from her own views on abortion and personal business dealings.

By the late eighties social liberals pushed for a total divorce of public and private morality. Teddy Kennedy, Gary Hart, and Bill Clinton may have "brought pain" to their marriages, but whatever they did in private did not reflect on what they would do as president. For folks who had argued in the sixties that "the personal is political," this tack was peculiar to say the least. It is not logically possible to politicize sexual behavior without also acknowledging that people who lie to their spouses or use others for immediate physical gratification might exhibit the same kind of selfish, deceptive tendencies as national leaders.

If social liberals and the media define morality differently than do religious conservatives, they also are quite clear as to what constitutes acceptable political behavior among church groups. Since the Southern Christian Leadership Conference champions civil rights, there is nothing wrong with black ministers mobilizing their congregations to vote against Republicans. The Christian Coalition, and before it the Moral Majority, in contrast, must not exhort congregations to vote against Democrats. Black Christians are good, white Christians—unless they are prochoice Episcopalians—are evil. As tax-exempt religious organizations, neither the SCLC nor the Christian Coalition may engage in political advocacy.

Both are, for tax purposes, "educational organizations." This is nonsense, of course, but it would be nice if the secular media and the Clinton administration, which has encouraged the IRS to go after the Christian Coalition, would come down as hard on black liberals as they do on white conservatives. By refusing to do so, social liberals only succeed in poisoning race relations and making a mockery of America's governmental and judicial institutions. (Of course, when Pat Robertson openly boasts—as he did in 1997—that the Christian Coalition intends to elect the next president, he should not be surprised that he attracts unwanted attention.)

As events of the recent past clearly demonstrate, race relations are not something requiring any further poisoning. Since the sixties, the black middle class has done well, if not even better than whites. Still, the problems of the black underclass loom large, and liberals and conservatives have offered their own conflicting prescriptions to deal with inner-city crime, drug abuse, poverty, and illegitimacy. If the implosion of the Great Society proved anything, poverty and anti-social behavior are not simply caused by the lack of jobs. Moral responsibility and personal behavior, as Robertson and black Representative John Lewis agree, weigh in heavily when it comes to perpetuating lives of misery and violence. So too, poor blacks have the right to police protection from criminal gangs. The hamstringing of law enforcement agencies and communities by the ACLU must come to an end. At the same time neighborhood groups and municipal officials must screen police officers closely to ensure that they do not intentionally provoke racial disorder. An environment of trust between police departments and the people being served has to be cultivated through strict and fair enforcement of the law.

Sadly, civil rights activists continue to flail at white racism, becoming in the process mirror images of their conservative enemies. The cause of honest political debate is not advanced when, as in 1980, the civil rights establishment warned blacks that Reagan would bring back segregation, deny them the vote, and tell rednecks that it "would be all right to kill niggers." It is equally insulting to religious conservatives when civil rights leaders reject assistance from Promise Keepers and the Christian Coalition to help rebuild burned-out southern black churches on the grounds that such organizations are "Trojan horses" for the Ku Klux Klan. In the same vein, blacks who have opened lines of communications with white social conservatives are dismissed as "Uncle Toms." As long as liberals call everyone who displeases them racists or anti-Semites—with the hypocritical exception of Jesse Jackson and Louis Farrakhan—there can be no hope for the improvement of relations among blacks, Jews, and white Christians. So too, every politically motivated charge of racism and anti-Semitism only deadens an increasingly cynical public to the evils of actual discrimination.

White conservatives, of course, have their failings when it comes to race. The civil rights leadership is able to keep the majority of blacks in the Democratic Party for a number of reasons. In the debate over affirmative action, for instance, black conservatives like Clarence Thomas and sympathetic whites like William Bennett prefer to credit minority success to individual initiative and merit, not quotas. Less kind, Senator Phil Gramm is wont to say that the black middle class and underclass are equally dependent upon government preferences and financial assistance. By implication, blacks are too lazy to study, work hard, and earn their professional status; they like living on "welfare." Libertarians would deny that is the message they intend to convey when they attack affirmative action, but that is what blacks hear. (It does not help matters any that in unguarded moments a few liberals express the same implicit rationale in defense of affirmative action. When the president of Rutgers claims that black students do not have the innate intelligence to compete with whites, you know that modern liberalism has reached an impasse.)

Civil rights leaders race-bait Republicans because they know that the majority of blacks are social conservatives. The Democratic Party's hold on the black vote is partly maintained by stirring up fear of white people. (Of course, it is possible to work both sides of the street. In the '92 presidential election Clinton played to the prejudices of some white Democrats while winking at the civil rights leadership.) Racial appeals and kinship, not moral issues, continue to shape black voting behavior. Republicans have missed their opportunity to rectify this situation for reasons far beyond the issue of quotas. The GOP's indifference to the Rust-belt cities generates black suspicion about conservative-white priorities. Urban decay is a problem tied to the self-destructive behavior of individual members of the underclass. However, explanations for the rise of inner-city poverty, crime, and anti-social behavior must also account for the disappearance of entry-level manufacturing jobs. McDonald's teaches discipline but does not pay well enough to support a family. A "McJob" should be a beginning, not an ending, point on the employment ladder.

The GOP, responsive to its suburban and free-market constituencies, has abandoned post-industrial cities, turning them into what conservative commentator Charles Murray rightly called "reservations" for the poor. Social pathologies cannot be confined to urban reservations. If only in the interest of self-preservation, Democratic and Republican suburbanites must offer cities something other than casinos, gentrified urban enclaves for Yuppie knowledge workers, hiring quotas at city universities, and football stadiums. The urban poor need jobs and spiritual uplift. Not one or the other, but both. For those who have no desire to acquire job skills, learn self-discipline, and find legitimate employment, there can be but one destiny: incarceration.

Republicans who complain that blacks look upon Big Government as a beloved friend would do well to look more critically at their own constituencies. Tobacco and wheat farmers certainly receive their share of federal subsidies, as do corporations lobbying Congress for lowering capital gains tax rates. Moreover, blacks (and New Deal–minded Reagan Democrats as well) might regard the GOP more favorably if Republicans offered policies to deal with urban decay. Further, free marketers need to make distinctions between blue-collar labor unions and middle-class public-employee organizations that seek to advance the agenda of social liberalism. Workers in the private sector have the right to bargain collectively and protect themselves from unfair treatment. (Union members, of course, should also have the right to protect themselves from their leaders. A union that collaborates in the creation of discriminatory wage scales that benefit Boomers at the expense of Baby Busters has no moral legitimacy.) There are some aspects of the New Deal order well worth keeping, just as the Great Society did a few things right when President Johnson advanced the cause of equal opportunity for blacks. Conservatives must make it abundantly clear (as do Bennett and Kemp) that they oppose quotas, not racial equality.

Republican leaders, though given to deriding social conservatives, are unlikely to turn their fire on themselves. That fact of life has become painfully obvious to larger numbers of conservatives who have come to see the GOP as little more than a bastion of privilege and selfishness. When the hypocrisy of GOP leaders is added to that of the civil rights establishment and the media, it is no wonder that the majority of Americans express great distrust of the national media and professional politicians. Only a minority of citizens even bothered to vote in the '96 presidential election.

In announcing his departure as director of the Christian Coalition in 1997, Ralph Reed emphasized the importance of grassroots activism. Having learned hard lessons from the '96 presidential campaign, Reed no longer regarded the Republican Party as an instrument of America's redemption: "The thing that is going to combat the social pathologies and the evils and the national sins . . . isn't going to be any political party," Reed told Christian Coalition leaders. "It's going to be the church of Jesus Christ, on its knees praying, with a sword and a spear in one hand and a breastplate of righteousness and a helmet of salvation and a revival that sweeps across the nation." Country-club Republicans and libertarians did not take Reed's words to heart. They had long discounted the prospect of massive defections by social conservatives. Where else could they go? Social conservatives would certainly not vote for the party of Clinton and Gephardt. Religious conservatives had just one option: to establish a third party. That, however, seemed improbable. Not since 1860 had a third party swept into power. Of course, Republican liberals and free marketers might well have recalled that the party of Lincoln grew out of precisely the same culture of religious revivalism (and frustration with the legal order) that Reed saw building to a climax in the early twenty-first century.[22]

Whether a religious revival could recruit enough foot soldiers to alter the established political order remains to be seen. If social conservatives could ally with economic populists—and, in the process, create a new style of orthodox Protestantism that looked more favorably upon some degree of federal regulation of the marketplace—their rivals would be overwhelmed. Pat Buchanan has pointed the way toward such a future, though he is too flawed a candidate to bring a such formidable coalition to life. William Bennett would be a suitable alternative but for the fact that he does not challenge the new economic order. Conservative populists do not want an apologist for corporate downsizing and the overseas relocation of American jobs.

Social conservatives and economic populists face problems that go well beyond contrasting ideological conceptions of the government, the individual, and the common good. Although supporters of the Christian Coalition and Focus on the Family are correct to point out that they are not illiterate, barefoot hillbillies, they still do not have the financial resources to take on either social liberals or libertarians. The Christian Coalition may raise millions of dollars but most of its donations—as is true for other Religious Right organizations—comes in small amounts from legions of the faithful. Relative to the wealth and power of CBS, Time-Warner, and Steve Forbes, there is simply no money in social conservatism.

The Coors brewing empire, in addition to funding the Heritage Foundation, also helps sponsors "Outfest," a gay-lesbian film festival held in Los Angeles. Coors, like Subaru of America, which targets lesbians in its advertising, knows that lifestyle liberals are a more lucrative market demographic than religious traditionalists. That fact explains why Disney extends benefits to the "lifetime companions" of its gay employees, sponsors gay days at its theme parks, and makes violent movies. Threats by the eighteen million members of the Southern Baptist Convention and the Assemblies of God to boycott Disney do not faze the corporation. Gays and social liberals have more money to spend than Baptists. Besides, the media predictably ridicule the proponents of the Disney boycott, branding them moral absolutists and religious nuts. President Clinton, raised in the Southern Baptist church, reassured Disney that he would ignore the boycott.[23]

While social liberals can seemingly count corporate America, the media, and the Clinton White House among its powerful allies, they are on the defensive. After all, Clinton had to reinvent himself as a conservative in order to eke out his victories in 1992 and 1996. Significantly, the mainstream Protestant churches are faring even worse than Democratic liberals. Efforts by Episcopalian and Evangelical Lutheran leaders to share clergy and churches speaks volumes about the fading prospects of both sects. Indeed, not only have Episcopalians been reeling from membership losses at home, their Third World counterparts are urging that the Americans be expelled from the Anglican communion. Asians, Africans, and Latinos find the American Episcopal Church's practice of gay ordination and blessing of same-sex marriages repulsive. In the sixties America's Episcopalians had been champions of Third World liberation. Now their purported comrades-in-arms call them pagans.[24]

So far as race is concerned most *religious* conservatives do not harbor ill will toward blacks. Paul Weyrich, Ralph Reed, and Pat Robertson have long sought to build interracial fellowship. Conversely, a few libertarians, notably those who attack quotas on the grounds that many blacks lack sufficient intelligence to be college professors, are not so well intentioned. The challenge for social conservatives is to eliminate quotas and combat inner-city crime while creating a climate of racial trust. At the same time, blacks must free themselves from their leaders and stop blaming all of life's setbacks on white racism. An interracial coalition built around shared moral values would deal a death blow to contemporary liberalism. Of course, social liberals and the civil rights establishment realize this and, therefore, race-bait white conservatives with gusto.

The restoration of moral order in America, as social conservatives see it, may require a diminution in individual liberties. Boomers and Baby Busters will have to change habits of many years' standing, whether voluntarily or by threat of fine and incarceration. Cultural commentators such as Neil Howe and William Strauss have remarked that millions of Boomers and Baby Busters are reevaluating their attitudes toward abortion, crime, drugs, and sexual liberation. Others, however, are not changing their ways. As had been true with the anti-slavery movement and Prohibition, when one group imposes its will upon another, the results may be bloody. Culture wars are the most vicious form of politics because they cut to the heart of how people identify themselves and what they think constitutes acceptable behavior.[25]

America's challenge, as the nation enters the twenty-first century, is to find a way out of its current political mess. Unless politicians overcome their poll-obsessed hypocrisy, the kind of profitless name-calling and duplicitous politics that we have seen in the past four decades are likely to continue. Politicians, however, are not entirely to blame. In a democracy political representatives are expected to be responsive to the desires of the people. Given that some voters want abortion, quotas, and gay rights, and others do not, contention and division are not surprising. Politicians are inclined to split the difference, simultaneously informing prolifers and prochoice partisans that they are with them in spirit but must bide their time for the most advantageous moment to take a stance. Presidents, after all, are people too.

When faced with a choice between raising entitlement spending on seniors or giving young families a tax break, Clinton and Reagan flinched. Reagan's solution to this dilemma—one that Clinton has emulated—was to protect senior entitlements and provide families with tax relief, hoping that the economy grew fast enough to absorb the costs. Politicians, understandably, gravitate toward policies that reward groups whose wealth and numbers are great. This fact explains in part why it is easier to scale back spending on welfare recipients than it is to trim Medicare or ban abortion.

As Reagan's and Clinton's presidencies clearly demonstrated, the New Deal order was dead. Neither leader, however, constructed a stable electoral coalition. Both were unwilling to embrace a socially conservative and economically populist agenda—in short, moral populism. Such a course of action would mean that the federal government punished racial discrimination without imposing quotas that hurt white males. Equal opportunity for all, special privilege to none. Moral populism would condemn corporations for relocating overseas in search of cheap labor and bar their products from the nation's shores. At the same time, businesses that treated their American workers well would receive federal tax breaks. Moreover, enlightened stock market investors in the U.S. would champion corporate restructuring when absolutely necessary, but not just for the sake of increasing dividends by a few dollars. (If moral arguments cannot persuade Boomer investors to look at more than the bottom line, then a case for pure self-interest may be made. As Walter Reuther, the late, great president of the UAW once observed, assembly-line robots may reduce labor costs, but they do not buy the consumer goods necessary to sustain economic growth.)

Moral populism would work at the state level to restrict abortion on demand but would also try to create a culture in which men and women eschewed premarital sex in the first place. (For public school districts that would mean teaching abstinence, not condom usage.) Moral populism would champion the notion of individual responsibility while recognizing that some people might need temporary government assistance. At last, moral populism would, in regard to gays, "condemn the sin, but not the sinner." In 1997, the American Catholic bishops underscored that very point.

As Richard Nixon observed after his political downfall, he had allowed his hatred for his enemies to consume, and ultimately, destroy him. Americans, regardless of race or religious belief (or lack thereof), must strive to find some common ground, to learn some measure of trust in one another, if they are not to destroy one another. For more than two centuries Americans—whether of English, Italian, or African descent— overcame many challenges that, arguably, were of greater menace than those facing the nation today. Slavery, the Civil War, the Great Depression, World War II, and, yes, even Vietnam—all divided Americans and posed a threat to the nation's democratic existence. Ultimately, perhaps, a just social order begins with a sense of personal decency and a belief in a moral power greater than the sum of us all.

Notes

Abbreviations: Gerald R. Ford Presidential Library (FPL); Billy Graham Archives, Wheaton College (BGA); University of Notre Dame Archives (NDA).

Notes to Introduction

1. Alessandra Stanley, "President Will Be Old Enough to Be (Gasp!) Me, Many Say," *New York Times,* 17 November 1992.

2. Alfonso A. Narvaez, "Alexander Barkan Dies at 81; Labor Federation Chief," *New York Times,* 20 October 1990.

3. Stanley, "President Will Be Old Enough to Be (Gasp!) Me, Many Say."

4. Peggy Noonan, *What I Saw at the Revolution: A Political Life in the Reagan Era* (New York: Random House, 1990).

5. "Excerpts of Gingrich Comments After Nomination," *New York Times,* 6 December 1994.

6. Alonzo Hamby, *Liberalism and Its Challengers: From FDR to Bush* (New York: Oxford University Press, 1990).

7. Michael Novak, "Errand into the Wilderness," in John H. Bunzel, ed., *Political Passages: Journeys of Change Through Two Decades, 1968–1988* (New York: Free Press, 1988), 239–72.

8. For the destruction of the New Deal coalition, see Hamby, *Liberalism and Its Challengers*; Kenneth J. Heineman, *Campus Wars: The Peace Movement at American State Universities in the Vietnam Era* (New York: New York University Press, 1993); Kenneth J. Heineman, "The Silent Majority Speaks: Antiwar Protest and Backlash, 1965-1972," *Peace and Change* 17 (October 1992): 402–33; Godfrey Hodgson, *America in Our Time: From World War II to Nixon, What Happened and Why* (New York: Vintage, 1978); Michael Kazin, *The Populist Persuasion: An American History* (New York: Basic Books, 1995); Everett Carll Ladd, Jr., *Where Have All the Voters Gone? The Fracturing of America's Political Parties* (New York: Norton, 1978); Christopher Lasch, *The Revolt of the Elites and the Betrayal of Democracy* (New York: Norton, 1995); E. J. Dionne, Jr., *Why Americans Hate Politics* (New York: Simon & Schuster, 1992).

9. James Davison Hunter, *Culture Wars: The Struggle to Define America* (New York: Basic Books, 1991), 111. Good discussions of religion and economics include John B. Judis, *William F. Buckley, Jr.: Patron Saint of the Conservatives* (New York: Simon & Schuster, 1990); William F. Buckley, Jr., *Gratitude: Reflections on What We Owe to Our Country* (New York: Random House, 1990); Patrick Allitt, *Catholic Intellectuals and Conservative Politics in America, 1950–1985* (Ithaca: Cornell University Press, 1993); Timothy A. Byrnes, *Catholic Bishops in American Politics* (Princeton: Princeton University Press, 1991); David J. O'Brien, *American Catholics and Social Reform: The New Deal Years* (New York: Oxford University Press, 1968); Monroe Billington and Cal Clark, "Catholic Clergymen, Franklin D. Roosevelt, and the New Deal," *Catholic Historical Review* 79 (January 1993): 65–82; Kenneth J. Heineman, "A Catholic New Deal: Religion and Labor in 1930s Pittsburgh," *Pennsylvania Magazine of History and Biography* 118 (October 1994): 363–94; Michael Novak, *Catholic Social Thought and Liberal Institutions* (New Brunswick, N.J.: Transaction, 1989).

10. William J. Bennett, *The Devaluing of America: The Fight for Our Culture and Our Children* (New York: Summit Books, 1992).

11. Karl Keating, *Catholicism and Fundamentalism: The Attack on "Romanism" by "Bible Christians"* (San Francisco: Ignatius Press, 1988).

12. *American Spectator,* 28 (28 August 1995).

13. Michael Lind, "Why Intellectual Conservatism Died," *Dissent* 42 (Winter 1995): 42–47; Michael Lind, "Should Jews Fear the 'Christian Right'?" *New York Times,* 2 August 1994; Michael Lind, "Rev. Robertson's Grand International Conspiracy Theory," *New York Review of Books,* 42 (2 February 1995): 21–25; Michael Lind, "On Pat Robertson," *New York Review of Books* 42 (20 April 1995): 67–71; James Atlas, "The Counter Counterculture," *New York Times Magazine* 19 (12 February 1995): 32, 34, 37–38, 54, 61–63; Lawrence H. Fuchs, "American Jews and the Presidential Vote," in Lawrence H. Fuchs, ed., *American Ethnic Politics* (New York: Harper & Row, 1968), 50–76.

14. For treatments of tensions between social conservatives and libertarians, see David Frum, *Dead Right* (New York: Basic Books, 1994); Nigel Ashford, "The Right After Reagan: Crack-Up or Comeback?" paper delivered at the Heritage Foundation, Washington, D.C., July 1994.

Notes to Chapter 1

1. Jesse Helms letter to Nelson Bell, 9 April 1968 (Nelson Bell Papers, Box 29, BGA); Nelson Bell letter to Robert D. Newell, 11 May 1968 (Nelson Bell Papers, Box 43, BGA); David J. Garrow, *Bearing the Cross: Martin Luther King, Jr., and the Southern Christian Leadership Conference* (New York: Morrow, 1986), 97; Taylor Branch, *Parting the Waters: America in the King Years, 1954–1963* (New York: Simon & Schuster, 1988), 227–28.

2. Nelson Bell letter to Howard H. Thompson, 21 August 1965 (Nelson Bell Papers, Box 52, BGA); Hazel M. Foster letter to Nelson Bell, 13 May 1968 (Nelson Bell Papers, Box 43, BGA); Stephan Lesher, *George Wallace, American Populist* (Reading, Mass.: Addison-Wesley, 1994), 349–50.

3. Montgomery (Ala.) *Advertiser,* 29 April 1968; Roy Reed, "Mississippi: 20 Years of Wide Racial Change," *New York Times,* 18 August 1983; Branch, *Parting the Waters,* 238–39, 242, 246–47.

4. Samuel Lubell, *The Hidden Crisis in American Politics* (New York: Norton, 19771), 71, 175.

5. *Ibid.,* 152; John Bodnar, *Remaking America: Public Memory, Commemoration, and Patriotism in the Twentieth Century* (Princeton: Princeton University Press, 1992), 213.

6. Robert Bork, "Civil Rights—A Challenge," *New Republic* 148 (31 August 1963): 21–24; John B. Judis, *William F. Buckley, Jr.: Patron Saint of the Conservatives* (New York: Simon & Schuster, 1988), 138–39, 168, 192–93.

7. Tom Weir, "All-White '63 Team Left Behind Racism to Play," *USA Today,* 29 March 1996.

8. John M. Perkins Interview with Paul Ericksen, June 1991 (John M. Perkins Oral Interview, BGA); Nicholas Lemann, *The Promised Land: The Great Black Migration and How It Changed America* (New York: Knopf, 1991), 1–58, 307–40.

9. Lemann, *The Promised Land,* 28–29, 31.

10. Jared Taylor, *Paved with Good Intentions: The Failure of Race Relations in Contemporary America* (New York: Carroll & Graf, 1992), 92; Betty Glad, *Jimmy Carter: In Search of the Great White House* (New York: Norton, 1980), 40; J. Morgan Kousser, *The Shaping of Southern Politics* (New Haven: Yale University Press, 1975).

11. Marshall Frady, "God and Man in the South," *Atlantic Monthly* 219 (January 1967): 37–42; "Public Statement by Eight Alabama Clergymen," 12 April 1963, (author's papers); Garrow, *Bearing the Cross,* 236–62; Taylor, *Parting the Waters,* 737–45.

12. Perry Deane Young, *God's Bullies: Power Politics and Religious Tyranny* (New York: Holt, Rinehart and Winston, 1982), 310–17.

13. Frances FitzGerald, *Cities on a Hill: A Journey Through Contemporary American Cultures* (New York: Simon & Schuster, 1986), 144–45.

14. E. Glenn Hinson, "Southern Baptists and the Liberal Tradition in Biblical Interpretation, 1845–1945," *Baptist History and Heritage* 19 (July 1984): 16–20; William A. Sloat II, "George Whitefield, African-Americans, and Slavery," *Methodist History* 33 (October 1994): 3–13.

15. Bill J. Leonard, "Southern Baptists and the Separation of Church and State," *Review and Expositor* 83 (Spring 1986): 195–207; Diane Ravitch, *The Troubled Crusade: American Education, 1945–1980* (New York: Basic Books, 1983), 4.

16. Thomas C. Berg, " 'Proclaiming Together'? Convergence and Divergence in Mainline and Evangelical Evangelism, 1945–1967," *Religion and American Culture* 5 (Winter 1995): 49–76; Ernest J. Sandeen, "Fundamentalism and American Identity," *Annals of the American Academy of Political and Social Science* 387 (January 1970): 56–65.

17. Berg, " 'Proclaiming Together'?" 49–76; Branch, *Parting the Waters,* 27–68, 305–8, 312–78.

18. Dan Morgan, *Rising in the West: The True Story of an "Okie" Family from the Great Depression Through the Reagan Years* (New York: Knopf, 1992).

19. Daniel Mark Epstein, *Sister Aimee: The Life of Aimee Semple McPherson* (New York: Harcourt Brace Jovanovich, 1993), 296–323.

20. William Saletan, "John Warner Just Keeps Hanging On," *American Spectator* 29 (June 1996): 38–43; David Edwin Harrell, Jr., *Pat Robertson: A Personal, Political, and Religious Portrait* (New York: Harper and Row, 1987), 10–11; Christopher Matthews, *Hardball: How Politics Is Played* (New York: Summit Books, 1988), 38.

21. John B. Donovan, *Pat Robertson: The Authorized Biography* (New York: Macmillan, 1988), 1–3, 39.

22. *Ibid.*, 19, 42–43.

23. *Ibid.*, 78; Harrell, *Pat Robertson,* 110; Jeffrey K. Hadden, "Religious Broadcasting and the Mobilization of the New Christian Right," *Journal for the Scientific Study of Religion* 26 (1987): 1–24; Lubell, *The Hidden Crisis in American Politics,* 75.

24. Francine du Plessix Gray, *Divine Disobedience: Profiles in Catholic Radicalism* (New York: Knopf, 1970), 4–7, 10–13, 39; Gary Wills, *Bare Ruined Choirs: Doubt, Prophecy, and Radical Religion* (Garden City, N.Y.: Doubleday, 1972), 67; Harvey G. Cox, "The 'New Breed' in American Churches: Sources of Social Activism in American Religion," *Daedalus* 96 (Winter 1967): 135–50.

25. William Au, *The Cross, the Flag, and the Bomb: American Catholics Debate War and Peace, 1960–1983* (New York: Praeger, 1987), 73, 121, 143–45; James W. Douglass, "Catholicism, Power, and Vietnamese Suffering," in Thomas E. Quigley, ed., *American Catholics and Vietnam* (Grand Rapids, Mich.: Eerdmans, 1968), 99.

26. James H. Smylie, "American Religious Bodies, Just War, and Vietnam," *Journal of Church and State* 11 (Autumn 1969): 383–408; Garrow, *Bearing the Cross,* 405–8; Kenneth Heineman, "The Silent Majority Speaks: Antiwar Protest and Backlash, 1965–1972," *Peace and Change* 17 (October 1992): 402–33; Christian Family Movement-Milwaukee, "St. Martin De Porres CFM Action Group Report," (Christian Family Movement-Milwaukee Papers, Box 1, NDA).

27. Edward Wynne, "Adolescent Alienation and Youth Policy," September 1976 (John F. Cardinal Dearden Papers, Box 11, NDA); FitzGerald, *Cities on a Hill,* 25–119; David Lance Goines, *The Free Speech Movement: Coming of Age in the 1960s* (Berkeley: Ten Speed Press, 1993), 587–89.

28. Cushing Strout, *The New Heavens and New Earth: Political Religion in America* (New York: Harper & Row, 1974), 319; Lubell, *The Hidden Crisis in American Politics,* 188, 210.

29. E. J. Dionne, Jr., *Why Americans Hate Politics* (New York: Simon & Schuster, 1992), 12, 36, 40, 46, 53, 84–85; Lucinda Franks, "Return of the Fugitive," *New Yorker* 70 (13 June 1994): 40–59; Jacob Cohen, "The Romance of Revolutionary Violence," *National Review* 45 (13 December 1993): 28–33; Peter Collier and David Horowitz, *Destructive Generation: Second Thoughts about the Sixties* (New York: Summit Books, 1989); Alan Wolfe, "Sociology, Liberalism, and the Radical Right," *New Left Review* 128 (July-August 1981): 3–27.

30. Dionne, *Why Americans Hate Politics,* 262; Frank S. Meyer, "Libertarianism or Libertinism?" *National Review* 21 (9 September 1969): 910; Margaret M.

Braungart and Richard G. Braungart, "The Life-Course Development of Left-and Right-Wing Youth Activist Leaders from the 1960s," *Political Psychology* 11 (1990): 243–82; Richard G. Braungart and Margaret M. Braungart, "The Childhood and Youth Experiences of Former Left- and Right-Wing Political Activist Leaders from the 1960s," paper presented at the Annual Meeting of the American Sociological Association, Pittsburgh, 20–24 August 1992; Christopher Lasch, "The Revolt of the Elites," *Harper's* 289 (November 1994): 39–49; Christopher Lasch, *The Revolt of the Elites and the Betrayal of Democracy* (New York: Norton, 1995).

31. Ravitch, *The Troubled Crusade,* 174; Jim Sleeper, *The Closest of Strangers: Liberalism and the Politics of Race in New York* (New York: Norton, 1990), 43–67, 91–115; Taylor, *Paved with Good Intentions,* 234.

32. Taylor, *Paved with Good Intentions,* 273; Dionne, *Why Americans Hate Politics,* 83; Todd Gitlin, *The Sixties: Years of Hope, Days of Rage* (New York: Bantam Books, 1989), 348–50; Collier and Horowitz, *Destructive Generation,* 21–66; Lesher, *George Wallace, American Populist,* 316; Lubell, *The Hidden Crisis in American Politics,* 117; Dinesh D'Souza, "Black America's Moment of Truth," *American Spectator* 28 (October 1995): 35–45.

33. Lesher, *George Wallace, American Populist,* 350; Peter Brown, *Minority Party: Why Democrats Face Defeat in 1992 and Beyond* (Washington, D.C.: Regnery Gateway, 1991), 216–18.

34. John J. Bukowczyk, *And My Children Did Not Know Me: A History of the Polish-Americans* (Bloomington: Indiana University Press, 1987); Michael Novak, *The Rise of the Unmeltable Ethnics: Politics and Culture in the Seventies* (New York: Macmillan, 1973); Thomas Bell, *Out of This Furnace: A Novel of Immigrant Labor in America* (Pittsburgh: University of Pittsburgh Press, 1991); Gary Wills, *Under God: Religion and American Politics* (New York: Simon & Schuster, 1990), 53.

35. Pittsburgh *Courier,* 24 July 1937; George W. Knepper, *Ohio and Its People* (Kent, Ohio: Kent State University Press, 1989), 375–76, 380; Taylor, *Parting the Waters,* 691, 788–89.

36. Heineman, "The Silent Majority Speaks," 402–33; Nicholas Lemann, "The Origins of the Underclass, Part I," *Atlantic Monthly* 257 (June 1986): 31–55; Lubell, *The Hidden Crisis in American Politics,* 288–89.

37. Nicholas Lemann, "The Origins of the Underclass, Part II," *Atlantic Monthly* 258 (July 1986): 54–68; Kenneth A. Briggs, "Protestantism in the City Divided on Racial Lines," *New York Times,* 20 August 1975.

38. Taylor, *Paved with Good Intentions,* 82, 303, 331; Charles Murray, *Losing Ground: American Social Policy, 1950–1980* (New York: Basic Books, 1984), 166, 169–70; Peter J. Ferrara, "Crime," in Peter J. Ferrara, ed., *Issues '94: The Candidate's Briefing Book* (Washington, D.C.: Heritage Foundation, 1994), 139–64; Sara McLanahan and Karen Booth, "Mother-Only Families: Problems, Prospects, and Politics," *Journal of Marriage and the Family* 51 (August 1989): 557–80.

39. Ravitch, *The Troubled Crusade,* 30–38; Peter Collier, with David Horowitz, *The Roosevelts: An American Saga* (New York: Simon & Schuster, 1994), 271.

40. Ravitch, *The Troubled Crusade,* 30–38; James Hennesey, *American Catho-*

lics: A History of the Roman Catholic Community in the United States (New York: Oxford University Press, 1981), 283, 286–87; Lesher, *George Wallace, American Populist* xv, 292.

41. Michael Barone, *Our Country: The Shaping of America from Roosevelt to Reagan* (New York: Free Press, 1990), 383–84; Murray, *Losing Ground,* 167–77; Ferrara, "Crime," 139–64. For a classic study of urban life, ethnicity, and social order, see Nathan Glazer and Daniel Patrick Moynihan, *Beyond the Melting Pot: The Negroes, Puerto Ricans, Jews, Italians, and Irish of New York City* (Cambridge: MIT Press, 1964).

42. Michael K. Brown and Steven P. Erie, "Blacks and the Legacy of the Great Society: The Economic and Political Impact of Federal Social Policy," *Public Policy* 29 (Summer 1981): 299–330; Thomas Byrne Edsall and Mary D. Edsall, *Chain Reaction: The Impact of Race, Rights, and Taxes on American Politics* (New York: Norton, 1991), 1–81; Murray, *Losing Ground,* 56–112.

43. Dionne, *Why Americans Hate Politics,* 12, 53, 91, 123; Michael Kazin, *The Populist Persuasion: An American History* (New York: Basic Books, 1995), 195–242.

44. Ravitch, *The Troubled Crusade,* 293; Judith Blake, "Abortion and Public Opinion: The 1960–1970 Decade," *Science* 171 (12 February 1971): 540–49; Michael K. Flaherty, "A White Lie," *American Spectator* 25 (August 1992): 37–38; James Davison Hunter, *Before the Shooting Begins: Searching for Democracy in America's Culture War* (New York: Free Press, 1994), 70; Jane Gross, "Patricia Ireland, President of NOW, Does She Speak for Today's Women?" *New York Times Magazine* 16 (1 March 1992): 16–18, 38, 54.

45. Dionne, *Why Americans Hate Politics,* 151; M. Timothy Iglesias, "CUF and Dissent: A Case Study in Religious Conservatism," *America* 155 (11 April 1987): 303–7.

46. Andrew M. Greeley, "What Is Subsidiarity? A Voice from Sleepy Hollow," *America* 153 (9 November 1985): 292–95.

47. Alfred O. Hero, Jr., *American Religious Groups View Foreign Policy: Trends in Rank-and-File Opinion, 1937–1969* (Durham: Duke University Press, 1973), 40–54; Mark Silk, *Spiritual Politics: Religion and America Since World War II* (New York: Simon & Schuster, 1988), 25–26; Patricia McNeal, *Harder Than War: Catholic Peacemaking in Twentieth-Century America* (New Brunswick: Rutgers University Press, 1992), xi, 1–70.

48. Dionne, *Why Americans Hate Politics,* 57; Harvey Klehr, John Earl Haynes, and Fridrikh Igorevich Firsov, *The Secret World of American Communism* (New Haven: Yale University Press, 1995).

49. Lawrence H. Fuchs, "American Jews and the Presidential Vote," in Lawrence H. Fuchs, ed., *American Ethnic Politics* (New York: Harper & Row, 1968), 50–76.

50. Godfrey Hodgson, *America in Our Time: From World War II to Nixon, What Happened and Why* (New York: Vintage, 1978), 67–98.

51. Heineman, "The Silent Majority Speaks," 402–33; Andrew M. Greeley, "Political Attitudes Among American White Ethnics," *Public Opinion Quarterly* 36 (Summer 1972): 213–20; H. Edward Ransford, "Blue Collar Anger: Reactions to Student and Black Protest," *American Sociological Review* 27 (June 1972): 333–46;

William L. Lunch and Peter W. Sperlich, "American Public Opinion and the War in Vietnam," *Western Political Quarterly* 32 (March 1979): 21–44; Philip E. Converse and Howard Schuman, " 'Silent Majorities' and the Vietnam War," *Scientific American* 222 (June 1970): 17–25.

52. Harold E. Quinley, "The Protestant Clergy and the War in Vietnam," *Public Opinion Quarterly* 34 (Spring 1970): 43–52; Kent Blevins, "Southern Baptist Attitudes Toward the Vietnam War in the Years 1965–1970," *Foundations* 23 (1980): 231–44; Mitchell K. Hall, "A Time for War: The Church of God's Response to Vietnam," *Indiana Magazine of History* 79 (December 1983): 1186–99; Bodnar, *Remaking America,* 161; Daniel Yankelovich, "What They Believe," *Fortune* 79 (January 1969): 70–71, 179–81.

53. Mark R. Levy and Michael S. Kramer, *The Ethnic Factor: How America's Minorities Decide Elections* (New York: Simon & Schuster, 1972), 122–58; Barone, *Our Country,* 307–35.

54. Barone, *Our Country,* 336–63; Hodgson, *America in Our Time,* 153–99.

55. Mark Stern, "Party Alignments and Civil Rights: Then and Now," *Presidential Studies Quarterly* 25 (Summer 1995): 413–27.

56. Michael Lind, "The Southern Coup: The South, the GOP, and America," *New Republic* 212 (19 June 1995): 20–29; Dionne, *Why Americans Hate Politics,* 179, 181; Barone, *Our Country,* 364–80.

57. Levy and Kramer, *The Ethnic Factor,* 140–90; Barone, *Our Country,* 364–80; Heineman, "The Silent Majority Speaks," 402–33; Gerald R. Ford Presidential Campaign, Opposition Research, "Ronald Reagan on Social Security" (President Gerald R. Ford Committee Records, Press Office, Ronald Reagan File, Box G5, FPL).

58. Lesher, *George Wallace, American Populist,* 283–85, 295.

59. *Ibid.,* 252, 338, 377; Jack Bass, *Taming the Storm: The Life and Times of Judge Frank M, Johnson, Jr., and the South's Fight over Civil Rights* (New York: Doubleday, 1993), 119, 216, 304–05, 311.

60. Lesher, *George Wallace, American Populist,* 269, 298; Ravitch, *The Troubled Crusade,* 142.

61. Bass, *Taming the Storm,* 391.

62. Lubell, *The Hidden Crisis in American Politics,* 110; Bill Iverson, Essex County Youth House, "Riot Report" 18 July 1967 (Nelson Bell Papers, Box 30, BGA).

63. Ze've Chafets, "The Tragedy of Detroit," *New York Times Magazine,* 14 (29 July 1990): 20–26, 38, 42, 50–51; Hodgson, *America in Our Time,* 430–39.

64. Lubell, *The Hidden Crisis in American Politics,* 109; Hodgson, *America in Our Time,* 430–39.

65. "Poll Finds Crime Top Fear at Home," *New York Times,* 28 February 1968; Robert B. Semple, Jr., "Nixon Scores Panel for 'Undue' Stress on White Racism," *New York Times,* 7 March 1968; Barone, *Our Country,* 418–19; Peter J. Ferrara, *Issues '94: The Candidate's Briefing Book* (Washington, D.C.: Heritage Foundation, 1994), 28.

66. Philip E. Converse, Warren E. Miller, Jerrold G. Rusk, and Arthur C. Wolfe, "Continuity and Change in American Politics: Parties and Issues in

the 1968 Election," *American Political Science Review* 63 (December 1969): 1083–1105.

67. Lubell, *The Hidden Crisis in American Politics* 75–76, 96; Lesher, *George Wallace, American Populist*, 412, 427, 423; Heineman, "The Silent Majority Speaks," 402–33; Converse et al., "Continuity and Change in American Politics," 1083–1105.

68. Lubell, *The Hidden Crisis in American Politics*, 145, 151; Lesher, *George Wallace, American Populist*, 428; J. Michael Ross, Reeve D. Vanneman, and Thomas F. Pettigrew, "Patterns of Support for George Wallace: Implications for Racial Change," *Journal of Social Issues* 36 (Spring 1976): 69–91; Anthony M. Orum, "Religion and the Rise of the Radical White: The Case of Southern Wallace Support in 1968," *Social Science Quarterly* 51 (December 1970): 674–88; Sheldon G. Levy, "Polarization of Racial Attitudes," *Public Opinion Quarterly* 36 (Summer 1972): 221–34.

69. Lesher, *George Wallace, American Populist*, 81–82; Frank B. Feigert, "Conservatism, Populism, and Social Change," *American Behavioral Scientist* 17 (November-December 1972): 272–78; William F. Buckley, Jr., *On the Firing Line: The Public Life of Our Public Figures* (New York: Random House, 1989), 161–66; Kazin, *The Populist Persuasion*, 1–7, 221–42.

Notes to Chapter 2

1. Ralph Reed, *Active Faith: How Christians Are Changing the Soul of American Politics* (New York: Free Press, 1996), 19.

2. William L. Lunch and Peter W. Sperlich, "American Public Opinion and the War in Vietnam," *Western Political Quarterly* 32 (March 1979): 21–44; Philip E. Converse and Howard Schuman, " 'Silent Majorities' and the Vietnam War," *Scientific American* 222 (June 1970): 17–25; Harlan Hahn, "Correlates of Public Sentiments about War: Local Referenda on the Vietnam Issue," *American Political Science Review* 64 (December 1970): 1186–98; Diane Ravitch, *The Troubled Crusade: American Education, 1945–1980* (New York: Basic Books, 1983), 216.

3. Edward Wynne, "Adolescent Alienation and Youth Policy," September 1976 (John F. Cardinal Dearden Papers, Box 11, NDA); Stephen E. Ambrose, *Nixon: The Triumph of a Politician, 1962–1972* (New York: Simon & Schuster, 1989), 499; Robert M. Teeter, Memorandum for H. R. Haldeman, "Catholic Vote," 6 January 1972 (Robert M. Teeter Papers, Committee to Reelect the President, Box 1, FPL); Robert M. Teeter, Memorandum for the Attorney General, "Pennsylvania Poll," 9 February 1972 (Robert M. Teeter Papers, Committee to Reelect the President, Box 1, FPL); Robert M. Teeter, Memorandum for H. R. Haldeman, "Louis Harris Issue Poll Analysis," 2 February 1972 (Robert M. Teeter Papers, Committee to Reelect the President, Box 1, FPL); Robert M. Teeter, Memorandum for the Attorney General, "Ohio Poll Analysis," 15 February 1972 (Robert M. Teeter Papers, Committee to Reelect the President, Box 1, FPL).

4. Ambrose, *Nixon*, 520–21, 523; Herbert Parmet, *Richard Nixon and His America* (Boston: Little, Brown, 1990), 595–97, 608–10.

5. John Pollock, *Billy Graham: Evangelist to the World* (Minneapolis: World

Wide Publications, 1979), 170–75; Charles Hirschberg, "The Eternal Crusader," *Life* 17 (November 1994): 104–16; William F. Buckley, Jr., *Execution Eve—And Other Contemporary Ballads* (New York: Putnam's Sons, 1975), 151–53.

6. Hirschberg, "The Eternal Crusader," 104–16; Patrick Allitt, *Catholic Intellectuals and Conservative Politics in America, 1950–1985* (Ithaca: Cornell University Press, 1995), 2–3. On Buckley and Nixon, see John B. Judis, *William F. Buckley, Jr.: Patron Saint of the Conservatives* (New York: Simon & Schuster, 1988); Gary Wills, *Nixon Agonistes: The Crisis of the Self-Made Man* (Boston: Houghton Mifflin, 1970); Gary Wills, *Confessions of a Conservative* (Garden City, N.Y.: Doubleday, 1979).

7. Charles D. Hadley, "Survey Research and Southern Politics: The Implications of Data Management," *Public Opinion Quarterly* 45 (Fall 1981): 393–401.

8. Richard A. Shaffer, "For a Plantation Hand, Progress of Blacks Seems Far Removed," *Wall Street Journal*, 17 October 1974.

9. Frances FitzGerald, *Cities on a Hill: A Journey Through Contemporary American Cultures* (New York: Simon & Schuster, 1986), 121–201; Jerry Falwell, "The Liberty University Story," *Liberty University Home Page*, World Wide Web, 30 May 1996.

10. Louis A. Zurcher, Jr., R. George Kirkpatrick, Robert G. Cushing, Charles K. Bowman, "Ad Hoc Anti-Pornography Organizations and Their Active Members: A Research Summary," *Journal of Social Issues* 29 (1973): 69–94; Louis A. Zurcher, Jr., R. George Kirkpatrick, Robert G. Cushing, and Charles K. Bowman, "The Anti-Pornography Campaign: A Symbolic Crusade," *Social Problems* 19 (Fall 1971): 217–38.

11. Zurcher et al., "Ad Hoc Anti-Pornography Organizations and Their Active Members," 69–94; Zurcher, et al., "The Anti-Pornography Campaign," 217–38; Nelson Bell letter to Carol Wilkie, 29 October 1971 (Nelson Bell Papers, Box 42, BGA). For a scathing critique of Nixon's pornography commission by social conservatives, see Tom Minnery, ed., *Pornography: A Human Tragedy* (Wheaton, Ill.: Tyndale House, 1986).

12. Helen Rose Fuchs Ebaugh and C. Allen Haney, "Shifts in Abortion Attitudes: 1972–1978," *Journal of Marriage and the Family* 42 (August 1980): 491–99.

13. *Ibid.*

14. Texas Catholic Conference, "An Open Letter from the Catholic Bishops of Texas on the Subject of Abortion," April 1971 (John F. Cardinal Dearden Papers, Box 1, Pamphlet Collection, NDA).

15. The Most Reverend Humberto S. Medeiros, Archbishop of Boston, "Homily on Abortion," 27 December 1970 (John F. Cardinal Dearden Papers, Box 1, Pamphlet Collection, NDA); A Joint Statement by the Catholic Bishops of Massachusetts on Abortion, "Killing or Caring? You Must Choose," February 1972 (John F. Cardinal Dearden Papers, Box 1, Pamphlet Collection, NDA); Father Geno Baroni, "United States Catholic Conference: National Task Force on Urban Problems," 1969 (John F. Cardinal Dearden Papers, Box 1, NDA).

16. Michael Novak, *The Rise of the Unmeltable Ethnics: Politics and Culture in the Seventies* (New York: Macmillan, 1973), 74–75; Michael Novak, "Errand into the Wilderness," in John H. Bunzel, ed., *Political Passages: Journeys of Change*

Through Two Decades, 1968–1988 (New York: Free Press, 1988), 239–72; Lawrence M. O'Rourke, *Geno: The Life and Mission of Geno Baroni* (New York: Paulist Press, 1991), 95, 269.

17. Novak, *The Rise of the Unmeltable Ethnics*, 75, 162–63, 166–67, 199; Novak, "Errand into the Wilderness," 239–72.

18. Patrick J. Buchanan, *Right from the Beginning* (Washington, D.C.: Regnery Gateway, 1990), 3–174, 217.

19. Tom Wells, *The War Within: America's Battle over Vietnam* (Berkeley: University of California Press, 1994), 319, 321, 459, 548; Patrick J. Buchanan, "Wallace Antidote to Liberals," San Diego *Union,* 1 March 1976; Stephen Glass, "Pat Speaks," *New Republic* 214 (18 March 1996): 17.

20. Richard M. Scammon and Ben J. Wattenberg, *The Real Majority* (New York: Coward-McCann, 1970), 234; Kenneth A. Briggs, "Protestantism in the City Divided on Racial Lines," *New York Times,* 20 August 1975.

21. "Buchanan's Past Comes out in Memo," Columbus (Ohio) *Dispatch,* 19 February 1996; Patrick J. Buchanan Memorandum for the Attorney General and H. R. Haldeman, 15 December 1971 (Working Assets Funding Service, World Wide Web, 1996); Patrick J. Buchanan Memorandum for the President, 24 March 1971 (Working Assets Funding Service, World Wide Web, 1996); Jeff Gillenkirk, "Before He Had a Heart: White House Memos Show Pat Buchanan Led Nixon's 1972 'Assault Team' " (Working Assets Funding Service, World Wide Web, 1996).

22. Larry Gerber, "Fight for Lennon's FBI File Finally Near End," Columbus (Ohio) *Dispatch,* 10 March 1996; Ambrose, *Nixon,* 500, 502.

23. Ambrose, *Nixon,* 555; Stephan Lesher, *George Wallace, American Populist* (Reading, Mass.: Addison-Wesley, 1994), 485.

24. E. J. Dionne, Jr., *Why Americans Hate Politics* (New York: Simon & Schuster, 1992), 48.

25. Daniel J. Baer and Victor F. Mosele, "Political and Religious Beliefs of Catholics and Attitudes Towards Involvement in the Vietnam War," *Journal of Psychology* 78 (July 1971): 161–64; Christian Family Movement-Milwaukee, George McGovern Campaign Materials (Christian Family Movement-Milwaukee Papers, Box 1, NDA); William Dean, "What Nixon Knew," *Christian Century* 111 (11 May 1994): 484–86.

26. Charles O. Rice, "The Radical Catholic," *Catholic World* 212 (July 1970): 156–60; Patrick J. McGeever, *Rev. Charles Owen Rice: Apostle of Contradiction* (Pittsburgh: Duquesne University Press, 1989), 92–135, 167–223.

27. David Caute, *The Great Fear: The Anti-Communist Purge Under Truman and Eisenhower* (New York: Simon & Schuster, 1978), 216; McGeever, *Rev. Charles Owen Rice,* 202–23; Bud and Ruth Schultz interview with Monsignor Charles Owen Rice, 7 March 1982 (Charles Owen Rice Papers, Box 13, Archives of an Industrial Society, University of Pittsburgh).

28. "The Evangelical Vote," *Newsweek* 80 (30 October 1972): 93; Ronald J. Sider, Evangelicals for McGovern, letter to Stephen Charles Mott, 14 November 1972 (Evangelicals for Social Action Papers, Box 1, BGA); W. T. Miller, Washington Bible College, letter to Evangelicals for McGovern, 8 November 1972 (Evan-

gelicals for Social Action Papers, Box 1, BGA); Evangelicals for McGovern, Fundraising Letter, 1972 (Evangelicals for Social Action, Box 1, BGA).

29. Stephen Charles Mott, Evangelicals for McGovern, letter to W. T. Miller, 5 January 1973 (Evangelicals for Social Action, Box 1, BGA); Richard V. Pierard, letter to W. T. Miller, 15 November 1972 (Evangelicals for Social Action, Box 1, BGA).

30. Michael McIntyre, "Religionists on the Campaign Trail," *Christian Century* 89 (27 December 1972): 1319–22.

31. Evangelicals for McGovern, Press Release, "Remarks of Senator George McGovern at Wheaton College," 11 October 1972 (Evangelicals for Social Action, Box 1, BGA); Louis Cassels, "Of God and Man," Terre Haute *Tribune*, Evangelicals for Social Action Newspaper and Magazine Clipping File (Evangelicals for Social Action, Box 1, BGA).

32. Tom Geoghegan, "Miami and the Seeds of Port Huron," *New Republic* 166 (2 September 1972): 16–18; Dionne, *Why Americans Hate Politics*, 46; M. Kent Jennings, "Residues of a Movement: The Aging of the American Protest Generation," *American Political Science Review* 81 (June 1987): 367–82; Ambrose, *Nixon*, 579–80.

33. Everett Carll Ladd, Jr., *Where Have All the Voters Gone? The Fracturing of America's Political Parties* (New York: Norton, 1978), 63–64; Scammon and Wattenberg, *The Real Majority*, 60–61; Irwin Unger, *The Best of Intentions: The Triumph and Failure of the Great Society Under Kennedy, Johnson, and Nixon* (New York: Doubleday, 1996), 345.

34. Ladd, *Where Have All the Voters Gone?*, 14, 65–66; Scammon and Wattenberg, *The Real Majority*, 60–61; Susan Welch, "Support Among Women for the Issues of the Women's Movement," *Sociological Quarterly* 16 (Spring 1975): 216–27; Andrew Levison, *The Working-Class Majority* (New York: Coward, McCann, & Geoghegan, 1974), 24–26.

35. Levison, *The Working-Class Majority*, 14; Gary Hart, *The Good Fight: The Education of an American Reformer* (New York: Random House, 1993), 6–7; Gary Wills, *Under God: Religion and American Politics* (New York: Simon & Schuster, 1990), 41–50; William Lee Miller, "Remembering Gary," *New Republic* 190 (16 April 1984): 11–12.

36. Ambrose, *Nixon*, 506–7.

37. *Ibid.*, 556, 588, 620–21, 623, 635, 648; John Hellemann, "Certain Defeat Liberated Dole," Columbus (Ohio) *Dispatch*, 10 November 1996.

38. Ambrose, *Nixon*, 554; Godfrey Hodgson, *America in Our Time: From World War II to Nixon, What Happened and Why* (New York: Vintage, 1978), 426; Carl Solberg, *Hubert Humphrey: A Biography* (New York: Norton, 1984), 430, 432–33.

39. Hunter S. Thompson, *Fear and Loathing on the Campaign Trail '72* (San Francisco: Straight Arrow Books, 1973); Gerald R. Ford Committee Records, Opposition Research, "Jimmy Carter," (President Ford Committee Records, Research Office, Opposition Research, Box 45, FPL); Gerald R. Ford Committee Records, Opposition Research, "Jimmy Carter," (President Ford Committee Re-

cords, Research Office, Box H39, FPL); Betty Glad, *Jimmy Carter: In Search of the Great White House* (New York: Norton, 1980), 206–7.

40. Ambrose, *Nixon*, 585; David Mixner, *Stranger Among Friends* (New York: Bantam Books, 1996), 65–70.

41. Archie Robinson, *George Meany and His Times* (New York: Simon & Schuster, 1981), 322–25.

42. Jeane Kirkpatrick, "The Revolt of the Masses," *Commentary* 55 (February 1973): 58–62; Paul R. Wieck, "McGovern's Jewish Problem," *New Republic* 166 (2 September 1972): 19–21; Kenneth Heineman, "The Silent Majority Speaks: Antiwar Protest and Backlash, 1965–1972," *Peace & Change* 17 (October 1992): 403–33.

43. Kirkpatrick, "The Revolt of the Masses," 58–62; Jeane J. Kirkpatrick, "Politics and the New Class," *Society* 17 (January/February 1979): 42–48; Andrew M. Greeley, "Catholic Chic," *Commentary* 55 (February 1973): 90–92.

44. Robert Timberg, *The Nightingale's Song* (New York: Simon & Schuster, 1995), 180.

45. Peggy Noonan, *What I Saw at the Revolution: A Political Life in the Reagan Era* (New York: Random House, 1990), 15–16.

46. Patrick J. Buchanan Memorandum to the President, 8 June 1972 (Working Assets Funding, World Wide Web, 1996); Dionne, *Why Americans Hate Politics*, 122–23, 234; Heineman, "The Silent Majority Speaks," 403–33; Arthur H. Miller, Warren E. Miller, Alden S. Raine, and Thad A. Brown, "A Majority Party in Disarray: Policy Polarization in the 1972 Election," *American Political Science Review* 70 (1976): 753–78; H. Edward Ransford, "Blue Collar Anger: Reactions to Student and Black Protest," *American Sociological Review* 27 (June 1973): 333–46; Ambrose, *Nixon*, 651.

47. Dionne, *Why Americans Hate Politics*, 122–23; Ambrose, *Nixon*, 636; S. Robert Lichter, Stanley Rothman, and Linda S. Lichter, *The Media Elite* (Bethesda: Adler & Adler, 1986), 22–23, 28–29.

48. Ronald Brownstein, *The Power and the Glitter: The Hollywood-Washington Connection* (New York: Pantheon Books, 1990), 204–7, 237–29.

49. Dionne, *Why Americans Hate Politics*, 47–48.

50. Buchanan, *Right from the Beginning*, 321; "Nixon Spewed Venom in Margin of Daily News Summary," Columbus (Ohio) *Dispatch*, 20 October 1996.

51. Dionne, *Why Americans Hate Politics*, 202; Richard Polenberg, *One Nation Divisible: Class, Race, and Ethnicity in the United States Since 1938* (New York: Viking, 1980), 240–41; Washington *Evening Star* (Washington, D.C.), 3 November 1972.

52. National Republican Heritage Groups [Nationalities] Council Newsletter, 1976 (Theodore C. Marrs Files, Conference File, Box 64, FPL).

53. Thomas Byrne Edsall and Mary D. Edsall, *Chain Reaction: The Impact of Race, Rights, and Taxes on American Politics* (New York: Norton, 1992), 86–87; Peter Ross Range, "Thunder from the Right," *New York Times Magazine* 5 (8 February 1981): 23–25, 64, 74–75, 81, 84.

Notes to Chapter 3

1. Michael Barone, *Our Country: The Shaping of America from Roosevelt to Reagan* (New York: Free Press, 1990), 516–18.

2. "Richard Nixon and American Religion," *Christian Century* 111 (11 May 1994): 488–89.

3. E. J. Dionne, Jr., *Why Americans Hate Politics* (New York: Simon & Schuster, 1992), 46–48, 270; Christopher Lasch, *The True and Only Heaven: Progress and Its Critics* (New York: Norton, 1991), 507–8.

4. Dionne, *Why Americans Hate Politics*, 122–23; Lasch, *The True and Only Heaven*, 505; Jules Witcover, *Marathon: The Pursuit of the Presidency, 1972–1976* (New York: Viking, 1977), 175–79.

5. Lasch, *The True and Only Heaven*, 478, 499.

6. Michael Novak, "Busing: Immoral?" 1975 (Robert A. Goldwin Files, Goldwin Name File, Box 26, FPL); Michael Novak, "The Vietnam of the 1970s: Busing," *A New America* (Newsletter of EMPAC [Ethnic Millions Political Action Committee]), July 1975 (Robert A. Goldwin Files, Goldwin Name File, Box 26, FPL); Michael Novak, "Blacks and Catholics—Two Fateful Migrations," MS ca. 1975 (Robert A. Goldwin Files, Goldwin Name File, Box 26, FPL).

7. Ronald J. Sider letter to Marlin Van Elderen, 18 June 1973 (Evangelicals for Social Action, Box 1, BGA); Ronald J. Sider, "News Release," 27 November 1973 (Evangelicals for Social Action, Box 1, BGA); Nadine Heiss, Testimony Submitted to the United States Senate Constitutional Amendments Subcommittee, 24 September 1973 (Gerald R. Ford Vice Presidential Papers, Issues File, Box 19, FPL); Altoona *Mirror*, 24 February 1974; James Hefley and Harold Smith, "What Should Johnny Read?" *Christianity Today* 28 (7 September 1984): 24–27.

8. Lasch, *The True and Only Heaven*, 482–83; Urie Bronfenbrenner, "The Calamitous Decline of the American Family," ca. 1976 (John F. Cardinal Dearden Papers, Pamphlet Collection, Box 11, NDA); Michael Novak, "The Family out of Favor," *Harper's* 272 (April 1976): 37–46.

9. Andrew Greeley, "In Search of the New Morality," Chicago *Tribune*, 16 March 1976; William Alex McIntosh, Letitia T. Alston, and Jon P. Alston, "The Differential Impact of Religious Preference and Church Attendance on Attitudes Toward Abortion," *Review of Religious Research* 20 (Spring 1979): 195–213.

10. Kenneth A. Briggs, "Bishops Ask Religious Teaching in the Public Schools," *New York Times*, 20 February 1976; William F. Willoughby, "Bishop's Remarks on Jews Criticized," Washington *Star*, 6 December 1975.

11. John Dart, "U. S. Catholics Reach Fork in the Road, Must Choose Between Mainstream or Minority," *New York Times*, 20 March 1975; Eileen Shanahan, "Equal Rights Test Is Near in Illinois," *New York Times*, 2 March 1975; Kent L. Tedin, "Religious Preference and Pro- Anti-Activism on the Equal Rights Amendment Issue," *Pacific Sociological Review* 21 (January 1978): 55–66.

12. Shanahan, "Equal Rights Test Is Near in Illinois"; Tedin, "Religious Preference and Pro- Anti-Activism on the Equal Rights Amendment Issue," 55–66; Kent L. Tedin, David W. Brady, Mary E. Buxton, Barbara M. Gorman, and Judy L. Thompson, "Social Background and Political Differences Between Pro- and

Anti-ERA Activists," *American Politics Quarterly* 5 (July 1977): 395–408; Bonnie Cook Freeman, "Antifeminists and Women's Liberation: A Case Study of a Paradox," *Women & Politics* 3 (Spring 1983): 21–38; David W. Brady and Kent L. Tedin, "Ladies in Pink: Religion and Political Ideology in the Anti-ERA Movement," *Social Science Quarterly* 56 (March 1976): 564–74; Margaret I. Miller and Helene Linker, "Equal Rights Amendment Campaigns in California and Utah," *Society* 11 (May-June 1974): 40–53; Joan Huber, Cynthia Rexroat, and Glenna Spitze, "A Crucible of Opinion on Women's Status: ERA in Illinois," *Social Forces* 52 (December 1978): 549–65; Theodore S. Arrington and Patricia A. Kyle, "Equal Rights Amendment Activists in North Carolina," *Signs* 3 (Spring 1978): 666–80; Kenneth A. Briggs, "Southern Baptists and Catholics Find Ties," *New York Times,* 19 September 1976.

13. Rosalind Rosenberg, "The Abortion Case," in John A. Garraty, ed., *Quarrels That Have Shaped the Constitution* (New York: Harper & Row, 1988), 351–79; Peter Leahy and Allan Mazur, "A Comparison of Movements Opposed to Nuclear Power, Fluoridation, and Abortion," *Research in Social Movements* 1 (1978): 143–54; Briggs, "Southern Baptists and Catholics Find Ties."

14. Mary Jo Neitz, "Family, State, and God: Ideologies of the Right-to-Life Movement," *Sociological Analysis* 42 (Fall 1981): 265–76; William Ray Arney and William H. Trescher, "Trends in Attitudes Toward Abortion, 1972–1975," *Family Planning Perspectives* 8 (May/June 1976): 117–24; Judith Blake, "The Supreme Court's Abortion Decisions and Public Opinion in the United States," *Population and Development Review* 3 (1977): 45–71; Donald Granberg, "Prolife or Reflection of Conservative Ideology? An Analysis of Opposition to Legalized Abortion," *Sociology and Social Research* 62 (April 1978): 414–29.

15. Leahy and Mazur, "A Comparison of Movements Opposed to Nuclear Power, Fluoridation, and Abortion," 143–54; Kenneth A. Briggs, "An Evangelical's Rise," *New York Times,* 30 July 1977; Missouri Synod Press Release, "Lutheran Leaders Urge Legal Protection for Unborn Children," 24 March 1976 (Office of the Press Secretary, David Gergen Files, Box 1, FPL).

16. Statement of Dr. Eugene W. Linse, Jr., Before the Subcommittee on Civil and Constitutional Rights, Committee on the Judiciary, House of Representatives, 24 March 1976 (Office of the Press Secretary, David Gergen Files, Box 1, FPL).

17. Celebrate Life Committee, "Practical Politics Kit," ca. 1975 (Joseph Breig Papers, Box 10, NDA).

18. Witcover, *Marathon,* 57–58; Dionne, *Why Americans Hate Politics,* 205.

19. Irving Kristol letter to Robert Goldwin, 28 January 1976 (James M. Cannon Files, Abortion File, Box 1, FPL); Irving Kristol, "On Corporate Capitalism in America," *Public Interest* 49 (Fall 1975): 124–41; Peter Steinfels, *The Neoconservatives: The Men Who Are Changing America's Politics* (New York: Simon & Schuster, 1979), 277–79. See John Podhoretz, *Hell of a Ride: Backstage at the White House Follies, 1989–1993* (New York: Simon & Schuster, 1993), for some pithy observations on preppies, Jews, and religious conservatives.

20. John D. Lofton, Jr., "Catholics Cheer Ford—But Why?" *Human Events* 36 (21 August 1976): 25–26; Warren S. Rustand letter to Randy Engel, 4 December 1974 (Theodore C. Marrs Files, Organizations File, Box 55, FPL); William W.

Nicholson Memorandum to Pam Needham, 18 November 1974 (Theodore C. Marrs Files, Organizations File, Box 55, FPL); Randy Engel letter to Warren Rustand, 11 November 1974 (Theodore C. Marrs Files, Organizations File, Box 55, FPL); Randy Engel letter to Theodore Marrs, 27 January 1975 (Theodore C. Marrs Files, Organizations File, Box 55, FPL).

21. Bobbie Greene Kilberg Memorandum to Jim Cavanaugh, 4 September 1976 (James M. Cannon Files, Abortion File, Box 1, FPL); Bobbie Greene Kilberg Memorandum to the President, 6 February 1976 (James M. Cannon Files, Abortion File, Box 1, FPL); Byron W. Daynes and Raymond Tatalovich, "Presidential Politics and Abortion, 1972–1988," *Presidential Studies Quarterly* 22 (Summer 1992): 545–61.

22. Michael Raoul-Duval Memorandum to Henry Cashen II, 14 July 1976 (Michael Raoul-Duval Files, Republican Party Platform File, Box 27, FPL); Dr. Melady and Dr. Lee Memorandum to Dr. Myron B. Kuropas, 25 June 1976 (Office of the Press Secretary, David Gergen Files, Box 1, FPL).

23. Meeting with the Executive Committee of National Conference of Catholic Bishops, 10 September 1976 (James M. Cannon Files, Abortion File, Box 1, FPL); Gerald R. Ford letter to Joseph Bernardin, 10 September 1976 (James M. Cannon Files, Abortion File, Box 1, FPL); Timothy A. Byrnes, "The Politics of the American Catholic Hierarchy," *Political Science Quarterly* 108 (1993): 497–514.

24. Michael Novak letter to Theodore C. Marrs, 1 April 1975 (Theodore C. Marrs Files, Marrs Name File, Box 61, FPL); Michael Novak letter to Robert Goldwin, 30 September 1975 (Robert A. Goldwin Files, Goldwin Name File, Box 26, FPL); Michael Novak letter to Gerald R. Ford, 2 October 1975 (Robert A. Goldwin Files, Goldwin Name File, Box 26, FPL); Special Voter Report to Gerald R. Ford, "Afro-Americans," 1976 (President Ford Committee Records, Special Voter Groups, Box C4, FPL); Michael Novak, "A Penny from the President?" *A New America*, April 1975 (Robert A. Goldwin Files, Goldwin Name File, Box 26, FPL).

25. Harold G. Bromwell letter to Gerald R. Ford, 1 March 1974 (Gerald R. Ford Vice Presidential Papers, Requests, Box 158, FPL); Gerald R. Ford letter to Harold G. Bromwell, 20 March 1970 (Gerald R. Ford Vice Presidential Papers, Requests, Box 158, FPL).

26. "Remarks of the President to National Religious Broadcasters Convention," 22 February 1976 (Robert T. Hartman Files, General Subject File, Box 13, FPL); "NAE in Washington: Bicentennial Faith," *Sojourners* 5 (March 1976).

27. Transcript of CBN Tape and Memorandum to the President on CBN, 5 August 1976 (Office of the Editorial Staff, Press Speeches, Box 37, FPL); Transcript of Thomas Road Baptist Church Tape, 21 June 1976 (Office of the Editorial Staff, Presidential Speeches, Box 35, FPL); David Edwin Harrell, Jr., *Pat Robertson*: A Personal, Political, and Religious Portrait (San Francisco: Harper & Row, 1987), 59; John B. Donovan, *Pat Robertson: The Authorized Biography* (New York: Macmillan, 1988), 115.

28. Witcover, *Marathon*, 46, 51, 167; Kevin Phillips, "GOP Obstacle to Conservatives," St. Petersburg *Times-Union*, 9 September 1976; Patrick Buchanan, "Ford's Nearsighted Visions," Chicago *Tribune*, 6 January 1976; Patrick Bu-

chanan, "Hardball Politics Begin," San Diego *Union,* 13 February 1976; R. W. Apple, Jr., "The Dilemma of the Republicans," *New York Times,* 10 March 1975; "GOP Role Sought by Conservatives," *New York Times,* 2 March 1975.

29. Ronald Reagan letter to Gerald R. Ford, 20 December 1974 (Richard Cheney Files, General Subject File, Box 13, FPL); President Gerald R. Ford Committee Records, Chairman's Office, File on Ronald Reagan, (President Ford Committee Records, Box A4, FPL); Gerald R. Ford letter to Nancy and Ronald Reagan, 13 May 1975 (White House Central File, Name File, Ronald Reagan, Box 2608, FPL); Pete Wilson report to Gerald R. Ford, 31 October 1975 (President Ford Committee Records, Press Office, Ronald Reagan File, Box G5, FPL.)

30. Henry Bellmon letter to Mary Louise Smith, 25 August 1975 (President Ford Committee Records, Chairman's Office, Ronald Reagan File, Box A4, FPL); "Citizens for Reagan" fundraising letter, 31 July 1975 (President Ford Committee Records, Chairman's Office, Ronald Reagan File, Box A4, FPL).

31. Dionne, *Why Americans Hate Politics,* 205–8; Peter Rose Range, "Thunder from the Right," *New York Times Magazine* 5 (8 February 1981): 23–25, 64, 74–75, 81, 84; John Calhoun Memorandum to Bill Baroody, 27 May 1976 (President Ford Committee Records, Staff Memoranda, Box B10, FPL); Jody Powell, *The Other Side of the Story* (New York: Morrow, 1984), 207; Witcover, *Marathon,* 419.

32. Calhoun Memorandum to Baroody; " 'Welfare Queen' Becomes Issue in Reagan Campaign," *New York Times,* 15 February 1976; Ford Attack Sheet on Reagan's Welfare Record, 1976 (President Ford Committee Records, Press Office, Ronald Reagan File, Box G5, FPL); Ford Fact Sheet, "Reagan Record in California," 1976 (President Ford Committee Records, Research Office, Ronald Reagan File, Box H41, FPL); L. William Seidman and Burton G. Malkiel Memorandum to President Gerald R. Ford, 1 April 1976 (James E. Connor Files, Staff Secretary, Subject File, Box 16, FPL); Rowland Evans and Robert Novak, "Reagan's Social Security Gaffe," *Washington Post,* 20 December 1975; Ford Campaign, "Ronald Reagan on Social Security," Fact Sheet, 1975 (President Ford Committee Records, Press Office, Ronald Reagan File, Box G5, FPL).

33. Dionne, *Why Americans Hate Politics,* 232; Kevin Phillips, "Conservative Profile Is Confusing," San Diego *Union,* 9 April 1975; "The President Ford Committee's Reaction to Reagan Announcement," 20 November 1975 (President Ford Committee Records, Chairman's Office, Ronald Reagan File, A4, FPL).

34. The Ad Hoc Committee in Defense of Life, *Lifeletter* #6, 6 April 1976, and *Lifeletter* #12, 23 August 1976 (Office of the Press Secretary, David Gergen Files, Box 1, FPL); James W. Malone, Testimony of the United States Catholic Conference Before the Republican Platform Committee, 1976 (James M. Cannon Files, Abortion File, Box 1, FPL); Michael J. Malbin, "The Conventions, Platforms, and Issue Activists," in Austin Ranney, ed., *The American Elections of 1980* (Washington, D.C.: American Enterprise Institute, 1981), 99–141.

35. Malbin, "The Conventions, Platforms, and Issue Activists," 99–141; *Lifeletter* #12, 23 August 1976; William A. Rusher, "Referendum on the ERA," Philadelphia *Inquirer,* 5 May 1976.

36. Betty Glad, *Jimmy Carter: In Search of the Great White House* (New York: Norton, 1980), 109–10.

37. *Ibid.*, 178, 247; Witcover, *Marathon*, 117, 127, 157, 296,

38. Glad, *Jimmy Carter*, 241–44, 247–48, 289, 328, 336, 338–39; Donovan, *Pat Robertson*, 181.

39. Witcover, *Marathon*, 114, 198, 293–94; Glad, *Jimmy Carter*, 337–38, 354; Thomas W. Ottenad, "McGovern Assails Carter in Wisconsin Talk, Backs Udall," *Washington Post*, 6 April 1976; John R. Coyne, Jr., "Niceguyin' His Way to the White House?" *National Review* 28 (14 May 1976): 501–4.

40. William A. Rusher, "Carter's Faith May Win Votes," Philadelphia *Inquirer*, 17 May 1976.

41. Glad, *Jimmy Carter*, 184, 332; E. Brooks Holifield, "The Three Strands of Jimmy Carter's Religion," *New Republic* 174 (5 June 1976): 15–17; Kenneth L. Woodward, John Barnes, and Laurie Lisle, "Born Again! The Year of the Evangelicals," *Newsweek* 88 (25 October 1976): 68–70, 75–76, 78; James Robison, "Who Are the Southern Baptists?" Chicago *Tribune*, 25 July 1976; Gary Wills, "The Plains Truth: An Inquiry Into the Shaping of Jimmy Carter," *Atlantic Monthly* 237 (June 1976): 49–54.

42. Glad, *Jimmy Carter*, 383; "Tax-Exempt Group Boosts Carter Campaign," *Human Events* 36 (10 April 1976): 5; Transcript of Jim Castelli interview with Jimmy Carter, *National Catholic News* (Washington, D.C.), 9 August 1976 (National Assembly of Religious Women Papers, Box 15, NDA).

43. Glad, *Jimmy Carter*, 384; Witcover, *Marathon*, 566; Mike Royko, "*Playboy* Still a Big No-No," Chicago *Daily News*, 30 September 1976.

44. Glad, *Jimmy Carter*, 384; Witcover, *Marathon*, 607; Donovan, *Pat Robertson*, 180; Ralph Reed, *Active Faith: How Christians Are Changing the Soul of American Politics* (New York: Free Press, 1996), 93, 106; David E. Anderson, "Year of the Evangelical?" 24 October 1976, UPI Tear Sheet, Gerald R. Ford Presidential Campaign (Office the Editorial Staff, Charles McCall Files, Box 94, FPL).

45. Harold Lindsell Newspaper Clipping File, 1976 (*Christianity Today* Papers, Box 24, BGA); Harold Lindsell letter to the editor of the Binghamton (N.Y.) *Sun*, 7 October 1976 (*Christianity Today* Papers, Box 24, BGA); Binghamton (N.Y.) *Sun*, "Such Language" (editorial), 28 September 1976; Harold Lindsell letter to Maxine K. Hedrich, 4 October 1976 (*Christianity Today* Papers, Box 24, BGA).

46. Kenneth Jordan letter to Harold Lindsell, 1976 (*Christianity Today* Papers, Box 24, BGA); C. W. Draper letter to Harold Lindsell, 27 September 1976 (*Christianity Today* Papers, Box 24, BGA); Maxine K. Hedrich letter to Harold Lindsell, 29 September 1976 (*Christianity Today* Papers, Box 24, BGA).

47. Glad, *Jimmy Carter*, 293–94. See Witcover, *Marathon*, for an extensive treatment of the Carter campaign's assertions of anti-Baptist prejudice in the media and among certain voters.

48. Andrew Greeley, "I'm Tired of Being a Democrat," Chicago *Tribune*, 17 August 1976; Andrew Greeley, " 'Ethnics' Is Code Word for Catholics," Chicago *Tribune*, 26 August 1976; Andrew Greeley, "Try These Solutions, Jimmy," Chicago *Tribune*, 24 August 1976; Michael Novak, "Carter's Nixon Image," Arlington (Va.) *Catholic Herald*, 5 August 1976.

49. Lawrence M. O'Rourke, *Geno: The Life and Mission of Geno Baroni* (New York: Paulist Press, 1991), 126–34.

50. Diane Ravitch, *The Troubled Crusade*: American Education, 1945–1980 (New York: Basic Books, 1983), 298; John Bodnar, *Remaking America: Public Memory, Commemoration, and Patriotism in the Twentieth Century* (Princeton: Princeton University Press, 1992), 234–37; William A. Rusher, "Carter Mollified the Liberal Democrats," Philadelphia *Inquirer*, 20 July 1976.

51. Glad, *Jimmy Carter*, 272–73, 308; Democratic National Platform on ERA, Abortion, and Civil Rights, 1976 (President Ford Committee Records, Staff Memoranda, Box B10, FPL); Jimmy Carter Presidential Campaign, "Jimmy Carter on Civil Rights," 1976 (National Assembly of Religious Women Papers, Box 15, NDA); Jimmy Carter Presidential Campaign, "Jimmy Carter on Crime," 1976 (National Assembly of Religious Women Papers, Box 15, NDA); Jimmy Carter Presidential Campaign, "Jimmy Carter Presidential Campaign," 1976 (National Assembly of Religious Women Papers, Box 14, NDA); Jimmy Carter Presidential Campaign, "Jimmy Carter on Welfare Program," 1976 (National Assembly of Religious Women Papers, Box 15, NDA); TNR. "Wary of Welfare," *New Republic* 174 (5 June 1976): 3–5.

52. Statement by Jimmy Carter on the American Family, 3 August 1976 (National Assembly of Religious Women Papers, Box 15, NDA); Glad, *Jimmy Carter*, 313, 375; .

53. O'Rourke, *Geno*, 126–34; "Jimmy Carter and the Democratic Platform Abortion Plank," 1976 (Office of the Press Secretary, David Gergen Files, Box 1, FPL); "Bernardin Hits Abortion Plank," *New York Times*, 4 July 1976; Glad, *Jimmy Carter*, 308.

54. Albert R. Hunt, "Carter and the Catholics," *Wall Street Journal*, 8 July 1976; Andrew Mollison, "Do Catholics Cut Carter's Chances?" Atlanta *Constitution*, 13 July 1976; Haynes Johnson, "Catholics Seen as Problem for Carter," *Washington Post*, 16 July 1976.

55. Witcover, *Marathon*, 319–26; Steven Brill, "Jimmy Carter's Pathetic Lies," *Harper's* 252 (March 1976): 77–88.

56. Witcover, *Marathon*, 129, 133, 350–51; Glad, *Jimmy Carter*, 245–46, 258; Ravitch, *The Troubled Crusade*, 313–14.

57. Witcover, *Marathon*, 245; Jim Templeton, "Six States to Decide Next U.S. President, Delegates to Area COPE Conference Told," Southern Illinois *Labor Tribune* (East St. Louis, Ill.), 1 April 1976.

58. Patrick Buchanan Memorandum to the President, Fall 1976 (Ford-Carter Debate Papers, Input Files, Box 29, FPL); Gallup Opinion Index, "Religion in America, 1975" (Charles McCall Files, Ford Presidential Campaign, Box 78, FPL).

59. Jerry V. Livadas, "The Winning of the White House 1976," 15 August 1976 (President Ford Committee Records, Research office, Box 29, FPL).

60. Rita E. Hauser Memorandum to Rogers C. B. Morton, 3 May 1976 (President Ford Committee Records, Staff Memoranda, Box B10, FPL); Reed, *Active Faith*, 82–83; Robert D. Novak, "Fiasco '76," *National Review* 28 (24 December 1976): 1396–98.

61. Dionne, *Why Americans Hate Politics*, 128, 140; Glad, *Jimmy Carter*, 381–82, 402.

62. Witcover, *Marathon*, 226, 554; Glad, *Jimmy Carter*, 401; Dionne, *Why Americans Hate Politics*, 227.

63. Dionne, *Why Americans Hate Politics*, 131, 227; Witcover, *Marathon*, 620; Glad, *Jimmy Carter*, 401–402; William Schneider, "The November 4 Vote for President: What Did It Mean?" in Austin Ranney, ed., *The American Elections of 1980* (Washington, D.C.: American Enterprise Institute, 1981), 212–62; Archie Robinson, *George Meany and His Times* (New York: Simon & Schuster, 1981), 352.

64. Witcover, *Marathon*, 546.

65. Gallup Opinion Index, "Religion in America, 1975"; Dionne, *Why Americans Hate Politics*, 124, 127.

66. Billy Graham letter to Gerald R. Ford, 24 November 1976 (White House Central Files, Name File, Box 1, FPL).

Notes to Chapter 4

1. Austin Ranney, "The Carter Administration," in Austin Ranney, ed., *The American Elections of 1980* (Washington, D.C.: American Enterprise Institute, 1981), 1–36; R. Emmett Tyrrell, Jr., *The Liberal Crack-Up* (New York: Simon & Schuster, 1984), 24, 39, 45, 157.

2. Paul Johnson, *Modern Times: From the Twenties to the Nineties* (New York: HarperCollins, 1991), 613–96.

3. *Ibid.*, 674; Jeane Kirkpatrick, "Dictatorships and Double Standards," *Commentary* 68 (November 1979): 34–45.

4. Johnson, *Modern Times*, 661; Christopher Matthews, *Hardball: How Politics Is Played* (New York: Summit Books, 1988), 137; Lou Cannon, *President Reagan: The Role of a Lifetime* (New York: Simon & Schuster, 1991), 820.

5. E. J. Dionne, *Why Americans Hate Politics* (New York: Simon & Schuster, 1992), 244, 277; Tyrrell, *The Liberal Crack-Up*, 50.

6. Michael Barone, *Our Country: The Shaping of America from Roosevelt to Reagan* (New York: Free Press, 1990), 579; Kevin P. Phillips, *Post-Conservative America: People, Politics, and Ideology in a Time of Crisis* (New York: Random House, 1982), 30. For the best discussion of the fall of smokestack industry in the seventies and eighties, see John P. Hoerr, *And the Wolf Finally Came: The Decline of the American Steel Industry* (Pittsburgh: University of Pittsburgh Press, 1988).

7. Tyrrell, *The Liberal Crack-Up*, 49–50; Burton Yale Pines, *Back to Basics: The Traditionalist Movement That Is Sweeping Grass-Roots America* (New York: Morrow, 1982), 321–22; Barone, *Our Country*, 580.

8. Joseph A. Califano, Jr., *Governing America: An Insider's Report from the White House and the Cabinet* (New York: Simon & Schuster, 1981), 368–71; Phillips, *Post-Conservative America*, 90; Thomas Byrne Edsall and Mary D. Edsall, *Chain Reaction: The Impact of Race, Rights, and Taxes on American Politics* (New York: Norton, 1992), 168.

9. Phillips, *Post-Conservative America*, 95, 97.

10. *Ibid.*, 93, 238; John R. Logan and Reid M. Golden, "Suburbs and Satellites: Two Decades of Change," *American Sociological Review* 51 (June 1986): 430–37; Barone, *Our Country*, 566.

11. Jody Powell, *The Other Side of the Story* (New York: Morrow, 1984), 39–40; Califano, *Governing America*, 78; Stacey Oliker, "Abortion and the Left: The Limits of 'Pro-Family' Politics," *Socialist Review* 56 (1981): 71–96; Pines, *Back to Basics*, 158; Susan Harding, "Family Reform Movements: Recent Feminism and Its Opposition," *Feminist Studies* 7 (Spring 1981): 57–75.

12. Oliker, "Abortion and the Left," 71–96; Barbara Ehrenreich, "The Women's Movements: Feminist and Antifeminist," *Radical America* 15 (Spring 1981): 93–101; Rosalind Pollack Petchesky, "Antiabortion, Antifeminism, and the Rise of the New Right," *Feminist Studies* 7 (Summer 1981): 206–46; Christopher Lasch, *The True and Only Heaven: Progress and Its Critics* (New York: Norton, 1991), 492; Edmund Fawcett and Tony Thomas, *The American Condition* (New York: Harper & Row, 1982), 84–85; Pines, *Back to Basics*, 161; Kant Patel, Denny Pilant, and Gary Rose, "Born-Again Christians in the Bible Belt: A Study in Religion, Politics, and Ideology," *American Politics Quarterly* 10 (April 1982): 255–72.

13. Frances FitzGerald, *Cities on a Hill: A Journey Through Contemporary American Culture* (New York: Simon & Schuster, 1986), 26–41, 46–68, 84.

14. Califano, *Governing America*, 229; Betty Glad, *Jimmy Carter: In Search of the Great White House* (New York: Norton, 1980), 456; Donald Granberg and Beth Wellman Granberg, "Abortion Attitudes, 1965–1980: Trends and Determinants," *Family Planning Perspectives* 12 (September/October 1980): 250–61; Donald Granberg, "The Abortion Activists," *Family Planning Perspectives* 13 (July/August 1981): 157–63.

15. William Martin, *With God on Our Side: The Rise of the Religious Right in America* (New York: Broadway Books, 1996), 169; Pines, *Back to Basics*, 121, 123, 172; S. Robert Lichter, Stanley Rothman, and Linda S. Lichter, *The Media Elite* (Bethesda: Adler & Adler, 1986), 238.

16. Califano, *Governing America*, 256–57; Matthews, *Hardball*, 100.

17. Califano, *Governing America*, 233–35; Gene I. Maeroff, "City U. Out-of-City Hiring Held Biased Against Jews," *New York Times*, 10 March 1975.

18. Sidney Hook and Miro Todorvich, "The Tyranny of Reverse Discrimination," *Change* 8 (December-January 1976): 42–43; Iver Peterson, "Rise in Black Students Brings Disputes on Law School Recruiting," *New York Times*, 7 April 1975; Mordeca Jane Pollock, "On Academic Quotas," *New York Times*, 4 March 1975; William McGowan, "The Fall of City College," *Wall Street Journal*, 4 October 1994.

19. Diane Ravitch, *The Troubled Crusade: American Education, 1945–1980* (New York: Basic Books, 1983), 286–88; Califano, *Governing America*, 231–33, 237, 241.

20. Califano, *Governing America*, 241; Edsall and Edsall, *Chain Reaction*, 124; Lasch, *The True and Only Heaven*, 497; Jared Taylor, *Paved with Good Intentions: The Failure of Race Relations in Contemporary America* (New York: Carroll & Graf, 1992), 138; Dinesh D'Souza, *The End of Racism: Principles for a Multiracial Society* (New York: Free Press, 1995), 224, 226.

21. Pines, *Back to Basics*, 313; Thomas Sowell letter to Robert A. Goldwin, 9 August 1975 (Robert A. Goldwin Files, Goldwin Name File, Box 27, FPL);

Thomas Sowell, " 'Affirmative Action' Reconsidered," *Public Interest* 50 (1976): 47–65.

22. Edsall and Edsall, *Chain Reaction,* 116–18, 143; John R. Logan and Mark Schneider, "Racial Segregation and Racial Change in American Suburbs, 1970–1980," *American Journal of Sociology* 89 (January 1984): 874–88.

23. Pines, *Back to Basics,* 133; Charles Murray, "White Welfare, White Families, 'White Trash,' " *National Review* 38 (28 March 1986): 30–34; Edsall and Edsall, *Chain Reaction,* 107.

24. Taylor, *Paved with Good Intentions,* 39; Edsall and Edsall, *Chain Reaction,* 112–13.

25. Powell, *The Other Side of the Story,* 74–75, 109–17, 150, 206, 290; Califano, *Governing America,* 417–18.

26. Lichter, Rothman, and Lichter, *The Media Elite,* 20–22, 28, 30, 32, 40–41, 45–47, 57, 64–65, 220–53.

27. Fawcett and Thomas, *The American Condition,* 158; Betty Glad, *Jimmy Carter: In Search of the Great White House* (New York: Norton, 1980), 417, 419, 421, 426–27, 451; Ranney, "The Carter Administration," 1–36.

28. "Transcript of President's Address to Country on Energy Problems," *New York Times,* 16 July 1979; Jeff Greenfield, *The Real Campaign: How the Media Missed the Story of the 1980 Campaign* (New York: Summit Books, 1982), 114–15.

29. Greenfield, *The Real Campaign,* 147–48; Nelson W. Polsby, "The Democratic Nomination," in Ranney, ed., *The American Elections of 1980,* 37–60.

30. Elizabeth Drew, *Portrait of an Election: The 1980 Presidential Campaign* (New York: Simon & Schuster, 1981), 78, 143, 160, 301; Greenfield, *The Real Campaign,* 70; Polsby, "The Democratic Nomination," 37–60.

31. Drew, *Portrait of an Election,* 32, 161; Greenfield, *The Real Campaign,* 55, 63, 67.

32. Powell, *The Other Side of the Story,* 186, 188.

33. Michael J. Malbin, "The Conventions, Platforms, and Issue Activists," in Ranney, ed., *The American Elections of 1980,* 99–141; Greenfield, *The Real Campaign,* 184–87; Drew, *Portrait of an Election,* 224, 253; Califano, *Governing America,* 291–92; Chester E. Finn, Jr., "Teacher Politics," *Commentary* 75 (February 1983): 29–41.

34. Michael Kazin, *The Populist Persuasion: An American History* (New York: Basic Books, 1995), 258; Martin, *With God on Our Side,* 171–73; Pines, *Back to Basics,* 121–22; Louise J. Lorentzen, "Evangelical Life Style Concerns Expressed in Political Action," *Sociological Analysis* 41 (1980): 144–54; John H. Simpson, "Status Inconsistency and Moral Issues," *Journal for the Scientific Study of Religion* 24 (1985): 155–62.

35. Martin, *With God on Our Side,* 171–73; John B. Donovan, *Pat Robertson: The Authorized Biography* (New York: Macmillan, 1988), 120; Pines, *Back to Basics,* 123.

36. Pines, *Back to Basics,* 140–41; Martin, *With God on Our Side,* 198–99; Ralph Reed, *Active Faith: How Christians Are Changing the Soul of American Politics* (New York: Free Press, 1996), 105; Fawcett and Thomas, *The American Condition,* 116; Michael Lienesch, *Redeeming America: Piety and Politics in the New Christian*

Right (Chapel Hill: University of North Carolina Press, 1993), 85; John G. Richardson and Julie E. Cranston, "Social Change, Parental Values, and the Salience of Sex Education," *Journal of Marriage and the Family* 43 (August 1981): 547–88.

37. FitzGerald, *Cities on a Hill,* 46–68; Lienesch, *Redeeming America,* 48; Pines, *Back to Basics,* 200; Harold Lindsell letter to Jason King, 30 March 1976 (*Christianity Today* Papers, Box 24, BGA); Jason King letter to Harold Lindsell, 25 March 1976 (*Christianity Today* Papers, Box 24, BGA).

38. "Abortion's Morning After," *New York Times,* 4 December 1978; Michael W. Traugott and Maris A. Vinovskis, "Abortion and the 1978 Congressional Elections," *Family Planning Perspectives* 12 (September/October 1980): 238–46; Peter Skerry, "The Class Conflict over Abortion," *Public Interest* 52 (1978): 69–84; Peter Ross Range, "Thunder from the Right," *New York Times Magazine* 5 (8 February 1981): 23–26, 74–75, 81, 84; Owen Ullmann, *Stockman: The Man, the Myth, the Future* (New York: Donald I. Fine, 1986), 111.

39. Phyllis Schlafly letter to the editor, *America* 148 (14 June 1980): 489; Donald Granberg, "The Abortion Activists," *Family Planning Perspectives* 13 (July/August 1981): 157–63; Juli Loesch, "Prolife, Pro-ERA," *America* 146 (9 December 1978): 435–36; Elizabeth Alexander and Maureen Fiedler, "The Equal Rights Amendment and Abortion: Separate and Distinct," *America* 148 (12 April 1980): 314–18; "ERA" Pro and Con," *Sunday Visitor* (Huntingdon, Ind.), 15 June 1980, 6–7.

40. Cliff Foster, "Friends and Foes of ERA Lobby Bishops," National Catholic News Service, 1 May 1978 (Conference of Major Superiors of Men, Box 31, NDA); Network, "Catholics and the Equal Rights Amendment," 1978 (National Assembly of Religious Women Papers, Box 11, NDA); Kathleen Cooney letter to Kathleen Keating, 30 January 1978 (National Assembly of Religious Women Papers, Box 10, NDA); Kathleen Keating letter to Kathleen Cooney, 3 April 1978 (National Assembly of Religious Women Papers, Box 10, NDA); Kathleen Keating letter to Wilma Kramer, 1978 (National Assembly of Religious Women Papers, Box 10, NDA); The Family Life Apostolate, Archdiocese of New Orleans, letter to National Assembly of Religious Women, 29 August 1977 (National Assembly of Religious Women Papers, Box 10, NDA); Kathleen Keating letter to the Family Life Apostolate, Archdiocese of New Orleans, 10 October 1977 (National Assembly of Religious Women Papers, Box 10, NDA).

41. Leslie Bennetts, "Abortion Foes, at Conference, Plan Strategy of Political Activism," *New York Times,* 21 January 1980.

42. George G. Higgins, "The Prolife Movement and the New Right," *America* 148 (13 September 1980): 107–10; Ronald E. Griescheimer letter to the Association of Chicago Priests, 28 April 1980 (Association of Chicago Priests Papers, Box 17, NDA).

43. Joan S. Carver, "The Equal Rights Amendment and the Florida Legislature," *Florida Historical Quarterly* 60 (April 1982): 455–91; Robert Booth Fowler, "The Feminist and Antifeminist Debate Within Evangelical Protestantism," *Women & Politics* 5 (Summer/Fall 1985): 7–39; Val Burris, "Who Opposed the ERA? An Analysis of the Social Bases of Antifeminism," *Social Science Quarterly* 64 (June 1983): 305–17; Matthew C. Moen, "School Prayer and the Politics of Life-Style Concern," *Social Science Quarterly* 65 (December 1984): 1065–71; Susan E.

Marshall and Anthony M. Orum, "Opposition Then and Now: Countering Feminism in the Twentieth Century," *Research in Politics and Society* 2 (1986): 13–34; Louis Bolce, Gerald De Maio, and Douglas Muzzio, "ERA and the Abortion Controversy: A Case of Dissonance Reduction," *Social Science Quarterly* 67 (June 1986): 299–314.

44. Martin, *With God on Our Side*, 181.

45. *Ibid.*, 178–88; Pines, *Back to Basics*, 140, 144; Pamela Johnston Conover, "The Mobilization of the New Right: A Test of Various Explanations," *Western Political Quarterly* 36 (December 1983): 633–49.

46. Evangelicals for Social Action, "Can My Vote be Biblical?" *Christianity Today* 24 (19 September 1980): 1035–38; "The White House Feud on the Family," *Christianity Today* 24 (2 May 1980): 47–48, 50; Martin, *With God on Our Side*, 189; Pines, *Back to Basics*, 149.

47. Pines, *Back to Basics*, 286–87, 295–96; Clyde Wilcox, "Fundamentalists and Politics: An Analysis of the Effects of Differing Operational Definitions," *Journal of Politics* 48 (November 1986): 1041–51; Stephen D. Johnson and Joseph B. Tamney, "Support for the Moral Majority: A Test of a Model," *Journal for the Scientific Study of Religion* 23 (1984): 183–96; George Vecsey, "Militant Preachers Try to Weld Fundamentalist Christians' Political Power," *New York Times*, 21 January 1980.

48. Pines, *Back to Basics*, 55; Phillips, *Post*-Conservative America, 48; Lienesch, *Redeeming America*, 98, 100, 114, 116–17, 119.

49. Edsall and Edsall, *Chain Reaction*, 132–34; Pines, *Back to Basics*, 297; Allan J. Mayer, "A Tide of Born-Again Politics," *Newsweek* 96 (15 September 1980): 28–29, 31–32, 36; Robert Zwier and Richard Smith, "Christian Politics and the New Right," *Christian Century* 97 (8 October 1980): 937–41; Daniel Yankelovich, "Stepchildren of the Moral Majority," *Psychology Today* 15 (November 1981): 5–6, 10; Bill Keller, "Evangelical Conservatives Move from Pews to Polls, But Can They Sway Congress?" *Congressional Quarterly* 38 (6 September 1980): 26–34; Kenneth A. Briggs, "Evangelicals Turning to Politics Fear Moral Slide Imperils Nation," *New York Times*, 19 August 1980; Martin E. Marty, "Fundamentalism as a Social Phenomenon," *Review and Expositor* 79 (Winter 1982): 19–29.

50. James Mann and Sarah A. Peterson, "Preachers in Politics: Decisive Force in '80?" *U.S. News & World Report* 89 (15 September 1980): 24–26; Martin, *With God on Our Side*, 205; Jerry Falwell, "The Maligned Moral Majority," *Newsweek* 98 (21 September 1981): 17; J. Milton Yinger and Stephen J. Cutler, "The Moral Majority Viewed Sociologically," *Sociological Focus* 15 (October 1982): 289–306; Charles L. Harper and Kevin Leicht, "Religious Awakenings and Status Politics: Sources of Support for the New Religious Right," *Sociological Analysis* 45 (Winter 1984): 339–53; Donna Day-Lower, "Who *Is* the Moral Majority? A Composite Profile," *Union Seminary Quarterly Review* 38 (1983): 335–49; Carol Mueller, "In Search of a Constituency for the 'New Religious Right,' " *Public Opinion Quarterly* 47 (Summer 1983): 213–29; Wesley E. Miller, Jr., "The New Christian Right and Fundamentalist Discontent: The Politics of Lifestyle Concern Hypothesis Revisited," *Sociological Focus* 18 (October 1985): 325–36; Emmett H. Buell., Jr., and Lee Sigelman, "An Army That Meets Every Sunday? Popular Support for the Moral

Majority in 1980," *Social Science Quarterly* 66 (June 1985): 426–34; John Herbers, "Ultraconservative Evangelicals a Surging New Force in Politics," *New York Times,* 17 August 1980; Anson Shupe and John Heinerman, "Mormonism and the New Christian Right: An Emerging Coalition?" *Review of Religious Research* 27 (December 1985): 146–57; Clyde Wilcox, "Popular Support for the Moral Majority in 1980: A Second Look," *Social Science Quarterly* 68 (March 1987): 157–66; Peter L. Berger, "The Class Struggle in American Religion," *Christian Century* 98 (February 1981): 194–99.

51. Bruce Buursma, "Evangelicals Give Reagan a 'Non-Partisan' Stump," *Christianity Today* 24 (19 September 1980): 50; Leo P. Ribuffo, "Liberals and That Old-Time Religion," *Nation* 231 (29 November 1980): 570–73; Frances FitzGerald, "A Disciplined, Charging Army," *New Yorker* 57 (18 May 1981): 53–54, 59–60, 63–64, 69–70, 73–74, 78, 81–82, 84, 89–90, 92, 95–96, 99–100, 103–4, 106–7, 109–33.

52. Greenfield, *The Real Campaign,* 230–31, 289; Cannon, *President Reagan,* 103.

53. Cannon, *President Reagan,* 520–21; Traugott and Vinovskis, "Abortion and the 1978 Congressional Elections," 238–46; Granberg and Granberg, "Abortion Attitudes, 1965–1980," 250–61; Sheila Rule, "Blacks, Reacting to Vote, Seek Way to Keep Gains," *New York Times,* 8 November 1980; Joseph B. Tamney and Stephen D. Johnson, "Religious Television in Middletown," *Review of Religious Research* 25 (June 1984): 303–13; Donovan, *Pat Robertson,* 169, 171; Martin, *With God on Our Side,* 188; E. J. Dionne, "Evangelicals' Vote Is a Major Target," *New York Times,* 29 June 1980; Michael W. Combs and Susan Welch, "Blacks, Whites, and Attitudes Towards Abortion," *Public Opinion Quarterly* 46 (Winter 1982): 510–20; Elaine J. Hall and Myra Marx Ferree, "Race Differences in Abortion Attitudes," *Public Opinion Quarterly* 50 (Summer 1986): 193–207

54. Dionne, "Evangelicals' Vote Is a Major Target"; Fawcett and Thomas, *The American Condition,* 114–15; Dudley Clendinen, "Rev. Falwell Inspires Evangelical Vote," *New York Times,* 20 August 1980.

55. Martin, *With God on Our Side,* 219; Arthur H. Miller and Martin P. Wattenberg, "Politics from the Pulpit: Religiosity and the 1980 Elections," *Public Opinion Quarterly* 48 (Spring 1984): 301–17; Jeffrey L. Brudney and Gary W. Copeland, "Evangelicals as a Political Force: Reagan and the 1980 Religious Vote," *Social Science Quarterly* 65 (December 1984): 1072–79; Cannon, *President Reagan,* 819; Greenfield, *The Real Campaign,* 139; Ronald Brownstein, *The Power and the Glitter: The Hollywood-Washington Connection* (New York: Pantheon, 1990), 290.

56. James L. Guth and John C. Green, "Politics in a New Key: Religiosity and Participation Among Political Activists," *Western Political Quarterly* 43 (1990): 153–79; Martin, *With God on Our Side,* 215, 217; Edward E. Plowman, "Conservative Network Puts Its Stamp on the Southern Baptists' Convention," *Christianity Today* 24 (18 July 1980): 50–51.

57. Edwin Warner, "New Resolve by the New Right," *Time* 116 (8 December 1980): 24, 27; Brownstein, *The Power and the Glitter,* 279–80.

58. Milton Himmelfarb, "Are Jews Becoming Republican?" *Commentary* 72 (August 1981): 27–31; Kathleen Murphy Beatty and Oliver Walter, "Religious Preference and Practice: Reevaluating Their Impact on Political Tolerance," *Public*

Opinion Quarterly 48 (Spring 1984): 318–29; Herbers, "Ultraconservative Evangelicals a Surging Force in Politics."

59. Martin, *With God on Our Side,* 212; Mayer, "A Tide of Born-Again Politics," 28–29, 31–32, 36.

60. "Pulpits and Politics, 1980," *Church and State* 33 (November 1980): 7–10; Donovan, *Pat Robertson,* 157–58; Harrell, *Pat Robertson,* 134.

61. Greenfield, *The Real Campaign,* 12, 34; Charles O. Jones, "Nominating Carter's Favorite Opponent: The Republicans in 1980," in Ranney, ed., *The American Elections of 1980,* 61–98; FitzGerald, "A Disciplined, Charging Army," 60; James Dunn, "Wise as Serpents, at Least: The Political and Social Perspectives of the Electronic Church," *Review and Expositor* 81 (Winter 1984): 77–92.

62. Drew, *Portrait of an Election,* 24, 274, 280; Michael J. Robinson, "The Media in 1980: Was the Message the Message?" in Ranney, ed., *The American Elections of 1980,* 177–211.

63. Martin, *With God on Our Side,* 213; Malbin, "The Conventions, Platforms, and Issue Activists," 99–141; Dudley Clendinen, " 'Christian New Right's' Rush to Power," *New York Times,* 18 August 1980; Cynthia H. Deitch, "Ideology and Opposition to Abortion: Trends in Public Opinion, 1972–1980," *Alternative Lifestyles* 6 (Fall 1983): 6–26; Robinson, "The Media in 1980," 177–211; Drew, *Portrait of an Election,* 190; Greenfield, *The Real Campaign,* 201.

64. Greenfield, *The Real Campaign,* 87, 89–90, 93; Drew, *Portrait of an Election,* 345.

65. Drew, *Portrait of an Election,* 184–85;

66. Greenfield, *The Real Campaign,* 151; William Schneider, "The November 4 Vote for President: What Did It Mean?" in Ranney, ed., *The American Elections of 1980,* 212–62 .

67. Phillips, *Post*-Conservative America, 39, 99, 226; Schneider, "The November 4 Vote for President," 212–62; Himmelfarb, "Are Jews Becoming Republican?" 27–31; Archie Robinson, *George Meany and His Times* (New York: Simon & Schuster, 1981), 356–405; Greenfield, *The Real Campaign,* 106–7, 196.

68. Greenfield, *The Real Campaign,* 106–7; Drew, *Portrait of an Election,* 270, 318; Himmelfarb, "Are Jews Becoming Republican?" 27–31; Phillips, *Post*-Conservative America, 164.

69. Phillips, *Post*-Conservative America, 91–92, 188; Donovan, *Pat Robertson,* 181; Harrell, *Pat Robertson,* 161; Albert R. Hunt, "The Campaign and the Issues," in Ranney, ed., *The American Elections of 1980,* 142–76; Schneider, "The November 4 Vote for President," 212–62.

70. Phillips, *Post*-Conservative America, 195, 232; Schneider, "The November 4 Vote for President," 212–62; Edsall and Edsall, *Chain Reaction,* 164; Jerome L. Himmelstein and James A. McRae, Jr., "Social Conservatism, New Republicans, and the 1980 Election," *Public Opinion Quarterly* 48 (Fall 1984): 592–605; Fawcett and Thomas, *The American Condition,* 179.

71. Greenfield, *The Real Campaign,* 295; Phillips, *Post-Conservative America,* 191; Barone, *Our Country,* 596.

72. Dionne, *Why Americans Hate Politics,* 277; Phillips, *Post-Conservative America,* 91.

Notes to Chapter 5

1. James M. Perry, "For the Democrats, Pam's is the Place for the Elite to Meet," *Wall Street Journal*, 8 October 1981; James Ring Adams, "Poor Pamela," *American Spectator* 28 (February 1995): 26–28, 30.

2. Tip O'Neill, with William Novak, *Man of the House: The Life and Political Memoirs of Speaker Tip O'Neill* (New York: Random House, 1987), 331–32, 349, 360.

3. Marjorie Hunter, "Conservative House Democrats Seek Bigger Voice," *New York Times*, 8 November 1980; O'Neill and Novak, *Man of the House*, 353–54; Dan Balz and Ronald Brownstein, *Storming the Gates: Protest Politics and the Republican Revival* (Boston: Little, Brown, 1996), 121; Sidney Blumenthal, "Reaganism on Fast-Forward," *New Republic* 190 (3 September 1984): 14–17.

4. Donald Granberg and James Burlison, "The Abortion Issue in the 1980 Elections," *Family Planning Perspectives* 15 (September-October 1983): 231–38; David Osborne, "The Great Society Revisited: Winning Battles, Losing the War," *Mother Jones* 11 (June 1986): 13–14, 16–21.

5. L. J. Davis, "Conservatism in America," *Harper's* 276 (October 1980): 21–26; James L. Guth and John C. Green, "Faith and Politics: Religion and Ideology Among Political Contributors," *American Politics Quarterly* 14 (July 1986): 186–200.

6. Zillah Eisenstein, "Antifeminism in the Politics and Election of 1980," *Feminist Studies* 7 (Summer 1981): 187–205; George McGovern, "The New Right and the Old Paranoia," *Playboy* 28 (January 1981): 118; Johnny Greene, "The Astonishing Wrongs of the New Moral Right," *Playboy* 28 (January 1981): 117–18, 248, 250, 252, 254–56, 258, 260, 262; "Religious Right Goes for Bigger Game," *U.S. News & World Report* 89 (17 November 1980): 42.

7. Owen Ullmann, *Stockman: The Man, the Myth, the Future* (New York: Donald I. Fine, 1986), 58, 60, 84, 111, 145, 159; John Judis, "Libertarianism: Where the Left Meets the Right," *Progressive* 44 (September 1980): 36–38.

8. Ullmann, *Stockman*, 91, 124, 147, 170; Judis, "Libertarianism," 36–38.

9. Ullmann, *Stockman*, 140, 167, 199; Martin Anderson, *Revolution* (New York: Harcourt Brace Jovanovich, 1988), xx, 114, 127, 129, 152.

10. Ullmann, *Stockman*, 236, 287; Anderson, *Revolution*, 175–79; Edwin Meese III, *With Reagan: The Inside Story* (Washington, D.C.: Regnery Gateway, 1992), 93, 150; Daniel Patrick Moynihan, *Family and Nation* (New York: Harcourt Brace Jovanovich, 1987), 120.

11. Ullmann, *Stockman*, 186–87, 227–28, 312–13; Meese, *With Reagan*, 158, 161; Michael Barone, *Our Country: The Shaping of America from Roosevelt to Reagan* (New York: Free Press, 1990), 621–22; "A Friendlier Congress for Ronald Reagan," *U.S. News & World Report* 89 (17 November 1980): 31–39.

12. Ullmann, *Stockman*, 216; Meese, *With Reagan*, 136–37.

13. Meese, *With Reagan*, 104, 107, 142–45; R. Emmett Tyrrell, Jr., *The Conservative Crack-Up* (New York: Simon & Schuster, 1992), 104, 107–8, 157, 163.

14. Kevin P. Phillips, *Post-Conservative America: People, Politics, and Ideology in a Time of Crisis* (New York: Random House, 1982), 49–50; Beth Spring,

"Republicans, Religion, and Reelection," *Christianity Today* 28 (5 October 1984): 54–58.

15. Tyrrell, *The Conservative Crack-Up*, 201, 259; "*Reason* Interview with Irving Kristol," *Reason* 14 (January 1983): 40–44; Byron E. Shafer, "The New Cultural Politics," *Political Science and Politics* 18 (Spring 1985): 221–31; Helen A. Moore and Hugh P. Whitt, "Multiple Dimensions of the Moral Majority Platform: Shifting Interest Group Coalitions," *Sociological Quarterly* 27 (Fall 1986): 423–39.

16. Guth and Green, "Faith and Politics," 186–200; Val Burris, "Business Support for the New Right: A Consumer Guide to the Most Reactionary American Corporations," *Socialist Review* 17 (January-February 1987): 33–63; J. Craig Jenkins and Teri Shumate, "Cowboy Capitalists and the Rise of the 'New Right': An Analysis of Contributors to Conservative Policy Formation Organizations," *Social Problems* 33 (December 1985): 130–45; Dan Clawson, Marvin J. Karson, and Allen Kaufman, "The Corporate Pact for a Conservative America: A Data Analysis of 1980 Corporate PAC Donations in Sixty-Six Conservative Congressional Elections," *Research in Corporate Social Performance and Policy* 8 (1986): 223–45; James L. Guth and John C. Green, "The Moralizing Minority: Christian Right Support Among Political Contributors," *Social Science Quarterly* 68 (September 1987): 598–610.

17. Niels Bjerre-Poulsen, "The Heritage Foundation: A Second-Generation Think Tank," *Journal of Policy History* 3 (1991): 152–72; Meese, *With Reagan*, 148, 315–19; Ann M. Reilly, "Reagan's Think Tank," *Dun's Review* 117 (April 1981): 110–14; Cal Thomas, *Occupied Territory* (Brentwood, Tenn.: Wolgemuth & Hyatt, 1987), 32.

18. Steven Pressman, "Religious Right: Trying to Link Poll Power and Lobby Muscle," *Congressional Quarterly* 42 (22 September 1984): 2315–19; "What Conservatives Think of Ronald Reagan: A Symposium," *Policy Review* 8 (Winter 1984): 12–19; Christopher Lasch, *The True and Only Heaven: Progress and Its Critics* (New York: Norton, 1991), 505–6; William Martin, *With God on Our Side: The Rise of the Religious Right in America* (New York: Broadway Books, 1996), 224, 227; Peter Ross Range, "Thunder from the Right," *New York Times Magazine* 5 (8 February 1981): 23–25, 64, 74–75, 81, 84; Richard V. Pierard, "Reagan and the Evangelicals: The Making of a Love Affair," *Christian Century* 100 (21–28 December 1983): 1182–85; Ralph Reed, *Active Faith: How Christians Are Changing the Soul of American Politics* (New York: Free Press, 1996), 115–17; Lou Cannon, *President Reagan: The Role of a Lifetime* (New York: Simon & Schuster, 1991), 128, 133; Stephen D. Johnson and Joseph B. Tamney, "Support for the Moral Majority: A Test of a Model," *Journal for the Scientific Study of Religion* 23 (1984): 183–96.

19. "What Conservatives Think of Ronald Reagan," 12–19; Martin, *With God on Our Side*, 223, 225; Walter Shapiro, "Politics and the Pulpit," *Newsweek* 104 (17 September 1984): 24–27.

20. E. J. Dionne, Jr., *Why Americans Hate Politics* (New York: Simon & Schuster, 1992), 290; Richard F. Fenno, Jr., *The Making of a Senator: Dan Quayle* (Washington, D.C.: Congressional Quarterly Press, 1989), 7, 14, 17–20; Seymour Martin Lipset and Earl Raab, "The Election and the Evangelicals," *Commentary* 71 (March 1981): 25–31.

21. Edwin Warner, "New Resolve by the New Right," *Time* 116 (8 December 1980): 24, 27; "Reagan and the Evangelicals," 1182–85; Terrel H. Bell, *The Thirteenth Man: A Reagan Cabinet Memoir* (New York: Free Press, 1988), 2, 53, 103–4, 130–31; Barone, *Our Country*, 589; Phillips, *Post-Conservative America*, 215.

22. Christopher Matthews, *Hardball: How Politics Is Played* (New York: Summit Books, 1988), 49, 195; O'Neill and Novak, *Man of the House*, 345, 348, 355; Barone, *Our Country*, 614, 624–25.

23. Barone, *Our Country*, 625, 629.

24. Ullmann, *Stockman*, 237; Robert Vasquez, "Saving a Steel Town," *New York Times*, 20 August 1980; Haynes Johnson, *Sleepwalking Through History: America in the Reagan Years* (New York: Norton, 1991), 117–19; Christopher Byron, "Booms, Busts, and Birth of a Rust Bowl," *Time* 120 (27 December 1982): 63, 66; Thomas Byrne Edsall, *The New Politics of Inequality* (New York: Norton, 1984), 104.

25. Lindsey Gruson, "As Steelworkers Strike, Mill Town Shows Decay," *New York Times*, 22 July 1985; Thomas Byrne Edsall and Mary D. Edsall, *Chain Reaction: The Impact of Race, Rights, and Taxes on American Politics* (New York: Norton, 1992), 199–200; Gregg Easterbrook, "Voting for Unemployment," *Atlantic Monthly* 251 (May 1983): 31–44; Robert M. Kaus, "The Trouble with Unions," *Harper's* 266 (June 1983): 23–35; Bill Keller, "Union Officials Stepping Up Their Efforts for Democrats," *New York Times*, 17 October 1984.

26. Marc Sellinger, "Authors Say Politics, As Usual, Need Cleaning Up," Columbus (Ohio) *Dispatch*, 30 June 1996; R. Emmett Tyrrell, *Boy Clinton: The Political Biography* (Washington, D.C.: Regnery Gateway, 1996), 19–32.

27. Lasch, *The True and Only Heaven*, 481–82; Edsall and Edsall, *Chain Reaction*, 194.

28. Edsall and Edsall, *Chain Reaction*, 212; Edsall, *The New Politics of Inequality*, 160–61; Sidney Blumenthal, "Steel and Roses," *New Republic* 190 (30 April 1984): 9–11.

29. , Blumenthal, "Steel and Roses," 9–11; M. Kent Jennings, "Residues of a Movement: The Aging of the American Protest Generation," *American Political Science Review* 81 (June 1987): 367–82.

30. Allen Hunter, "In the Wings: New Right Ideology and Organization," *Radical America* 15 (Spring 1981): 113–38; Roger Wilkins, "Smiling Racism," *Nation* 239 (3 November 1984): 437; Roy Reed, "Mississippi: 20 Years of Wide Racial Change," *New York Times*, 18 August 1983.

31. Glenn C. Loury, "The Moral Quandary of the Black Community" *Public Interest* 59 (Spring 1985): 9–22; Frances X. Clines, "President Talks to Black Leader," *New York Times*, 11 September 1984.

32. Moynihan, *Family and Nation*, 97, 99, 168, 183; Nicholas Lemann, "The Origins of the Underclass, Part II," *Atlantic Monthly* 258 (July 1986): 54–68; Ann Hulbert, "Children as Parents," *New Republic* 190 (10 September 1984): 15–23.

33. Frances FitzGerald, *Cities on a Hill: A Journey Through Contemporary American Cultures* (New York: Simon & Schuster, 1986), 81; Tom Bethell, "*Roe's* Disparate Impact," *American Spectator* 29 (June 1996): 18, 20; Sidney Blumenthal,

Pledging Allegiance: The Last Campaign of the Cold War (New York: Harper-Collins, 1990), 187–88.

34. Lucius J. Barker, *Our Time Has Come: A Delegate's Diary of Jesse Jackson's 1984 Presidential Campaign* (Urbana: University of Illinois Press, 1988), 62–63, 70–71, 74–75, 77.

35. William A. Henry II, *Visions of America: How We Saw the 1984 Election* (Boston: Atlantic Monthly Press, 1985), 78; Barker, *Our Time Has Come*, 79–80.

36. Barker, *Our Time Has Come*, 72, 75, 84, 146; Ed Magnuson, "Stirring Up New Storms," *Time* 124 (9 July 1984): 8–10.

37. Barker, *Our Time Has Come*, 121, 149, 177, 199; Benjamin Ginsberg, *The Fatal Embrace: Jews and the State* (Chicago: University of Chicago Press, 1993), 145–46, 148–49, 152–53; Lucy S. Dawidowicz, "Politics, the Jews, and the '84 Election," *Commentary* 79 (February 1985): 25–30; "Jackson and the Jews," *New Republic* 190 (19 March 1984): 9–10; Barbara Reynolds, "Jackson and the Pols," *New Republic* 190 (30 April 1984): 11–13.

38. Barone, *Our Country*, 641; Jane Gross, "Patricia Ireland, President of NOW, Does She Speak for Today's Women?" *New York Times Magazine* 16 (1 March 1992): 16–18, 38, 54; Robert W. Merry, "Lobbyist Wexler Advises Ferraro," *Wall Street Journal*, 17 September 1984; Henry, *Visions of America*, 176, 179; Ronald Brownstein, *The Power and the Glitter: The Hollywood-Washington Connection* (New York: Pantheon, 1990), 293.

39. "The Reagan 45," *New Republic* 190 (16 April 1984): 5–7; Sidney Blumenthal, "The GOP 'Me Decade'," *New Republic* 190 (17 and 24 September 1984): 12–15.

40. Suzanne Garment, *Scandal: The Culture of Mistrust in American Politics* (New York: Random House, 1991), 275–81; Henry, *Visions of America*, 201, 205–6.

41. Henry, *Visions of America*, 191; Geraldine A. Ferraro, *Ferraro: My Story* (New York: Bantam Books, 1985), 218; Robert D. McFadden, "O'Connor-Ferraro Dispute on Abortion Unresolved," *New York Times*, 11 September 1984.

42. Ferraro, *Ferraro*, 213–14, 221–22, 232, 236; United States Catholic Conference Staff Analysis of "The New Voluntarism," 28 February 1982 (John F. Cardinal Dearden Papers, Box 35, NDA); John Cardinal O'Connor and Mayor Edward I. Koch, *His Eminence and Hizzoner: A Candid Exchange* (New York: Morrow, 1989), 336; National Conference of Catholic Bishops, "Abortion: Questions and Answers," 1983 (National Assembly of Religious Women, Box 11, NDA); Timothy A. Byrnes, "The Politics of the American Catholic Hierarchy," *Political Science Quarterly* 108 (1993): 497–514; Kenneth A. Briggs, "Bishops' Debate," *New York Times*, 17 October 1984; Joe Klein, "Abortion and the Archbishop," *New York Magazine* 17 (1 October 1984): 36–43; Kenneth L. Woodward, "Politics and Abortion," *Newsweek* 104 (20 August 1984): 66–67.

43. "Testimony of Terence Cardinal Cooke of New York, Chairman, Committee for Prolife Activities, National Conference of Catholic Bishops," 5 November 1981 (John F. Cardinal Dearden Papers, Box 35, NDA); O'Connor and Koch, *His Eminence and Hizzoner*, 334.

44. Sydney H. Schanberg, "Thoughts of an Infidel," *New York Times*, 8 September 1984; John Herbers, "Kennedy Chides Church Leaders on Role of State,"

New York Times, 11 September 1984; "Excerpts from Kennedy's Remarks on Religion," *New York Times,* 11 September 1984.

45. Charles Krauthammer, "The Church-State Debate," *New Republic* 190 (17 and 24 September 1984): 15–18; Tom Minnery, ed., *Pornography: A Human Tragedy* (Wheaton, Ill.: Tyndale House, 1986), 22; Michael Oreskes, "Abortion Debate Is Held a Threat to Rights Bill," *New York Times,* 22 May 1984; Woodward, "Politics and Abortion," 66–67; Richard P. McBain, *Caesar's Coin: Religion and Politics in America* (New York: Macmillan, 1987), 101–68.

46. Ralph Reed, *Active Faith: How Christians Are Changing the Soul of American Politics* (New York: Free Press, 1996), 21–22, 85.

47. Woodward, "Politics and Abortion," 66–67; Stephen L. Carter, *The Culture of Disbelief: How American Law and Politics Trivialize Religious Devotion* (New York: Basic Books, 1993), 62; Suzanne Staggenborg, "Life-Style Preferences and Social Movement Recruitment: Illustrations from the Abortion Conflict," *Social Science Quarterly* 68 (December 1987): 779–97; Moynihan, *Family and Nation,* 148.

48. FitzGerald, *Cities on a Hill,* 87–92; Andrea J. Baker, "The Portrayal of AIDS in the Media: An Analysis of Articles in the *New York Times,*" in Douglas A. Feldman and Thomas M. Johnson, eds., *The Social Dimensions of AIDS: Method and Theory* (New York: Praeger, 1986), 179–93; Martin, *With God on Our Side,* 241.

49. V. S. Naipaul, "Among the Republicans," *New York Review of Books* 25 (October 1984): 5–12; Martin, *With God on Our Side,* 242, 248; Stephen Glass, "Pat Speaks," *New Republic* 214 (18 March 1996): 17; William Scobie, "Unholy Crusade on a Sexual Battlefront," *MacLean's* 94 (4 May 1981): 13–14; Rodney Clapp, "What the Democrats Believe," *Christianity Today* 28 (19 October 1984): 32–36.

50. Beth Spring, "These Christians Are Helping Gays Escape from Homosexual Lifestyles," *Christianity Today* 28 (21 September 1984): 56–58; Beth Spring, "A Woman Who Cares About Gays in Washington, D.C.," *Christianity Today* 28 (21 September 1984): 58, 60; Michael Stephen, "On Homosexual Priests," *New York Times,* 18 August 1980.

51. O'Connor and Koch, *His Eminence and Hizzoner,* 223–53, 297–98, 302, 308.

52. Sidney Blumenthal, "The Righteous Empire," *New Republic* 190 (22 October 1984): 18–24; James M. Perry, "Church and State: Candidates' Views on Religion Remain Big Campaign Issue," *Wall Street Journal,* 18 September 1984; Balz and Brownstein, *Storming the Gates,* 216.

53. Richard Pierard, "Religion and the 1984 Election Campaign," *Review of Religious Research* 27 (December 1985): 98–114; "Partisan Politics: Where Does the Gospel Fit?" *Christianity Today* 28 (9 November 1984): 15–17; Beth Spring, "Some Christian Leaders Want Further Political Activism," *Christianity Today* 28 (9 November 1984): 46–47, 49.

54. Clyde Wilcox, "America's Radical Right Revisited: A Comparison of the Activists in Christian Right Organizations from the 1960s and the 1980s," *Sociological Analysis* 48 (Spring 1987): 46–57; Clyde Wilcox, "Evangelicals and Fundamentalists in the New Christian Right: Religious Differences in the Ohio Moral Majority," *Journal for the Scientific Study of Religion* 26 (September 1986): 355–61; Clyde Wilcox, "Religious Attitudes and Anti-Feminism: An Analysis of the Ohio

Moral Majority," *Women & Politics* 7 (Summer 1987): 59–77; Clyde Wilcox, "Religious Orientations and Political Attitudes: Variations Within the New Christian Right," *American Politics Quarterly* 15 (April 1987): 274–96; Jeffry Will and Rhys Williams, "Political Ideology and Political Action in the New Christian Right," *Sociological Analysis* 47 (Summer 1986): 160–68; James L. Guth, "Political Converts: Partisan Realignment Among Southern Baptist Ministers," *Election Politics* 3 (1985/1986): 2–6; Sari Thomas, "The Route to Redemption: Religion and Social Class," *Journal of Communication* 35 (Winter 1985): 111–22; Clapp, "What the Democrats Believe," 32–36.

55. John Herbers, "Moral Majority and Its Allies Expect a Harvest of Votes for Conservatives," *New York Times,* 4 November 1984; "The Role Religion Plays," *Newsweek* 104 (17 September 1984): 31–32; Kenneth L. Woodward, "Faith, Hope, and Votes," *Newsweek* 104 (17 September 1984): 34–35.

56. Shapiro, "Politics and the Pulpit," 24–27; "Critics Fear That Reagan Is Swayed by Those Who Believe in a 'Nuclear Armageddon'," *Christianity Today* 28 (14 December 1984): 48, 51; Randy Frame, "Prolife Activists Escalate the War Against Abortion," *Christianity Today* 28 (9 November 1984): 40–42; Frances X. Clines, "Reporter's Notebook: Few Blacks in Reagan Crowds," *New York Times,* 8 September 1984; "Reagan Defends His Statements," *New York Times,* 8 September 1984.

57. Herbers, "Moral Majority and Its Allies Expect a Harvest of Votes for Conservatives"; Adam Clymer, "Moral Majority Starts Ad Campaign to Counter Critics," *New York Times,* 26 March 1981; Jim Buie, "Praise the Lord and Pass the Ammunition," *Church and State* 37 (October 1984): 4–8; Shapiro, "Politics and the Pulpit," 24–27.

58. Beth Spring, "Fundamentalists Go to Capital to Discuss God, Not Government," *Christianity Today* 28 (18 May 1984): 76; Pierard, "Religion and the 1984 Election Campaign," 98–114; Tim LaHaye, "The Election of Our Lifetime," *Religious Broadcasting* 16 (July-August, 1984): 14–15; Spring, "Some Christian Leaders Want Further Political Activism," 46–47, 49; Kenneth L. Woodward, "Playing Politics at Church," *Newsweek* 104 (9 July 1984): 52.

59. Shapiro, "Politics and the Pulpit," 24–27; Henry, *Visions of America,* 225, 244; Barone, *Our Country,* 646; George J. Church, "The Promise: 'You Ain't Seen Nothin' Yet!' " *Time* 124 (19 November 1984): 38–41.

60. Francis X. Clines, "Reagan Plays His Campaign Song at Country Music's Capital," *New York Times,* 14 September 1984; Bernard Weinraub, "Mondale Defends Himself on Religion Issue in South," *New York Times,* 14 September 1984.

61. John Herbers, "Church Issues Spread to State Races," *New York Times,* 19 September 1984; Robert S. Erikson, Thomas D. Lancaster, and David W. Romero, "Group Components of the Presidential Vote, 1952–1984," *Journal of Politics* 51 (May 1989): 337–46; Barone, *Our Country,* 646; William Bole, "Is the GOP Becoming God's Own Party?" *Church and State* 38 (January 1985): 12–13.

62. Edsall and Edsall, *Chain Reaction,* 173, 181–82; Evan Thomas, "Every Region, Every Age Group, Almost Every Bloc," *Time* 124 (19 November 1984): 42, 45.

63. Gerald M. Boyd, "Bush Subjected to Heckling in a Steel Town," *New York Times,* 4 November 1984, 62; Barone, *Our Country,* 645–46.

64. Barone, *Our Country,* 645–46; Henry, *Visions of America,* 191, 261.

65. Beth Spring, "Born-Again Minnesotans Play Political Hardball," *Christianity Today* 28 (21 September 1984): 68–70; Church, "The Promise," 38–41; Paul Taylor, *See How They Run: Electing the President in an Age of Mediaocracy* (New York: Knopf, 1990), 248.

66. Edsall and Edsall, *Chain Reaction,* 179; Stephen D. Johnson and Joseph B. Tamney, "The Christian Right and the 1984 Presidential Election," *Review of Religious Research* 27 (December 1985): 124–33; John H. Simpson, "Socio-Moral Issues and Recent Presidential Elections," *Review of Religious Research* 27 (December 1985): 115–23; Charles Krauthammer, "America's Holy War," *New Republic* 190 (9 April 1984): 15–19.

67. Moynihan, *Family and Nation,* 68–69; James M. Perry, "Candidates' Views on Religion Remain Big Campaign Issue," *Wall Street Journal,* 18 September 1984.

68. Reed, *Active Faith,* 22, 116–17; Balz and Brownstein, *Storming the Gates,* 318.

Notes to Chapter 6

1. Edwin Meese III, *With Reagan: The Inside Story* (Washington, D.C.: Regnery Gateway, 1992), 223, 238; Martin Anderson, *Revolution* (New York: Harcourt Brace Jovanovich, 1988), 405.

2. George J. Church, "An Interview with the President," *Time* 128 (8 December 1986): 18–22, 27; Sidney Blumenthal, *Pledging Allegiance: The Last Campaign of the Cold War* (New York: HarperCollins, 1990), 35. I thank Dr. Kyle Sinisi for his thoughts about North.

3. Jack W. Germond and Jules Witcover, *Whose Broad Stripes and Bright Stars? The Trivial Pursuit of the Presidency, 1988* (New York: Warner Books, 1989), 45, 47; John B. Judis, "Black Donkey, White Elephant: Race and American Politics," *New Republic* 198 (18 April 1988): 25–28.

4. Robert H. Bork, *The Tempting of America: The Political Seduction of the Law* (New York: Free Press, 1990), 268, 283–86; Suzanne Garment, "The War Against Robert H. Bork," *Commentary* 85 (January 1988): 17–26.

5. Garment, "The War Against Robert H. Bork," 17–26; Gary Wills, *Under God: Religion and American Politics* (New York: Simon & Schuster, 1990), 272, 315–16.

6. Bork, *The Tempting of America,* 323–26, 337–43; Garment, "The War Against Robert H. Bork," 17–26.

7. Jack Kemp, "GOP Victory in 1988," *Policy Review* 12 (Summer 1988): 2–9; Bork, *The Tempting of America,* 310; David Brock, *The Real Anita Hill: The Untold Story* (New York: Free Press, 1993), 67.

8. Jules Witcover, *Crapshoot: Rolling the Dice on the Vice Presidency* (New York: Crown, 1992), 374–75; Germond and Witcover, *Whose Broad Stripes and Bright Stars?* 233–34; Bob Woodward and David S. Broder, *The Man Who Would Be President: Dan Quayle* (New York: Simon & Schuster, 1992), 78–79.

9. Kevin Phillips, *The Politics of Rich and Poor: Wealth and the American Electorate in the Reagan Aftermath* (New York: Random House, 1990), 10, 21, 124, 138–40, 179–80, 207.

10. William C. Frederick, "Corporate Social Responsibility in the Reagan Era and Beyond," *California Management Review* 25 (Spring 1983): 145–57; Martin Tolchin, "Shifting Burden to the Private Sector," *New York Times,* 22 July 1985.

11. "Higher Incomes Have Not Trickled Down," *Christianity Today* 32 (22 April 1988): 42–43; Harold B. Smith, "Supply-Side Morality," *Christianity Today* 32 (2 September 1988): 14–15.

12. Peggy Noonan, *What I Saw at the Revolution: A Political Life in the Reagan Era* (New York: Random House, 1990), 38.

13. *Ibid.,* 160, 163, 240, 241–43, 265, 314; John B. Judis, "The Conservative Wars," *New Republic* 195 (11 and 18 August 1986): 15–18; M. E. Bradford, "On Being a Conservative in a Post-Liberal Era," *Intercollegiate Review* 21 (Spring 1986): 15–18.

14. Rob Gurwitt, "1986 Elections Generate GOP Power Struggle," *Congressional Quarterly* 44 (12 April 1986): 802–7; Michael Kazin, *The Populist Persuasion: An American History* (New York: Basic Books, 1995), 265; Fred Barnes, "Sore Winners," *New Republic* 199 (5 December 1988): 16–18; Charles Colson, "So Much for Our 'Great Awakening'," *Christianity Today* 32 (13 May 1988): 72; David Aikman, "Washington Scorecard," *Christianity Today* 32 (21 October 1988): 22–23.

15. R. Emmett Tyrrell, Jr., *The Conservative Crack-Up* (New York: Simon & Schuster, 1992), 217; P. J. O'Rourke, *Holidays in Hell* (New York: Vintage Books, 1988), 95–96; David S. Broder, "The American Voters' New Stripes," *Washington Post,* 19 October 1987.

16. "Sizing Up the Reagan Revolution," *Christianity Today* 32 (21 October 1988): 17–21; "Where We Succeeded, Where We Failed: Lessons from Reagan Officials for the Next Conservative Presidency," *Policy Review* 12 (Winter 1988): 44–57; Barnes, "Sore Winners," 16–18; Kim A. Lawton, "Too Close to Call?" *Christianity Today* 32 (21 October 1988): 34–35; Blumenthal, *Pledging Allegiance,* 52, 67; Peter Goldman and Tom Matthews, *The Quest for the Presidency: The 1988 Campaign* (New York: Simon & Schuster, 1989), 188.

17. "Study Shows Church Kids Are Not Waiting," *Christianity Today* 32 (18 March 1988): 54–55; "Suicides Blamed on Music's Satanic Spell," *Christianity Today* 32 (18 March 1988): 53; Terry C. Muck, "A Sexpert's Ethics," *Christianity Today* 32 (2 September 1988): 15; Lloyd Billingsley, "Rock Video: 24-Hour-a-Day Pacifier for 'TV Babies'," *Christianity Today* 28 (13 July 1984): 70.

18. Julia Duin, "Mainline Methodists Denounce Liberal Trends," *Christianity Today* 32 (5 February 1988): 51–52; "Lutherans Affirm Gay Policy," *Christianity Today* 32 (22 April 1988): 40; "Statement on Gay Rights Legislation Aired," Chicago *Catholic,* 18 July 1986; National Assembly for Religious Women, "Regarding a Proposed Gay Rights Chicago City Ordinance," March 1986 (National Assembly for Religious Women Papers, Box 11, NDA).

19. Charles Colson, "A Remedy for Christian 'Homophobia': Coercive Enlightenment," *Christianity Today* 32 (15 July 1988): 72; Charles MacKenzie, "Just Say No to Uncle Sam's Money," *Christianity Today* 32 (2 September 1988): 12;

Terry Muck, "Too Much of a Good Thing?" *Christianity Today* 32 (13 May 1988): 14–15; "Bill May Not Force Schools to Help Fund Abortions," *Christianity Today* 32 (4 March 1988): 40–41.

20. James Davison Hunter, "Modern Pluralism and the First Amendment: The Challenges of Secular Humanism," *Brookings Review* 8 (Spring 1990): 20–27; Paul C. Vitz, "Religion and Traditional Values in Public School Textbooks," *Public Interest* 60 (Summer 1986): 72–90; David Briggs, "Religious Groups Trying to Surmount Barriers," *Patriot-News* (Harrisburg, Pa.), 28 December 1990.

21. Brain D. Ray, "The Kitchen Classroom: Is Home Schooling Making the Grade?" *Christianity Today* 32 (12 August 1988): 23–26; David Sharp, "Your Kids' Education Is at Stake," *USA Today* Weekend, 14–16 March 1997; Leslie Kaufman, "Life Beyond God," *New York Times Magazine* 18 (16 October 1994): 48–51, 70, 73.

22. Rodney A. Smolla, *Jerry Falwell v. Larry Flynt: The First Amendment on Trial* (New York: St. Martin's Press, 1988), 1–3, 7–8; "Falwell Loses *Hustler* Suit," *Christianity Today* 32 (8 April 1988): 48; Tom Minnery, ed., *Pornography: A Human Tragedy* (Wheaton, Ill.: Tyndale House, 1986), 9, 31, 40; James Davison Hunter, *Before the Shooting Starts: Searching for Democracy in America's Culture War* (New York: Free Press, 1994), 70.

23. Minnery, *Pornography*, 34, 51, 69, 83; Cal Thomas, *Occupied Territory* (Brentwood, Tenn.: Wolgemuth & Hyatt, 1987), 157–58.

24. Randy Frame, "Citizens Battle a Booming Pornography Business," *Christianity Today* 28 (7 September 1984): 72–73; Minnery, *Pornography*, 25–26, 199–200, 207, 209; Jean Bethke Elshtain, "The New Porn Wars," *New Republic* 190 (25 June 1094): 15–20; "A 'Conservative Court' Is Still Uncertain," *Christianity Today* 32 (4 November 1988): 37.

25. E. J. Dionne, Jr., "A Liberal's Liberal Tells Just What Went Wrong," *New York Times,* 22 December 1988; Suzanne Garment, *Scandal: The Culture of Mistrust in American Politics* (New York: Times Books, 1991), 191–97; Lyn Cryderman, "Church Groups Urged to Join Dirty Battle," *Christianity Today* 32 (22 April 1988): 43; Goldman and Matthews, *The Quest for the Presidency*, 361.

26. Francis Wilkinson, "The Gospel According to Randall Terry," *Rolling Stone* 23 (5 October 1989): 85–86, 91–92; Lyn Cryderman, "A Movement Divided," *Christianity Today* 32 (12 August 1988): 48–49.

27. Wilkinson, "The Gospel According to Randall Terry," 85–86, 91–92; Randy Frame, "Atlanta Gets Tough," *Christianity Today* 32 (4 November 1988): 34–36.

28. Kim A. Lawton, "Republicans or Reaganites?" *Christianity Today* 32 (16 September 1988): 38–39; William Martin, *With God on Our Side: The Rise of the Religious Right in America* (New York: Broadway Books, 1996), 268–69, 284; E. J. Dionne, Jr., "Michigan GOP Is Split on Eve of Vote," *New York Times,* 14 January 1988; David Shribman, "Michigan Results Expose Weakness of Robertson and Other Republican Presidential Contenders," *Wall Street Journal,* 7 August 1986; John C. Green and James L. Guth, "The Christian Right in the Republican Party: The Case of Pat Robertson's Supporters," *Journal of Politics* 50 (1988): 150–65; Corwin E. Smidt and James M. Penning, "A Party Divided? A Comparison of

Robertson and Bush Delegates to the 1988 Michigan Republican State Convention," *Polity* 23 (Fall 1990): 127–38.

29. Germond and Witcover, *Whose Broad Stripes and Bright Stars?* 87; Martin, *With God on Our Side,* 260.

30. Martin, *With God on Our Side,* 272, 289–90; Blumenthal, *Pledging Allegiance,* 97; John B. Donovan, *Pat Robertson: The Authorized Biography* (New York: Macmillan, 1988), 185; James L. Guth and John C. Green, "Robertson's Republicans: Christian Activists in Republican Politics," *Election Politics* 4 (1987/1988): 9–14; James M. Penning, "Pat Robertson and the GOP: 1988 and Beyond," *Sociology of Religion* 55 (1994): 327–44.

31. Martin, *With God on Our Side,* 268, 271, 278, 281–82, 289; Blumenthal, *Pledging Allegiance,* 89; Kim A. Lawton, "Pat's Big Surprise: The Army Is Still Invisible," *Christianity Today* 32 (8 April 1988): 44–45; Dan Morgan, *Rising in the West: The True Story of an "Okie" Family from the Great Depression Through the Reagan Years* (New York: Knopf, 1992), 480; Harold Smith, "NAE Sets Politics Aside in Favor of 'Spiritual' Agenda," *Christianity Today* 32 (8 April 1988): 54, 56; Kim A. Lawton, "Iowa Christians and the Race for the Oval Office," *Christianity Today* 32 (15 January 1988): 50–52, 55.

32. Martin, *With God on Our Side,* 282–83; Beth Spring, "A Study Finds Little Evidence that Religious TV Hurts Local Churches," *Christianity Today* 28 (18 May 1984): 70–71; S. Dennis Ford, "The Electronic Church's Aesthetic of Evil," *Christian Century* 98 (28 October 1981): 1095–97; Jeffrey K. Hadden, "Religious Broadcasting and the Mobilization of the New Christian Right," *Journal for the Scientific Study of Religion* 26 (March 1987): 1–24; Donovan, *Pat Robertson,* 206; David Edwin Harrell, Jr., *Pat Robertson: A Personal, Political, and Religious Portrait* (San Francisco: Harper & Row, 1987), 213; Michael Lienesch, *Redeeming America: Piety and Politics in the New Christian Right* (Chapel Hill: University of North Carolina Press, 1993), 232.

33. Harrell, *Pat Robertson,* 204; Donovan, *Pat Robertson,* 195; Excerpts from Pat Robertson speech "A Strong Warning that Moral Decay Is Basic Trouble Facing the Nation," *New York Times,* 14 January 1988; Thomas, *Occupied Territory,* 13, 26.

34. Charles E. Shepard, *Forgiven: The Rise and Fall of Jim Bakker and the PTL Ministry* (New York: Atlantic Monthly Press, 1989), xv, 42, 85; Martin, *With God on Our Side,* 275–76; Donovan, *Pat Robertson,* 202; Harrell, *Pat Robertson,* 55; Blumenthal, *Pledging Allegiance,* 69; Corwin Smidt, " 'Praise the Lord' Politics: A Comparative Analysis of the Social Characteristics and Political Views of American Evangelical and Charismatic Christians," *Sociological Analysis* 50 (Spring 1988): 53–72; Randy Frame, "PTL: A Year After the Fall," *Christianity Today* 32 (18 March 1988): 44–45; Louise M. Bourgault, "The 'PTL Club' and Protestant Viewers: An Ethnographic Study," *Journal of Communication* 35 (Winter 1985): 132–48.

35. Lawrence Wright, *Saints and Sinners* (New York: Knopf, 1993), 50–51, 60–61, 68–70, 75–81; Julia Duin, "Why the Assemblies Dismissed Swaggart," *Christianity Today* 32 (13 May 1988): 36–37, 39; Stewart M. Hoover, "The Religious

Television Audience: A Matter of Significance, or Size?" *Review of Religious Research* 29 (December 1987): 135–51;

36. Sean Wilentz, "God and Man at Lynchburg," *New Republic* 198 (25 April 1988): 30–34; Razelle Frankl and Jeffrey K. Hadden, "A Critical Review of the Religion and Television Research Report," *Review of Religious Research* 29 (December 1987): 111–24; Shepard, *Forgiven,* 199; Martin, *With God on Our Side,* 276; Michael Hirsley, "Mainline Protestants Trying to Stem Losses," Chicago *Tribune,* 7 May 1991; Donovan, *Pat Robertson,* 172; Harrell, *Pat Robertson,* 78–79; Blumenthal, *Pledging Allegiance,* 103; Martin, *With God on Our Side,* 270; Harold B. Smith, "Call Them Unelectable," *Christianity Today* 32 (4 March 1988): 15; Kim A. Lawton, "Unification Church Ties Haunt New Coalition," *Christianity Today* 32 (5 February 1988): 46–47.

37. Kim Lawton, "Candidates Court Religious Broadcasters," *Christianity Today* 32 (4 March 1988): 32–33.

38. Blumenthal, *Pledging Allegiance,* 167–68; Germond and Witcover, *Whose Broad Stripes and Bright Stars?* 217–18, 268.

39. Blumenthal, *Pledging Allegiance,* 216–18; Germond and Witcover, *Whose Broad Stripes and Bright Stars?* 286–87; Goldman and Matthews, *The Quest for the Presidency,* 137–40.

40. Germond and Witcover, *Whose Broad Stripes and Bright Stars?* 212, 214, 260; Blumenthal, *Pledging Allegiance,* 126–27; Goldman and Matthews, *The Quest for the Presidency,* 83, 95.

41. Germond and Witcover, *Whose Broad Stripes and Bright Stars?* 212, 214, 260; Paul Taylor, *See How They Run: Electing the President in an Age of Mediaocracy* (New York: Knopf, 1990), 63.

42. Elizabeth O. Colton, *The Jackson Phenomenon: The Man, the Power, and the Message* (New York: Doubleday, 1989), 25, 47–48, 85, 118, 175, 177, 214, 219, 221.

43. *Ibid.,* 181, 188–89; Morton M. Kondracke, "Nunn's Story," *New Republic* 199 (5 December 1988): 15–16; Peter Collier and David Horowitz, "McCarthyism: The Last Refuge of the Left," *Commentary* 85 (January 1988): 36–41; Judis, "Black Donkey, White Elephant," 25–28; Germond and Witcover, *Whose Broad Stripes and Bright Stars?* 294–95; Taylor, *See How They Run,* 136, 141; William Schneider, "The Democrats in '88," *Atlantic Monthly* 259 (April 1987): 37–59.

44. Randy Frame, "Twenty Years after King: How Far Have We Come?" *Christianity Today* 32 (8 April 1988): 42–43; Germond and Witcover, *Whose Broad Stripes and Bright Stars?* 327; Jewell Handy Gresham, "The Politics of Family in America," *Nation* 249 (24/31 July 1989): 116–22; Sara McLanahan and Karen Booth, "Mother-Only Families: Problems, Prospects, and Politics," *Journal of Marriage and the Family* 51 (August 1989): 557–80; Michael Novak, "The Content of Their Character," *National Review* 38 (28 February 1986): 47.

45. Thomas Byrne Edsall and Mary D. Edsall, *Chain Reaction: The Impact of Race, Rights, and Taxes on American Politics* (New York: Norton, 1992), 236; Jared Taylor, *Paved with Good Intentions: The Failure of Race Relations in Contemporary America* (New York: Carroll & Graf, 1992), 79–80, 92, 273; Jim Sleeper, *The Closest of Strangers: Liberalism and the Politics of Race in New York* (New York: Norton, 1990), 203–7, 254–56, 315–16.

46. Taylor, *Paved with Good Intentions*, 11, 312–15.

47. *Ibid.*, 352–53; Ze'ev Chafets, "The Tragedy of Detroit," *New York Times Magazine* 14 (29 July 1990): 20–26, 38, 42, 50–51.

48. Carlyle C. Douglas, "Urban League Head Assails Reagan's Civil Rights Record," *New York Times*, 22 July 1985; James S. Gibney, "The Berkeley Squeeze," *New Republic* 199 (11 April 1988): 15–17; Chester E. Finn, Jr., " 'Affirmative Action' Under Reagan," *Commentary* 73 (April 1982): 17–28.

49. "Run Jesse," *Christianity Today* 32 (13 May 1988): 43; Harrell, *Pat Robertson*, 137; Vinson Synan, "The Quiet Rise of Black Pentecostals," *Charisma* 11 (June 1986): 45–55; Randall L. Frame, "Race and the Church: A Progress Report," *Christianity Today* 32 (4 March 1988): 16–17; Thomas, *Occupied Territory*, 76–77.

50. Noonan, *What I Saw at the Revolution*, 304; E. J. Dionne, Jr., *Why Americans Hate Politics* (New York: Simon & Schuster, 1992), 311–12.

51. Peter Brown, *Minority Party: Why Democrats Face Defeat in 1992 and Beyond* (Washington, D.C.: Regnery Gateway, 1991), 218.

52. Taylor, *See How They Run*, 190–92; Goldman and Matthews, *The Quest for the Presidency*, 301, 305–6; Germond and Witcover, *Whose Broad Stripes and Bright Stars?* 163.

53. Taylor, *See How They Run*, 208–10; Goldman and Matthews, *The Quest for the Presidency*, 364; Blumenthal, *Pledging Allegiance*, 307.

54. Germond and Witcover, *Whose Broad Stripes and Bright Stars?* 162–63, 337; Taylor, *See How They Run*, 192, 204–05, 223.

55. Goldman and Matthews, *The Quest for the Presidency*, 341; Taylor, *See How They Run*, 119–20.

56. Germond and Witcover, *Whose Broad Stripes and Stars?* 352.

57. Taylor, *See How They Run*, 165, 174; Ronald Brownstein, *The Power and the Glitter: The Hollywood-Washington Connection* (New York: Pantheon, 1990), 376.

58. Taylor, *See How They Run*, 174–78; Tyrrell, *The Conservative Crack-Up*, 232.

59. Taylor, *See How They Run*, 167, 180–81.

60. Kim A. Lawton, "Religious Groups Push Platform Agenda," *Christianity Today* 32 (15 July 1988): 41–42; "Democrats Losing Catholics?" *Christianity Today* 32 (7 October 1988): 38; Kim A. Lawton, "Democrats Gain Momentum," *Christianity Today* 32 (2 September 1988): 38–40; Morgan, *Rising in the West*, 486; Gary Wills, "The Secularist Prejudice," *Christian Century* 107 (24 October 1994): 969–73.

61. Goldman and Matthews, *The Quest for the Presidency*, 173; Blumenthal, *Pledging Allegiance*, 202; Dionne, *Why Americans Hate Politics*, 309.

62. Dan Balz and Ronald Brownstein, *Storming the Gates: Protest Politics and the Republican Revival* (Boston: Little, Brown, 1996), 67–69.

63. Colton, *The Jackson Phenomenon*, 255; Blumenthal, *Pledging Allegiance*, 240–41, 288; Goldman and Matthews, *The Quest for the Presidency*, 415; Ruy Teixeira, "What If We Held an Election and Everybody Came?" *American Enterprise* 3 (July-August 1992): 52–59; Paul R. Abramson, John H. Aldrich, and David W.

Rohde, *Change and Continuity in the 1992 Elections* (Washington, D.C.: Congressional Quarterly Press, 1994), 106.

64. Taylor, *See How They Run*, 20; Germond and Witcover, *Whose Broad Stripes and Bright Stars?* 424; Balz and Brownstein, *Storming the Gates*, 71; Schneider, "The Democrats in '88," 37–59; William Schneider, "Tough Liberals Win, Weak Liberals Lose," *New Republic* 199 (5 December 1988): 11–15; Martin Peretz, "Why Dukakis Lost," *New Republic* 199 (28 November 1988): 14–18.

65. Goldman and Matthews, *The Quest for the Presidency*, 414; Balz and Brownstein, *Storming the Gates*, 305–6; Michael Barone, *Our Country: The Shaping of America from Roosevelt to Reagan* (New York: Free Press, 1990), 668; Dionne, *Why Americans Hate Politics*, 315–16; Taylor, *See How They Run*, 238; Schneider, "Tough Liberals Win, Weak Liberals Lose," 11–15; Everett Carll Ladd, "The 1988 Elections: Continuation of the Post-New Deal System," *Political Science Quarterly* 104 (1989): 1–18.

66. Ralph Reed, *Active Faith: How Christians Are Changing the Soul of American Politics* (New York: Free Press, 1996), 23.

Notes to Chapter 7

1. David Horowitz, "Coalition Against the U.S.," *National Review* 43 (25 February 1991): 36–38. I participated in the Ames, Iowa, demonstration.

2. Dinesh D'Souza, *Illiberal Education: The Politics of Race and Sex on Campus* (New York: Free Press, 1991), 16, 18, 136, 143–44; John P. Rouche, "Marxism and the American Professor," *Collegian* (Toledo, Ohio), 7 May 1990; Alan Wolfe, "The Feudal Culture of the Postmodern University," *Wilson Quarterly* 20 (Winter 1996): 54–66; Jane E. Larson and Clyde Spillenger, " 'That's Not History': The Boundaries of Advocacy and Scholarship," *Public Historian* 12 (Summer 1990): 33–43; Christopher Lasch, "Academic Pseudo-Radicalism: The Charade of 'Subversion'," *Salmagundi* 88/89 (Fall 1990): 25–36.

3. George Sim Johnston, "Pope Culture," *American Spectator* 28 (July 1995): 26–29; Michael Novak, "The Revolution That Wasn't," *Christianity Today* 34 (23 April 1990): 18–20; Jack W. Germond and Jules Witcover, *Mad as Hell: Revolt at the Ballot Box, 1992* (New York: Warner Books, 1993), 50; "The American '80s: Disaster or Triumph? A Symposium," *Commentary* 90 (September 1990): 13–52.

4. Germond and Witcover, *Mad as Hell*, 45, 51; Adam Walinsky, "The Crisis of Public Order," *Atlantic Monthly* 67 (July 1995): 39–54.

5. Geoffrey T. Holtz, *Welcome to the Jungle: The Why Behind Generation X* (New York: St. Martin's, Griffin, 1995), 148, 151–52, 155, 158.

6. Frederick Standish, "UAW: What Direction Should It Take?" Pittsburgh *Post-Gazette*, 12 June 1989; Peter T. Kilborn, "No Breaking the Ice with Labor Chief," *New York Times*, 21 February 1992; Lee Iacocca, " 'Japan Bashing' Is a Code Term for Racism," Detroit *Free Press*, 23 April 1990; "U.S. Workers Hit Recession, Not Japanese," Columbus (Ohio) *Dispatch*, 6 February 1992; David Kusnet, *Speaking American: How the Democrats Can Win in the Nineties* (New York: Thunder's Mouth Press, 1992), 173; Michael Duffy and Dan Goodgame,

Marching in Place: The Status Quo Presidency of George Bush (New York: Simon & Schuster, 1992), 244, 248.

7. "Charles Murray," *National Review* 43 (8 July 1991): 29–30; "The American '80s," 13–52.

8. Christopher Lasch, "The Revolt of the Elites," *Harper's* 289 (November 1994): 39–49.

9. Suzanne Garment, *Scandal: The Culture of Mistrust in America* (New York: Times Books, 1991), 234–35, 237, 240–41; Germond and Witcover, *Mad as Hell*, 43.

10. Barry A. Kosmin and Seymour P. Lachman, *One Nation Under God: Religion in Contemporary American Society* (New York: Harmony Books, 1993), 226–27.

11. *Ibid.*; David Frum, *Dead Right* (New York: Basic Books, 1994), 63.

12. Aaron Wildavsky, "What Was So Bad About the '80s, Anyway?" *New York Times,* 17 May 1992; Robert Rector, "Poverty in U.S. Is Exaggerated by Census," *Wall Street Journal,* 25 September 1990; Adam Meyerson, "The Limits of Tyranny: And Other Lessons from the Gulf," *Policy Review* 15 (Spring 1991): 2–3; William J. Bennett, *The Devaluing of America: The Fight for Our Culture and Our Children* (New York: Summit Books, 1992), 146, 148.

13. Frum, *Dead Right,* 84, 96; Jason DeParles, "How Jack Kemp Lost the War on Poverty," *New York Times Magazine* 17 (28 February 1993): 26, 47–48, 56, 58; Jack Kemp, "Tackling Poverty: Market-Based Policies to Empower the Poor," *Policy Review* 14 (Winter 1990): 2–5; Jason DeParles, "The Civil Rights Battle Was Easy Next to the Problems of the Ghetto," *New York Times,* 17 May 1992.

14. Frum, *Dead Right,* 23, 84; John Podhoretz, *Hell of a Ride: Backstage at the White House Follies, 1989–1993* (New York: Simon & Schuster, 1993), 17–18, 20, 31, 84–85, 88.

15. Podhoretz, *Hell of a Ride,* 94–95, 124; Ralph Reed, *Active Faith: How Christians Are Changing the Soul of American Politics* (New York: Free Press, 1996), 15–16; William Martin, *With God on Our Side: The Rise of the Religious Right in America* (New York: Broadway Books, 1996), 312–16, 324; Stephen Bates, *Battleground: One Mother's Crusade, the Religious Right, and the Struggle for Control of Our Classrooms* (New York: Poseidon Press, 1993), 278; Duffy and Goodgame, *Marching in Place,* 208.

16. Podhoretz, *Hell of a Ride,* 79, 110; Duffy and Goodgame, *Marching in Place,* 47, 90, 95, 201, 218, 222; Charles Kolb, *White House Daze: The Unmaking of Domestic Policy in the Bush Years* (New York: Free Press, 1994), 17.

17. Patrick J. Buchanan, "CBS: 'Conservative Broadcasting System'?" *Human Events* 45 (16 February 1985): 137; Patrick J. Buchanan, "America First—and Second, and Third," *National Interest* 19 (Spring 1990): 77–82; Germond and Witcover, *Mad as Hell,* 143, 147.

18. Frum, *Dead Right,* 132, 136–37; Germond and Witcover, *Mad as Hell,* 152; John B. Judis, "The Conservative Crack-Up," *American Prospect* 3 (Fall 1990): 30–42; Jeffrey Bell, "The Wrong Man on the Right," *New York Times,* 3 March 1992.

19. Germond and Witcover, *Mad as Hell,* 231–33; Stephen Glass, "Pat Speaks," *New Republic* 214 (18 March 1996): 17.

20. Glass, "Pat Speaks," 17; Germond and Witcover, *Mad as Hell,* 135–36;

Benjamin Ginsberg, *The Fatal Embrace: Jews and the State* (Chicago: University of Chicago Press, 1993), 223; John B. Judis, "Buchanan Gives Democrats High Hopes," *In These Times* 15 (11–17 December 1991): 3, 10; John B. Judis, "The Conservative Wars," *New Republic* 195 (11 and 18 August 1986): 15–18; A. M. Rosenthal, "Buchanan's Free Ride," *New York Times,* 21 February 1992.

21. Steven A. Holmes, "Buchanan Sees Foreign Influence in Bush's Camp," *New York Times,* 14 March 1992; Robin Toner, "Marching Through Georgia, Sights on Buchanan," *New York Times,* 26 February 1992; Frum, *Dead Right,* 181–82.

22. Germond and Witcover, *Mad as Hell,* 235–36; Frum, *Dead Right,* 72; Ginsberg, *The Fatal Embrace,* 229.

23. Peter Brown, *Minority Party: Why Democrats Face Defeat in 1992 and Beyond* (Washington, D.C.: Regnery Gateway, 1991), 78, 81, 84–85, 95–96; Thomas Byrne Edsall and Mary D. Edsall, *Chain Reaction: The Impact of Race, Rights, and Taxes on American Politics* (New York: Norton, 1992), 280–81; Joseph A. Califano, Jr., "Don't Blame LBJ," *New York Times,* 14 May 1992; Coretta Scott King, "After Years of Stalemate, It's Time to Reopen Lyndon Johnson's War on Poverty," Detroit *Free Press,* 11 August 1989; George Lipsitz, "Toxic Racism," *American Quarterly* 47 (September 1995): 416–27; Robert Rector, "Combating Family Disintegration: Crime and Dependence, Welfare Reform and Beyond," *Heritage Foundation Backgrounder #983,* 8 April 1994 (Washington, D.C.: Heritage Foundation, 1994).

24. Jim Sleeper, *The Closest of Strangers: Liberalism and the Politics of Race in New York* (New York: Norton, 1990), 34, 152; D'Souza, *Illiberal Education,* 134–36; Gordon MacInnes, *Wrong for All the Right Reasons: How White Liberals Have Been Undone by Race* (New York: New York University Press, 1996), 106; Molefi Kete Asante and Diane Ravitch, "Multiculturalism: An Exchange," *American Scholar* 60 (1991): 267–76; Molefi Kete Asante, "The Afrocentric Idea in Education," *Journal of Negro Education* 60 (1991): 170–80.

25. B. Drummond Ayres, Jr., "Marion Barry's Toughest Campaign: A Bid for Respect as Well as Office," *New York Times,* 3 November 1990; "Two Trials Reflect City's Two Worlds," *New York Times,* 24 March 1992.

26. Carl F. Horowitz, "Searching for the White Underclass," *National Review* 47 (11 September 1995): 52, 54–56; William Schneider, "The Suburban Century Begins," *Atlantic Monthly* 270 (July 1992): 33–44; Brown, *Minority Party,* 69, 91.

27. Peter B. King, "Ice-T Is Hot and Bothered," Pittsburgh *Press,* 16 February 1992; Bob Wagner, "Mel-Man and His Special Delivery," *In Pittsburgh,* 12–18 February 1992; Dinesh D'Souza, *The End of Racism: Principles for a Multiracial Society* (New York: Free Press, 1995), 513–14.

28. David Brock, *The Real Anita Hill: The Untold Story* (New York: Free Press, 1993), 34, 42, 61,86. 88.

29. *Ibid.,* 3, 9, 11–12, 17, 79–80; Germond and Witcover, *Mad as Hell,* 237.

30. Brock, *The Real Anita Hill,* 3, 11–12, 335–43; Elizabeth Wright, "Black America and the Thomas Nomination," *Wall Street Journal,* 24 July 1991.

31. Brock, *The Real Anita Hill,* 63, 70; William J. Bennett, "A New Civil Rights Agenda," *Wall Street Journal,* 1 April 1991; Frum, *Dead Right,* 62.

32. Frum, *Dead Right*, 146–47; Brown, *Minority Party*, 164–65; Judis, "The Conservative Crack-Up," 30–42; Mark Stern, "Party Alignments and Civil Rights: Then and Now," *Presidential Studies Quarterly* 25 (Summer 1995): 413–27; Duffy and Goodgame, *Marching in Place*, 102.

33. James Bovard, "Job-Breakers: The EEOC's Assault on the Workplace," *American Spectator* 27 (March 1994): 32–37.

34. Frum, *Dead Right*, 143; Robert Vernon, *L.A. Justice: Lessons from the Firestorm* (Colorado Springs: Focus on the Family, 1993), 16, 28; Michael White, "Rioters Stole Futures, Hopes," Columbus (Ohio) *Dispatch*, 27 April 1997; Michael White, "Riots' Legacy Still Exacting Toll on L.A.," Columbus (Ohio) *Dispatch*, 27 April 1997; Jared Taylor, *Paved with Good Intentions: The Failure of Race Relations in Contemporary America* (New York: Carroll & Graf, 1992), 119; "Even a Burned House Can't Defeat Firefighter," Columbus (Ohio) *Dispatch*, 19 May 1996.

35. Vernon, *L.A. Justice*, 2, 35, 50; Charlotte Allen, "The King Cops and Double Jeopardy," *Wall Street Journal*, 20 May 1992.

36. Frum, *Dead Right*, 149; Edsall and Edsall, *Chain Reaction*, 280–81; William Tucker, "All in the Family," *National Review* 47 (6 March 1995): 36–39, 44, 76; Walinsky, "The Crisis of Public Order," 39–54; R. W. Apple, Jr., "Politicians Warily Gauge the Effects of Los Angeles's Rioting at the Polls," *New York Times*, 17 May 1992.

37. Joe Maxwell, "Black Southern Baptists," *Christianity Today* 39 (15 May 1995): 27–31; Kosmin and Lachman, *One Nation Under God*, 216, 235; Nathan O. Hatch and Michael S. Hamilton, "Can Evangelism Survive Its Success?" *Christianity Today* 36 (5 October 1992): 21–31.

38. "Robertson Regroups 'Invisible Army' into New Coalition," *Christianity Today* 34 (23 April 1990): 35.

39. Erin Saberi, "From Moral Majority to Organized Minority: Tactics of the Religious Right," *Christian Century* 110 (11–18 August 1993): 781–84; Steve Bruce, *The Rise and Fall of the New Christian Right: Conservative Protestant Politics in America, 1978–1988* (Oxford: Clarendon Press, 1990); Judis, "The Conservative Crack-Up," 30–42.

40. Robert Sullivan, "An Army of the Faithful," *New York Times Magazine* 17 (25 April 1993): 32–44; "Open Season on Christians?" *Christianity Today* 34 (23 April 1990): 34–36; William Strauss and Neil Howe, *The Fourth Turning: An American Prophecy* (New York: Broadway Books, 1997), 195.

41. James M. Perry, "Christian Right Maps Route to Power in Efforts at the Local Level to Oppose Homosexual Rights," *Wall Street Journal*, 25 November 1992; "Homosexual Bill Threatens Family Values," *Christianity Today* 36 (5 October 1992): 59; Peter Steinfels, "At Methodists' Conference, Compromise and Close Vote on Church Policy," *New York Times*, 17 May 1992; Roy Beck, "Washington's Profamily Activists," *Christianity Today* 36 (9 November 1992): 20–23, 26.

42. James M. Penning, "Pat Robertson and the GOP: 1988 and Beyond," *Sociology of Religion* 55 (1994): 327–44; Kim A. Lawton, "A Republican God?" *Christianity Today* 36 (5 October 1992): 50–52.

43. Germond and Witcover, *Mad as Hell*, 396–98; Mona Charen, "Urban Cri-

sis Stems from Family Breakdown," Columbus (Ohio) *Dispatch,* 21 May 1992; Mona Charen, "Liberal Elitists Squirm Because Quayle Is Right," Columbus (Ohio) *Dispatch,* 24 May 1992; Reed, *Active Faith,* 140.

44. Kim A. Lawton, "Bush Affirms Role of Religion in Public Life," *Christianity Today* 35 (29 April 1991): 38–39; Mark A. Noll, "The Politicians' Bible," *Christianity Today* 36 (26 October 1992): 16–17; Germond and Witcover, *Mad as Hell,* 406–8; Peter Schrag, "The Great School Sell-Off," *American Prospect* 12 (Winter 1993): 34–43.

45. Podhoretz, *Hell of a Ride,* 154–55, 185; Germond and Witcover, *Mad as Hell,* 414–15.

46. Germond and Witcover, *Mad as Hell,* 410–13; Frum, *Dead Right,* 15.

47. L. Brent Bozell III, Lynne Cheney, and S. Robert Lichter, "Press Objectivity: R. I. P.," *American Enterprise* 7 (March/April, 1996): 34–38; Ellen Ladowsky, "Bill Clinton Is No Victim of the Press," *New York Times,* 24 March 1992; Tom Rosenstiel, *Strange Bedfellows: How Television and the Presidential Candidates Changed American Politics, 1992* (New York: Hyperion, 1992), 64–65; Germond and Witcover, *Mad as Hell,* 279.

48. Rosenstiel, *Strange Bedfellows,* 49–53,145–46;

49. Germond and Witcover, *Mad as Hell,* 287–88, 378, 420; Ronald Brownstein, *The Power and the Glitter: The Hollywood-Washington Connection* (New York: Pantheon, 1990), 362, 378–79; Gwen Ifill, "Clinton Goes Eye to Eye with MTV Generation," *New York Times,* 17 June 1992.

50. Germond and Witcover, *Mad as Hell,* 89–90, 260; R. W. Apple, Jr., "Tsongas Appears to Gain in States with Voting Today," *New York Times,* 3 March 1992; Christopher Hitchens, "Voting in the Passive Voice: What Polling Has Done to American Democracy," *Harper's* 287 (April 1992): 45–52; Gwen Ifill, "Clinton Task: Making Message Heard," *New York Times,* 21 February 1992.

51. Germond and Witcover, *Mad as Hell,* 291–94, 304; MacInnes, *Wrong for All the Right Reasons,* 14–16; Gwen Ifill, "Clinton Stands by Remark on Rapper," *New York Times,* 15 June 1992; Sheila Rule, "Rapper, Chided by Clinton, Calls Him a Hypocrite," *New York Times,* 17 June 1992; R. W. Apple, Jr., "Jackson Sees a 'Character Flaw' in Clinton's Remarks on Racism," *New York Times,* 19 June 1992.

52. Lisa Schiffren, "Bill and Hillary at the Trough," *American Spectator* 26 (August 1993): 20–23; Neil A. Lewis, "Clinton's Coalition Proves a Money-Making Dynamo," *New York Times,* 3 March 1992; Charles Lewis, *The Buying of the President* (New York: Avon Books, 1996), 34–73; Germond and Witcover, *Mad as Hell,* 283; R. Emmett Tyrrell, *Boy Clinton* (Washington, D.C.: Regnery Gateway, 1996), 51–122.

53. David Mixner, *Stranger Among Friends* (New York: Bantam Books, 1996), 203–18, 250, 254; Jane Gross, "Patricia Ireland, President of NOW, Does She Speak for Today's Women?" *New York Times Magazine* 16 (1 March 1992): 16–18, 38, 54; "A Gay Rights Law Is Voted in Massachusetts," *New York Times,* 1 November 1989; Al Kamen, "Pacific Isle for an Activist?" *Washington Post,* 20 July 1994;

54. Mixner, *Stranger Among Friends,* 203–18, 250, 254; Kilborn, "No Breaking the Ice with Labor Chief"; Germond and Witcover, *Mad as Hell,* 343, 346.

55. Duffy and Goodgame, *Marching in Place*, 105; Kusnet, *Speaking American*, 118–19; Kolb, *White House Daze*, 287.

56. Rosenstiel, *Strange Bedfellows*, 281–82; Kevin Coyne, *Domers: A Year at Notre Dame* (New York: Viking, 1995), 33–34, 38; George Embrey, "Pennsylvania Rebounds Under Moderate Democrat Casey," Columbus (Ohio) *Dispatch*, 16 October 1994; Frum, *Dead Right*, 65; "Transcript of Speech by Clinton Accepting Democratic Nomination," *New York Times*, 17 July 1992; Gwen Ifill, "Clinton's Standard Campaign Speech: A Call for Responsibility," *New York Times*, 26 July 1992; Paul R. Abramson, John H. Aldrich, and David W. Rohde, *Change and Continuity in the 1922 Elections* (Washington, D.C.: Congressional Quarterly Press, 1994), 54–55; Germond and Witcover, *Mad as Hell*, 284–85, 339.

57. Germond and Witcover, *Mad as Hell*, 274–75, 308, 321; Duffy and Goodgame, *Marching in Place*, 265; Frum, *Dead Right*, 198; Rosenstiel, *Strange Bedfellows*, 180, 187, 265; Everett Carll Ladd, "The 1992 Vote for President Clinton: Another Brittle Mandate?" *Political Science Quarterly* 108 (1993): 1–28; Lyman A. Kellstedt, John C. Green, James L. Guth, and Corwin E. Smidt, "Religious Voting Blocs in the 1992 Election: The Year of the Evangelical?" *Sociology of Religion* 55 (1994): 307–26.

58. Brown, *Minority Party*, 62, 65, 294–95, 304; Kolb, *White House Daze*, 350; Edsall and Edsall, *Chain Reaction*, 270; Abramson et al., *Change and Continuity in the 1992 Elections*, 38,76, 85, 133; Frum, *Dead Right*, 25; Germond and Witcover, *Mad as Hell*, 441–42, 506–07; Ladd, "The 1992 Vote for President Clinton," 1–28.

59. Brown, *Minority Party*, 63; Kolb, *White House Daze*, 350; Abramson et al., *Change and Continuity in the 1992 Elections*, 133; Rosenstiel, *Strange Bedfellows*, 72–73; Schneider, "The Suburban Century Begins," 33–44; Seymour Martin Lipset, "The Significance of the 1992 Election," *Political Science and Politics* 26 (March 1993): 7–16.

60. Frum, *Dead Right*, 26; Abramson et al., *Change and Continuity in the 1992 Elections*, 133–34, 323; Fred Barnes, "The Family Gap," *Reader's Digest* 71 (July 1992): 48–54; Dennis B. Roddy, "Hard Times Force State Voters to Rethink Loyalties," Pittsburgh *Press*, 16 February 1992; Rhodes Cook, "Clinton Struggles to Meld a Governing Coalition," *Congressional Quarterly* 51 (7 August 1993): 2175–19; Ladd, "The 1992 Vote for President Clinton," 1–28.

61. Abramson et al., *Change and Continuity in the 1922 Elections*, 173–74, 269; Dan Balz and Ronald Brownstein, *Storming the Gates: Protest Politics and the Republican Revival* (Boston: Little, Brown, 1996), 307; Ladd, "The 1992 Vote for President Clinton," 1–28; Kellstedt et al., "Religious Voting Blocs in the 1992 Election," 307–26; James M. Penning, "Pat Robertson and the GOP: 1988 and Beyond," *Sociology of Religion* 55 (1994): 327–44; Seth Mydans, "Christian Conservatives Counting Hundreds of Gains in Local Votes," *New York Times*, 21 November 1992.

62. Penning, "Pat Robertson and the GOP," 327–44; Mydans, "Christian Conservatives Counting Hundreds of Gains in Local Votes"; Kim A. Lawton, "Seeking Common Ground," *Christianity Today* 36 (14 December 1992): 40–41, 62; Kim A. Lawton, "The Family Man," *Christianity Today* 36 (9 November 1992): 26–28.

63. E. J. Dionne, Jr., *Why Americans Hate Politics* (New York: Simon & Schus-

ter, 1992), 342; Balz and Brownstein, *Storming the Gates,* 153–54; Guy M. Condon, "You Say Choice, I Say Murder," *Christianity Today* 35 (24 June 1991): 20–23.

Notes to Chapter 8.

1. David Mixner, *Stranger Among Friends* (New York: Bantam Books, 1996), 267–68, 286–87.

2. *Ibid.,* 272, 284; Paul R. Abramson, John H. Aldrich, and David W. Rohde, *Change and Continuity in the 1992 Elections* (Washington, D.C.: Congressional Quarterly Press, 1994), 3.

3. Abramson et al., *Change and Continuity in the 1992 Elections,* 2–3; Roger K. Lowe, "Anti-Gay Rights Law Overruled," Columbus (Ohio) *Dispatch,* 21 May 1996; "High Court Term Comes to a Close," Columbus (Ohio) *Dispatch,* 4 July 1996.

4. Maureen Dowd, "Grow Up, Mr. President," *New York Times,* 4 June 1997; Lisa Schiffren, "Bill and Hillary at the Trough," *American Spectator* 26 (August 1993): 20–23; R. Emmett Tyrrell, Jr., *Boy Clinton: The Political Biography* (Washington, D.C.: Regnery Gateway, 1996), 102, 138–40, 197–99, 201–3, 208–10, 224–25, 248; Charles Lewis, *The Buying of the President* (New York: Avon Books, 1996), 34–48; Mona Charen, "Why Does Press Ignore McDougal?" Columbus (Ohio) *Dispatch,* 27 September 1996; "Mrs. Clinton Aided Client with Dubious Document, FDIC Says," Columbus (Ohio) *Dispatch,* 24 September 1996; "Two Clinton Donors on Trial in Bank Fund Misuse," Columbus (Ohio) *Dispatch,* 17 June 1996; "Subcommittee to Probe Commodities Deals," Columbus (Ohio) *Dispatch,* 26 June 1996; "Whitewater Heat Building for Clinton," Columbus (Ohio) *Dispatch,* 30 May 1996; Leslie Phillips, "Whitewater Witness: No Cronyism," *USA Today,* 12 May 1996; Stephen Labaton, "Clinton Aide Testifies on Campaign Deal in 1990," *New York Times,* 27 June 1996; "Travel Office Report Lashes Out at Clinton," Columbus (Ohio) *Dispatch,* 19 September 1996; Francis X. Clines, "For Keeper of the Files, a Bad Day," *New York Times,* 27 June 1996; Paul Richter and Ronald J. Ostrow, "Unanswered Questions Surround FBI Files Furor," Denver *Post,* 23 June 1996; William M. Welch, "Explanation of FBI Files Is Challenged," *USA Today,* 20 June 1996; William M. Welch, "In Files Probe, Heat Stays On," *USA Today,* 2 July 1996; Robert Simon, "Fishy Odor Lurks over Clintonites' Abuse of FBI Files," Columbus (Ohio) *Dispatch,* 13 June 1996; Maureen Dowd, "Aldrich's Tale Illuminates Culture Clash," Columbus (Ohio) *Dispatch,* 2 July 1996.

5. Lynette Rice, "Networks Say No," Denver *Post,* 22 June 1996.

6. Karen S. Peterson, "Single Life Gaining on Couplehood," *USA Today,* 13 March 1996; "Singles Find It Easy to End up Doubles," Columbus (Ohio) *Dispatch,* 17 May 1996.

7. Catherine Candisky, "GOP Slams Clinton on Anti-Drug Effort," Columbus (Ohio) *Dispatch,* 29 August 1996; "Decline in Social Health Plagues Children," Columbus (Ohio) *Dispatch,* 14 October 1996; "More Children Being Born to Unwed Parents, Study Says," *Washington Post,* 20 July 1994; "More Teenagers Use Marijuana, Survey Says," Columbus (Ohio) *Dispatch,* 20 December 1996; Georgie

Anne Geyer, "Clinton White House Lacks Moral Outrage in Drug War," Columbus (Ohio) *Dispatch*, 27 August 1996; Tim Friend, "Teens' Use of Drugs Rises Seventy-Eight Percent," *USA Today*, 20 August 1996; "Dole Hammers Away at Clinton's Drug Policies," Columbus (Ohio) *Dispatch*, 19 September 1996.

8. Vivian S. Toy, "Sex Shops Greet New Law with Wink, Nod, and Lawsuit," *New York Times*, 16 October 1996; Tony Snow, "Curfews Won't Tame Teens," *USA Today*, 3 June 1996; Mona Charen, "Dole Would Appoint No Soft Judges," Columbus (Ohio) *Dispatch*, 13 June 1996; Joseph Sorrentino, "A Felony's a Felony, Whether You're a Kid or Adult," *USA Today*, 11 June 1996; Gina Kolata, "Experts Are at Odds on How Best to Tackle Rise in Teenagers' Drug Use," *New York Times*, 18 September 1996; Linda Chavez, "Self-Esteem's Dark Side Emerges," *USA Today*, 21 February 1996; Fox Butterfield, "Bills Target Jailhouse Separation of Youths," Denver *Post*, 24 June 1996.

9. Snow, "Curfews Won't Tame Teens"; Doug Levy, "USA Almost Flunks Violence Report Card," *USA Today*, 12 June 1996; Doug Levy, "Schools Are Unable to Offer Protection Against Violence," *USA Today*, 12 June 1996; William Grady, "Juvenile Home Still Precarious," Chicago *Tribune*, 9 June 1996.

10. "Man Burglarizes Home of Good Samaritans," Columbus (Ohio) *Dispatch*, 16 January 1996; "Mayor of Gary, Indiana, Declares Emergency," Columbus (Ohio) *Dispatch*, 13 September 1996; Debbie Howlett, "Gary, Indiana, in National Spotlight—for Homicides," *USA Today*, 23 September 1996.

11. John Larrabee, "Conn. Troopers Help Bridgeport Vet the Violence," *USA Today*, 8 October 1996; Debbie Howlett, "Feds Asked to Help Quell Gang War," *USA Today*, 17 July 1996; "Atlanta Safe, Police Prepared, Chief Asserts," *USA Today*, 17 July 1996.

12. David Kopel, "Gun-Carrying Citizens Deter Serious Crime," Columbus (Ohio) *Dispatch*, 22 July 1996; "Civilians Take on Border Guard Role," *USA Today*, 16 May 1996.

13. Frank H. Henson, "Vocational Education Really Pays," Columbus (Ohio) *Dispatch*, 30 October 1996; Dinesh D'Souza, *The End of Racism: Principles for a Multiracial Society* (New York: Free Press, 1995), 322.

14. James K. Glassman, "Voucher Program Helps Poor Kids, New Data Show," Columbus (Ohio) *Dispatch*, 5 September 1996; George F. Will, "Flowers Bloom in Education's Barren Wasteland," Columbus (Ohio) *Dispatch*, 16 September 1996; "High Marks for School Choice," Columbus (Ohio) *Dispatch*, 13 August 1996; Mona Charen, "Educrats See Deadly Peril: Competition," Columbus (Ohio) *Dispatch*, 11 September 1996; John Leo, "Catholic School Funding Helps Urban Areas," Lancaster (Ohio) *Eagle-Gazette*, 24 July 1996; Deborah Sharp, "Schools Bulging at the Seams," *USA Today*, 4 November 1996.

15. Cal Thomas, "Branson Is Town That Slime Forgot," Youngstown (Ohio) *Vindicator*, 22 June 1995; Charles Trueheart, "Welcome to the Next Church," *Atlantic Monthly* 278 (August 1996): 37–40, 42–44, 46–47, 50, 52–54, 56–58; David Briggs, "New Study Finds Generation X is Keeping the Faith," Lancaster (Ohio) *Eagle-Gazette*, 18 January 1997; Sylvia Brooks, "A Holy Roll of the Dice," Columbus (Ohio) *Dispatch*, 4 December 1995; "Record Labels See the Light: Spiritual Songs Sell," *USA Today*, 23 April 1996.

16. Hans Johnson, "Broken Promise?" *Church and State* 48 (May 1995): 9–12; Edward Gilbreath, "Manhood's Great Awakening," *Christianity Today* 39 (6 February 1995): 20–28; Jena Recer, NOW Intern, "Whose Promise Are They Keeping?" NOW Home Page, World Wide Web, 30 May 1996.

17. Robert D. Putnam, "Signs of Antisocial Society Are Everywhere," Columbus (Ohio) *Dispatch,* 31 December 1995; Andrew Peyton Thomas, "The Death of Jeffersonian America?" *Weekly Standard* 1 (26 August 1996): 26–29.

18. Andrea Stone, "Not Boomers, Not Xers, They Are Tweeners," *USA Today,* 22–24 March 1996; Laura Myers, "Whom Do You Trust? Not Government, Three of Four Say," Salt Lake City *Tribune,* 1 August 1995; Richard Benedetto, "Today's Political Jokes Show Respect Is a Lost Art," *USA Today,* 1 April 1996.

19. Sandy Grady, "Perot and Choate, His Running Mate, Sing the Same Tune," Columbus (Ohio) *Dispatch,* 13 September 1996; "Economists Challenge Buchanan's Statistics," *USA Today,* 22 February 1996; Ted Gregory, "Casinos Dealing Economy a Bad Hand, Study Says," Chicago *Tribune,* 10 June 1996.

20. Merrill Goozner, "Autos," Chicago *Tribune,* 9 June 1996; Keith Bradsher, "New Approach for Auto Union in Ford Accord," *New York Times,* 18 September 1996; "Steelworkers Vow to Continue Strike," Columbus (Ohio) *Dispatch,* 20 October 1996.

21. Lester C. Thurow, "Changes in Capitalism Render One-Earner Families Extinct," *USA Today,* 27 January 1997; William R. Mattox, Jr., "Too Pooped to Parent," *USA Today,* 8 August 1996; "Most Would Sacrifice to Buy a Home," Columbus (Ohio) *Dispatch,* 3 June 1996; R. C. Longworth, "The Shrinking Middle Class," Columbus (Ohio) *Dispatch,* 8 October 1995;

22. Peter F. Drucker, "The Age of Social Transformation," *Atlantic Monthly* 276 (November 1994): 53–80; Michael Lind, "To Have and Have Not: Notes on the Progress of the American Class War," *Harpers'* 290 (June 1995): 35–39, 42–47; Susan Page, "Robust New Hampshire Still Queasy from Economic Ups and Downs," *USA Today,* 14 February 1996; Richard Wolf, "Medicaid Outcome Will Affect All," *USA Today,* 9 September 1996; Albert J. Dunlap, "Would You Pick Surgery or Death?" *USA Today,* 12 June 1996.

23. Lind, "To Have and Have Not," 35–39, 42–47; Cathy Hainer, "Fancy This, Fancy That," *USA Today,* 25 June 1996; Beth Belton, "Degree-Based Earnings Gap Grows Quickly," *USA Today,* 16 February 1996; Steven A. Holmes, "Survey Shows Rich Get Richer," Denver *Post,* 20 June 1996; R. C. Longworth Sharman Stein, "The Middle Class Blues," Columbus (Ohio) *Dispatch,* 8 October 1995.

24. James MacGregor Burns Remarks on President Bill Clinton's First Six Months, International Society of Political Psychology Conference, Cambridge, Massachusetts, 1995.

25. John McLaughlin, "Mighty Mario," *National Review* 38 (14 March 1986): 22; Dan Balz and Ronald Brownstein, *Storming the Gates: Protest Politics and the Republican Revival* (Boston: Little, Brown, 1996), 56; David Gonzalez, "In Brooklyn, These Foes Say Injustice Is Not Blind," *New York Times,* 11 May 1996.

26. John B. Judis, "A Taxing Governor," *New Republic* 203 (15 October 1990): 22, 24, 26, 28, 31; John Chalfant, "Burch Hits Voinovich on National Ambitions," Columbus (Ohio) *Dispatch,* 4 October 1994.

27. Balz and Brownstein, *Storming the Gates*, 13, 22–26, 151; Kim A. Lawton, "Mrs. Smith Takes on Washington," *Charisma* 22 (August 1996): 36–40.

28. Jeffrey H. Birnbaum, "The Gospel According to Ralph," *Time* 145 (15 May 1995): 29–33; John F. Persinos, "Has the Christian Right Taken Over the Republican Party?" *Campaigns and Elections* 15 (September 1994): 21–24; George W. Gerner, "Catholics and the 'Religious Right'," *Commonweal* 122 (5 May 1995): 15–20; "Parties Seek Catholic Voters," Lansing (Mich.) *State Journal*, 15 May 1996; Tony Snow, "No, Not 'Extremists'," *USA Today*, 26 February 1996.

29. Balz and Brownstein, *Storming the Gates*, 90–93, 204–8, 225; Gordon MacInnes, *Wrong for All the Right Reasons: How White Liberals Have Been Undone by Race* (New York: New York University Press, 1996), 188; E. J. Dionne, Jr., "The Political Crisis," *Commonweal* 122 (5 May 1995): 11–14; Rhodes Cook, "Dixie Voters Look Away: South Shifts to the GOP," *Congressional Quarterly* 52 (12 November 1994): 3230–31.

30. Katharine Q. Seelye, "Shifting Campaign Strategy to Tax Cutting, Dole Meets with Forbes," *New York Times*, 23 May 1996; Dick Armey, "Freedom's Choir," *Policy Review* 18 (Winter 1994): 27–34.

31. Phil Gramm Commencement Address, Liberty University, Lynchburg, Va., 6 May 1995 (World Wide Web, 30 May 1996).

32. Ralph Reed, *Active Faith: How Christians Are Changing the Soul of American Politics* (New York: Free Press, 1996), 240; David Frum, *Dead Right* (New York: Basic Books, 1994), 185–86; Joseph Spear, "Many Republican Critics Never Served," Lancaster (Ohio) *Eagle-Gazette*, 7 June 1996.

33. Balz and Brownstein, *Storming the Gates*, 323–24.

34. Steven V. Roberts, "The Heavy Hitter: James Dobson Speaks for a 'Parallel Culture' Washington Has Ignored," *U.S. News & World Report* 118 (24 April 1995): 34, 39; James Dobson, "Why I Use 'Fighting Words': A Response to John Woodbridge's 'Culture War Casualties,'" *Christianity Today* 39 (19 June 1995): 27–30; John D. Woodbridge, "Culture War Casualties: How Warfare Rhetoric Is Hurting the Work of the Church," *Christianity Today* 39 (19 June 1995): 18–26; John D. Woodbridge, "Why Words Matter: A Response to James Dobson," *Christianity Today* 39 (19 June 1995): 31–32; Bob Ewegen, "Murphy's Law Would Cripple Our Charities," Denver *Post*, 24 June 1996.

35. Balz and Brownstein, *Storming the Gates*, 325; Frum, *Dead Right*, 165, 167; Steven V. Roberts, "Church Meets State," *U.S. News & World Report* 118 (24 April 1995): 26–30; "My Guy: Why My Presidential Candidate Is Mr. Right," *Policy Review* 19 (Summer 1995): 6–16.

36. William Saletan, "John Warner Just Keeps Hanging On," *American Spectator* 29 (June 1996): 38–43; William M. Welch, "Virginia's Warner Facing His Most Difficult Election Ever," *USA Today*, 4 June 1996; Robin Toner, "Political Briefs: The Campaigns for the Senate," *New York Times*, 30 May 1996.

37. Gary Wills, "The Visionary," *New York Review of Books* 42 (23 March 1995): 5–8; Michael Lind, "On Pat Robertson," *New York Review of Books* 42 (20 April 1995): 67–71; Michael Lind, "Rev. Robertson's Grand International Conspiracy Theory," *New York Review of Books* 42 (2 February 1995): 21–25; Richard John

Neuhaus, "Anti-Semitism and Our Common Future," *National Review* 47 (10 July 1995): 52–57; Michael Lind, "The Southern Coup: The South, the GOP, and America," *New Republic* 212 (19 June 1995): 20–29; Michael Lind, "Why Intellectual Conservatism Died," *Dissent* 42 (Winter 1995): 42–47.

38. Neuhaus, "Anti-Semitism and Our Common Future," 52–57; "Fired House Historian Defended by Colleagues, Students," Columbus (Ohio) *Dispatch*, 12 January 1995.

39. Neuhaus, "Anti-Semitism and Our Common Future," 52–57; Jon Meacham, "What the Religious Right Can Teach the New Democrats," *Washington Monthly* 25 (April 1993): 42–48; Michael Raphael, "Reform Rabbi Urges Separate Religion," Columbus (Ohio) *Dispatch*, 6 April 1996; Sylvia Brooks, "Rabbis Back Same-Sex Marriage," Columbus (Ohio) *Dispatch*, 29 March 1996.

40. Nina J. Easton, "Merchants of Virtue," *Los Angeles Times Magazine* 11 (21 August 1994): 16, 18, 20, 40–42; "Should Jews Fear the 'Christian Right'?" *New York Times*, 2 August 1994; Marjorie Stinchcombe, "Religious Conservatives Up Close," *The American Enterprise* 6 (November-December 1995): 24–28, 35–38, 48–52, 62–66, 74–77; Jeffrey L. Sheler, "Mending Fences Between the Christian Right and Jews," *U.S. News & World Report* 118 (24 April 1995): 32.

41. Ralph Reed, "Casting a Wider Net," *Policy Review* 17 (Summer 1993): 31–35; Gerald F. Seib, "Christian Coalition Hopes to Expand by Taking Stands on Taxes, Crime, Health Care, and NAFTA," *Wall Street Journal*, 7 September 1993; Leslie Kaufman, "Life Beyond God: The Christian Right Is Going Secular," *New York Times Magazine* 18 (16 October 1994): 48–52, 73.

42. "Christian Coalition Seeks Social Issues 'Contract', as Anti-Semitism Charges Continue to Swirl," *Church and State* 48 (May 1995): 14–15; Paul Tough, "A Revolution or Business as Usual?" *Harper's* 290 (March 1995): 43–53; Ralph Reed, "Conservative Coalition Holds Firm," *Wall Street Journal*, 13 February 1995; Ralph Reed, ed., *Contract with the American Family* (Nashville, Tenn.: Moorings, 1995), x.

43. David Briggs, "Conservatives Feel Abandoned: GOP Avoids Issues, Group's Leader Says," Columbus (Ohio) *Dispatch*, 22 July 1995; William L. Anderson, "Onward Christian Soldiers?" *Reason* 25 (January 1994): 28–34; Seib, "Christian Coalition Hopes to Expand by Taking Stands on Taxes, Crime, Health Care, and NAFTA"; Reed, *Active Faith*, 144; Edward Ericson, Jr., "Puppet Masters: Ralph Reed, Pat Buchanan, and the Right's Secret Plan for America," Columbus (Ohio) *Guardian*, 21–27 March 1996.

44. David Shribman, "Hey Marlene, How's the Rhetoric in Iowa?" *Chicago Tribune*, 11 August 1995; Richard Benedetto, "Buchanan's Chances Put at Slim and None," *USA Today*, 14 February 1996; Mimi Hall, "Party Doesn't Mean Politics in Louisiana," *USA Today*, 31 January 1996; Lori Sharn, "Buchanan Fails to Win Christians' Faith," *USA Today*, 5 March 1996; Judy Keen, "Textile Worries vs. Tech Hopes," *USA Today*, 1 March 1996.

45. Maureen Dowd, "Buchanan the Bully Brawls Just Like He Did in School," Columbus (Ohio) *Dispatch*, 14 September 1995; Robert D. Novak, "Pat Buchanan, Populist Republican," *National Review* 47 (14 August 1995): 33–36; Patrick J. Buchanan, "Mexico: Who Was Right?" *New York Times*, 25 August 1995; James L.

Srodes and Arthur Jones, *Campaign 1996: Who's Who in the Race for the White House* (New York: HarperCollins, 1996), 109–13.

46. John B. Judis, "Taking Buchananomics Seriously," *New Republic* 214 (18 March 1996): 18–20; Steven Stark, "Right-Wing Populist," *Atlantic Monthly* 278 (February 1996): 19–20, 28–29.

47. Dowd, "Buchanan the Bully Brawls Just Like He Did in School"; "Record Company Accused of Welching on Clean-Lyrics Vow," Columbus (Ohio) *Dispatch,* 11 December 1996; Judy Keen, "Buchanan's Rise Worries GOP Center," *USA Today,* 20 February 1996; Mimi Hall, "Pat Buchanan's Strong Words Get Second Look," *USA Today,* 22 February 1996; Mimi Hall, "Buchanan Still Clutching the Wild Card," *USA Today,* 27 March 1996; Lawton, "Mrs. Smith Takes on Washington," 36–40; Judy Keen, "Buchanan Banking on Simplicity," *USA Today,* 21 February 1996; Del Jones, "Candidates Pick on Party's Traditional Allies," *USA Today,* 15 February 1996; James W. Coons, "Buchanan's Plan Would Ruin Economy," Columbus (Ohio) *Dispatch,* 21 February 1996; "On the Prowl," *American Spectator* 30 (July 1997): 16–17; Jacob Weisberg, "The Coming Republican Crack-Up," *New York Magazine* 29 (4 March 1996): 18–25; Easton, "Merchants of Virtue," 16, 18, 20, 40–42; William J. Bennett, "Revolt Against God," *Policy Review* 18 (Winter 1994): 19–24.

48. Weisberg, "The Coming Republican Crack-Up," 18–25; "Forbes Windfall?" *USA Today,* 1 March 1996; Patrick J. Buchanan, "A Flawed Flat Tax and the Way Out," *New York Times,* 17 January 1996; John B. Judis, 'White Squall: The Majority Party Cracks Up," *New Republic* 214 (11 March 1996): 28–30; Judi Hasson, "Strong Finishes Boost Buchanan, Alexander," *USA Today,* 13 February 1996; Judy Keen, "Religious Right May Not be in Forbes' Corner," *USA Today,* 25 January 1996; Bob Minzesheimer, "Forbes: Attack Ads Backfired in Iowa," *USA Today,* 15 February 1996.

49. Frum, *Dead Right,* 4; Cal Thomas, "Dole Should Surrender Nomination Now," Columbus (Ohio) *Dispatch,* 18 July 1996; "Allies Bad-Mouthing Dole Campaign," Columbus (Ohio) *Dispatch,* 16 July 1996; Robert D. Novak, "Dole's Stilted Visit to Ohio Fails to Rally Republicans' Morale," Columbus (Ohio) *Dispatch,* 17 September 1996; James Bennet, "Weekly Grabs Attention on the Right," *New York Times,* 23 May 1996; Jude Wanniski, "Kemp Stays in Battle While Others Flee," *USA Today,* 30 October 1996; Judi Hasson, "Kemp Scolds GOP for Not Backing Dole," *USA Today,* 28 October 1996.

50. Todd S. Purdum, "Clinton Plans a New Vision Once Again," *New York Times,* 23 January 1995.

51. Sandy Grady, "Clinton Is Right: Hateful Rhetoric Must Be Curbed," Columbus (Ohio) *Dispatch,* 26 April 1995; Ann McFeatters, "Clinton Criss-Crossing Country to Gain Steam," Columbus (Ohio) *Dispatch,* 26 April 1995; Tony Snow, "Clinton Mistakes Grief as Call to Arms," Columbus (Ohio) *Dispatch,* 29 April 1995; L. Brent Bozell III, "The Official Media Versus the GOP," *National Review* 47 (12 June 1995): 46, 48–49; John Corry, "Meeting the Enemy," *American Spectator* 28 (July 1995): 48–49.

52. Richard Benedetto, "Poll Points Toward Conservative Electorate," *USA Today,* 22 May 1996; Richard Gooding, "Top Clinton Aide and the Sexy Call

Girl," *Star*, 10 September 1996; Richard Gooding, "My Last Night with Dick Morris," *Star*, 24 September 1996; Richard Benedetto, "If the Poll Is King, Then the President Is Just a Pawn," *USA Today*, 27 January 1997; Tony Mauro and Debbie Howlett, "Into the Courts, Away from Congress," *USA Today*, 11 September 1996; Maureen Dowd, "No Bridge Too Far," *New York Times*, 23 May 1996.

53. Todd S. Purdum, "Clinton Would Sign Bill Barring Recognition to Gay Marriages," *New York Times*, 23 May 1996; Susan Page, "Welfare Overhaul a Dramatic Shift," *USA Today*, 1 August 1996; Richard Wolf, "Clinton to Sign Welfare Bill," *USA Today*, 1 August 1996; Clarence Page, "Clinton Shows He's Mastered Lesson from Disgraced Morris," Columbus (Ohio) *Dispatch*, 17 September 1996; Jessica Lee and Richard Wolf, "The GOP Congress: Revolutionaries and Realists," *USA Today*, 30 September 1996; Richard Benedetto, "Clinton Runs, Keeping Congress at His Side," *USA Today*, 30 September 1996; William M. Welch, "Welfare Bill Rouses Liberal Clinton Allies," *USA Today*, 22 August 1996; Cal Thomas, "Senate Stands Firmly Against Moral Outrage," Columbus (Ohio) *Dispatch*, 13 September 1996; Jill Lawrence, "Gay Bills' Only Effect Right Now: Politics," *USA Today*, 11 September 1996; Bruce Dunford, "Hawaii Court Case Still Could Have Ramifications," *USA Today*, 11 September 1996.

54. "Clinton Touts Border Program," Columbus (Ohio) *Dispatch*, 11 June 1996; "Clinton Backs Teen Curfews," Lancaster (Ohio) *Eagle-Gazette*, 31 May 1996; Maureen Dowd, "Undisciplined Clinton Turns Tough on Kids," Columbus (Ohio) *Dispatch*, 5 June 1996; Mimi Hall, "Clinton Sings Praises of Teen Curfews," *USA Today*, 31 May 1996; "Clinton Pledges Money to Cut Down on Truancy," Columbus (Ohio) *Dispatch*, 4 July 1996; Neil MacFarquhar, "Clinton, Visiting New Jersey, Warns Children About Smoking," *New York Times*, 8 May 1996.

55. Bill Nichols, "No 'New Tricks' in Drug Strategy," *USA Today*, 30 April 1996; "Clinton Proposes Drug Tests for Teens," Columbus (Ohio) *Dispatch*, 20 October 1996; Jessica Lee, "Clinton's Latest Crime Weapon: Cell Phones," *USA Today*, 17 July 1996; Ron Fournier, "Clinton Shoots at Big, Easy Targets," Columbus (Ohio) *Dispatch*, 3 August 1996; "Clinton Touts Public Lists to Find Deadbeat Parents," Columbus (Ohio) *Dispatch*, 23 July 1996; Bill Nichols and William M. Welch, "Clinton Takes Aim at Deadbeat Dads," *USA Today*, 19 July 1996; "Drug Tests Cause a Stir," Columbus (Ohio) *Dispatch*, 16 July 1996.

56. Jessica Lee, "Clinton Fires Back at Hecklers by Zeroing in on Dole's Record," *USA Today*, 30 October 1996; Maureen Dowd, "In Run for Re-Election, Clinton Starts Thinking Small," Columbus (Ohio) *Dispatch*, 26 July 1996; Susan Page, "Clinton Picks Up Support of CEOs," *USA Today*, 8 October 1996; "Clinton Claiming the Credit," Columbus (Ohio) *Dispatch*, 29 October 1996; Martin Crutsinger, "$28.8 Billion Reduction in Deficit Is Expected," *USA Today*, 17 July 1996.

57. "Ad Touts Clinton's Support of Religion," Columbus (Ohio) *Dispatch*, 15 October 1996; Alison Mitchell, "Clinton, Touring Midwest, Seems to Take a Page from 'Morning in America'," *New York Times*, 18 September 1996.

58. Robert W. Merry, "Milwaukee Mayor Exemplifies New Breed of Democrat," Columbus (Ohio) *Dispatch*, 10 September 1996; Davis S. Broder, "Democrats' 'Unity' Won't Last Beyond Election Day," Columbus (Ohio) *Dispatch*,

28 August 1996; Susan Page, "For Liberals, Clinton only Choice," *USA Today*, 26 March 1996; Susan Page, "Labor Urged to Put Off Its Endorsement," *USA Today*, 22 March 1996; Maureen Dowd, "Democratic Party a No-Show at Own Convention," Columbus (Ohio) *Dispatch*, 30 August 1996; "Gay Rights Groups Decry Clinton on Same-Sex Marriage," Columbus (Ohio) *Dispatch*, 23 September 1996.

59. Susan Page, "Clinton Vows to 'Fix' Medicare," *USA Today*, 6 September 1996; Alison Mitchell, "Clinton Seeks Florida Votes with a Focus on Medicare," *New York Times*, 6 September 1996; "Clinton Woos Florida Seniors," Columbus (Ohio) *Dispatch*, 6 September 1996; "Social Security Being Reshaped Behind Scenes," Columbus (Ohio) *Dispatch*, 10 October 1996.

60. Ron Freeman, "Media Should Put Church Burnings in Perspective and Quit the Race-Baiting," Kansas City *Star*, 25 June 1996; Gary Fields and Richard Price, "Arsons Symbolic of Racial Divide," *USA Today*, 1 July 1996; Gary Fields and Richard Price, "Why Are Churches Burning?" *USA Today*, 2 July 1996; Ronald Smothers, "After Fires, Some Black Churches Face Trouble with Insurance," *New York Times*, 3 July 1996; Steven A. Holmes, "Clinton Seeks $6 Million to Halt Church Fires," *New York Times*, 3 July 1996; Gary Fields, "Clinton Lends Hand to Tennessee Church," *USA Today*, 20 August 1996; Susan Page, "Clinton to Urge Healing in Visit to Site of Arson," *USA Today*, 11 June 1996; Virginia Culver, "Church Blazes Decried," Denver *Post*, 21 June 1996; "Clinton at Arson Site Urges Racial Harmony," Columbus (Ohio) *Dispatch*, 13 June 1996; Tom Curley, "Church Fires Spark a New Call for Action," *USA Today*, 10 October 1996; Debbie Howlett, "Churchgoers, Pastors Refuse to Live in Fear," *USA Today*, 20 June 1996; Lori Sharn, Deborah Sharp, and Gary Fields, "Leave Politics 'Out': Clinton, Governors Take Stand Against Fires," *USA Today*, 20 June 1996; Ken Hamblin, "The Wolf Is at the Door," Denver *Post*, 23 June 1996.

61. "U. S. Investigates Attacks on 216 Places of Worship," Kansas City *Star*, 20 June 1996; Tom Curley, "Parishioners Forgive Arson Suspect," *USA Today*, 21 June 1996; Robyn Meredith, "Solving Church Fires Not an Easy Task," Denver *Post*, 22 June 1996; John F. Harris, "Politics Set Aside as Leaders Assail Burning of Churches," Denver *Post*, 20 June 1996; "Racism Not Behind Most Fires, Data Show," Columbus (Ohio) *Dispatch*, 5 July 1996; Eric Harrison, "Christian Coalition Meets Black Pastors," Indianapolis *Star*, 19 June 1996; J. Sebastian Sinisi, "Group Aids Black Churches," Denver *Post*, 23 June 1996.

62. M. D. Carnegie, "March Madness," *American Spectator* 28 (December 1995): 50–52; "Pat Robertson Denounces Louis Farrakhan," Christian Broadcasting Network Press Release, 17 October 1995, World Wide Web, 1995; Kevin Sack, "Tensions over Racism and Anti-Semitism Have Surfaced in Georgia House Campaign," *New York Times*, 16 October 1996.

63. Laura S. Washington, "The Color of Fear: Blacks and Whites on Common Ground," Chicago *Tribune*, 10 June 1996; Leonard Pitts, "Behavior, Not Race, Led to Ban," Columbus (Ohio) *Dispatch*, 14 July 1996; Peter Applebome, "Bitter Racial Rift in Dallas Board Reflects Ills in Many Other Cities," *New York Times*, 25 June 1996; Zoe Ingalls, "Faculty Notes: White Professor Sues Rutgers for Racial Bias," *Chronicle of Higher Education*, 2 November 1994; Andrea Hamilton, "Black Mid-

dle Class Is Faring Well, Feeling Worse, Some Say," Columbus (Ohio) *Dispatch*, 21 April 1996.

64. "California Vote Focuses Racial Preferences Fight," Columbus (Ohio) *Dispatch*, 10 November 1996; Terry Eastland, "End Affirmative Action—Starting in California," *USA Today*, 21 March 1996; George F. Will, "Welcome California Initiative Likely to Ban Government Racism," Columbus (Ohio) *Dispatch*, 16 July 1996; "Democratic, GOP Chairmen Discourage Election Race-Baiting," Columbus (Ohio) *Dispatch*, 30 July 1996; Terry Eastland, "Quota King," *American Spectator* 29 (May 1996): 33–35, 71; John Zipperer, "Is Discrimination Destined to Stay?" *Christianity Today* 39 (15 May 1995): 42–44; Paul Craig Roberts and Lawrence M. Stratton, Jr., "Color Code: How We Got Quotas," *National Review* 47 (20 March 1995): 36–38, 40, 44–48, 50–51, 80; D'Souza, *The End of Racism*, 289–336.

65. Alan D. Miller, "OU President's Tenure Decision Jangles Campus," Columbus (Ohio) *Dispatch*, 10 January 1996; "Review and Outlook: Riled at Rutgers," *Wall Street Journal*, 13 February 1995.

66. Tony Snow, "Don't Count Dole Out Yet," *USA Today*, 29 April 1996; Darrel Rowland, "Dole's Views More Popular Than He Is," Columbus (Ohio) *Dispatch*, 15 May 1996; Richard Benedetto, "World War II Service Loses Luster as Badge of Honor," *USA Today*, 25 March 1996; Roger K. Lowe, "Candidates Talk Entitlements: Will Winner Take Action?" Columbus (Ohio) *Dispatch*, 20 October 1996; Richard Benedetto, "Clinton Leads Dole Despite Character Gap," *USA Today*, 21 June 1996; Richard Benedetto, "Character Bullets Are Bouncing Off Clinton," *USA Today*, 21 June 1996; Richard Benedetto, "Clinton Shifts Emphasis Away from Character," *USA Today*, 9 September 1996.

67. James Bennet, "Democrats Use Early Ads in Michigan to Help Clinton and Beat Republicans," *New York Times*, 23 April 1996; Catherine Candisky, "Dole Needs to Win 'Soccer Moms'," Columbus (Ohio) *Dispatch*, 4 October 1996; Ronald D. Utt, "How Congress Won the Budget War," *Heritage Foundation F.Y.I.*, 17 June 1996 (Washington, D.C.: Heritage Foundation, 1996).

68. Judy Keen, "Dole Remains in Control, Despite Behind-Scene Sniping," *USA Today*, 30 October 1996; Judi Hasson, "Dole Denounces 'Wink and Nod' Clinton Policies," *USA Today*, 17 September 1996; "NAACP Leader Tried 'To Set Me Up,' Dole Says," Columbus (Ohio) *Dispatch*, 12 July 1996; "Dole Touts Anti-Crime Agenda," Columbus (Ohio) *Dispatch*, 17 September 1996;

69. Maureen Dowd, "First Boomer Caters to Selfish Cohorts," Columbus (Ohio) *Dispatch*, 13 September 1996; Judy Keen, "Dole's Can-Do Commentary Does Not Always Connect," *USA Today*, 28 October 1996.

70. Sandy Grady, "With Bridges Burned, Dole Must Sell Himself to Voters," Columbus (Ohio) *Dispatch*, 14 June 1996; Judy Keen, "Dole's Record: Action Over Ideology," *USA Today*, 17 May 1996; John Hellemann, "Certain Defeat Liberated Dole," Columbus (Ohio) *Dispatch*, 10 November 1996.

71. Denise Dick, "GOP Grapples with Abortion," Lancaster (Ohio) *Eagle-Gazette*, 8 May 1996; Judy Keen, "California Governor to Fight Abortion Plank," *USA Today*, 30 April 1996; Sara Rimer, "Weld Joins Move to Drop GOP Anti-Abortion Plank," *New York Times*, 8 May 1996; Tanya Mellich, "My Party Has

Turned Its Back on Women," *USA Today,* 14 February 1996; Richard Benedetto, "Abortion Platform Could Trip up GOP," *USA Today,* 13 May 1996.

72. Chip Brown, "Senator Raps 'Kamikaze' Critics," Denver *Post,* 22 June 1996; Bob Minzesheimer, "New Jersey Governor Casts a Big Shadow in GOP," *USA Today,* 18 July 1996; Bob Minzesheimer, "In Texas, Abortion Litmus Test," *USA Today,* 20 April 1996.

73. "GOP Senator Gains Support," Denver *Post,* 23 June 1996; Robert D. Novak, "Incumbent-Protection Measures Divide GOP," Columbus (Ohio) *Dispatch,* 3 July 1996; Adriel Bettelheim, "Abortion Splits GOP Delegates," Denver *Post,* 21 June 1996; Mona Charen, "Republican Platform Should Never Compromise with Moral Evil of Abortion," Columbus (Ohio) *Dispatch,* 12 July 1996.

74. Jill Lawrence, "Molinari Bubbling to GOP Top," *USA Today,* 17 July 1996; "Reed: Our Goal Is to Save Congress," *USA Today,* 31 October 1996; Howard Fineman, "The Fight Inside the Tent," *Newsweek* 127 (13 May 1996): 24–27; Ralph Reed, " 'We Stand at a Crossroads': The Religious Right Must Give Ground—Or Risk Irrelevance," *Newsweek* 127 (13 May 1996): 28–29.

75. William Raspberry, "Fear of Slippery Slope Inhibits Decision-Makers," Columbus (Ohio) *Dispatch,* 2 October 1996; Janet L. Folger, "Partial-Birth Abortion Too Common, Never Necessary to Protect Women," Columbus (Ohio) *Dispatch,* 25 September 1996; Mike Royko, "Abortion Lies Lead to Rebuke," Columbus (Ohio) *Dispatch,* 3 March 1997.

76. Richard Wolf, "Late-Term Abortion Ban OK'd," *USA Today,* 28 March 1996; Jonathan Riskind, "Senate Can't Override Veto of Late Abortion Ban," Columbus (Ohio) *Dispatch,* 27 September 1996.

77. Susan Page, "Cardinals Blast Abortion Veto," *USA Today,* 17 April 1996; Susan Page, "Clinton's Abortion-Ban Veto Risks Catholic Vote," *USA Today,* 17 April 1996.

78. "Catholics Launch Assault on Clinton Abortion Veto," *USA Today,* 1 July 1996; Darrel Rowland, "Thought Kept at Bay, Critics Go," *USA Today,* 13 August 1996; Roger K. Lowe and Catherine Candisky, "Parties Vie for Catholic Voters," Columbus (Ohio) *Dispatch,* 22 September 1996.

79. Steven V. Roberts, "Republicans Watch a Bitter Feud with Anxiety," *New York Times,* 22 July 1985; Jack Kemp, "GOP Contract—My Amendments," *Wall Street Journal,* 23 September 1994.

80. "Kemp Scores at Rally in Buffalo," Columbus (Ohio) *Dispatch,* 19 August 1996; Mike Feinsilber, "Enthusiastic Kemp Missed Some Chances Along the Way," Columbus (Ohio) *Dispatch,* 12 August 1996; Judi Hasson, "Kemp Peppers Inner Cities With 'Empowerment' Message," *USA Today,* 10 September 1996; Robert D. Novak, "Kemp Manages to Stay True to Self Without Hurting His Running Mate," Columbus (Ohio) *Dispatch,* 2 October 1996.

81. "Clinton Went After Cash as Early as '93," Columbus (Ohio) *Dispatch,* 20 March 1997; "Fund-Raising: Democrats Return $1.5 Million More in Questionable Donations," *The News Virginian* (Waynesboro, Va.), 1 March 1997; Mary McGrory, "Both Parties Hypocritical on Campaign Financing," Columbus (Ohio) *Dispatch,* 23 October 1996; Joseph Perkins, "Gore in Four Years? Don't Bet On It," Lancaster (Ohio) *Eagle-Gazette,* 29 January 1997; Tony Snow, "Clinton Beggar

Image Tacky for Nation," Lansing (Mich.) *State Journal,* 22 February 1997; "Did Foreign Donors Sway Clinton Policy?" Columbus (Ohio) *Dispatch,* 18 October 1996; Dave Hobson, "Full Accounting of INS Errors Due," Lancaster (Ohio) *Eagle-Gazette,* 25 November 1997; David H. Mayer, "Clinton's Presidency Is Most Corrupt," Columbus (Ohio) *Dispatch,* 19 October 1996; Jill Lawrence, "Democrats' Fund-Raising Mire Deepens," *USA Today,* 31 October 1996; Jill Lawrence, "Burned by Criticism, Democrats Release Documents," *USA Today,* 30 October 1996; Bradley H. Smith, "Foreign Contributions Taint Democrats," Columbus (Ohio) *Dispatch,* 1 November 1996; Robert D. Novak, "Huang Proved His Value to Indonesians," Columbus (Ohio) *Dispatch,* 31 October 1996; David S. Broder, "In Second Term, Will Ethics Bring Clinton Down?" Columbus (Ohio) *Dispatch,* 30 October 1996; Mary McGrory, "Democrats' Fund-Raising Scandals Taint Even Gore," Columbus (Ohio) *Dispatch,* 30 October 1996.

82. Richard Benedetto, "Character Plays Diminished Role in '90s Campaigns," *USA Today,* 24 June 1996; Mike Rosen, "Media Stung by Charges of Liberal Bias," Denver *Post,* 21 June 1996.

83. "NPR Apologizes for Remark That Upset Christian Group," Columbus (Ohio) *Dispatch,* 23 December 1995; Jeff Jacoby, "New Study Shows Heavy Leftist Bias in National Media," Columbus (Ohio) *Dispatch,* 14 June 1996; Frank Rich, "Happy New Year? How Dole Spent Rosh Ha-Shanah," *New York Times,* 18 September 1996; Richard Benedetto, "All Bob Dole May Need Is a Miracle," *USA Today,* 16 September 1996; Georgie Anne Geyer, "Evidence Proves Media's Liberal Bias," Columbus (Ohio) *Dispatch,* 8 November 1996; John Corry, "The Goldberg Deviation," *American Spectator* 29 (April 1996): 46–48; Cal Thomas, "Media's Liberal Bias Becomes More Evident," Columbus (Ohio) *Dispatch,* 18 May 199; Howard Kurtz, "Does the Evening News Still Matter?" *TV Guide* 44 (12 October 1996): 20–23.

84. Cal Thomas, "Big Media Spew Anti-Republican Bias," Columbus (Ohio) *Dispatch,* 15 August 1996; "Ruccia's Camp Makes the Most of the Backlash," *Other Paper* (Columbus, Ohio), 17–23 October 1996.

85. R. Emmett Tyrrell, Jr., "The Game of Politics Will Proceed," Lancaster (Ohio) *Eagle-Gazette,* 7 November 1996; Norm Brewer, "Democratic Candidates Unlock Power of the Purse," *USA Today,* 2 May 1996; William M. Welch, "Unions to Spend Millions on Democrat Hopefuls," *USA Today,* 22 March 1996; Carey Goldberg, "Thousands March to Battle New Right," *New York Times,* 15 April 1996; "Abortion Rights League to Attack Freshmen in House," Columbus (Ohio) *Dispatch,* 14 July 1996; Alan Johnson, "Party Leaders Urge Ohioans to Help Net Congress," Columbus (Ohio) *Dispatch,* 29 August 1996; Jessica Lee, "House Minority Leader Eyes the Recapture of Congress," *USA Today,* 29 August 1996; Richard Wolf, "Democrats' Favorite Demon: Gingrich," *USA Today,* 29 August 1996; James Bennet, "Democrats Defend Clinton on Immigration in Striking Manner," *New York Times,* 27 June 1996; Jonathan Riskind, "New Buzzword to Assail Voters," Columbus (Ohio) *Dispatch,* 29 July 1996; "Congressional Leaders Square Off in TV Debate," Columbus (Ohio) *Dispatch,* 30 September 1996; William M. Welch, "In Democrats' Ads, Everything's Coming Up Gingrich," *USA Today,* 7 October 1996; James Bennet, "Democrats' Attack Ads Home in on

Dole," *New York Times,* 4 April 1996; Jim Norman, "At Least One Pollster Was Right on Target," *USA Today,* 7 November 1996.

86. George F. Will, "Turnout Keeps Declining as Voters' Alienation Rises," Columbus (Ohio) *Dispatch,* 31 October 1996; Mimi Hall, "Clinton Wins Over 'Soccer Moms'; Dole the Young," *USA Today,* 7 October 1996; Bob Minzesheimer, "Turnout Takes a Record Downturn," *USA Today,* 7 November 1996; Bob Minzesheimer, "South Continues on an Increasingly Republican Course," *USA Today,* 6 November 1996; John Green, Lyman Kellstedt, James Guth, and Corwin Smidt, "Who Elected Clinton: A Collision of Values," *First Things* (August-September 1997): 35–40.

87. Dudley Buffa, "A Set of Voters Wired for the Future," *USA Today,* 30 October 1996; James Bradshaw, "GOP Still Rules Ohio Delegation," Columbus (Ohio) *Dispatch,* 6 November 1996; George F. Will, "On Balance, Outcome of Voting Favors Republicans," Columbus (Ohio) *Dispatch,* 7 November 1996; Richard Benedetto, "Voter Anger Appears to Be a Thing of the Past," *USA Today,* 30 October 1996; Alan Johnson, "President Finds Favor in Parma: Reagan Democrats Shift Allegiance Back to Roots," Columbus (Ohio) *Dispatch,* 22 October 1996; "Election '96," *USA Today,* 7 November 1996.

88. Adam Clymer, "Voters Dividing Almost Evenly in House Races, Survey Finds," *New York Times,* 6 November 1996; Adrianne Flynn, "Shifting Politics," Columbus (Ohio) *Dispatch,* 8 December 1996.

89. David Frum, "GOP, We Could Have Won," *USA Today,* 7 November 1996; David Frum, "The Campaign's Casualties," *New York Times,* 6 November 1996.

90. Amitai Etzioni, *The New Golden Rule: Community and Morality in a Democratic Society* (New York: Basic Books, 1996), 3–33.

Notes to Epilogue.

1. Robert H. Bork, *Slouching Towards Gomorrah: Modern Liberalism and American Decline* (New York: Simon and Schuster, 1996), 130–33.

2. "Son of Time-Warner's Chief Is Found Slain in Apartment," *New York Times,* 4 June 1997.

3. Bill Maxwell, " 'Gangsta' Rappers Shield Own Children Well," Columbus (Ohio) *Dispatch,* 4 November 1995; "Gangs Find Reason to Fight Again," Columbus (Ohio) *Dispatch,* 6 October 1996; "For Rap Star Tupac Shakur, Violence Spills from His Lyrics into His Life," Columbus (Ohio) *Dispatch,* 11 September 1996; "Bullet Wounds Claim Rapper Tupac Shakur," Columbus (Ohio) *Dispatch,* 14 September 1996; "Record Company Accused of Welching on Clean-Lyrics Vow," Columbus (Ohio) *Dispatch,* 11 December 1996.

4. Sarah Glazer, "Boston Fights Crime—And Wins," Columbus (Ohio) *Dispatch,* 11 May 1997; "Toledo Shoots Down Gun Control Proposals," Columbus (Ohio) *Dispatch,* 6 April 1997.

5. "Florida Prisons Turn Violent Felons Loose," Columbus (Ohio) *Dispatch,* 13 March 1997; "Los Angeles Seeks to Widen Ban Against Gang Clustering,"

Columbus (Ohio) *Dispatch,* 11 July 1997; Bork, *Slouching Towards Gomorrah,* 317–43.

6. "Los Angeles Seeks to Widen ban on Gang Clustering"; Haya El Nasser, "Poll: Whites Increasingly Accept Blacks," *USA Today,* 11 June 1997; "A 'Retreat of Civil Rights'," *USA Today,* 21 May 1997.

7. Mireya Navarro, "National Baptist Leader Denies Misconduct Accusations," *New York Times,* 12 July 1997.

8. Paul Davidson, "So, How Much Money Does It Take to Be Rich?" *USA Today,* 20–22 June 1997; "School Is Serious Business for Pupils at Cape Cod Elementary," Columbus (Ohio) *Dispatch,* 26 May 1997.

9. "Survey: Most Companies Not Hiring the Poor," Columbus (Ohio) *Dispatch,* 26 May 1997; Dennis Fiely, "College Is Like a Job, Guide Says," Columbus (Ohio) *Dispatch,* 21 May 1997.

10. "Newspaper: Migrants to Florida Returning to Ohio," Columbus (Ohio) *Dispatch,* 5 May 1997.

11. Linda P. Harvey, "Should Ohio Limit Use of Family-Planning Clinic Funds? Yes: Abortions Are Agencies' Real Goal," Columbus (Ohio) *Dispatch,* 20 May 1997; Gina Kolata, "Nomadic Group of Anti-Abortionists Uses New Tactics to Make Its Mark," *New York Times,* 24 March 1992.

12. Linda Bowles, "Clinton Gives Presidential Seal to Homosexuals," Lancaster (Ohio) *Eagle-Gazette,* 10 May 1997; Carol Clurman, "Gay Rights: What's the Agenda?" *USA Today* Weekend, 28 February–2 March, 1997.

13. William M. Welch and Jessica Lee, "Clinton Leaves His Own Party Split," *USA Today,* 2 May 1997; Jessica Lee, "Republicans Are 'Fired Up!', Democrats 'Will Have to See'," *USA Today,* 2 May 1997; William M. Welch, "Gephardt Says He'll Oppose Bipartisan Budget Agreement," *USA Today,* 21 May 1997.

14. Tom Watson, "Gingrich: 'Let's Get on with It'," *USA Today,* 27 January 1997; "Some Conservatives See Little to Like in Lott," Columbus (Ohio) *Dispatch,* 5 May 1997; Michael Reagan, "Reagan: 'Bye to GOP," *USA Today,* 17 April 1997; Fred Barnes, "No Confidence: How Newt Gingrich's Congressional Lieutenants Have Begun to Turn on Him," *Weekly Standard* 2 (30 June 1997): 17–20; John Podhoretz, "The Handcuffed Republicans," *Weekly Standard* 2 (30 June 1997): 20–23.

15. "TV Ratings Deal Could Doom 'Family Hour' Bill," Columbus (Ohio) *Dispatch,* 14 July 1997.

16. Bill Nichols, "Clinton Will Renew China Trade Status," *USA Today,* 20 May 1997.

17. Arianna Huffington, "Limbaugh Leads Summit Grinches," Columbus (Ohio) *Dispatch,* 25 April 1997.

18. William F. Buckley, Jr., *Gratitude: Reflections on What We Owe to Our Country* (New York: Random House, 1990), xiv, xx, 17–18, 25, 36, 47, 53, 56–57, 134.

19. *Ibid.,* xiv, xx, 17–18, 36, 47, 53, 56–57, 134; Michael Lind, "Why Intellectual Conservatism Died," *Dissent* 42 (Winter 1995): 42–47.

20. David Frum, *Dead Right* (New York: Basic Books, 1994), 3–4; Bork, *Slouching Towards Gomorrah,* 151, 336.

21. "Layoffs Feed Stock-Market Frenzy," Columbus (Ohio) *Dispatch*, 20 September 1997.

22. "Reed: Whites Must Repent, Help Blacks," Columbus (Ohio) *Dispatch*, 11 May 1997.

23. David Briggs, "Protesters Saying Down with Mickey," Lancaster (Ohio) *Eagle-Gazette*, 19 July 1997; "Niche Marketing Helps Auto Makers Stand Out," Columbus (Ohio) *Dispatch*, 19 July 1997; Clifford Rothman, "Hollywood Throws Its Support Behind Outfest," *USA Today*, 11 July 1997.

24. Ed Briggs, "Episcopalians Accept Pact with Lutherans," Columbus (Ohio) *Dispatch*, 19 July 1997; Terry Mattingly, "U.S. Episcopalians Are Out of Step," Lancaster (Ohio) *Eagle-Gazette*, 19 July 1997.

25. William Strauss and Neil Howe, *The Fourth Turning: An American Prophecy* (New York: Broadway Books, 1997), 25–253.

Index

ABC, 119, 138, 198, 202

Abernathy, Ralph, 15

Abortion: Berrigan on, 6; blacks on, 6, 10, 90, 114; Bork on, 153–54; Buchanan on, 6; Bush on, 119, 131–32; and Carter, 81–82, 86–87, 90, 98, 111; and Catholics, 49–52, 71–72, 74–75, 86–87, 89, 109, 140–42, 240, 256; Clinton on, 205, 245; conservatives' opposition to, 49–52, 79, 113, 115, 131, 163–64, 173, 178, 209, 216, 220, 222, 223–24, 266; Dole on, x, 11, 238–41; Ferraro on, 140–42; gag rules concerning information on, 211; as issue with voters, 12, 71–75, 108–10, 148, 208; Jackson on, 6, 90; as liberal cause, 30, 64, 67, 71–75, 85, 106, 127, 141; libertarians on, 222; and McGovern, 60; under Nixon, 65; partial-birth, 239–40, 242, 245, 250; Reagan on, 1, 115, 130, 165, 181; supporters of, 49, 251; Supreme Court's ruling on, 7, 49, 71, 81, 109, 141, 142, 211. *See also* National Abortion Rights Action League; Operation Rescue; Planned Parenthood; Right to Life Amendments

Abzug, Bella, 98

Achtenberg, Roberta, 204, 210

ACLU. *See* American Civil Liberties Union

ACT-UP, 166

AFDC (Aid to Families with Dependent Children), 28, 31, 96. *See also* Welfare

Affirmative action ("Quotas"): blacks' support for, 99, 172–73, 235–36; Buchanan on, 190–91; Clinton on, 211, 235; controversies over, 101–3, 249, 264; and Dole, 238; and EEOC, 37; under Ford, 75; for gays, 106; as

a kind of welfare, 261; liberals on, 10, 179; New Deal policies on, 4; under Nixon, 65; and organized labor, 135

Afghanistan, 94

AFL-CIO, 2, 41, 60, 120, 134–35, 242. *See also* Kirkland, Lane; Meany, George; Sweeney, John

AFSCME (American Federation of State, County, and Municipal Employees), 92, 105, 147, 153, 205, 207; as white-collar union, 2, 135

Agnew, Spiro, 66

Agricultural subsidies, 4, 16, 262

AIDS, 143–44, 159, 166, 210

Aid to Families with Dependent Children (AFDC), 28, 31, 96. *See also* Welfare

Akron (Ohio), 41

Alabama, 38, 42, 206, 245. See also *Names of specific cities in*

Alabama State University, 38

Alcohol, 11, 17, 18–19

Allaire, Paul, 232

All in the Family (television show), 61, 64

Al Smith Dinner (New York City), 114

Altoona (Pennsylvania), 68–69

AMA (American Medical Association), 213, 233

American Civil Liberties Union (ACLU): and abortion, 109; and affirmative action, 101; and Bork nomination, 153; candidates supported by, 118, 146; and censorship, 107, 162–63, 213; and crime, 29, 248, 260; and nativity displays, 150; and religion in public schools, 160–61; support for, 162, 176

325

About the Author

Kenneth J. Heineman, an associate professor of history at Ohio University, is the author of *Campus Wars: The Peace Movement at American State Universities in the Vietnam Era* (New York University Press, 1993). He has published articles on recent American history in *The Historian,* the *Journal of Popular Film & Television, Peace and Change,* the *Pennsylvania Magazine of History and Biography,* and *Pittsburgh History.* Edited essays and excerpts of his work have also appeared in *Give Peace a Chance: Exploring the Vietnam Antiwar Movement* (Syracuse University Press, 1992, Melvin Small and William D. Hoover, editors), *The American Record: Images of the Nation's Past since 1865* (McGraw-Hill, 1995, William Graebner and Leonard Richards, editors), and *The American Record: Images of the Nation's Past Since 1941* (McGraw-Hill, 1997, William Graebner and Jacqueline Swansinger, editors). In 1996 professor Heineman was one of the young historians featured in a *Linguafranca* cover story "Who Owns the Sixties? The Opening of a Scholarly Generation Gap."